A Democratic Theory of Truth

A Democratic Theory of Truth

Linda M. G. Zerilli

The University of Chicago Press   CHICAGO AND LONDON

The University of Chicago Press, Chicago 60637
The University of Chicago Press, Ltd., London
© 2025 by The University of Chicago
All rights reserved. No part of this book may be used or reproduced in any manner whatsoever without written permission, except in the case of brief quotations in critical articles and reviews. For more information, contact the University of Chicago Press, 1427 E. 60th St., Chicago, IL 60637.
Published 2025
Printed and bound by CPI Group (UK) Ltd, Croydon, CR0 4YY

34 33 32 31 30 29 28 27 26 25   1 2 3 4 5

ISBN-13: 978-0-226-83902-8 (cloth)
ISBN-13: 978-0-226-83904-2 (paper)
ISBN-13: 978-0-226-83903-5 (e-book)
DOI: https://doi.org/10.7208/chicago/9780226839035.001.0001

Library of Congress Cataloging-in-Publication Data

Names: Zerilli, Linda M. G. (Linda Marie-Gelsomina), 1956– author.
Title: A democratic theory of truth / Linda M. G. Zerilli.
Description: Chicago : The University of Chicago Press, 2025. | Includes bibliographical references and index.
Identifiers: LCCN 2024035540 | ISBN 9780226839028 (cloth) | ISBN 9780226839042 (paperback) | ISBN 9780226839035 (ebook)
Subjects: LCSH: Truth—Political aspects. | Democracy. | Truthfulness and falsehood.
Classification: LCC BD171 .Z43 2025 | DDC 121—dc23/eng/20240905
LC record available at https://lccn.loc.gov/2024035540

♾ This paper meets the requirements of ANSI/NISO Z39.48-1992 (Permanence of Paper).

For Gregor
To the memory of my mother, Marie Antoinette Stillitano Zerilli (1930–2022)

Sometimes you have to take an expression out of the language,
to send it for cleaning,
—& then you can put it back into circulation.
WITTGENSTEIN, *CULTURE AND VALUE*

Contents

List of Abbreviations * xi
Preface * xiii

INTRODUCTION. DEMOCRATIC POLITICS
AND THE PROBLEM OF TRUTH * 1

1. TO BRING THINKING DOWN TO EARTH * 23

2. CRITIQUE AS A POLITICAL PRACTICE
OF FREEDOM * 47

3. FACT-CHECKING AND TRUTH-TELLING IN
AN AGE OF ALTERNATIVE FACTS * 63

4. IDEOLOGY AND THE ORDINARY * 95

5. FEMINISM, CRITIQUE, AND THE
REALISTIC SPIRIT * 127

6. THE PROBLEM OF DEMOCRATIC PERSUASION * 149

CONCLUSION. A REALISTIC PICTURE OF
DEMOCRACY AND TRUTH * 177

Acknowledgments * 191
Notes * 195
Index * 251

Abbreviations

The following abbreviations have been used in this book; publication information for editions cited can be found at the first citation of each item in the notes.

DT	Michel Foucault, *Discourse and Truth and Parrhesia*
GL	Michel Foucault, *On the Government of the Living: Lectures at the Collège de France 1979–1980*
GS	Michel Foucault, *The Government of Self and Others: Lectures at the Collège de France, 1982–1983*
"IP"	Hannah Arendt, "Introduction *into* Politics"
"LP"	Hannah Arendt, "Lying in Politics"
OC	Ludwig Wittgenstein, *Über Gewissheit / On Certainty*
OT	Hannah Arendt, *The Origins of Totalitarianism*
PI	Ludwig Wittgenstein, *Philosophical Investigations*
"PP"	Hannah Arendt, "Philosophy and Politics"
"TP"	Hannah Arendt, "Truth and Politics"
"WC"	Michel Foucault, "What Is Critique?"

Preface

"The modern growth of worldlessness, the withering away of everything *between* us, can also be described as the spread of a desert." So begins the short and enigmatic epilogue to Hannah Arendt's "Introduction *into* Politics."[1] Reflecting on the worry animating my book, I returned to her 1955 text, wondering whether democratic citizens were now so habituated to this "desert-world" that we had come to feel at home in it. But what could this mean? Arendt reminds us that the problem of worldlessness is misdiagnosed when described as an inner state of being. Believing that "the desert is in ourselves," we seek individualized ways to endure and risk falling into further world-eroding forms of "escapism."

Around the corner, however, lurks a far "greater danger," warns Arendt. "There are sandstorms in the desert," which are none other than "the totalitarian movements" we thought to have defeated once and for all. "Well-adjusted to the conditions of the desert," these movements patiently await their moment, taking advantage of the empty space between us to sow distrust of each other and of a shared public world in which our plural existence could be expressed in words and deeds.[2] In the view of many contemporary critics, this moment has all but arrived. The startling rise of demagogic leaders and the surprising attractions of authoritarianism in formally liberal-democratic societies at home and abroad is a red flag for what lies ahead.

Although many phrases are invoked to describe the precarity of democracy today, perhaps none resonates more than "post-truth." That we express the dangers facing democratic citizens as a loss of truth can initially seem unsurprising. There can be no sense of a public world if the participants do not see themselves as inhabiting a shared reality. How can we engage in meaningful debate about the world we have in common if the exchange of plural opinions is little more than citizens expressing their own "alternative" facts. The rapid rise of disinformation and conspiracy theories, and the continuing loss of confidence in the possibility of impartial evidence, have led to a situation in which highly partisan opinions threaten to devolve into a state where no one believes anything anymore. As Arendt put it: "The ideal subject of totalitarianism is not the convinced Nazi or the convinced Communist, but people for whom the distinction between fact and fiction (*i.e.*, the reality of experience) and the distinction between true and false (*i.e.*, the standards of thought) no longer exist."[3]

In the face of this danger, it can seem imperative to affirm the existence of objective Truth and hold to account anyone who doubts that such Truth exists. This includes not only conspiracy theorists, political opportunists, and brazen liars but also scholars who have been critical of calls to ground democracy in foundational truths, whatever they might be. Isn't it time to put aside our differences, circle the wagons, and defend Truth against all comers? After all, democracy is at stake.

In this book, I defend the importance of truth for democracy. However, it is not the idea of objective Truth that has supposedly been lost, according to critics in the now vast "post-truth" debate. This is the idea of Truth that Michel Foucault critically described as having "force" in itself, Truth that compels submission from those who first track its presence.[4] The received idea of Truth does not build a common world but destroys what lies between us, leaving behind nothing but an uninhabitable desert. It is a Truth that has nothing to do with citizen opinions, nothing with what we say, think, or do—nothing to do with us. Truth denialism is a grave danger to democracy. But so, too, is this form of objective Truth. Falling prey to the ideal of Truth is as dangerous for democracy as being truth denialists—and, more importantly, it does not constitute an effective critical strategy against the apologists of "alternative facts." Instead, it provokes and incites them, for it refuses to countenance the subject dependence of any humanely possible idea of truth. It drives citizens into the skeptical despair of truth denialism, where corrosive doubt holds sway and the distinction between true and false ceases to exist.

I have titled this work *A Democratic Theory of Truth* not to survey different philosophical theories of truth (e.g., correspondence, coherence, semantic, or pragmatic) but to consider what happens when we take seriously the Socratic idea that there is truth in opinion. From the standpoint of democratic politics and the plurality that is its *conditio per quam*, this is the idea of truth that matters, the only world-building idea of truth. Crucially, it is the only form of truth to help us survive the sandstorms now gathering in the desert.

INTRODUCTION

Democratic Politics and the Problem of Truth

What form of critique is called for in our "post-truth" times? How might we meet the challenges of democratic citizenship in contexts where factuality is under assault and "alternative facts" are viewed as equally legitimate ways of describing "reality"? Whatever their disagreements, authors of the voluminous critical literature on post-truth see in the ongoing hemorrhaging of objective facts to subjective opinion a genuinely new threat to democracy, which calls for united strategies of resistance.[1] Many embrace ideals of Truth and Objectivity that are indifferent to the plurality of human experience and democratic citizens' particular standpoints on the public world. Animated by the fear of relativism, according to which all perspectives on the world are equally valid, with none being more accurate to how things are, debates over post-truth repeat the long-standing distrust of human experience, perspective, and opinion that characterizes the Western philosophical tradition.

In this book, I reclaim plurality as the basis for a critical political practice that restores the rightful place of citizen opinion in the debate about democracy and truth. Interrogating the lure of "factualism," I show that those critics who would restore the authority of objective facts misunderstand the fate of facts, truth, and reality in the more general problem of democratic erosion. To describe our current predicament as "post-truth" is to name a condition in which the political norm is to lie, be indifferent to facts, and appeal to irrational emotions. Consequently, argue post-truth critics, we must recommit ourselves to objectivity, rational discourse, and truthfulness in politics; recognize the merely subjective nature of opinions; and hold political actors accountable to rigorous fact-checking standards.[2] These demands raise my guiding question: What concept of "truth" is presupposed in the post-truth debate?

Contemporary denouncements of post-truth generally assume a universal conception of truth waiting to be reclaimed by democratic citizens that does not depend on the historically contingent practices with which we distinguish truth from falsity.[3] They assume that truth is *eo ipso* valuable for democratic politics and that citizens should always be guided by truth. And, not least, they assume that truth—its value and existence—does not depend in any way on us. Instead, it is only a matter of recognizing and affirming objective truth beyond what we think, say, or do and declaring it the fundamental condition of democratic politics.

According to the received conception of truth, the part played by citizen-subjects in determining the existence or value of truth is always already given in the structure of truth itself. As Michel Foucault parses this view of truth: "The truth is sufficient unto itself for making its own law. And why? Quite simply because the coercive force of truth resides within truth itself. In the search for and manifestation of the truth, what constrains me, what determines my role, what calls on me to do this or that, what obliges me in the procedure of the manifestation of the truth is the structure of truth itself. It is truth itself, and that's all" (*GL*, 95). In short, I submit myself to what is true *because* it is true. In the state of post-truth, it is said that various interests converge or conspire to occlude, distort, and erode our grasp of truth and the ground to distinguish truth from falsity, leaving ordinary citizens unbound to truth's otherwise inherent guiding force. What if the "coercive force of truth" did not depend on truth alone, as critics assume, but on us?

In his later work, Foucault questions the received notion that "truth itself determines its regime, makes the law, and obliges me. It is true, and I submit to it. I submit to it, since it is true, and I submit inasmuch as it is true" (*GL*, 96).[4] He introduces the idea of historically situated "games of truth" on the one hand and "regimes of truth" on the other. Although this distinction is more analytic than real—there are no games of truth without regimes of truth, and vice versa—it serves Foucault initially to dispute the suprahistorical idea of truth that has nothing to do with the plural ways in which contingent games of truth are played and nothing to do with us.

Foucault grants that "truth is *index sui*." In other words, "only the truth can legitimately show the true[;] . . . only the game of truth and falsity can demonstrate what is true." However, he adds, "it is not the truth that so to speak administers its own empire, that judges and sanctions those who obey or disobey it" (i.e., the truth is *index sui* but not "*rex sui*," "*lex sui*," or "*judex sui*") (*GL*, 96).

> It is not true that the truth constrains only by truth. . . . [Instead], even in the event of something being recognized as self-evident, there is always . . .

a certain assertion that does not belong to the logical realm of observation or deduction, in other words, as assertion that does not belong exactly to the realm of the true or false, that is rather a sort of commitment, a sort of profession. In all reasoning there is always this assertion that consists in saying: if it is true, then I will submit; it is true, *therefore* I submit; it is true, therefore I am bound. But this "therefore" of the "it is true, therefore I submit; it is true, therefore I am bound," is not a logical "therefore," it cannot rest on any self-evidence, nor is it univocal moreover. (*GL*, 96)[5]

Denying that the subject's submission to truth is given in the game of truth itself, Foucault does not deny that there is truth or try to reduce truth to power, as critics who align him with "post-truth" accuse, argues Daniele Lorenzini in his transformative reading.[6] He never denied that "in any *game of truth*, that is, in any regulated system for the production of truth claims (when it is considered in terms of its formal structure, and not of the individuals who concretely engage with it), 'only the truth can legitimately show the true' and establish the distinction between true and false statements."[7] Criteria of truth are internal to the game, Foucault agreed, but the game itself has no intrinsic force; it cannot compel those who play it to submit to the practical consequences that follow from deciding on the epistemic validity of "x."[8]

What binds subjects to truth and obliges them to "manifest truth" is the "therefore" that links the "I submit" to the "it is true." This "therefore" is not given in the formal rules of the "game" but constitutes the specific "regime of truth." Foucault explains: "Truth is above all a system of obligations.... What is important in this question of truth is that a certain number of things actually pass for true, and that the subject must produce them himself, or accept them, or submit to them. So, what has been and will be at issue is the truth as bond, as obligation, and also as politics, and not the truth as content of knowledge or as formal structure of knowledge."[9]

To illuminate the subject's part in constituting these "bonds of what could be called veridiction," Foucault makes visible the distinction between a game and a regime of truth that disappears behind the received idea of truth as containing its own binding force (e.g., especially in the games of logic and science that I examine in chapter 4).[10] This "distinction," explains Lorenzini, marks the difference between "the epistemic acceptance of a given truth claim and the practical submission to that claim. While *acceptance* of the truth can be explained at the level of the game of truth, that is, by relying on the formal structure and rules, *submission* to the truth (giving the truth the right and power to govern one's, and others', conduct) must be addressed at a different level, that of the regime of truth."[11]

The distinction between game and regime significantly affects how we think about the democratic problem of truth.[12] For one thing, as we will see in chapter 6, it helps explain why citizens with vastly different political views can agree on the facts—it is not always a problem of lies and fake news—but draw contrasting, if not incommensurable, conclusions for their own public lives. It provokes questions about the public conditions under which democratic citizens bind themselves to truth (using the "therefore"), that is, how they manifest and become "subjects of truth" or "alethurgic" subjects. A regime of truth points not only to citizen-subjects themselves but also to the specific political context in which subjects might or might not bind themselves to any game of truth.

Indeed, what interests Foucault is how this binding of oneself to truth connects with what he calls "the government of men by the truth" (*GL*, 11). "Why, in what form, in a society like ours, is there such a deep bond between the exercise of power and the obligation for individuals to become themselves essential actors in the procedures of manifestation of the truth, in the procedures of alethurgy needed by power?," he asks (*GL*, 80–81). How is the affirmation of truth (and not just its denial, as post-truth critics hold) connected to political rule?

For Foucault, "power has no intrinsic legitimacy" and any form of power is contingent—it could have been otherwise (*GL*, 77).[13] The manifestation of truth binds subjects to, and authorizes, specific forms of power, lending the latter the appearance of necessity. Instead of assuming that we should bind ourselves to something simply because it is true (i.e., has epistemic validity), we should *both* contest the idea that there is no truth ("post-truth") and problematize the intrinsic value of truth for democratic politics. "Shifting the accent from the 'it is true' to the force we accord truth" with Foucault, we can critically examine how "men have gradually bound themselves in and through the manifestation of truth" to different forms of power (*GL*, 101).[14] We can question how games and regimes of truth might bind us to practices of freedom but also to what Hannah Arendt calls "politics as rule": a historically tenacious idea of what *must* be the case for all sociopolitical life that finds support in the suprahistorical conception of truth that has nothing to do with us.

Truth and Opinion

"Every claim in the sphere of human affairs to an absolute truth, whose validity needs no support from the side of opinion, strikes at the very roots of all politics," writes Arendt.[15] For her, the "despotic character" of truth resides in the idea that it has nothing to do with us in the specific sense of citizen opinion, the free public exchange of which is "the hallmark of all political thinking" ("TP," 236, 237). Arendt's adamant claim that "antipolitical" truth has no place in the public realm, however, needs to be balanced with her equally adamant claim that in the absence of accepted factual truths there would be no public realm and no opinions to exchange. For her, the "compelling force of [factual] truth" forms the scaffolding of the public realm but, as such "force," should be excluded from the political debate ("TP," 236).

This containment strategy, however, must be squared with Foucault's claim that the "force of truth" lies not in the "game of truth" itself but in the "regime": the "therefore" by which subjects submit themselves to the practical consequences that follow from the "it is true." I will examine this objection in chapters 1 and 4. For now, however, we might focus on Arendt's admission that factual truths, being contingent (they could always have been "otherwise"), are "vulnerable." She writes, "In other words, factual truth is no more self-evident than opinion, and ... opinion-holders find it relatively easy to discredit factual truth as just another opinion" ("TP," 238, 239). For Arendt, the fragility of truth and the ever-present possibility of its denial seems to inhere in the contingent nature of factual truth itself.

Notwithstanding its supposedly intrinsic "coercive force," factual truth is also at grave risk of being "manipulate[d] ... out of the world," giving rise to what Arendt describes as the "lying world order."[16] In her well-known account, twentieth-century totalitarianism was such a world. It invented what she calls "modern political lies." By contrast with familiar uses of the "traditional political lie," which intentionally misrepresents reality to deceive a political opponent, the modern lie aims not to mislead us or to falsify reality but to recreate it ("TP," 247). Arendt explains:

> Fascist propaganda ... was not satisfied with lying but deliberately proposed to transform its lies into reality. ... For such a fabrication of a lying reality no one was prepared. The essential characteristic of fascist propaganda was never its lies. ... The essential thing was that they exploited the age-old Occidental prejudice which confuses reality with truth, and made that "true" which until then could only be stated as a lie. It is for this reason that any argumentation with fascists ... is so extremely senseless: it is as though one were to debate with a potential murderer as to whether his future victim were dead or alive, completely forgetting that man can kill and that the murderer, by killing the person in question, could promptly provide proof of the correctness of this statement.[17]

With this transformation, the political lie introduces what Peg Birmingham, citing Arendt, calls "a mutation into the history of the lie."[18] As Arendt puts it, "One can say that to some extent fascism has added a new variation to the old art of lying—the most devilish variation—that of *lying* the truth."[19]

The "mutation" performed by the modern political lie does more than transform the lie into reality. Its political power goes beyond the creation of a fictitious world. The more intractable problem associated with the new modern art of "lying the truth," Arendt writes, is "a peculiar kind of cynicism—an absolute refusal to believe in the truth of anything, no matter how well this truth may be established. In other words, the result of a consistent and total substitution of lies for factual truth is not that the lies will now be accepted as truth, and the truth be defamed as lies, but that the sense by which we take our bearings in the real world—and the category of truth vs. falsehood is among the mental means to this end—is being destroyed" ("TP," 252). With that destruction goes deep skepticism about all truth claims: "If everybody always lies to you, the consequence is not that you believe the lies, but rather that nobody believes anything any longer."[20] The corrosiveness of the modern lie—which I argue to be most relevant to, but also occluded by, debates on post-truth—is worldly disorientation and the disintegration of citizens' credulity regarding facts and factual truth. Disintegration and disorientation go hand in hand with dismissing citizen opinions as cognitively worthless and with the shrinkage of the public space in which opinions can be formed and exchanged.[21]

The modern political lie is not restricted to terror-ruled regimes. In essays written after *The Origins of Totalitarianism*, Arendt doggedly examined the persistence and transformation of the modern political lie in contemporary democratic governments. In her scathing reading of the Pentagon Papers that I examine in chapter 3, Arendt forcefully argues that brazen "defactualization," reality-denying "image-making," and the destruction of the "distinction between true and false" are a standing threat to modern democracies. The modern lie is a complex reality-creating *and* destroying phenomenon that employs truth claims not to dissimulate truth (conceal, hide, or distort) but to undermine the basis of distinguishing between true and false and, with it, the belief that factual truth exists, that it needs support from opinion, and that it is world giving.

The erosion of belief such that nothing can count as evidence is a familiar trope of philosophical skepticism. In a typical skeptical argument, the skeptic puts forth a hypothesis that can account for all the data on which those beliefs rest but is incompatible with the beliefs themselves.[22] Famously dramatized by Descartes, our ordinary beliefs can be accounted for by the hypotheses that we are dreaming or hallucinating or, worse, that an "evil demon" is manipulating the entire content of what we take as real.[23] (We could be "brains in a vat" for all we know.)[24] Key to this form of skepticism is that no possible sensory evidence could distinguish between states in which we are dreaming and are awake, whether a demon is at work or not. Within the modern Western tradition's view of knowledge as certainty, the states are, as Samir Okasha puts it, "empirically equivalent."[25]

Accordingly, how can we be sure that the news we read is the news when all "news" looks identical to "fake news"? How do we know the faces we see on the internet depict real people when the web is awash in "deep-fakes." How do we know our favorite celebrity said "x" when social media sites are routinely hijacked by AI and human-sounding bots? The entirety of our existence could be a computer simulation.[26] The "evil demon" famously evoked by Descartes (also dear to conspiracy theorists) could be "the deep state," the "liberal media," "MAGA republicans," "democratic socialism," or "corporate capitalism," depending on your political point of view.[27] It should not surprise us that fact-checked evidence meant to prove otherwise in each case is increasingly disregarded or treated as further cause for doubt. Radical skepticism arises when "no possible data could tell apart the skeptical hypothesis and the beliefs the skeptic is attacking."[28] There is no possible counterevidence to assuage doubt.[29]

Arendt took Descartes's external world skepticism to express in acute terms the broader problem of subjectivism and worldlessness that characterize the modern age. She examines Cartesian doubt less as a philosophical argument, let alone a causal agent, but more as politically symptomatic of the modern loss of faith in the world-giving power of the senses and common sense, the "sixth sense" that fits sense experiences into a shared world.[30] Cartesian doubt is corrosive and all embracing. Arendt writes:

> The outstanding characteristic of Cartesian doubt is its universality, that nothing, no thought, and no experience, can escape it.... Cartesian doubt did not simply doubt that human understanding may not be open to every truth or that human vision may not be able to see everything, but that intelligibility to human understanding does not constitute a demonstration of truth, just as visibility did not at all constitute proof of reality. This doubt doubts that such a thing as truth exists at all, and discovers thereby that the traditional concept of truth, whether based on sense perception or on reason or on belief in divine revelation, had rested on the twofold assumption that what truly is will appear of its own accord and that human capabilities are adequate to receive it.[31]

Cartesian doubt evacuated the human senses as world giving and truth revealing; it denied intelligibility to human understanding as the measure of truth. It is "an even more disastrous blow to human confidence in the world and the universe than is indicated by a clear-cut separation of being and appearance," writes Arendt. Appearances are no longer understood as hiding "a true being which forever escapes the notice of man," as they were in metaphysics and ancient skepticism. "This Being, on the contrary, is tremendously active and energetic: it creates its own appearances, except that these appearances are delusions."[32]

As we will see in chapter 3, Cartesian doubt "used the nightmare of non-reality as a means of submerging all worldly objects into the stream of consciousness and its processes," writes Arendt.[33] Basic material objects such as "the 'seen tree'" come to figure in consciousness as radically distinct from any sense experience that could be shared.[34] Commonsense reasoning is reduced to "the playing of the mind with itself, which comes to pass when the mind is shut off from all reality and 'senses' only itself."[35] It is reasoning that happens to be the same in everyone but has lost all connection to reality and others. "What men now have in common is not the world but the structure of their minds" and the power of logical thinking cut free from the constraints of reality.[36] "This dissolution of objective reality into subjective states of mind or, rather, into subjective mental processes" and the loss of a common world that this entails are radically disorienting. They form the preconditions for the modern lie.[37]

Describing Cartesian skepticism as doubting "that such a thing as truth exists at all," Arendt could be read as describing the problem we call "post-truth." But this is an illusion. For her, the political problem of truth (mainly factual truth) is not, as it were, the loss of truth. Instead, it is a broader problem of modern subjectivism and worldlessness, compounded by the consumerism and loneliness of mass society. It is a problem of the constitution and maintenance of "the common world" that is bypassed by calls to reinstate the received notion of objective truth in which there would be no exchange of opinion and no debate. Although the modern lie in democratic regimes does not attain the totalitarian "total substitution of lies for factual truth," Arendt recognized—as should we—that loneliness, isolation, and a profoundly restricted public realm have generated a deep cynicism regarding factuality in democratic mass societies that is growing.[38] Any discussion of post-truth needs to begin there, and not with nostalgia for a supposedly lost Truth.

Arendt's response to the modern lie's ongoing threat to democratic politics is not to double-down on the received conception of objective truth, as did many intellectuals of her generation, like most post-truth critics today. From Plato to the present, this is the idea of truth as binary—either a proposition corresponds to reality, or it does not—and of opinion as a deficient truth claim. As Arendt will show us in chapter 1, truth on the Platonic account expresses *phainetai* ("it shows itself") in contrast to *dokei moi* ("it appears/seems to me"). Compromised by human forms of subjectivity and the perspectival, situated, and affective nature of human thought, opinion is merely subjective. It can never express truly objective knowledge.

"While the Platonic truth concept [*phainetai*] is criticized in modernity," writes Guido Niccolò Barbi, "the internal paradigm of truth [as binary] remains largely the same: truth describes phenomena as they are, independently of any singular point of view."[39] Its central doctrine—that all human knowledge is perspectival (subject dependent), and as such (merely) subjective (not objective)—persists in the inherited view of truth critically described by Foucault: truth has "coercive force" in itself and nothing to do with us (*GL*, 95). Truth "shows itself" and bypasses any "admixture of human subjectivity," to borrow James Conant's apt phrase.[40] "Anything properly termed an 'appearance' [*to* a subject] is *ipso facto* not a glimpse of reality."[41] Conant continues:

> It also gives rise . . . to the following fateful formula for specifying in substantive terms what it means for a property to be *objective*. Any property that is not (in the above sense) subjective (i.e., subject-dependent) is objective. Objective knowledge of the world, thus understood, must involve knowledge of properties of the world that in no way depend upon the effects such properties typically have upon the cognizing subjects. This has the following consequence: objective knowledge will be possible only for those beings who are able to piece together a picture of the universe which eschews all description in terms of properties that can be understood only through an essential reference to their effects on such beings.[42]

This fateful view of objectivity has decisive consequences for democratic politics. It binds truth to science, cognitive expertise, and epistemic competence (e.g., epistocracy), and, not least, it erodes ordinary citizens' view of opinion. As no exercise of human subjectivity can produce objective knowledge, opinion—one's own and that of one's fellow citizens—is ipso facto merely subjective. Singular perspective, how the world appears to each of us, can never bring the shared world into view. We therefore need a new problematization of truth.

Two Problematizations of Truth

Arendt teaches that a conception of truth and objectivity that excludes opinion denies what she argues to be the latter's world-giving power. To reconceptualize opinion as the condition of politically relevant truth, its "force" for citizen-subjects, is to refuse the principle of bivalence and the transcendent demand to which the political sphere has been reduced. The dokei moi, as Arendt will show us in chapter 1, is neither "subjective fantasy and arbitrariness, but also not something absolute and valid for all."[43] Instead, it is the means to create a shared world. Notwithstanding her argument about its antipolitical nature, Arendt reconceives truth as something that requires the support of opinion. In this way, she problematizes truth anew. I will now read her approach in tandem with what Foucault calls the "great problematization of truth," that is, how truth has been identified and discussed as a problem in specific registers of human life, including politics.

To think politically about the problem of truth, we first need to recognize the nonnecessary relation that Foucault discovers in the problematization of truth in ancient Greek society. As I argue in chapter 3, for him, a discourse of truth cannot be reduced to "the reality of the things of which it speaks."[44] Truth is a supplement added to reality. Put otherwise, the question of what is real is not the same as what is true: "The fact that the sky is blue will never be able to account for the fact that I say that the sky is blue," writes Foucault.[45] Foucault does not deny what "our most ordinary and common games of truth" take for granted, writes Lorenzini, namely, that "correspondence with reality does make it possible to establish the truth value of a statement: 'It is because the sky is blue that it is true to say: the sky is blue.'"[46] His aim is not to deny the "epistemic legitimacy of these games of truth, but to problematize the idea that their historical emergence can be accounted for solely by referring to the existence of a given reality."[47] Rightly putting to rest the charge that for Foucault "reality is but a function of discourse," Lorenzini finds in the later writings on truth an effort to reconstruct the singular and historical event of the game of truth in any given domain.[48]

Distinguishing between what is real and what is true, Foucault examines the emergence of true discourse in domains originally devoid of truth, including politics.[49] His approach to truth resonates in essential ways with Arendt's genealogical account of truth and the Greek polis. As I show in chapter 2, Arendt disputes the idea that politics has always been organized around the problem of truth. She describes the rise of the Platonic Academy as a new but antipolitical space of (philosophical and intellectual) freedom that pitted the few against the many, the quest for singular truth against plural opinion, which lives on in contemporary debates about academic freedom and the role of experts in democratic institutions. Each thinker genealogically disarticulates truth and politics to critically examine their historical origins and eventual entanglement in ways essential for rethinking democracy and the problem of truth today.

For both Arendt and Foucault, the political problem of truth arises from its long-standing historical entanglement with democracy. Democracy is the condition of true discourse; it is only in democratic societies that truth can emerge as nonnecessary, contingent. Authoritarian regimes, by contrast, typically root their claim to necessary truth in the absolute truth of religion and inheritance of tradition, excluding it from political debate. Bradford Vivian observes: "Regimes of truth amenable to authoritarian power (including those that circulate within formally democratic institutions) frequently traffic in especially pernicious metaphysical verities. Such verities concern the alleged truths of the great leader, of national destiny and might, of blood and soil, of spirit and will."[50] Absolute truth in the modern political realm is created through the "modern political lie" that constructs fictive worlds and erects such verities on the eroded public ground of corrigible plural opinions and the ability to distinguish true from false.

Discerning a "new problematization" of truth in fifth-century Athens, Foucault identifies a shift in the understanding of *parrhesia*, or the freedom to speak frankly.[51] Democracy, as an institutional system of equality, cannot determine who should have the right and the aptitude to tell the truth.[52] But not everyone who speaks frankly tells the truth. There can be "bad *parrhesia*" (*DT*, 124). The new Greek debate was about the relationship between parrhesia and democratic institutions. Foucault explains: "On the one side, democracy is a *politeia*, a constitution, where the *demos*, the people exercise power, and where everybody is equal before the law. But isn't it a fact that such a constitution is condemned to give place to any kind of *parrhesia*, even to the worst? And, on the other side, since *parrhesia* is given even to the worst citizens, isn't it a fact that this *parrhesia* becomes a danger for the city and for the democracy itself, since the overwhelming influence of bad orators leads necessarily to tyranny?" (*DT*, 124).

"The discovery of this problem—this kind of necessary antinomy between *parrhesia*, freedom of speech, [and] the relation to truth and democratic institutions," argues Foucault, set the terms and "the point of departure for a very long and impassioned [Greek] debate" (*DT*, 124). From Arendt's perspective, the fundamental shift brought about by the crisis of parrhesia is the turn away from the political realm. As we will see in chapter 3, this is the *philosophical* idea of parrhesia that holds the most interest for Foucault. "No longer linked to the *agora* as the public place where political discussions and decisions take place," this "new parrhesiastic practice" had grave consequences for democratic politics that continue to resonate today (*DT*, 157).[53]

"The problem [of democracy and *parrhesia*] sounds to us rather familiar," writes Foucault (*DT*, 124). Indeed, it captures the pessimistic mood of the contemporary debate over post-truth and democratic erosion (*DT*, 157). Such familiarity can hide from view the historical moment of discovery when *political parrhesia* became a problem, *philosophical parrhesia* arose in its place, and the free public exchange of opinions came to be seen as opposed to telling the truth.[54] It underwrites the assumption that to restore the commitment to true discourse is to return democracy to its real origin in Truth, which has been lost to excessive and rampant "bad *parrhesia*." And yet Foucault is clear: "Nothing is more inconsistent than a political regime that is indifferent to truth; but nothing is more dangerous than a political system that claims to lay down the truth."[55] This is the real danger that the post-truth debate conceals from view. Democracy has historically accommodated competing claims to truth and the right of ignorant and even irresponsible speakers to exercise the freedom to spread falsehoods as an instrument of power. That belongs to parrhesia and to *isegoria*, the equal right to speak in public. Nevertheless, the problem of knowing who is telling the truth persists if democratic citizens are to forestall the formation of a political regime whose claim to truth brokers no debate, for it transcends the political realm.

Foucault's study of parrhesia brings to light a crucial distinction between thinking about the problem of truth as being able to determine whether truth claims are veridical, on the one hand, and being able to discern who can tell the truth and why telling the truth matters, on the other hand. These related but different abilities, he avers, represent "two sides, two major aspects" of "the great problematization of truth" as it originated in ancient Greek society (*DT*, 224, 223). "One [side] is concerned with the question of how to make sure that a statement is true, that its reasoning is correct, and that we are able to get access to truth. And the other [side] is concerned with the question of the importance for individuals, for the community, for the city, for society, of telling the truth and of having people telling the truth and of recognizing which people are able to tell the truth" (*DT*, 224). The side concerned with the correct reasoning that determines if a statement is true is what Foucault calls "the analytics of truth." It can be traced back to "the great tradition in Western philosophy" (*DT*, 224). The side concerned with the importance of telling the truth is "the tradition of the question," which "is at the root, at the foundation of what we could call the critical tradition of philosophy in our society" (*DT*, 224).

Taking up these two distinct problematizations of truth, I read the post-truth debate as centered on "the analytics of truth," that is, on correct reasoning and veridicality, where the "force of truth" lies in the truth itself and it is only a matter of democratic citizens remaining cognitively alert to its presence: tracking truth. This first problematization of truth circles around issues associated with the "traditional lie," such as exposing falsehoods, errors, and deliberate dissimulation. Accordingly, it focuses on fact-checking and related knowledge practices concerning access to unbiased information and the ability to process it objectively. Essential though correct reasoning surely is, I argue in chapters 3 and 4 that it can operate without citizens recognizing truth as politically significant.[56] The citizen-subject might agree on the epistemic validity of a claim ("it is true") and yet refuse to draw pragmatic consequences from that agreement ("therefore, I submit"). For truth to have "force," there must be not only a game but also a regime of truth, which has everything to do with us and the political context in which games of truth are played. This includes authoritarian or totalitarian regimes and liberal-democratic ones characterized by loneliness, worldlessness, and a lifeless public realm.

Reducing truth-telling to correct reasoning, "the analytics of truth" misconstrues the genuine threat to democracy: growing cynicism toward parrhesia and the citizen opinion that Arendt holds to be essential to the fate of factual truth in the political realm. The crisis of parrhesia opens an abyss in the distinction between true and false, making possible the fictional realities of eternal verities beloved by authoritarian leaders and governments. Lost is what Foucault calls parrhesia's primary feature, its "function as criticism. Criticism of oneself, the speaker himself, or criticism of the interlocutor" (*DT*, 43). The crisis of parrhesia, then, is a crisis of critique: who can know the truth and tell it; who can tell the truth, and who will be believed?

Responses to this crisis have run the gamut of epistocratic arguments from Plato to the present, which would limit the political rights of citizens and entrust political rule to an "educated" class of citizens whose putative cognitive superiority could, in principle, trump participation as the main legitimating principle of political authority.[57] A democracy that relinquished civic-political participation as its legitimating principle would no longer qualify as a democracy. Consequently, "epistocratic" arguments in modern liberal democracies are typically clothed in the technocratic language of the administrative state, which serves as an object of fierce criticism for both Arendt and Foucault.

Epistocratic arguments respond to but in no way solve the crisis of parrhesia: how will we know who can tell the truth, and why should citizens trust "experts"? According to Foucault, the problem of truth-telling and the truth-teller, which figures in the second great problematization of truth, is not a brief for epistocracy but an attempt to forestall arguments for its necessity. Such arguments take hold when average citizens are not trusted to make the right decisions or even to decide who is capable. Consequently, citizens are called on to give up the right to decide in matters of common concern and even to decide which people are making the correct decisions and can tell the truth. They are, in effect, called on to give up their right to an opinion that could have any public meaning whatsoever. Further, as the 1920s debate between Walter Lippmann and John Dewey vividly showed, once cognitive competence becomes the primary criterion for meaningful participation in everyday affairs, the ordinary citizen's opinion, no matter how informed, will never rise to satisfy technocratic criteria of knowledge.[58] Thus, technocracy reduces citizen opinion to subjective perspectives with no claim to knowledge and risks morphing into various forms of authoritarianism, for which truth is no longer contingent but necessary and fixed.

Arendt and Foucault view truth as a problem that inheres in democracy, a problem that cannot be eradicated without destroying democracy or solved by epistemological (e.g., epistocratic) means. They raise the issue of truth as something other than a problem of the criteria for true statements and correct reasoning, which can be traced back to Greek philosophy, beginning with Plato, Aristotle, Chrysippus, and Sextus Empiricus (*DT*, 223). I've argued that within the frame of the first problematization of truth, "post-truth" appears to be a strictly epistemic matter and that this diagnosis fails to grapple adequately with the related phenomena of the modern political lie, worldlessness, and an inert public realm. The modern lie is less a problem of correct reasoning than a loss of worldly orientation and the ability to distinguish true from false. We come to inhabit the fictitious worlds spawned in the absence of a robust public realm with its exchange of opinions about how the common world appears to each of us.

The problem of truth-telling expressed by the crisis of parrhesia gave rise to the second great problematization of truth: how can we decide who is telling the truth when all have the right to speak publicly (isegoria)? How can we contain "bad *parrhesia*" if its possibility is also that of democracy itself? "For there to be democracy there must be *parrhesia*; for there to be *parrhesia* there must be democracy," writes Foucault.[59] Epistocratic arguments and their refutation have defined no small part of the debate over democratic erosion and post-truth. They circle better and worse ways of limiting bad parrhesia, which must have consequences for the possibility of democracy itself. Whatever side one takes in this debate, we risk devising a cure worse than the disease. How might we leave the terms of the discussion behind and build out the critical "tradition of the question" in ways that can facilitate democratic critique and truth-telling today?

Critique and Truth-Telling in a Realistic Key

Reframing the debate about post-truth through the critical tradition and the problem of truth-telling rather than correct reasoning, I advance a democratic theory of truth and democratic critique in a *realistic spirit*.[60] My argument is rooted in ordinary language philosophy and takes its cue from Cora Diamond's book *The Realistic Spirit: Wittgenstein, Philosophy, and the Mind*, which explores the attitude toward worldly reality expressed in the philosopher's work.[61] Diamond interprets Wittgenstein's realistic stance as a critical response to the surprising affinity between the antirealist (e.g., empiricist) *and* realist idea that some underlying regularity must secure the proper relationship of our judgments to reality.[62] This realistic attitude is distinguished from metaphysical realism and antirealism about facts, truth, and meaning.[63]

The surprising affinity between realism and antirealism, writes Diamond, can be found in the shared "style of answer to questions of the general type: *Where is* the reality which must guide us here? Where is the reality to which our mode of thought must be responsible?"[64] The realist and antirealist "accept the same pair of alternatives." "Both views conceive the situation this way: [either] *there is* a logical reality independent of and external to our modes of thought and expression, *or there is not* and the logical structures of our thought and expression are fundamentally arbitrary."[65] The realist and the antirealist "share a conception: either there is something where we are both looking for a reality, or there is not, and we are without objective standards; that is what they both think."[66] Both think that reality is to be sought external to the modes of expression; they disagree only on whether such a reality exists.[67]

Like the realist, the antirealist assumes a transcendent perspective on meaning *must* be the condition of objectivity and related epistemic ideals (which ironically concedes the realist view). From what position concerning language and our experience would we need to stand to occupy that perspective? The interpretation of Wittgenstein as an antirealist assumes that there is a genuine philosophical question for him as to the existence of metaphysical features of reality, underlying structural or logical characteristics of language, which he supposedly answered negatively and decisively. "The criticism of the metaphysical demand by Wittgenstein is never that what is demanded *is not there*, that there are no facts of the kind which is necessary if the demand is to be met [i.e., mind independent]," objects Diamond.[68] Pace his putative antirealism, Wittgenstein views the idea of a transcendent perspective not as a *"mistake"* but as a *"fantasy"*—a picture of how things *must* be.[69] When envisioning ourselves as occupying it, we speak as if we "were looking down onto the relation between ourselves and some reality, some kind of fact or real possibility."[70] Are we not looking for reality in the wrong place?

"Look somewhere *else*: that is what we can hear in Wittgenstein's later philosophy; look where you do not think there can be any reason for looking," writes Diamond.[71] This place consists in our ordinary "nonmetaphysical methods of distinguishing the real and the unreal," which the realist counsels us to mistrust and the antirealist embraces at the expense of any claim to objectivity.[72] By contrast with the realist and the "metaphysical spirit," Wittgenstein teaches that reality is not to be found external to or beyond our affective modes of expression but *in* them. And contrary to the antirealist, he shows those modes are not arbitrary but objective, just as Conant describes: "We need to be able to regard our modes of sensibility as involving operations of subjectivity *and* as affording us genuine glimpses of the world."[73]

Wittgenstein makes visible the fantasy—the "picture [that holds] us captive"—that leads both realists and antirealists to think our linguistic practices depend for their stability on a prior reality whose truth has nothing to do with us.[74] At the same time, he seeks to redirect attention from looking beyond our life with words to the practices themselves. In a famous, difficult, but also clarifying passage of *Philosophical Investigations* he responds to an imaginary interlocutor thus: "'So you are saying that human agreement decides what is true and what is false?'—It is what human beings *say* that is true and false; and they agree in the *language* they use. That is not agreement in opinions but in form of life" (*PI*, §241). Wittgenstein's claim is not that *whatever* human beings say is true (subjectivism), but that whatever is true is spoken by us (subject dependent). Truth is, as Foucault held, a supplement added to reality ("The sky is blue") that originates in our ordinary life with language and in nonepistemic (versus antirealist) forms of agreement that Wittgenstein calls "certainty" (*Gewissheit*). I examine his argument in chapters 4 and 6.

Critical questioning in a realistic spirit facilitates awareness of philosophical and political fantasies that seek "the criteria of truth, reality, objectivity, and meaning . . . outside rather than within our practices," as John Gunnell, reflecting on the lesson of Wittgenstein, describes the ongoing task for critical political thought.⁷⁵ In chapter 1, we will see how Arendt's radical and realistic reformulation of "thinking" locates the "metaphysical spirit" at work in the philosopher's fantasy of a reality to be found beyond the appearing and contingent world of human affairs. Like Wittgenstein, Arendt recognizes that we continue to live in the ruins of metaphysics and that to declare ourselves antirealists is to remain in the grip of the picture or fantasy of what must be the case for our practices to be objective or make claims to truth. Arendtian realistic critical thinking works with an ordinary conception of truth rooted in the exchange of plural opinion. Modeled by Socrates in the space of appearances that is the agora, such thinking examines received concepts in cases where we reach a stalemate between opposing views or are confronted with something strange, unexpected, surprising, or new.

Critics who denounce post-truth as the impending death of democracy and those who grudgingly accept it as the price for democratic pluralism both entangle us further in the metaphysical fantasy about what truth and objectivity require. They share the same surprising affinity of the realist and the antirealist: either there is an independent reality, and we need to keep looking for it, or there is none, and our fate is post-truth. Both make our knowledge and experience of objective reality dependent on something wholly external to what we say and do. This "[narrow] conception of objectivity," to speak with Alice Crary, is based on an impossible "abstraction requirement" that strictly excludes the use of our affective propensities as if they were, in Conant's phrase, "irremediably distorting."⁷⁶ Rather than seek the elimination of any "admixture of subjectivity," the realistic spirit adopts what Crary calls "the alternative, philosophically heterodox conception of objectivity." According to this "wider conception," she writes, objectivity is conceived as capacious enough to encompass what are typically seen as "problematically subjective [human] properties."⁷⁷ Working from the narrow conception, the debate over post-truth has us looking for reality in the wrong place: everything we need for critical thinking and democratic truth-telling is already available in our public acting and speaking, in what we say and do.

The Difficulty of Reality

A realistic orientation toward the world does not assume that facing reality is easy—far from it. Diamond speaks of "the difficulty of reality," that is, "experiences in which we take something in reality to be resistant to our thinking it, or possibly to be painful in its inexplicability, difficult in that way, or perhaps awesome and astonishing in its inexplicability. *We take things so*. And the things we take so may simply not, to others, present the same kind of difficulty—of being hard or impossible or agonizing to get one's mind round."[78] We may find ourselves alone when experiencing the difficulty of reality; others may find reality presents no real problem that our ordinary concepts cannot handle. Citing Stanley Cavell, Diamond calls this a form of "deflection," when we move from an awareness of something that makes impossible demands on our thinking to familiar concepts that deny anything radically new or disturbing presents itself at all.[79]

To take Cavell's example, one might translate human finitude and the radical separateness of human beings into a philosophical "problem of other minds," a known trope in the skeptic's conceptual toolbox.[80] Or, to take Diamond's, when confronted with the suffering of animals slaughtered for human consumption, we deflect that painful reality into the philosopher's tool kit for "how we should treat animals. Should we eat them, should we grant them rights? And so on. Philosophy knows how to do this. It is hard, all right, but that is what university philosophy departments are for, to enable us to learn how to discuss hard problems, what constitutes a good argument, what is distorted by emotion, when we are making assertions without backing them up."[81] Such cases, she writes, are characterized by "a repudiation of the everyday; with a sense of being shouldered out from our ways of thinking and speaking by a torment of reality. . . . The repudiation may be heard as expressing such-and-such position in an intellectualized debate; . . . opposite sides in the debate may have more in common than they realize."[82]

The deflection of reality can also take the form of something that exceeds our expectations, experience, and concepts. Relating the story told by Ruth Klüger in her memoir *Still Alive: A Holocaust Girlhood*, Diamond retells the terrified young Ruth's experience of wonder at a girl, also forcibly held at Auschwitz, who, risking her own life, saved Ruth's. "Klüger says when she tells her story in wonder, 'people wonder at my wonder. They say, okay, some persons are altruistic. We understand that. It doesn't surprise us. The girl who helped you was one of those who liked to help.'"[83] Klüger asks us to confront rather than deflect her wonder with a well-known concept (altruism). Elsewhere, Diamond describes this possibility of the unexpected thus: "Reality may surprise us, not only by showing us what *is* the case, when we had not expected it was, but also by showing us something beyond what we had ever taken to be possible, beyond anything we had thought of at all. Our conception of what is possible might be altered by reality to include something not merely beyond anything we had imagined, but beyond anything we *could* imagine, given our finite capacity to imagine things."[84]

Arendt also speaks of facing what she calls "reality" and criticizes the received idea that "comprehension" involves turning the unknown into the known. In the first preface to *The Origins of Totalitarianism*, she forcefully declares:

> The conviction that everything that happens on earth must be comprehensible to man can lead to interpreting history by commonplaces. Comprehension does not mean denying the outrageous, deducing the unprecedented from precedents, or explaining phenomena by such analogies and generalities that the impact of reality and the shock of experience are no longer felt. It means, rather, examining and bearing consciously the burden which our century has placed on us—neither denying its existence nor submitting meekly to its weight. Comprehension, in short, means the unpremeditated, attentive facing up to, and resisting of, reality—whatever it may be. (*OT*, viii)

"Facing up to reality," as Deborah Nelson observes, "appears countless times in slightly different phrasing throughout Arendt's entire body of writing." Striking here is the idea—call it a demand—that her readers, too, need to face reality, with little concession to how painful or disorienting—in a word, difficult—that might be. We should face reality in an "unpremeditated" way, which, Nelson clarifies, "implies openness and defenselessness, a refusal to assemble in advance the tools or the categories to apprehend a set of facts that may defy both."[85] Those tools are what Arendt calls the "commonplaces" or ordinary concepts that reassure us in the face of the "unprecedented," something radically unknown, a phenomenon that exceeds our received concepts, experience, and ideas. "In this sense, it must be possible to face and to understand the outrageous fact that so small (and, in world politics, so unimportant) a phenomenon as the Jewish question and antisemitism could become the catalytic agent for first, the Nazi movement, then a world war, and finally the establishment of death factories" (*OT*, viii). We must first face reality if we are ever to resist it.

There are ways of interpreting such "small" facts that lead to no comprehension at all but instead to denying that anything "outrageous" and "unprecedented" has occurred (e.g., judging antisemitism to be not the mere catalyst but the *cause* of these events). Comprehension as a critical practice is not a positivist question of assembling facts qua evidence to justify truth claims, as antirealist verificationism would have it. We can recognize what is new in such facts and how facts unsettle what we already think is at stake. Instead of assuming that facts alone tell us everything we need to know, Arendt examines how our interpretation of facts through received concepts might distort reality and close our eyes to what has occurred, to its surprising, novel, or even unprecedented character. Guided by what Alice Crary called the "narrow conception of objectivity,"[86] verification procedures too often employ facts in ways that eliminate their contingency and subject dependence, blocking them as vehicles for feeling "the impact of reality and the shock of experience," as Arendt put it (*OT*, viii).

Further, claims about reality—past or present—are underdetermined by the data on which they are based. That is what the skeptic (e.g., historical revisionist) exploits. More facts cannot fix underdetermination by the data, as if the facts speak for themselves. Factualists who insist on verification conditions face the well-known objection that few empirical statements can be conclusively established or verified and that they rest on forms of nonepistemic and nonpropositional "certainty." This is a point that Arendt stresses when describing the endless possibilities for lying in politics (chapter 3).[87]

The difficulty of reality can involve something other than unprecedented, surprising, or novel events. It more often concerns attending to, bringing into view, or taking notice of the ordinary itself. Facing reality can involve learning a new way of seeing what has gone unnoticed because of its familiarity. "One is unable to notice something—because it is right before our eyes," writes Wittgenstein, whose discussion of "seeing aspects" I discuss in chapter 6 (*PI*, §129).[88] We take things for granted and fail to appreciate their strangeness as if it is just how things are (and always were, perhaps always will be). To take things in this way may be *realist* in the conventional sense. However, it is not *realistic*, for it deflects the difficulty of reality with sedimented concepts (e.g., "animal rights," "altruism," "women's work," "political rule"). Bringing these things to our attention, "lighting them up," as feminist ordinary language philosopher Nancy Bauer puts it, is a practice of realistic critique.[89] To adopt the realistic spirit is to recognize, as Hanna Pitkin writes of Wittgenstein's teaching, that "sometimes it is not easy to see the obvious; sometimes we have to learn to see, and the learning can be a slow and difficult process. It is almost a matter of forming new habits of thought."[90]

To attend to the ordinary is not to leave everything just as it was. Typically ascribed to the quietism said to characterize Wittgenstein's work, this received idea of the ordinary misunderstands the difficulty of learning to see and "understand something that is already in plain view," as he puts it (*PI*, §89). Reaching for the external standpoint, the place outside human practice where Truth is said to dwell, it bypasses that difficulty in search of the "hidden." Noticing the taken for granted, seeing it under a different aspect (e.g., that the "force of truth" depends on us), aims at a transformation, not confirmation, of the given. There can be, in Toril Moi's marvelous phrase, a "revolution of the ordinary" that comes from paying "attention to particulars."[91]

What could the realistic spirit be in democratic political theory? What difficulty of reality does one face there? Could there be a political theory that is not deflected from such difficulty? Wittgenstein and Arendt teach that we need to reorient ourselves in the ordinary realm of human action and speech and learn to see what is in plain view from different points of view, for only through multiple perspectives can the world we have in common be critically comprehended and judged. We need to affirm the subject dependence of objectivity and our world-giving, corrigible affective propensities, how the world seems to each of us, as the basis for a realistic form of democratic critique.

Foucault, too, is deeply attuned to the critical resources of the ordinary. "We have known for a long time that the role of philosophy is not to discover what is concealed, but rather to make visible what precisely is visible—which is to say, to make appear what is so close, so immediate, so intimately linked with ourselves that we cannot perceive it," he writes.[92] The model for thinking critically without leaving the plane of the ordinary, observes Foucault, is none other than "Anglo-American" ordinary language philosophy:

> Anglo-Saxon analytic philosophy does give itself the task of reflecting on the being of language or the deep structures of speech; it reflects on the everyday use of speech we make in the different kinds of discourse. In a similar manner, I think we could imagine a philosophy that would seek to show what these relations of power are about, what their forms, stakes, and objectives are.... Anglo-Saxon philosophy seeks to tell that language never fails nor shows anything. Rather, language is played. Hence, the importance of the notion of game....
>
> Relations of power too are played; they are games of power that we should study in terms of tactics and strategy, rule and accident, stakes and objective. It's a little bit in this direction that I have tried to work.[93]

If Foucault has a critical "method," it is this. Approaching truth as an ordinary language "game," rather than a suprahistorical force that transcends what we say and do, he develops a realistic critique that makes "visible precisely what is visible" but remains unseen from the external perspective where such Truth dwells. Getting into view what is so "intimately linked with ourselves," as we will see in chapter 2, is what he calls an "ontology of ourselves."[94]

My argument for a realistic democratic critique, based on learning to see what is in plain view, follows from a wager: the problem of post-truth is not—in the first place—one of false belief, false consciousness, or ideological distortion. Instead, as I argue in chapters 3, 4, and 6, it is better characterized as a problem of what David Owen astutely calls "aspectival captivity." This is the state of being held captive by a picture or perspective, that is, by a system of judgments, themselves neither true nor false, that provides the framework in which we count what *can* be true or false, subject to the activity of judging politically, and so part of the common world.[95] When held captive to a picture or perspective, we cannot countenance the existence of other pictures or perspectives in which to decide what could count as true or false. It is as if we were frozen in one or another "game of truth" with no sense that there might be others in which the world becomes intelligible as shared. We are blind to the potential truth-value of other perspectives and to our ability to see differently.

As a diagnosis of what ails us, "post-truth" itself is not a real condition but a picture that holds us hostage to the suprahistorical idea of truth and its narrow conception of objectivity. Let us aspire to loosen the grip of this picture and facilitate a better understanding of our current predicament and our imaginative capacity to face and resist it. A realistic democratic theory of truth begins in the ordinary, with what we do and say in everyday language. There, the truths relevant to politics will be found because they do indeed depend on us.

❋ 1 ❋
To Bring Thinking Down to Earth

The question is whether thinking and other mental activities which are invisible and soundless are meant to appear to begin with or whether they can never find an adequate home in the world.

ARENDT, "THINKING"

"Thinking," part 1 of Arendt's *The Life of the Mind*, is a subversive text.[1] It brings the traditional philosophical activity of thinking back down to earth, wholly recalibrating its relationship to the realm of appearances and, thus, to the political realm. However, this radical reformulation of thinking is hard to see. Arendt often ventriloquizes well-known voices of Western philosophy; consequently, it is not always clear *who* is speaking about the activity of thinking. For some readers, the philosophical voice signals Arendt's homecoming to the tradition in which this student of Heidegger and Jaspers was formally trained. For Ronald Beiner, Arendt's last and unfinished work on thinking, willing, and judging as autonomous "mental activit[ies]," rather than "feature[s] of political life," represents a turn away from the *vita activa* to the *vita contemplativa*; it represents a withdrawal from the political realm tout court.[2]

In previous work, I questioned this reading of the later Arendt, but my focus was on the activity of judging.[3] Here, I am concerned with thinking, a faculty that, compared with willing and judging, seems to withdraw most from the world of appearances and the public realm. To make political sense of Arendt's concern with thinking, I begin with what she calls the "two rather different origins" of her "preoccupation with mental activities": the trial of Adolf Eichmann, on the one hand, and the Western philosophical tradition's distortion of both the vita activa and the vita contemplativa, on the other hand (15; 3). The two seemingly unconnected origins share a resolutely political concern: how to face and, where appropriate, resist reality and affirm a shared world.

From Contemplation to Thinking

"The title I gave to this lecture series [the Gifford Lectures], *The Life of the Mind*, sounds pretentious," writes Arendt, "and to talk about Thinking seems to me so presumptuous that I feel I should start less with an apology than with a justification" (15; 3). After all, Arendt admits to having "neither claim nor ambition to being a 'philosopher' or what Kant, not without irony, called the *Denker von Gewerbe*, the 'professional thinkers'" (15; 3). Instead, she describes herself as a rogue intellectual traveler who "ventures forth from the relatively safe fields of political science and theory into these rather awesome matters." Why not leave the topic of thinking in the hands of "the experts"? she asks.

What initially appears as a concession to the "professional thinkers" (i.e., the philosophers) quickly becomes a radical redefinition of their subject matter. Arendt makes two seemingly unrelated moves: (1) she sets out the Eichmann trial as the worldly problem that first "prompted" her interest in the subject matter of thinking, and (2) she raises doubts about the professional thinkers' ability to recognize the distinctiveness of their own intellectual activity. Arendt wonders whether her central thesis regarding "the banality of evil" can support an unexplored connection between thinking and wrongdoing. "Could the activity of thinking as such . . . be among the conditions or even actually 'condition' men in such a way that they abstain from evil-doing?" (17; 5). In her controversial view, Eichmann was "quite ordinary, commonplace, and neither demonic nor monstrous" (16; 4), less driven by fierce political convictions than an inability to think. His demeanor was characterized not by "stupidity but *thoughtlessness*" (16; 4). Although the philosophers have nothing to say about the political case of Eichmann, perhaps they can shed light on what it means to think.

However, this hope is quickly dashed, and almost immediately Arendt names a second and, at first glance, only indirectly related reason for writing a book on thinking. The Eichmann trial had raised "moral questions, originating in factual experience" that did not seem answerable within the Western philosophical tradition (17; 6). This worry, in turn, she continues,

> renew[ed] in me certain doubts which had plagued me ever since I had finished a study of what my publisher wisely called "The Human Condition," but which I had intended more modestly as an inquiry into "The Vita Activa." I had been concerned with the problem of Action, the oldest concern of political theory, and what had always troubled me in this concern was that the very term under which I reflected on this matter, namely, *Vita activa*, was coined by those who themselves were devoted to

the contemplative way of life and who looked upon all kinds of being alive from this perspective. (17; 6)

This philosophical prejudice, which valued "complete quietness in contemplating" (18–19; 7) over everything else, unsurprisingly dismissed Action and, more generally, the Vita Activa, flattening out what Arendt argues to be the fundamentally different activities of labor, work, and action.[4] More surprisingly, this same leveling gesture appears in the philosophers' account of their own domain, the vita contemplativa, where active thinking is subordinated to passive contemplation as the highest state of mind. Arendt clarifies: "The thinking activity, according to Plato the soundless dialogue we carry on with ourselves, only serves to open the eyes of the mind, and even the Aristotelian *nous* is an organ for seeing and beholding the truth. In other words, thinking ends and aims at contemplation, and contemplation is no activity but a passivity, it is the point where mental activity comes to rest" (18; 6).

Suppose active thinking was but a stage to be transcended by passive contemplation in the quest for truth. In that case, we may wonder whether truth is the proper object of thinking according to the "professional thinkers" or if they should be deferred to as "experts" on the topic.

Invoking the "curious sentence" from Cicero (citing Cato), which had closed *The Human Condition*, Arendt proposes an idea of thinking that contests, right from the start, the authority of the traditional account: "Never is he [man] more active than when he does nothing, never is he less alone than when he is by himself" (19; 7–8). When read together with the Eichmann vignette, this sentence points subversively toward an image of thinking that is radically different from what the professional thinkers assumed: thinking might be active, not passive; it might strive for some unsettled relation to the plural and contingent realm of human affairs, rather than the solitariness, stillness, and speechlessness of contemplation.

The relationship between thinking and wrongdoing, the problem of Eichmann, cannot be posed, let alone answered, from within the vita contemplativa, where the activity of thinking has been wholly subsumed under the passivity of contemplation. To make sense of Eichmann's wrongdoing, Arendt must recover thinking as a distinctive activity and dislodge the idea, "as old as Western philosophy," that "contemplation is the highest state of mind" (18; 6), the end against which all other human activities (including thinking) should be measured and toward which they should strive. She will release thinking from its subordinate relationship to contemplation and the quest for eternal truth and bring thinking back down to earth, to the realm of appearances, where it has its original home.

Thoughtlessness

Exploring the possible connection between thinking and wrongdoing, Arendt claims that Eichmann was thoughtless but not stupid. Why insist that Eichmann was lacking not in knowledge but in the ability to think? Why not focus on what he claimed to know or not know about, say, what was happening to the Jews and other groups singled out for state-organized extermination, about the brazen falsification of scientific evidence to support the supposed natural superiority of the Aryan race, or about the Nazi invention of such tales as the Elders of Zion as proof of a universal Jewish conspiracy? What is at stake for Arendt and for us today in the difference between knowing and thinking?

One thing that is at stake, says Arendt, is this: "If . . . the ability to tell right from wrong should have anything to do with the ability to think, then we must be able to 'demand' its exercise in every sane person, no matter how erudite or ignorant, how intelligent or stupid, he may happen to be" (24; 13). "Thoughtlessness is not stupidity, it can be found in highly intelligent people," she asserts (24; 13). This claim is akin to remarks in the *Lectures on Kant's Political Philosophy* that intelligence does not guarantee the ability to judge, and that this ability is something we can expect of everyone: we have no more need for professional thinkers than for professional judges.[5] It is a normative claim about what citizens can demand from each other.

Arendt's point is not that all citizens should know (and follow) a shared rule of conduct collectively distilled through acts of thinking. "Should the problem of good and evil, should our ability to tell right from wrong be connected with our faculty of thought," she writes, it is "not in the sense that thinking could ever produce the good deed as its result" (16; 5). Thinking does not produce rules of conduct that, once learned, can be applied to the particulars of everyday life. Thinking is not knowing what is good.

But that is not all. Arendt shows that the ability to tell right from wrong turns on citizens' ability to face the "shock of reality" rather than avoid it as did Eichmann, using "clichés, stock phrases, adherence to conventional, standardized codes of expression and conduct" (16; 4). She notes that these "have the socially recognized function of protecting us against reality, that is, against the claim on our thinking attention that all events and facts arouse by virtue of their existence" (16; 4). They form the *Vorurteile*, the prejudices or prejudgments, whose otherwise essential role in our lives Arendt does not dispute: "If we were responsive to this claim all the time, we would soon be exhausted; the difference in Eichmann was only that he clearly knew of no such claim at all" (16; 4).

For Arendt, "the unpremeditated attentive facing up to and resisting of reality—whatever it may be" requires what Deborah Nelson described as an "openness and defenselessness, a refusal to assemble in advance the tools or the categories to apprehend a set of facts that may defy both."[6] The problem is not with ordinary language and given concepts, whose pragmatic function protects us against the unending demand the everyday world makes on our attention. Instead, it is when ordinary concepts no longer orient us in the everyday world but conceal or disfigure it. At that point, they become a grab bag of banalities and platitudes that animate rule following as a mechanical decision procedure indifferent to the particulars of any given case. As a preliminary definition, the failure to think—the problem of Eichmann—is the inability to recognize when specific ordinary concepts have exhausted their orienting function.[7]

Eichmann's inability to think is not a failure of knowledge, and wrongdoing does not result from something in the world that he does not know. Eichmann may not know much about the world, but the claim that reality ought to make on his thinking attention concerns something other than that. The question arises about what makes—or ought to make—a claim on one's attention. What in the world makes us think? What is this reality against which prejudices and prejudgments typically protect us but toward which we must remain receptive if we are to avoid wrongdoing?

Being receptive to the call of reality involves not only cognitive abilities but also the need and quest for meaning. In the text, Arendt moves directly from the difference between stupidity and absence of thought to Kant's distinction between "*Vernunft* and *Verstand*, 'reason' and 'intellect'" (24; 13). The former faculty concerns the quest for meaning, while the latter concerns the search for knowledge.[8] What it means to *know* something to be the case is in some politically significant way different from what it means to seek the *meaning* of what may be the case. This difference, explored below, is implicit in her claim that Eichmann was thoughtless but not stupid. Something is at stake in the quest for meaning for affirming a shared world. As Arendt sees it, the unthinking but not stupid Eichmann knows many facts, but he is blind to their meaning, that is, to the reality that calls on him to respond. Instead, his knowledge supported the refusal "to share the earth with the Jewish people and the people of a number of other nations."[9]

Thinking in the Ruins of Metaphysics

The connection between thinking and a shared everyday world may seem counterintuitive. After all, Arendt describes thinking's quest for meaning as leaving the world of appearances behind. How are we to make sense of this concession to traditional philosophical accounts?

When one reflects on thinking, she remarks, one is tempted to fall back into the various "metaphysical fallacies" of Western philosophy. Thinking seems to move in what the tradition described as the supersensory realm, the "true world" of (Platonic) ideas forever above and apart from the sensory realm, the "apparent world" of human affairs. Affirming the "modern deat[h] ... of ... metaphysics," Arendt nevertheless identifies thinking as harboring an experience that mimics "the metaphysical fallacies ... [that] contain the only clues we have to what thinking means to those who engage in it—something of great importance today and about which, oddly enough, there exist very few direct utterances" (22, 23; 11, 12). Clues are all we have because, for the philosophers, thinking was a mere way station to what ultimately mattered: Truth and contemplation of eternal things.

The subsumption of thinking under contemplation is a consequence of belief in "the dichotomy of Being and Appearance" (33; 25) or, more precisely, of "the evaluation of Being versus Appearance, which is at the bottom of all two-world theories" (47; 42), Arendt remarks. In the metaphysical view of reality, thinking that does not end in contemplation cannot get behind the appearance and grasp truth: phainetai ("it shows itself"). Such thinking remains hostage to appearances and stuck in the "mode of an it-seems-to-me, *dokei moi*" (29; 21). Accordingly, dokei moi, which is by definition active (i.e., it involves the "me" to which something appears), can never attain actual knowledge. Contemplation, by contrast, is passive: Being shows itself; it does not appear-*to*-me. Truth should only describe phenomena as such and be indifferent to any relation between phenomena and observer. Truth should tell only what appears as it is, independently from its singular appearance in dokei moi. Something is either true or false—the bivalence principle—regardless of the observer's ability to recognize it. I have no say in phainetai, what shows itself.

As argued in the introduction, the search for truth choreographed by the two-world theory is a quest for what Cora Diamond called a metaphysical "elucidation, the demand that a philosophical account of what I mean make clear how it is fixed, out of all possible continuations, out of some real semantic space, *which* I mean."[10] Philosophical realists think they need something independent of context, experience, and the speaking subject to distinguish between the real and the illusions. With this belief in hand, the philosophical realist looks past how ordinary experience provides the clues we need to tell that difference. The realist does not see that the concept of the word "real" merely floats free and is what Diamond called a "fantasy." She explains: "A fantasy of what it is for a term to mean something is what leads us to philosophical fantasy about what we are getting at when we distinguish the real from the chimerical" (e.g., true forms versus mere shadows in the Platonic cave).[11]

For Arendt, "this traditional hierarchy [of Being versus Appearance] does not arise out of our ordinary experiences in the world of appearances. Its source is rather the not-at-all ordinary experience of the thinking ego" (47; 42). Saying as much, Arendt at once grants this experience of the two-world theory as subjectively real but redescribes it as a "metaphysical delusion," for "the thinking ego obviously never leaves the world of appearances altogether" (105; 110). Thinking beings still appear to others when they think. By granting the subjective experience of thinking as a withdrawal from the world of appearances in which, objectively speaking, we still are, Arendt does not declare the philosopher's fantasy or delusion wrong. Instead, she makes political sense of this subjective experience by revealing its denied objective conditions of possibility: the reality of the appearing world.

Arendt's response to the philosophical tradition's "metaphysical delusion" is therapeutic and radical. It shifts our focus from a rejection of metaphysics, as if it presented a set of propositions that are either true or false, to a critical account of how we misunderstand what we do when we think. "The two-world theory," she observes, "is a metaphysical delusion although by no means an arbitrary or accidental one; it is the most plausible delusion with which the experience of thought is plagued" (105; 110). Rather than deny the experience that philosophy affirms (a loss of worldly reality when engaged in thinking), Arendt makes political sense of it. Doing so will allow her to distinguish thinking from contemplation and restore the former to its "original" home. By contrast with the eventual home of contemplation in the Platonic Academy (where, as we will see in the next chapter, the thinking few took flight from the so-called unthinking many), this original home of thinking is the space of appearances, whose locus classicus is for Arendt the agora, where Socrates thought together with other citizens.

Arendt's critical therapeutic approach to thinking is akin to Wittgenstein's approach to skepticism. For him, skepticism could not be refuted (as, for example, G. E. Moore had famously tried to do when he outstretched his two hands to prove the "existence of external things"); it could, at best, be exposed as a fantasy or delusion.[12] Skeptics must be brought to recognize the conditions of their doubting practice: there can be no doubt without end; every doubt has its conditions of certainty. To reveal something as a fantasy or delusion differs from proving it false. Criteria of correctness are out of place here. Notwithstanding her characterization of the two-world theory as one among other "metaphysical *fallacies*," Arendt recognizes that metaphysics is not an error we can correct but, as Wittgenstein put it, a "picture" that holds us "captive" (*PI*, §115).[13] To recover thinking from its fate in contemplation's quest for absolute truth, Arendt first attempts to make this picture visible and, with Socrates, offers a different picture.

Looking for clues in the metaphysical fallacies to what thinking might be, Arendt does not aim to resurrect metaphysics—not desirable and, in any case, impossible, in her view.[14] Instead, she highlights an aspect of thinking that keeps metaphysics alive as an ongoing temptation to which we, political thinkers and democratic citizens in the grip of philosophical prejudices, are susceptible—and dangerously so. When we think, we are prone to misinterpret our thinking practice, failing to see it as an activity concerned primarily with meaning, not knowledge or truth, and as an activity located in the contingent and ordinary realm of human affairs, something we can expect of each other, not as "professional thinkers" but as citizens.

Alternatively, those who wish to refashion thinking after metaphysics may recognize that the two-world theory is no longer credible and resign themselves to life in the "apparent world," where appearances are all there is. "What has come to an end is the basic distinction between the sensual and the supersensual, together with the notion, at least as old as Parmenides, that whatever is not given to the senses—God or Being or the First Principles and Causes (*archai*) or the Ideas—is more real, more truthful, more meaningful than what appears, that it is not just *beyond* sense perception but *above* the world of the senses" (21; 10). But to this once suspect sensory realm of appearances, Arendt warns, there is no return. Quoting Nietzsche, she tells us: "We have abolished the true world. What has remained? The apparent one perhaps? Oh no! With the true world we have also abolished the apparent one" (22; 11).

Does this leave any new form of thinking stranded between a fantasy or delusion of metaphysical truth and a world-destroying nihilism? Recognizing how metaphysical temptation persists despite the recognition "that 'the elimination of the suprasensual also eliminates the merely sensual, and thereby, the difference between them'" (Arendt, quoting Heidegger on Nietzsche, 22; 11), Arendt (like Nietzsche) sees that thinking cannot simply relocate itself from the vita contemplativa, where it was in the service of contemplation of eternal things, to the vita activa, where it can now operate freely in a realm of pure appearances. The idea of appearance remains hostage to a two-world grammar of "mere appearance." All that has changed after metaphysics is the sober awareness that "mere appearances" are our "fate." They can never be objective or world giving, as positivism claimed them to be.[15]

In the ruins of metaphysics, the problem of thinking is different and more fraught than we had imagined. "In other words," writes Arendt, "once the always precarious balance between the two worlds is lost, no matter whether the 'true world' abolishes the 'apparent one' or vice versa, *the whole framework of references, in which our thinking was accustomed to orient itself, breaks down. In these terms, nothing seems to make much sense anymore*" (22; 11; my emphasis). For thinking to reorient rather than merely relocate itself in the realm of appearances, to borrow James Conant's description of a similar problem in Nietzsche, "the fateful (pre-Kantian) concept of the 'true world' and its equally fateful counterpart concept of a 'mere appearance' [must] disappear together."[16] Taking leave of the "true world" is not enough; the received idea of appearance must be radically rethought.

Return to Appearances

Perhaps it was her insight into the disorientation of thinking after metaphysics that led Arendt to title chapter 1 "Appearance," whose first section is "*The world's phenomenal nature*" (27; 19). That's a rather startling way to open a book on thinking that some readers have called her "homecoming" to philosophy, to the "life of the mind."[17] In contrast to the philosophers, she begins with and never leaves the appearing world that thinking, understood as aiming for and ending in contemplation, must, in their view, transcend. From the first sentence, Arendt opens the scene of a bustling and diverse world of appearance that is nothing like its counterpart in the two-world theory.

> The world men are born into contains many things, natural and artificial, living and dead, transient and sempiternal, all of which have in common that they *appear* and hence are meant to be seen, heard, touched, tasted and smelled, to be perceived by sentient creatures, endowed with the appropriate sense organs. Nothing could appear, the word "appearance" would make no sense, if such recipients of appearances did not exist— living creatures able to acknowledge, recognize, and to react in flight or desire, in approval or disapproval, in blame or praise to what is not merely

there but appears to them and is meant for their perception. In this world, into which we appear from a nowhere and from which we disappear into a nowhere, *Being and Appearing coincide*. Dead matter, natural and artificial, changing and unchanging, depends in its being, that is, in its appearingness, on the presence of living creatures. Nothing and nobody exists in this world whose very being does not presuppose a *spectator*. In other words, nothing that is, insofar as it appears, exists in the singular; everything that is is meant to be perceived by somebody. Not Man but men inhabit this planet. *Plurality is the law of the earth.* (27; 19)

Arendt does not turn the two-world theory on its head, revaluing the devalued term (appearance). As Nietzsche already recognized, that inversion makes sense only within the metaphysical grammar both he and Arendt reject. Appearance is now declared not superior but identical to Being: "Being and Appearance coincide." With this claim, Arendt melds the two worlds into one: to be is to appear, and to appear is to be. But to be and appear are never singular or stable in the way that Being, the object of contemplation, must remain in the two-world theory. She describes an appearing plural world of men, not Man, bristling with a limitless variety that will become food for a new form of thinking and idea of appearance in the ruins of metaphysics. "The almost infinite diversity of its appearances, the sheer entertainment value of its views, sounds, and smells ... is hardly ever mentioned by the thinkers and philosophers" (28; 20), she notes. For them, such change and contingency could never sustain contemplation of eternal things and reveal Truth.

Further, Arendt's vibrant-appearing world implicitly challenges what it means to think in the Western tradition: the unity of being and thought and the sublation of active thinking into passive contemplation of eternal things. In "What Is Existenz Philosophy?," she describes that which "the whole of western philosophy ... since Parmenides had dared not to doubt: *'to gar auto esti noein te kai einai.'*"[18] Excepting Kant, this unity of thought and being reaches into "all the so-called schools of modern philosophy," including pragmatism and phenomenology, establishing a philosophical consensus about the proper objects of thought, the activity of thinking, and the conditions of truth.[19] For Arendt, the persistence of this unity through Western philosophy, "despite all its variety and apparent contradictions," speaks to the tenacious problem of how to be "at home" in a world that is not of our own making.[20] "The modern feeling of homelessness in the world has always ended up with things torn out of their functional context," she writes.[21] "Its philosophical basis lies in the fact that though the functional context of the world, in which also I myself am involved, can always justify and explain that there are, for example, tables and chairs generally, nevertheless it can never make me grasp conceptually that *this* table *is*. And it is the existence of *this* table, independent of tables in general, which evokes the philosophical shock."[22] Although philosophers have invented different ways of describing and reacting to this shock of the particular that exceeds the concept, most have refused to face it, choosing to transform "alien Being into consciousness" (Husserl) or otherwise fleeing "the knowledge that the What can never explain the That."[23]

Affirming that Being and Appearance coincide, Arendt interrupts any return to the unity of thought and Being, modern philosophy's response to the "dreadful collision against bare reality [the *this*]."[24] In *Thinking*, the virtual explosion of particulars qua ways to be seen is matched only by the limitless ways to perceive. "Living beings, men and animals, are not just in the world, they are *of the world*, and this precisely because they are subjects and objects—perceiving and being perceived—at the same time" (28; 20). To be is at once to appear to others and be perceived by others, and in explicitly sensory ways (seen, smelled, touched).

Appearance is defined not in relation to its opposite, Being, but to spectators, who are also appearances. The vibrant senses here are vehicles less of information (knowledge of the other) than of sociability. Appearing actively solicits the attention of others. Arendt explains:

> In contrast to the inorganic thereness of lifeless matter, living beings are not mere appearances. To be alive means to be possessed by an urge toward self-display which answers the fact of one's own appearingness. Living things *make their appearance* like actors on a stage set for them. The stage is common to all who are alive, but it *seems* different to each species, different also to each individual specimen. Seeming—the it-seems-to-me, *dokei moi*—is the mode, perhaps the only possible one, in which an appearing world is acknowledged and perceived. To appear always means to seem to others, and this seeming varies according to the standpoint and the perspective of the spectators. In other words, every appearing thing acquires, by virtue of its appearingness, a kind of disguise which indeed may but does not have to hide or disfigure it. Seeming corresponds to the fact that every appearance, its identity notwithstanding, is perceived by a plurality of spectators. (29; 21)

In Arendt's view, being alert to dokei moi, not contemplating phainetai as if it could show itself independent of appearances, is the proper mode of apprehending reality in a shared world of appearances. Being and thought are not one; being and appearance are. The flight into consciousness can never answer to modern philosophy's shock of "alien Being," the "*this*" that exceeds the concept, and the Being "man" did not create. All these ways of "being at home in the world" amount to a failure to be *in* and *of* the world, to face the shock of reality. In Arendt's account, the shock concerns not just those new events (e.g., totalitarianism) that expose the exhaustion of inherited concepts but also the heterogeneity of plural appearances that cannot be subsumed under a rule. Sharing the world as spectators and actors, as subjects and objects, is the realistic basis of being at home in a world. Arendt writes:

> Since sentient beings—men and animals, to whom things appear and who as recipients guarantee their reality—are themselves also appearances, meant for and able both to see and be seen, to hear and be heard, to touch and be touched, they are never mere subjects and can never be understood as such; they are no less "objective" than stone and bridge. The worldliness of living things means that there is no subject that is not also an object and appears as such to somebody else who guarantees its "objective" reality. What we usually call consciousness [e.g., "Descartes's *Cogito me cogitare ergo sum*"], the fact that I am also aware of myself and therefore in a sense can also appear to myself, would never suffice to guarantee reality.... Seen from the perspective of the world, every creature that is born into it arrives well-equipped to deal with a world in which Being and Appearing coincide; they are fit for worldly existence. (27–28; 19–20)

Here, what Conant called "the fateful (pre-Kantian) concept of the 'true world' and its equally fateful counterpart concept of a 'mere appearance'" have indeed disappeared together.[25]

Arendt's world of appearance is not the "apparent world" that Nietzsche, as Arendt says, recognized as the detritus of a lost "true world" into which philosophical thought takes flight. I said previously that Arendt grants the experience of the two-world theory as subjectively real but redescribes it as a "delusion," for "the thinking ego obviously never leaves the world of appearances altogether" (105; 110). We can now see why. The denied objective and *prior* condition of this subjective experience is the reality of the shared appearing world and the appearance of the thinking subject. As she transitions directly to section 2, "Two-World Theory," Arendt suggests how we can flesh out the full significance of this insight and make sense of why the previous section focused on the phenomenal nature of the world:

> We may find a first consoling hint regarding this subject [whether thinking can "appear" and "find an adequate home in the world"] when we turn to

the old metaphysical dichotomy of (true) Being and (mere) Appearance, because it too actually relies on the primacy, or at least on the priority of appearance. In order to find out what truly *is*, the philosopher must *leave* the world of appearances among which he is naturally and originally at home—as Parmenides did when he was carried upward [in *The Way of Truth*] ... "far from the beaten path of men" and as Plato did in the Cave parable. The world of appearances is *prior* to whatever region the philosopher may *choose* as his "true" home but into which he was not born. It has always been the very appearingness of this world that suggested to the philosopher, to the human mind, the notion that there should exist something which is not appearance.... When the philosopher takes leave of the world given to our senses and turns-about (Plato's periagōgē) to the life of the mind, he takes his clue from the former, looking for something that would be revealed to him that would explain it as its underlying truth. This truth—*a-lētheia*, that which is disclosed (Heidegger)—can be conceived only as another "appearance," another phenomenon originally hidden but of a supposedly higher order, thus signifying the lasting predominance of appearance. Our mental apparatus, though it can withdraw from *present* appearances, remains geared to Appearance. (31; 23–24)

Metaphysical thinking is a "delusion" because it forgets or denies that shared and prior worldly condition of appearance, just as the skeptic ignores or denies the conditions of doubt. In this way, traditional philosophers misunderstand their thinking activity, which has been concerned not with Being but with "another appearance" all along. And though Kant too remained captivated by the idea of something that is not appearance (e.g., "the thing in itself"), argues Arendt, it was he who broke open the fantasy or delusion of knowing a Being that was not an appearance. For Arendt, it is not Nietzsche but Kant who radically reoriented thinking, severing it from the philosophical quest for truth.

It was first Kant who destroyed "the old identity of Being and thought and with it a pre-established harmony between Man and the world," declares Arendt in "What Is Existenz Philosophy?"[26] His "proof of the antinomy-structure of Reason, and his analysis of synthetic propositions that proves that in every proposition in which something is asserted about Reality we go beyond the concept (the *essentia*) of a given thing—had already robbed man of the ancient security in Being."[27] Kant's critical epistemology refuses objective knowledge of anything that cannot be experienced, and supersensible objects, like God, immortality, freedom, or the soul, lie outside the limits of our finite conditions of human sensibility. With knowledge now confined to objects of experience in the realm of appearances (i.e., sensation or intuition), the question arises: What can thinking be? Freed from contemplation as the way to knowledge of eternal things, thinking must be reoriented in a world where such knowledge is impossible and the sense of "homelessness" unresolved.

Arendt credits Kant with radically reorienting thinking in the metaphysical world. His key move was to sever thinking from knowing; if tethered to truth, thinking remains subordinate to the passive contemplation of eternal things. It can never actively speak to how things are in the ever-changing world of human affairs. However, Kant's discovery of "the scandal of reason" (25; 14) and consequent demolition of the unity of Being and thought could only go so far in reorienting thinking in the appearing world. "Although he insisted on the inability of reason to arrive at knowledge, especially with respect to God, Freedom, and Immortality which to him were the highest objects of thought, he could not part altogether with the conviction that the final aim of thinking as of knowledge is truth and cognition" (66; 63), observes Arendt. Kant freed thinking from contemplation, only to put it in the service of knowledge, which "uses thinking as a means to an end [truth]" (67; 64).

Even the "distinction between truth and meaning," though "the necessary consequence of Kant's crucial distinction of reason and intellect" (61; 57–58) was never articulated by him, remarks Arendt. In fact, "a clear-cut line of demarcation between these two altogether different modes of speech cannot be found in the history of philosophy" (61; 58), she adds.[28] Why did Arendt think it important to develop the distinction between truth and meaning that no one before Kant had recognized only to betray it in the quest for truth? How is this distinction "decisive for any inquiry into the nature of human thinking" and for the problem Arendt named as making that inquiry necessary: the possible relationship between thinking and wrongdoing (61; 57–58)? How is thinking's unique "critical capacity" connected to meaning instead of truth as the mode for orienting oneself anew in the sociohistorical and political world (60; 56)?

New Objects of Thought

Hostage to "the enormous weight of the tradition of metaphysics," Arendt observes, Kant was unable to conceive of the difference between thinking and knowing beyond a conventional view of topics that could be "*proved to be unknowable*, and while he justified reason's need to think beyond the limits of what can be known, he remained unaware of the fact that man's need to reflect encompasses nearly everything that happens to him, things he knows as well as matters he can never know" (12; 14). Expanding the range of potential thought-objects to include ordinary objects of everyday life, Arendt enlarges the field of meaning beyond the supersensible world of thought-objects discussed by Kant (e.g., God, the soul, immortality, freedom). In his view, these objects cannot appear, be experienced, and thus known. Arendt's reorientation of thinking in the ruins of metaphysics focuses not on what lies beyond the power of cognition but on objects that appear in human affairs. These ordinary objects *can* be known using the intellect/understanding (*Verstand*) as outlined in Kant's first *Critique*. But they can also animate the need of reason (*Vernuft*) to think beyond what can be cognized in its endless quest for meaning.

Arendt's extension of Kant's revolution in thought expands the range of thinkable objects. It redefines how something becomes an object for reason and thinking when it could also be one for understanding and cognition. Nothing in the object itself *determines* what it can be for us.[29] Just as the botanist's determinative judgment sees in the flower the reproductive organ of a plant, while the artist's reflective judgment of taste finds an expression of beauty, so too can we approach identical worldly objects in contrasting ways. Orientation is the choice to treat an object in one way or the other, and so to place it in the world in a specific way. This choice is normative: though based on feeling, orientational judgment is a matter of how one places oneself in relation to objects in the empirical world. I can be held responsible for how things appear to me and how I orient myself in the world.

Arendt's expansion of the field of meaning is also a transformation of thinking; it alters the scope of thinking, both the range of its potential objects and who can be a thinker. Although she grants that certain "thought-objects, concepts, ideas, categories, and the like, became the special subject matter of 'professional' philosophy, there is nothing in the ordinary life of man that cannot become the food for thought, that is, be subjected to the twofold transformation which prepares a sense object into a suitable thought-object" (76; 77–78). In "Some Questions of Moral Philosophy," Arendt explicitly disputes philosophy's exclusive claim on the thinking activity and elaborates on the ordinary objects of thought:

> Thinking as an activity can arise out of every occurrence; it is present when I, having watched an incident in the street or having been implicated in some occurrence, now start considering what has happened, telling it to myself as a kind of story, preparing it in this way for its subsequent communication to others, and so forth....
>
> However, while thinking in this nontechnical sense is certainly no prerogative of any special kind of men, philosophers or scientists, etc.—you will find it present in all walks of life and may find it entirely absent in what

we call intellectuals—it cannot be denied that it certainly is much less frequent than Socrates supposed, although one hopes a bit more frequent than Plato feared.[30]

Recognizing that not all men think while insisting that all men *can* think, Arendt brings thinking and the thinking subject down to earth, so to speak, by anchoring them via an unlimited proliferation of worldly objects in the contingent realm of human affairs. Only then can thinking be expected of citizens and become a genuinely political affair.

Notwithstanding the potential for any object to become a candidate both for meaning and for knowledge, it is crucial to Arendt's reformulation of thinking that these registers remain distinct. Giving explicit propositional form to the teaching that Kant's crucial distinction between reason and intellect implied but never clearly articulated, let alone accepted or carried through, she writes: "*The need of reason is not inspired by the quest for truth but by the quest for meaning. And truth and meaning are not the same.* The basic fallacy, prior to all specific metaphysical fallacies, is to interpret meaning according to the model of truth" (26; 15).

Why would the interpretation of meaning on the model of truth (i.e., according to rules of cognition and logic) constitute the "basic fallacy" that is "before all specific metaphysical fallacies"? The metaphysical fallacy of the true versus the apparent world, for example, would be parasitic on the basic fallacy of confusing truth and meaning insofar as the quest for knowledge of a true world requires that we halt the endless search for meaning and its proliferation of "thought-objects." That is why thinking must ultimately end in contemplation: the beholding of something fixed, which holds out the promise—realized or not—of knowledge.

"The temptations to this equation [between meaning and truth]—ultimately the refusal to accept and think through Kant's distinction of reason and intellect, the 'urgent need' to think and the 'desire to know'—are very great, and by no means due only to the weight of tradition" (26; 15), comments Arendt. Hegel, Heidegger, and German idealism are just three examples of this refusal, and each is guilty of failing to think politically in some way. The list extends to Eichmann and those like him who were unable to think in part because they confused knowing with meaning. But how exactly does this reduction of meaning to knowing matter for politics?

Socratic Thinking

This question can be pursued by turning to the section in "Thinking" titled "The Answer of Socrates," which also appears in Arendt's essay "Thinking and Moral Considerations." Here, Arendt is focused on the early Platonic dialogues in which Socrates is engaged in an ordinary public practice of thinking about "very simple, everyday concepts, such as arise when people open their mouths and begin to talk." Arendt continues:

> The introduction usually runs as follows: to be sure, there are happy people, just deeds, courageous men, beautiful things to see and admire, everybody knows about them. The trouble starts with our usage of nouns, presumably derived from those adjectives which we apply to particular cases as they *appear* us (we *see* a happy man, *perceive* the courageous deed or the just decision), that is, with such words as *happiness, courage, justice*, etc., which we now call concepts and which Solon called the "non-appearing measure" (*aphanes metron*) "most difficult for the mind to comprehend, but nevertheless holding the limits of all things," and which Plato somewhat later called ideas perceivable only by the eyes of the mind. These words are part and parcel of our everyday speech, and still we can give no account of them; when we try to define them, they get slippery; when we talk about their meaning, nothing stays put anymore, everything begins to move. (160–61; 170)

Arendt's diagnosis of the attempt to fix the meaning of concepts beyond any specific context of use recalls Wittgenstein's account of metaphysical conceptions of meaning. Both thinkers recognize that all concepts (e.g., happiness, courage, justice) originated in some *activity*, such as seeing or perceiving and, so, in the world of appearances. We forget this original activity when looking for something that persists beyond any appearance, context, or activity: a (timeless) universal. This is the philosophical form of thinking aimed at truth and ending in contemplation.

Thinking in Arendt's Socratic account is aporetic: its aim is not to render motionless a concept-word so as "to open the eyes of the mind" (Plato) (18; 6) or activate "*nous*[,] . . . an organ for seeing and beholding the truth" (Aristotle) (18; 6). On the contrary, thinking reactivates the original activity that gave rise to a concept that is now fixed. Shaking the concept free of its sedimented meanings, thinking reveals the origin in human practice and an original act of judgment. Thinking about "happiness" or "courage" is coming back to the authentic experience of "see[ing] the happy man, perceiv[ing] the courageous deed." Thinking returns to this initial activity of concept formation, not to the fixed concept ("happiness" or "courage") or unchanging object of passive contemplation.

The ordinary word "house," for example, can stand for many things ("for the mud-hut of a tribe, for the palace of a king, the country home of a city dweller," etc.) (161; 171). The word at once relies on meanings rooted in experience and occludes them from view. "The word *house*, Solon's 'unseen measure,' 'holds the limits of all things' pertaining to dwelling; it is a word that could not exist unless one presupposes thinking about being housed, dwelling, having a home. As a word, *house* is shorthand for all these things, the kind of shorthand without which thinking and its characteristic swiftness . . . would not be possible at all." And yet, Arendt adds, "*the word 'house' is something like a frozen thought which thinking must unfreeze*, defrost as it were, whenever it wants to find out its original meaning" (161; 171). This process of thinking, Arendt adds, "does not produce definitions and in this sense is entirely without results" (162; 171).

The unfreezing of a concept-word is modeled for Arendt in the public thinking activity of Socrates in the agora. Publicity is central to Arendt's appropriation of the Kantian inheritance and effort to distance Socrates from Plato. It is based on Kant's comment in "What Does It Mean to Orient Oneself in Thinking?" that to take away "people's freedom publicly to communicate their thoughts also takes from them the freedom to think."[31] To think correctly, one must be in dialogue with others, including oneself. Besides relocating the scene of thinking from the Academy to the agora, Arendt inscribes plurality into the soundless thinking ego as a two-in-one dialogue: There is an "original duality or the split between me and myself which is inherent in all consciousness" (74; 75), she remarks. Even when I think in solitude, I am not "lonely," for "I keep myself company" (173; 185).[32]

For Arendt, the Socratic practice of thinking *in* the world of appearance models the definitive feature of critical thought: its status as an unending activity that "produces no end result" (118; 123). The business of thinking is not the production of new concepts but the constant questioning of sedimented terms. Such examination begins not in the solitary stillness of contemplation but in the active exchange of *doxa* (opinion). Socratic thinking is an endless practice that stays in the world of appearances, refusing the external standpoint (withdrawal and contemplation) demanded by the philosophical quest for Truth. The proximity of thinking to the ordinary world and opinions of others is typically understood as risking submission to the given.[33] Proximity is a liability to critical thought because individual perspectives are understood to be irremediably distorting. Socratic thinking, by contrast, proceeds initially by creating not distance but proximity to the *doxai* of his interlocutors, how the world appears differently to each of them. Socrates practices what Arendt elsewhere calls "representative thinking," thinking from standpoints other than one's own.[34] How the world appears to each of us can be subjected to critical thought because dokei moi is not "merely subjective" but normative. I have a say in how the world appears to me and how I receive it. I can notice what is "in plain view" or look beyond it for a "reality" that I take to be "hidden," that is, for what lies beyond appearance.

For Arendt's Socrates, critical leverage concerning appearances taken at face value is not to be found by getting behind them but by perspectival movement within the dimension or on the plane of appearance itself.[35] Arendt's Socrates gains critical traction on plural opinions because he treats them as ways of receiving the world that can be better or worse, in the sense not just of correct cognition but of finding meaning in the things of a shared world. For Arendt's Socrates, it is a matter not of choosing meaning over truth but of seeing that the quest for truth absent the quest for meaning would create sterile knowledge of the world (dead facts) that failed to face reality and speak to it as shared. Consequently, as Valeria Pashkova and Mikhail Pashkov parse Arendt, "Truth-seeking in relation to the quest for meaning manifests itself in the very commitment of a thinking individual to the ongoing process of examining and re-examining how the world appears to her as well as how the same world may appear to others, and continuously constituting and reconstituting a meaning of the world and all phenomena in it."[36] It is not enough to seek truth; one must practice truthfulness, which involves subjecting one's own doxa to the kind of ongoing critical questioning that can arise only through the exchange of doxai in the public space. "Just as nobody can know beforehand the other's *doxa*, so nobody can know by himself and without further effort the inherent truth of his own opinion," as Arendt puts the lesson of Socrates ("PP," 81).

In Arendt's Socratic account, "the quest for meaning . . . relentlessly dissolves and examines anew all accepted doctrines and rules" (166; 176). "There are no dangerous thoughts; thinking itself is dangerous, but nihilism is not its product" (166; 176). Nihilism negates "the current, so-called positive values, to which it remains bound" (166; 176), for example, appearance over Being. Insofar as all critical thought goes through this "stage," nihilism is "an ever-present danger of thinking," Arendt concedes—and quickly qualifies:

> But this danger does not arise out of Socratic conviction that an unexamined life is not worth living but, on the contrary, out of the desire to find results which would make further thinking unnecessary. Thinking is equally dangerous to all creeds and, by itself, does not bring forth any new creed. Its most dangerous aspect from the viewpoint of common sense, is that what was meaningful while you were thinking dissolves the moment you

want to apply it to everyday living. When common opinion gets hold of the "concepts," that is, the manifestations of thinking in everyday speech, and begins to handle them as though they were the results of cognition, the end can only be a clear demonstration that no man is wise. Practically, this means that each time you are confronted with some difficulty in life you have to make up your mind anew. (166; 176–77)

Arendt suggests that when we treat meanings "as though they were the results of cognition" (265; 176), we refreeze the concept that thinking was intended to unfreeze. In the next paragraph, Arendt explains the political consequences of not thinking:

By shielding people against the dangers of examination, it teaches them to hold fast to whatever the prescribed rules of conduct may be at a given time in a given society. What people then get used to is less the content of the rules . . . than the *possession* of rules under which to subsume particulars. If somebody appears who . . . wishes to abolish the old "values" or virtues, he will find it easy enough, provided he offers a new code, and he will need relatively little force and no persuasion—the proof that the new values are better than the old—to enforce it. The firmer men held to the old code, the more eager they will be to assimilate themselves to the new one, which in practice means that it will be easier to make those obey who were the most respectable pillars of society, the least likely to indulge in thoughts, dangerous or otherwise, than those who to all appearances were the least reliable elements of the old order. (166–67; 177)

Among other examples from totalitarianism, Arendt says that the meaninglessness of traditional moral commandments, such as "Thou shalt not kill" in Nazi Germany, shows how easily reliance on an old code could become the basis for obedience to a new one (167; 177).

In "Thinking and Moral Considerations," Arendt asserts:

It [thinking] remains a marginal affair except in emergencies. For thinking as such does society little good, much less than the thirst for knowledge in which it is used as an instrument for other purposes. It does not create values, it will not find out, once and for all, what "the good" is, and it does not confirm but rather dissolves accepted rules of conduct. Its political and moral significance comes out only in those rare moments in history when [quoting Yeats] "Things fall apart: the centre cannot hold; / Mere anarchy is loosed upon the world," when "The best lack all conviction, while the worst / Are full of passionate intensity."[37]

Are these passages evidence of the ultimately limited role that she gave to thinking in political life? After all, thinking has no apparent use value: it does not tell one how to act or judge, and it dissolves existing concepts rather than forming new ones.[38]

Notwithstanding these remarks, Arendt no more invites a rarefied conception of thinking than (her critics claim) she does of action. This reading misses how she embeds thinking in everyday practice and, through the example of Socrates, in the public sphere. Expanding the range of potential thought-objects and thinkers, Arendt reclaims thinking from the philosophical tradition before Kant, in which thinking was wholly subordinated to the passive contemplation of eternal things. Arendt also retrieves thinking from a particular interpretation of Kant (and the tradition that claimed him as the defender of modern science) that distinguished reason (*Vernuft*) from intellect (*Verstand*) only to subordinate the quest for meaning to the search for truth.

Reason or the faculty of thought, Arendt explains, "does not ask what something is or whether it exists at all—its existence is always taken for granted—*but what it means for it to be*" (61; 57). Recall modern philosophy's "dreadful collision against bare reality," the discovery that "the What can never explain the That." That tables exist generally "can never make me grasp conceptually that *this* table *is*," wrote Arendt.[39] The confusion of meaning with truth is a refusal to face the shock of reality, the "this" (the particular) that confronts us with a problem of meaning that cannot be grasped, let alone settled, by subsumption under a concept. In political life, the "difficulty of reality" is evaded with "cliches, stock phrases, adherence to conventional, standardized codes of expression and conduct" (16; 4).

Thinking is not something that people decide to do today (when, say, they find themselves in a state of emergency), having not done it yesterday or the day before that. Thinking is an ordinary habit of not resting content with inherited rules of conduct or meaning. Those individuals who never questioned the rules of moral conduct before 1933 were unlikely to challenge the new rules after Hitler was elected and the Nazis consolidated power. If you do not develop the habit of thinking before an emergency arises, it is doubtful that you will "when the chips are down."[40] That, in a nutshell, was Eichmann's problem.

Should we be thinking all the time, and question all our concepts at once? This way of putting the question again misses Arendt's contribution. She grants the place of ordinary concepts and prejudgments (*Vorurteile*) as necessary to navigate everyday life's otherwise overwhelming sensory experience. Her concern is neither to set restrictions on thinking nor to proscribe its unlimited exercise. It is to show how we misunderstand our activity when we confuse thinking with knowing. Recognizing when thinking rather than knowing is called for is the task of orienting oneself in the political world. Confusing the two can have serious political consequences. Subsuming the new case at hand under known concepts, we evade what Cora Diamond called the "difficulty of reality," denying that anything radically novel or disturbing presents itself at all.[41]

Conclusion

"Could the activity of thinking as such, the habit of examining whatever happens to come to pass or to attract attention, regardless of results and specific content, could this activity be among the conditions or even actually 'condition' men in such a way that they abstain from evil-doing" (17; 5)? Arendt's opening question led to a wide-ranging exploration of thinking whose distilled lesson was a (Kantian) warning against confusing meaning and knowing. I have suggested various ways in which Eichmann modeled this equation for her, but more needs to be said.

For one thing, why would this confusion, which Arendt described as the "basic fallacy" (26; 15) on which rest the other metaphysical fallacies, be of central concern in late modernity, when contemplation, as classical philosophy understood it, has been rendered obsolete by the development of science and technology? Insisting on the continued relevance of this fallacy after "the demise of metaphysics" (23; 12), Arendt's point cannot be that the activities of knowing and thinking are unrelated; no knowledge would be possible if thinking did not spark our desire to know, including the vast enterprise of science, as she admits.[42] The problem that persists in modernity is the refusal or inability to recognize what is called for in a specific situation. When placed in the world in one way, any object can be an object of cognition and, when placed in another, an object of thought. Knowing how to put things in the world appropriately belongs to orientation and recognizing that truth and meaning are not the same.

Arendt's critique is directed at a failure of orientation, exemplified by Eichmann. But there are other failures as well. There is a form of philosophical reasoning (e.g., German idealism) that she sees as part of a general tendency to "pursu[e] the Cartesian ideal of certainty as though Kant had never existed; they believed in all earnest that the results of their speculations possessed the same kind of validity as the results of cognitive processes" (26; 16). And there is the commonsense reasoning of science. Despite the awareness that truth can be no more than "provisional verities" to be exchanged for "more accurate verities" as science progresses, "what science and the quest for knowledge are after is *irrefutable* truth, that is, such propositions as human beings are not free to reject; they are compelling" (62; 59), Arendt claims. Pursuing these truths sets the putative neutrality of the scientific method over and against the partiality of opinion or how things appear to each of us.

The problem that both forms of reasoning share is a refusal to recognize the world-giving place of human affective propensities in any credible conception of objectivity. The problem of the modern age, Arendt argues, was no longer the philosophers' vita contemplativa, understood as the wonder-filled activity of beholding the divine and everlasting, for which everything human was felt to be a distraction or irritant. The problem was placing the Archimedean point within man, as in Descartes's analytical geometry. The "world-alienation [of man]," whose "shortest and most fundamental expression . . . is contained in Descartes' famous *de omnibus dubitatum est*," writes Arendt, "is so difficult to perceive *as a basic condition of our whole life* because out of it, and partly at least out of its despair, did arise the tremendous structure of the human artifice we inhabit today, in whose framework we have even discovered the means of destroying it together with all non-man-made things on earth."[43]

Arendt describes science as a prolonged extension of commonsense reasoning, and both are indifferent to the quest for meaning.[44] But if common sense keeps us connected to reality, as she claims, whereas thinking "withdraws from the sensually given and hence also from the feeling of realness, given by common sense" (57; 52), how might the activity of thinking get us closer to facing reality? Indeed, if Arendt's project is one of bringing thinking down to earth, shouldn't we follow the trail of common sense, which leads directly back to appearances and "guarantees reality," rather than thinking, "which subjects to doubt everything it gets hold of" (57; 52)? Isn't this the problem of Cartesian doubt just described? But Descartes assuaged his doubt by taking refuge in consciousness, not appearances, where he sought an unrealistic ideal of certainty that became modern science's unending quest.

Furthermore, Arendt reminds us that "it is ultimately common-sense reasoning that ventures out into the realm of sheer speculation in the theories of the scientists, and the chief weakness of this kind of common sense in this sphere has always been that it lacks the safeguards inherent in sheer thinking, namely its critical capacity, which . . . [we have seen, also] harbors within itself a highly self-destructive tendency" (60; 56). "Thinking, the quest for meaning, is out of order because it produces no end result which could survive the activity, which could make sense after the activity of thinking has come to its end" (118; 123). Put otherwise, it is not thinking's endless quest for meaning but commonsense reasoning's reduction of meaning to truth, as expressed through modern science, that affirms that "everything is possible"—for Arendt, the foundational claim of totalitarianism and the fictive world of the modern lie (*OT*, 437).

Arendt was no enemy of common sense. On the contrary, she describes its decline in terms of the pervasive sense of unreality that characterizes totalitarianism and extends to modern mass societies. But common sense can also close our eyes to the specific object or event that exceeds the concept (knowledge) and makes a demand (meaning) on our thinking attention.[45] Socrates figures thinking in the world for Arendt not because he—like Descartes—refuses the authority of common sense. Instead, Socrates brings thinking into proximate contact with the commonsense reasoning expressed in doxa and rooted in "it-seems-to-me." "Everything is possible" when you bypass the proximate view gained through critical engagement with different ways the world appears to each of us. That was the nonthought of Eichmann.

Arendt called Eichmann thoughtless. The fatal "flaw in Eichmann's character was his almost total inability ever to look at anything from the other fellow's point of view."[46] Eichmann refused any other perspective that might disturb him or challenge a worldview organized around the stringent "logicality" of the movement to which he was devoted (*OT*, 472). Although she called Eichmann "banal," a man without deep convictions, Arendt in no way ruled out his being an idealogue in the precise sense she gave that term. As Roger Berkowitz explains, "Eichmann was an idealogue in the totalitarian sense, someone who was ideologically committed less to a particular idea (the destruction of the Jews) than to the belonging to a movement that required the destruction of the Jews as its logical conclusion."[47] Failing to think from the perspectives of others was the failure to think tout court, for it "locked [him] in the logical coherence of his own simplified view of the world."[48] Logic, wrote Arendt, is "the capability to press on to conclusions with a total disregard for all reality and all experience."[49] And truth was just wherever logic led: "You can't say A without saying B and C and so on, down to the end of the murderous alphabet" (*OT*, 472).

Perhaps it was not so much the quest for knowledge and truth—be it via ancient contemplation, modern philosophy, science, or commonsense reasoning—but the total disregard for reality exemplified in the coercive logic of the idealogue Eichmann's nonthought that inspired Arendt to embrace the one "mental activity" that is always and everywhere "out of order"—the disruptive but enlivening power of thinking. She remarks: "The only possible metaphor of which one may conceive for the life of the mind is the sensation of 'being alive.' *Without the breath of life the human body is a corpse; without thinking the human mind is dead*" (118; 123).

In the next chapter, we will see how the disruptive and enlivening power of thinking as a public practice can animate a critique of political rule.

※ 2 ※

Critique as a Political Practice of Freedom

What does it mean to think about critique as a *political* practice? The answer to this question may seem obvious: insofar as critique aims at exposing forms of unjust power, critique is political. Is critique political, however, if it arises not in public spaces concerning different and often conflicting points of view but in private or institutional areas where opinions converge? Thinking about such questions, I am not searching for an analytic definition of critique, as if critique meant one thing or happened in one kind of space. Instead, I aim to retrieve the origins of critique in the public space as a practice of freedom: speaking and acting with citizens and strangers about matters of common concern.

A political genealogy of critique is even more important today when the practice of critique in advanced capitalist liberal democracies such as the United States seems to be mostly restricted to the activity of "professional thinkers" and the space of the academy, which is at once charged with preserving the tradition of critical thought and maligned for harboring an arrogant intellectual elite. But the academy, as both Michel Foucault and Hannah Arendt will show us in their different ways, is not the original home of critique; it is where critique retreats when it loses its footing in the political realm. Critique was born not inside the relatively sheltered intellectual spaces of the academy but in this public space, where it opposed the tenacious idea of politics as rule, according to which the few have natural governing authority over the many.

Grasping this inaugural task of critique can help make sense of our contemporary predicament, in which even the more limited conception of critique as academic freedom is under siege. Rather than settling for what is ultimately an illusory safe harbor in the academy at the price of indifference to the political realm, Arendt and Foucault invite us to reorient our thinking around forms of critique that contest the politics of rule and engage the always contingent and uncertain realm of human affairs.

Critique as the Art of Not Being Governed

In his writings on Kant and the Enlightenment, Foucault describes critique as "the art of not being governed like this and at this price."[1] Critique is neither the anarchic refusal of all modes of governance nor the acceptance of whatever mode of governance may contingently arise. Foucault connects the emergence of critique to the historical development of "governmentalization" ("WC," 23) and the modern form of rationality. Alongside the developing "art of governing people and methods of doing this," he argues, arose the question: "How *not* to be governed" ("WC," 23). Critique is a quotidian skill cultivated in continuous interplay with hegemonic arts of governing, which originated in doctrines of reason of state in sixteenth-century Europe through the advent of liberalism in the eighteenth century up to the neoliberalism of the present day.

I seek to retrieve what is specifically political or—more precisely—politically public in Foucault's idea of critique as a practice of not being governed (in a certain way). To do this, I will distinguish the *political* concept of critique from two related ideas, both of which have been widely discussed in the secondary literature: the *philosophical* idea of critique as an "ontology of ourselves"[2] or "ontology of the present" (*GS*, 21), on the one hand, and the *ethical* idea of critique as "self-transformation"[3] on the other hand. I contrast my reading with the well-known interpretations of John Rajchman and Judith Butler, each offering insightful accounts of philosophical and ethical conceptions. I aim to tease out the strand of Foucault's thinking that concerns a politically public practice of critique, which may or may not be articulated with these other conceptions. Because Foucault himself often folds the political concept of critique into either philosophical or ethical conceptions, my interpretation tries to reconstruct the political conditions under which critique as the desire and the "will not to be governed thus, like this, in this way" could gain traction ("WC," 56).

In his 1978 lecture "What Is Critique?," delivered to the French Society of Philosophy, Foucault sets out the basic parameters of his rereading of the Kantian inheritance, specifically the relationship between the demand of *Aufklärung* (*Sapere Aude!*) and the idea of critique (the limits to knowledge). According to John Rajchman, the lecture "is notable in at least two ways."

> First, in addressing this Society (rather than, for example, later debating with the social historians), Foucault was taken with the rather dramatic notion that French philosophers . . . might assume "responsibility" for

a new lumière "breaking through the academic window," which would allow them to play a distinctive role in a larger European and international debate; secondly, at the same time, in putting the accent on the political stakes in this larger debate, Foucault introduces the notion of governmentality through which Kant's own idea of "man's release from his self-incurred tutelage" would be linked to the refusal "to be governed like that"—precisely the passages in which Foucault talks of a "politics of truth."[4]

In Rajchman's telling, "What Is Critique?," like all of Foucault's "lectures on enlightenment, . . . [is] tied up with the problem of the 'public use of reason' or the 'intellectual' vocation or role of philosophy."[5] But this reading—though valid in essential respects—risks unduly prejudicing our understanding of Foucault's return to Kant as an attempt "to rethink the very idea of critique in philosophy," to cite Rajchman, with politics as that which is partly at stake in this rethinking but not the site of the rethinking itself.[6] Although this interpretation seems perfectly plausible—Kant, after all, was himself a philosopher who rethought critique—it can lead to a restrictive understanding of what it might have meant for Kant to use one's reason publicly—Arendt, as we will see, has a different reading—and, more importantly, what it might mean for us. Consequently, the second "notable" aspect of Foucault's lecture, "the refusal 'to be governed like that'" and the entire question of counter arts of governing, could appear as if it were synonymous with a (philosophical) practice of intellectual elites.

The point here is not to deny that Foucault was interested in "the complex of post-war French philosophy," as Rajchman notes.[7] After all, he was addressing a philosophical society. Beyond that context, he may have been engaged in a broader attempt "to invent a new style of critique," a new kind of critical philosophy that could hold its own against "Post-Kantian German critical thought."[8] Dominated by the towering figure of Jürgen Habermas, the German reception of Kant had come increasingly to understand its mission as one of rescuing enlightenment and the Kantian inheritance from the so-called nihilism of Foucault and other French "poststructuralist" thinkers. Nevertheless, we also know that Foucault was skeptical of elites and anyone who claimed to have keys to the kingdom of critique and social transformation. We need instead to consider how an "agonistic collectivity in critical thought," to invoke Rajchman's evocative phrasing of Foucault's project, arises in and through a specific and, at times, fraught relation to the political realm.[9]

The political basis of intellectual critique is confirmed in Foucault's account of governmentalization and responses to emerging modes of governance. Alongside the developing sixteenth-century "art of governing men and the methods of doing it"—he observes in "What Is Critique?"—"arose the question of how *not* to be governed *like this*" ("WC," 22). Historically speaking, the critique of unjust power and the wish "not to be governed" took at least three forms: (1) questions regarding the truth of Scripture and the authority of the church to interpret it ("WC," 25), (2) claims to "universal and imprescriptible rights, to which all government . . . must submit" ("WC," 25), and (3) demands for valid reasons for any truth claims advanced by secular and ecclesiastical authorities ("WC," 25–26).

Critique as an "art of not being governed" is not a refusal of all governance but a differentiated relation to various forms of power. Foucault explains:

> I do *not* mean here that governmentalization was opposed in a kind of standoff with the opposite affirmation, "We don't want to be governed, and we don't want to be governed *at all*." What I mean is that we find a perpetual question in this great anxiety about the way of governing and research into ways of governing. This question is how not to be governed *like this*, by these people, in the name of these principles, in view of these particular goals, and by means of these particular processes: not like this, not for this, not by them. ("WC," 23)

Critique does not aim to reinstate illusory prepolitical freedom but points to the need to refigure political relations to foster collective resistance to power. "Not wanting to be governed in this particular way is about not wanting to accept these particulars laws, because they are unjust, because . . . they conceal an essential illegitimacy," Foucault writes ("WC," 25). Critique faces off arts of governing as "a way of being wary, challenging these arts, limiting them, finding the right balance, and transforming them, of seeking to escape from these arts of governing, or at any rate, displacing them through an essential reluctance" ("WC," 24). "Critique is the art of voluntary insubordination, of considered indocility. Critique essentially performs the function of desubjectification in the play of . . . the politics of truth" ("WC," 26).

The question for us now is how critique understood as "desubjectification" in the game of truth can be practiced and defended as a *political* claim; a claim to not be governed in *these* ways, on the one hand, and to *other* possibilities for being governed or, as I prefer to put it, other modes of being politically in common, on the other hand.

Critique as an Ethical Practice of Desubjugation

Distinguishing between "the will not to be governed at all" and "the will not to be governed like this, by them, at this price,'" Foucault rejects the idea of "the decisive will not be governed" as "an originary freedom" ("WC," 56). Nevertheless, in answer to questions, Foucault qualifies: "I was not referring to something like a fundamental anarchism, or an originary freedom that was absolutely and fundamentally resistant to any governmentalization. I didn't say this, but that doesn't mean I am absolutely excluding it" ("WC," 56).

One could proceed here to argue along now-familiar lines that Foucault needs recourse to origins to rescue the idea of human freedom from his "totalizing" conception of power. Although the genealogist and archaeologist Foucault appears to have such recourse at times, I agree with Rudi Visker that, for Foucault, "there is no power without the possibility of resistance, and this resistance is guaranteed by the freedom present in every power relation. Power can only be exerted over free subjects and can only be exerted so far as they are free. If this freedom disappears, then we must speak, rather, of violence: a slave in chains is not being subjected to power but to physical compulsion."[10] That said, granting freedom as the very condition of power does not answer the problem of the legitimacy of a *particular* form of resistance. The question is whether this problem can be solved only through recourse to the normative "foundations" posited by (moral) philosophy, as Habermas and like-minded critics hold.

Judith Butler's commentary on Foucault's lecture creatively struggles with just these issues of normativity and the recourse to origins. "Foucault finds a way to say 'originary freedom,' and I suppose that it gives him great pleasure to utter these words, pleasure and fear. He speaks them, but only through staging the words, relieving himself of an ontological commitment, but releasing the words themselves for a certain use. Does he refer to originary freedom here? Does he seek recourse to it? Has he found the well of originary freedom and drunk from it?"[11]

Rather than attempt to ground his claim to originary freedom, as proponents of universal rights historically have (ontologically), and as many neo-Kantians demand we do (epistemologically), Foucault takes what Butler calls the "oddly brave" risk of a speech act whose validity can have no epistemological or ontological guarantee.[12] Absent any "foundational anchor," freedom is affirmed "by the artful performance of its release from its usual discursive constraints, from the conceit that one might only utter it knowing in advance what its anchor must be," Butler observes.[13]

Foucault calls into question "the regime of truth" in which he, qua subject, has been formed and performs critique as "desubjugation" through his utterance.[14] His claim to an originary freedom is an attempt to posit a value that he, qua subject, "knows" he cannot philosophically ground. Like Nietzsche's performative account of the origin of morals, Foucault's "speech act inaugurates the value, and becomes something like an atopical and atemporal occasion for the origination of values," asserts Butler.[15]

To make sense of Butler's capacious freedom-centered interpretation of Foucault's speech act, we need to grasp the idea of critique that they advance in his name. In Butler's account, the philosophical conception of critique (i.e., the "ontology of ourselves" or "of the present") meets an ethical idea of critique (i.e., "desubjugation" qua "self-transformation"). Foucault is not concerned with the normative question that dominates the Frankfurt School idea of critique. "The primary task of critique will not be to evaluate whether its objects—social conditions, practices, forms of knowledge, power, and discourse—are good or bad, valued highly or demeaned, but to bring into relief the very framework of evaluation itself," Butler observes.[16] For Foucault, "the relation [to this framework and its norms] will be 'critical' in the sense that it will not comply with a given category, but rather constitute an interrogatory relation to the field of categorization itself, referring at least implicitly to the limits of the epistemological horizon within which practices are formed." Critique, then, is "the very practice that exposes the limits of that epistemological horizon itself," explains Butler. "Moreover, the critical practice in question turns out to entail self-transformation in relation to a rule of conduct. How, then, does self-transformation lead to the exposure of this limit?"[17]

Through "self-stylization" and "self-transformation," Butler's Foucault practices critique; he forms himself as an ethical subject whose actions cannot be subsumed under inherited rules of conduct. This process is imbricated with but also different from the philosophical conception of critique or "ontology of ourselves," by which the subject identifies the limits to being and knowing as specific regimes of truth set them out. According to Butler, the boundaries themselves are revealed in the very act of their transgression by which the subject shapes itself as ethical.[18] "To gain a critical distance from established authority means for Foucault not only to recognize the ways in which the coercive effects of knowledge are at work in subject-formation itself, but to risk one's very formation as a subject" through the suspension of "judgment," Butler writes.[19] Released from the demands of judgment, which "subsum[es] a particular under an already constituted category," Foucault forms himself as an *ethical subject* against but also within a regime of truth.[20] "Paradoxically, self-making and desubjugation happen simultaneously when a mode of existence is unsupported by what he calls the regime of truth," observes Butler.[21]

Butler's interpretation responds to the (Habermasian) charge that Foucault lacks normative grounding for critique. But what might we overlook when we fold the idea of critique into an ethical act of self-transformation concerning given categories of identity? For instance, what counts as a person? What counts as a coherent gender? What qualifies as a citizen? We need to probe more closely into the worldly conditions of an act of desubjugation (figured as the claim to originary freedom). What does such an act take for granted?

The Political Conditions of Desubjugation

The question (from Jean-Louis Bruch) that prompts Foucault at once to deny and retain the possibility of originary freedom also elicits a more explicitly political conception of critique as a way of making collective claims in a public space. Bruch's question focuses on the difference between two interlocutions in Foucault's lecture: "the decisive will not to be governed" and "not being governed like this" ("WC," 55). When asked by Bruch whether "the decisive will not to be governed" needs to be "the subject of an examination and be called into question which itself would be an essentially philosophical move" ("WC," 55), Foucault replies that he "was not referring to an original anarchism but also not excluding it." He continues:

> If we wanted to explore this dimension of critique I believe to be so important both because it's part of philosophy and also not part of it. In exploring this dimension of critique and the base of the critical attitude, we might be referred back to something like the historical practice of revolt and the nonacceptance of a real government, on the one hand, and on the other, the individual experience of the rejection of governmentality....
>
> ... Perhaps we should now be examining what the will not to be governed like this and so on might be both in its individual and collective forms of experience. We must now raise the problem of the will. . . . But since this problem of the will is a problem that Western philosophy has always treated with infinite precautions and difficulty, let us say that I've tried to avoid it as much as possible. Let's just say [this question] is inevitable. ("WC," 56–57)

Describing critique as both an individual and a collective experience, I would argue, only makes sense as a *"politics of desubjugation"* if we insist on the conjunctive "and" ("WC," 57). Indeed, we will miss what is distinctive about this political conception of critique as collective action if we fold it into desubjugation as an individual act of will. What facilitates such an act and makes it more than a subjectively isolated expression of resistance? Does Foucault's claim to originary freedom not need to be connected to a political idea of critique as collective action to have worldly traction?

The fraught place of originary freedom in Foucault's text points to the aporia of the will when it comes to freedom. In Arendt's view, the problem with claiming originary freedom is the problem of thinking about freedom as an inner state, a conception of freedom that has exerted tremendous influence on the Western tradition of philosophical thought. In this tradition, she observes, "free will and freedom became synonymous notions, and the presence of freedom was experienced in complete solitude."[22] Other people immediately turn this idea of freedom as free will into a problem and a mirage. The part of critique that "is both part of philosophy and also not part of it," as Foucault writes ("WC," 56), is what Arendt calls the transformation of the "I-Will" into the "I-Can."[23] Whereas "philosophical" freedom, focused on the self's relation to itself, requires no more than an I-will, "independent of circumstances and of attainment of the goals the will has set," writes Arendt, "political freedom ... consists in being able to do what one ought to will."[24] For the few Enlightenment thinkers such as Montesquieu who retain the political conception of freedom, she notes, "it was obvious that an agent could no longer be called free when he lacked the capacity to do—whereby it is irrelevant whether this failure is caused by exterior or by interior circumstances."[25] To be felicitous, a claim to freedom must involve more than a subject engaged in a willful desubjugation, for the I-will inevitably relies on an I-can and others in the political community.

An adequate response to Arendt would have to take up the later Foucault's complex relation to Greco-Roman Stoicism, in which the modern problem of the will is radically rethought with his understanding of freedom as a self-care practice.[26] In this chapter, I will only note that in the writings on critique, Foucault presupposes but does not adequately explore its mutually imbricated individual and collective nature. Consequently, critique can at times sound, as Butler's reading shows, as if it turned solely on the subject's ability to elude the presumably limiting power of concepts and categories of identity—and yet it is also Foucault who gave us a political and public account of critique in the sense of the collective historical practice of revolt animated by the desire not to be governed this way.

The politically public conception of critique that I am trying to tease out of Foucault becomes more visible in his January 5, 1983, lecture at the Collège de France (*GS*, 1–23).²⁷ Here, Foucault argues that *Aufklärung* calls forth two distinct forms of critical thinking: an "analytic of truth" that focuses on the limits of cognition and the rules for proper reasoning as exemplified in Kant's first *Critique*, on the one side; and "another type of question, of critical questioning" as exemplified in Kant's response to the French Revolution, on the other side (*GS*, 20). "This other critical tradition does not pose the question of the conditions of the possibility of a true knowledge; it asks the question: What is present reality? What is the present field of our experiences? What is the present field of possible experiences?" (*GS*, 20). Foucault describes his reading of Kant as reflecting the "philosophical choice" to pursue critique as an "ontology of the present, . . . an ontology of ourselves" rather than as "an analytical philosophy of truth in general" (*GS*, 21). This critical project or ontology takes Kant's account of political revolution as its object. It does so by seeking the genealogy of critique in the phenomenon of revolutionary enthusiasm and its transmission in what Arendt, reading Kant on the same world-historical event, describes as a practice of public reason and reflective judgment.

In Foucault's telling, the question for Kantian philosophy of enlightenment is not to decide "what part of the [French] Revolution should be retained and set up as a model" for future political revolt.²⁸ That would accord with the subsumptive model of judgment that Kant called determinative and that Butler rightly rejects as having any role to play in Foucauldian critique. Kant's response is an attempt to make sense of the will for revolution and the enthusiasm that gripped spectators like him, though they might not—as Kant did not—condone insurrection as a moral act. The question to which the Revolution was (for Kant) an answer was whether one could speak of the "progress of the human race."²⁹ The answer, however, came not in the form of the Revolution itself as "a noisy, spectacular occurrence," writes Foucault.³⁰ Rather, "what is significant is the way the Revolution operates as spectacle, the way it is generally received by spectators who are not participants, but observers, witnesses, and who, for better or worse, let themselves be caught up in it" (*GS*, 17).³¹ It is their "enthusiasm for the Revolution," observes Foucault, "that is [for Kant] the sign of a moral disposition of humanity; this disposition manifests itself in two permanent ways: the right of every people to provide itself with the political constitution which appears good to the people itself; and the lawful and moral principle of a constitution framed in such a way as to avoid . . . war."³²

Put otherwise, critique is figured not as the actual historical revolt against arbitrary power that was at issue in Foucault's response to Bruch, but as the *relation* to the event (e.g., enthusiasm) that harbors a judgment: the right of a people to decide the question of which art of governance is appropriate for them. It is a judgment based on neither the success nor the failure of the Revolution, which characterizes historicist and determinative forms of judgment, but on radical contingency: the Revolution did not have to happen. Yet it did happen, and—moreover—it could happen again: "For this event is too important . . . not to be recalled to memory by the peoples at the occasion of each favourable circumstance, so that they would then be aroused to a repetition of new attempts of this kind," comments Foucault.[33] The event becomes a story for Kant, to cite Arendt's reading, whose "importance lies precisely not at its end [or its content] but in its opening up new horizons for the future."[34]

What breaks apart sedimented ways of being and acting, then, is not the willful act of an individual subject claiming originary freedom and suspending judgment tout court; it is the relation to the spectacle of collective liberation (the Revolution). To see this relation in its proper political register, however, we need to foreground the public character of spectators in Kant's account. Publicity is central to Arendt's reading: "What constituted the appropriate public realm for this particular event were not the actors but the acclaiming spectators," she writes.[35] To see what is public here, she observes, we need to distinguish Kant's revolutionary spectator from the tradition's ideal of spectatorship based on "the superiority of the contemplative way of life." That ideal is "as old as the hills; it is, in fact, among the oldest, most decisive, notions of philosophy," remarks Arendt.[36]

Historically first realized in Plato's Academy, where the cave of opinions could be left behind in search of the truth of everlasting things, it is an ideal for which meaning (or truth) is revealed only to those who restrain themselves from acting and, indeed, from any involvement in the contingent and messy realm of human affairs. It is an ideal of contemplative spectatorship that underwrites "the turning away from the polis, an *a-politia*, so to speak, or indifference to politics," she writes, as the condition of all genuinely critical thought.[37] This is the received idea of thinking as withdrawal from the world of appearances, which we examined in the last chapter.

"Kant's view is different: one withdraws also to the 'theoretical,' the onlooking standpoint of the spectator, but this position is the position of the Judge," and the standard of judgment is progress, observes Arendt.[38] Progress, we have seen, is not a rule that can be applied but an example that opens horizons for the future. Kant's spectator is no philosopher in his study, shutting out the world of human affairs, but a member of the reading and writing public. Spectators exist in the plural. Foucault sees this plurality, too, but his interpretation leaves open the question of how plural spectators relate to each other through the event and how their shared enthusiasm indicates a practice of spectatorship that departs from a merely contemplative (philosophical) form. To answer this question, we must first grasp what Kant understood by the *"public use of one's reason."*[39]

Both Arendt and Foucault examine the distinction between the private and public uses of reason, though Foucault does not adequately probe what makes reason public (rather than, say, not private).[40] In "What Is Enlightenment?" for example, he follows Kant's famous essay to open the fundamental problem: "knowing how the use of reason can take the public form that it requires."[41] Kant's answer, he argues, proposes a sort of contract between the sovereign and his subjects, which renders the duty to obey consistent with universal reason. "Let us leave Kant's text here," Foucault advises, to open the more pressing question of what the Enlightenment can mean *for us*, namely, "the permanent reactivation of an attitude—that is, of a philosophical ethos that could be described as a permanent critique of our historical era."[42] He clarifies: "But the Kantian question was that of knowing [*savoir*] what limits knowledge [*connaissance*] must renounce exceeding, it seems to me that the critical question today must be turned back into a positive one: In what is given to us as universal, necessary, obligatory, what place is occupied by whatever is singular, contingent, and the product of arbitrary constraints? The point, in brief, is to transform the critique conducted in terms of necessary limitation into a practical critique that takes the form of a possible crossing-over [*franchissement*]."[43] That is what Foucault calls "philosophy as the problematisation of a present-ness" and characterizes as the legacy of Kant.[44]

Arendt would remind us that the critical stance celebrated by Foucault holds only insofar as critique is practiced beyond the solitary confines of the philosopher's study and in dialogue with the opinions of other citizens. For Kant, reason is public rather than private, not only when we think beyond the confines of our social roles, what Kant called being a mere "cog in a machine." We must also think beyond the confines of the philosophical ideal of spectatorship. "Critical thinking [for Kant] is possible only where the standpoints of all others are open for inspection. Hence, critical thinking, while still a solitary business, does not cut itself off from all others," remarks Arendt. On the contrary, "the more people participate in it, the better."[45] "By the force of imagination it makes the others present and thus moves in a space that is potentially public, open to all sides."[46] The individual practice of critique is not separate from but irreducibly connected to this potentially public space. Arendt explains:

Freedom of speech and thought, as we understand it, is the right of an individual to express himself and his opinion in order to be able to persuade others to share his viewpoint. This presupposes that I am capable of making up my mind all by myself and that the claim I have on the government is to permit me to propagandize whatever I have already fixed in my mind. Kant's view of this matter is very different. He believes that the very faculty of thinking depends on its public use; without "the test of free and open examination," no thinking and opinion-formation are possible. Reason is not made "to isolate itself but to get into community with others."[47]

The idea of critique that Arendt would have us retrieve, then, is not that of the epistemological Kant who would expose the limits of knowledge; it is the political Kant who would remind us of the public conditions of critical thinking. Foucault also recognizes that Kant's key legacy lies in the idea of critique as a genuine political problem. For Kant, he observes, "the use of reason must be free and public. Enlightenment is thus not merely the process by which individuals would see their own personal freedom of thought guaranteed. There is Enlightenment when the universal, the free, and the public uses of reason are superimposed on one another."[48] The "critical tradition" that Foucault traces back, not to the first Greek problematization of truth, the "analytics of truth," and so to the epistemological Kant, but to a different—Arendt would say political and aesthetic—Kant, however, cannot take hold in the absence of the public use of reason.

Such use involves what Kant called the "enlargement of the mind," writes Arendt, citing Kant, which is "accomplished by 'comparing our judgment with the possible rather than the actual judgment of others, and by putting ourselves in the place of any other man.'" Arendt famously calls the Kantian practice of public reasoning and political thinking "representative," imaginatively thinking from standpoints, not one's own ("TP," 237).[49] It is only then, from standpoints not our own, that we can see the contingency of our own standpoint and engage in the "ontology of ourselves"; only then that we can see what is given to us as universal, necessary, or obligatory, as "singular, contingent, the product of arbitrary constraints"; and only then that we can take up the Enlightenment with Foucault as giving "new impetus to the undefined work of freedom" and the ongoing "problematization of a present-ness."[50]

Conclusion

If problematizing present-ness is to be more than "an empty dream of freedom," as Foucault observes, "this historico-critical attitude must also be an experimental one":

I mean that this work done at the limits of ourselves must, on the one hand, open up a realm of historical inquiry and, on the other, put itself to the test of reality, of contemporary reality, both to grasp the points where change is possible and desirable, and to determine the precise form this change should take. This means that the historical ontology of ourselves must turn away from all projects that claim to be global or radical. In fact, we know from experience that the claim to escape from the system of contemporary reality so as to produce the overall programs of another society, of another way of thinking, another culture, another vision of the world, has led only to the return of the most dangerous traditions.[51]

As mentioned in the introduction, the "ontology of ourselves" turns away from abstract projects of liberation in favor of attending to what is visible but remains unseen in ordinary life: namely, that which is so intimately connected with us that we do not notice it.

Foucault departs from the utopian Enlightenment tradition, which sought solace in moralized and ultimately unrealistic forms of critique that skip "the political aporia," to borrow Reinhardt Koselleck's phrase.[52] Realistic practices of critique need to resist moving outside the political realm to search for what Arendt and Foucault show as illusory freedom. According to Arendt, Plato's founding of the Academy outside the walls of ancient Athens, mainly as a response to what he saw as the tenuous status of philosopher-citizens after the trial and execution of Socrates, continues to influence "our idea of academic freedom today" ("IP," 133). By restricting the exchange of opinions to a sphere that is populated by the few rather than the many, the Academy effectively introduced "a new concept of freedom into the world," one that is hostile to plurality and, as such, intended as "a fully valid substitute for the marketplace, the agora, the central space for freedom in the polis" where Socratic thinking engaged with the doxai of other citizens ("IP," 131). This turning away from politics, however, haunts the freedom of critical thought for which it appears to be the condition.

Freedom from politics or retreat to a space outside politics as the condition of genuine critique remains essential for our understanding, insofar as it both casts suspicion on the opinions of the many as a vital source of critical thought and makes it challenging to grasp politics as the original home of both freedom *and* critique. On the contrary, we tend to see politics as the *object* of critique, which can be practiced only from wholly *outside* politics. This way of thinking often leads to a moralized and unrealistic conception of critique (Koselleck), the public basis of which is occluded, or it leads to a philosophical concept of critique that opposes the unpredictable and contingent world of human affairs.[53] It leads us to think that securing the future of critique is to shore up the boundaries of whatever intellectual home we inhabit. Freedom to criticize is then understood to be that which it is the job of politics to secure, namely, the absolute freedom of spaces of critical thinking outside of politics, such as the university, into which many of us have indeed retreated today.[54]

Many of these spaces, as Foucault will show us in chapter 4, are not free but governed by the protocols of truth demonstration that belong to the scientific game of truth. Not just anyone who retreats to spaces "outside" politics can "manifest truth." Foucault writes:

> Universities, learned societies, canonical teaching, schools, laboratories, the interplay of specialization and professional qualification, are all ways of organizing the rarity of those who can have access to a truth that science posits as universal. It will be the abstract right of every individual to be a universal subject, if you like, but to be one in fact, concretely, will necessarily entail rare individuals being qualified to perform the function of universal subject. In the history of the West since the 18th century, the appearance of philosophers, men of science, intellectuals, professors, laboratories, etcetera, is directly correlated with this extension of the standpoint of scientific truth and corresponds precisely to the rarefaction of those who can know a truth that is now present everywhere and at every moment.[55]

In other words, truth demonstration also relies—as does any other truth event—on sorting those qualified to recognize this omnipresent truth from those who cannot, the very basis for the difference between the few and the many on which Plato's Academy was founded.

The original separation of politics and critique that Arendt identifies with the Academy and finds characteristic of the modern university fails to sustain but instead endangers critical thought: endangers because the indifference, if not hostility, to politics that characterizes our academic spaces and understanding of critique, leads us to lose track of the worldly conditions of such thought, which both Foucault and Arendt have shown to be irreducibly political. By "political," I do not mean politicized in the way that the heated debates about "political correctness" assume. These debates presuppose that, ideally, the university should be a free space of critical inquiry that is free to the extent that it has wholly divorced itself from the political realm.[56] Such a university would extend the politics of rule that was the original target of critique, albeit in the protected form of an academic elite, sheltered from the vicissitudes of politics and the opinions of the many. Current debates confirm the problem I have described.

"The few, wherever they have isolated themselves from the many—be it in the form of academic indifference or oligarchic rule—have manifestly ended up depending on the many, particularly in all those matters of communal life requiring concrete action," warns Arendt ("IP," 133). Written in the 1950s, these prescient words capture the genuine dilemma faced today by those of us worried about the future of true discourse and critique, and about the limits of a defense of academic freedom that is blind to critique's original home and continuing condition in the political realm. It is in the political realm, as we will see in the next chapter, that the debate over who is capable of telling the truth and who will be recognized as a truth-teller will be found.

3

Fact-Checking and Truth-Telling in an Age of Alternative Facts

> To be clear, there are not "alternative facts." There are certainly alternative interpretations of the facts, or alternative data sets, or, in this case, potentially different crowd-size estimates from experts. But a "fact," in the words of Merriam-Webster is "something that has actual existence" or "a piece of information presented as having objective reality."
>
> **FACTCHECK.ORG**

In a now infamous NBC *Meet the Press* interview on January 22, 2017, then US councilor to the president Kellyanne Conway defended former press secretary Sean Spicer's false statement about the number of people who attended Donald Trump's presidential inauguration. The ceremony, claimed Spicer, had drawn the "largest audience to ever witness an inauguration, period, both in person and around the globe." When asked by the interviewer, Chuck Todd, how Spicer could "utter a provable falsehood," Conway replied that Spicer "gave alternative facts." Todd responded, "Look, alternative facts are not facts. They're falsehoods."[1]

Spicer's claim was swiftly fact-checked.[2] Conway's redescription of it as an "alternative fact" was widely mocked on social media and sharply criticized by journalists and fact-checking organizations in the United States and abroad. The phrase was described as Orwellian. Within four days of the interview, sales of Orwell's dystopian masterpiece *1984* had skyrocketed and reached the top of Amazon's best-seller list. "Many Americans have become accustomed to President Trump's lies," *The New York Times* cautioned. "But as regular as they have become, the country should not numb itself to them."[3] Trump's "daily deluge of fabrications, deceptions, shams, pretenses, untruths, deceits, mendacities, and 'demonstrable falsehoods,'" observes Mary Dietz, "have been tallied, fact-checked, parsed, characterized, and cataloged on the websites PolitiFact and FactCheck.org and by the country's newspapers of record, including an interactive enumeration in *The New York Times*. As of January 20, 2021, *The Washington Post* reported more than 30,573 'false or misleading claims' made by Trump."[4] More recently, Trump's response to the 2023 criminal indictments brought by the Justice Department and the State of Georgia for election tampering has been characterized by the exponential growth of false claims and an equally dizzying attempt on the part of the critical press to keep count.

Although essential, fact-checking practices can leave us wondering what democratic citizens might do with the exposure of alternative facts as falsehoods. How can we avoid becoming numb to them? Revelations that President Trump lied then or now are increasingly met with a shrug of the shoulders: "So what else is new?" That the lies are brazen and easily countered by rudimentary forms of evidence (e.g., National Park Service tallies, or photographs of the crowds at presidential inaugurations) may well be the linchpin for understanding what is new in the age-old game of lying and politics. In the past, this game was played by previous administrations seeking to justify or conceal their political interests and actions; it reached its US apogee with Watergate, the Pentagon Papers, and the resignation of Richard Nixon in 1974. With Trumpism, however, we seem to have moved from this register of the traditional or deliberate lie into another register: the modern lie. Lies become secondary to what Arendt calls the "fundamental attitude that excludes the very distinction between truth and falsehood."[5] The consequences are far more corrosive of democratic politics than anything cooked up by inveterate liars like Nixon.

In the register of the deliberate lie, it may be a strange comfort to believe that when Conway, Spicer, or any Trump supporter *looks* at the images comparing Trump's and Obama's respective inaugurations, they see what Chuck Todd saw.[6] But they consciously refuse to acknowledge what they see as having any political consequence for the liar. It's as if they say, "Trump exaggerates, even lies—so what? He's got our back." "Having our back" could mean putting conservatives on the Supreme Court, ending NAFTA, putting tariffs on Chinese goods, making Europeans pay "their fair share" for NATO, or keeping the "wrong kind" of immigrant out of the United States. On this view of the problem of "post-truth" democracies, people *know* they are being lied to but refuse to *acknowledge* it. They refuse to accord the lie any public significance because buying into it pays. Accordingly, material interests outweigh fidelity to truth, but truth itself remains, in principle, knowable. It assumes that citizens are poised to recognize what is right before their eyes if only their material interests could be adequately aligned with what is real. It is a view of mystification and deception familiar to anyone who has worked on the classic question of ideology, where how things appear is a distortion of what is, but a distortion in which subjects are invested because it aligns with what they take their interests to be. Leaving aside the knotted problem of ideological discourse—I'll return to it in chapter 4—on this account of post-truth, reality is there to be seen by all those interested in seeing it.

Though she did not subscribe to an interest-based theory of ideology, Hannah Arendt's trenchant critique of the Nixon administration and its handling of the Vietnam War seemed to take for granted the conception of truth on which it was based. In *Crises of the Republic*, Arendt's 1972 essay "Lying and Politics" vividly describes "deception, self-deception, image-making, ideologizing, and defactualization" as par for the course in the Nixon administration; yet what remains, she suggests, is the tenacity of reality.[7] Liars will be exposed for what they are, as the disgraced Nixon ultimately was, and factual truth will prevail.

Dietz questions whether Arendt's reading of the Pentagon Papers can help us make sense of new and unprecedented varieties of lying in politics, such as those associated with Trump.[8] The wars in Vietnam and the Iraq and Afghanistan wars were characterized by massive prevarication on the part of political leaders, she observes, but "we weren't in a polity where substantial segments of the US citizenry had been talked into believing that it's the press and not the President that dissembles before our own lying eyes."[9] I agree with Dietz that this is one reason why "Lying and Politics" does not translate seamlessly to our current political predicament and that we need to attend to what is genuinely new in our situation. Nevertheless, when read together with her account of totalitarianism, Arendt's 1972 text incisively identifies what Cathy Caruth calls "the violence of the modern lie, [namely] the absolute loss of the reality that it denies."[10] Arendt can help us understand what is happening in our age of alternative facts and the limits of fact-checking as a counterpolitical practice against the loss of reality.

Knowing versus Acknowledging

"What calls for further close and detailed study is the fact," writes Arendt, "that the Pentagon papers revealed little significant news that was not available to the average reader of dailies and weeklies; nor are there any arguments, pro or con, in the 'History of US Decision-Making Process on Vietnam Policy' [portions of which, known as "the Pentagon Papers," were leaked by Daniel Ellsberg to *The New York Times* in 1971] that have not been debated publicly for years in magazines, television shows, and radio broadcasts."[11] Strangely, Arendt never explains this fact, save as testimony to the existence and importance of "the fourth branch of government"—a free press. By 1971, opposition to the Vietnam War had been ongoing for six years, much of the information revealed in the Pentagon Papers had already been mobilized in direct action to end the war, and approximately 61 percent of Americans thought the war was a mistake.[12] Although some facts were new (i.e., had not been known or reported by the media) and other known facts were put into a coherent narrative, it was less the revelation of something utterly unknown than shock at the brazen lies devised to hide facts that made the Pentagon Papers public dynamite.[13]

Compare the shock waves Ellsberg's truth-telling disclosure created throughout the public sphere with the equally bold lies told to justify the 2003 invasion of Iraq. In previous work, I have considered the American reception of the Downing Street memos that describe a secret meeting on July 23, 2002, between Tony Blair and British intelligence and defense figures to discuss a possible war with Iraq.[14] The memos show how war hawks of the George W. Bush regime sought to preempt the work of UN inspectors in the political firestorm around Saddam Hussein's fabled weapons of mass destruction. The exposure of the memos by London's *Sunday Times* on May 1, 2005, led to a massive uproar in Britain and nearly cost Blair the election; in the United States, its disclosure was barely reported by the media, noted by a few opposition senators in a May 5, 2005, letter to President Bush, but mainly dismissed by journalists and citizens alike as "old news."[15]

This stark difference in the respective receptions of the Downing Street memos and the Pentagon Papers suggests that public facts, once discovered, do not speak for themselves. A highly significant fact (e.g., the Bush administration's attempt to "fix" the facts of Saddam Hussein's Iraq to justify US military intervention) can become public without becoming politically significant or having consequences for those concerned. What would it take for a fact to be politically acknowledged as such?

A plausible response to this question cannot settle for showing what is objectively true; more than fact-checking is needed. Arendt's concern with the precarious status of factual truths begins with their contingency—every fact could have been otherwise—and this contingency lends itself not only to denial but also to multiple and often competing interpretations—something that positivists and empiricists tend to overlook. Arendt's "hermeneutic-phenomenological notion of experience," observes Marieke Borren, rejects the "strong empiricist [positivist] conception [that] holds that experience is a pure source of knowledge which mirrors reality 'out there,' independent of language and interpretation, to which we have immediate access" in the form of facts.[16] In the "absolute conception of the world" a fact mirrors what is given in reality wholly independent of its reception by a perceiving subject.[17] For Arendt, by contrast, "we are never merely passive receivers of sense data, but always also actively taking part in the constitution of their meaning. The meaning of a phenomenon is always its meaning for us. We always experience something as something, for example, as a political, private or social phenomenon (the 'as-structure' of understanding)," explains Borren.[18] And this contribution is not merely private or individual. We take up or receive facts as members of sociopolitical communities and their embedded values and ideas of what ought to count.

Keenly aware of the interpretive elasticity of factual truths, an Arendtian approach to endangered factual truths cannot settle for straightforward fact-checking. It requires a nuanced understanding of what checking a fact entails. To state a fact is to do more than enact the correspondence between a proposition and how things are. As Heidegger argues, "the old received definition of truth, *veritas est adaequatio Intellectus ad rem, homoiôsis*," is not wrong but incomplete.[19] Mark Wrathall explains that, for Heidegger, correspondence involves more than "a relationship between mental representations and facts or states of affairs in the world."[20] Instead, "Heidegger suggests that correspondence is a characteristic of our orientation to the world—in particular, of our 'assertive being toward what is asserted.' Our beliefs and assertions correspond not by representing some state of affairs just as it is, but by giving us an orientation to things that 'lets the state of affairs appear just as it is.' True beliefs and assertions are true because they make possible a perceiving that 'lets what is itself be encountered as it is.'"[21] In this way, to state a fact "'lets' what is 'be seen' (*apophanis*) in its uncoveredness." In other words, "a true assertion uncovers a state of affairs by elevating it into salience or prominence, thus allowing it to be seen." That is what Heidegger calls "the basic achievement of speech."[22]

Arendt accepts this originally Greek understanding of what it means to speak truthfully and to state a fact. Like Heidegger, she does not dismiss but complicates the idea of correspondence, insisting that speaking beings call attention to things in the world as they appear through action and speech. Correspondence is not a matter of getting behind appearances but noticing things as they appear. For Arendt, however, calling attention to something in plain view that remains unseen (e.g., facts everyone already knows but refuses to acknowledge) raises a specific *political* problem of "orientation." Our ability to "'le[t]' what is 'be seen'" is conditioned—though not determined—by the presence or absence of a public realm in which our words can be exchanged, heard, and judged. That is why, as we saw in the previous chapter, critical thinking, the ability to question received ideas and values, always involves the political form of orientation to the world that takes the perspectives of others into account.

Recognizing the part played by the perceiver in what is perceived, grasping how reality comes into view through speech acts that elevate features of the world into salience, and appreciating the importance of the public space in assuming a critical stance toward truth claims, Arendt invites us to identify the limits of our current fact-checking practices. What if the obsessive positivistic fact-checking that has become second nature to those who would contest the "delusional reality show" of Trumpism,[23] bypassing the problem of meaning and plurality, worked against the public acceptance of checked facts, that is, their veracity and their significance? What if fact-checking undermines the place of opinion and dokei moi ("it seems to me") in what comes to count as real and meaningful? What, then, is the fate of factual truths, including those that are doggedly checked?

Action and the Lie

"That concealment, falsehood, and the role of the deliberate lie became the chief issues of the Pentagon papers, rather than illusion, error, miscalculation, and the like, is mainly due to the strange fact that the mistaken decisions and lying statements consistently violated the astoundingly accurate factual reports of the intelligence community," remarks Arendt ("LP," 14). In other words, the facts were there, the facts had been checked, but the facts were ignored—and not just ignored but deliberately denied. The deliberate lie is different from "error or illusion." Whereas the latter "intend[s] to say what is or how something appears to me [*dokei moi*]," the "deliberate falsehood or lie" such as "Belgium invaded Germany in August 1914" (discussed below) "is clearly an attempt to change the record, and as such, it is a form of *action*" ("TP," 245). Arendt's initial focus on the uses of the deliberate lie in her reading of the Pentagon Papers, however, gives way to a far more menacing account of lying, in which the agency associated with the intentional act of lying is outrun by the spontaneous movement of the lie itself: the lie as a form of action. This feature of the lie makes it especially relevant to grasping the political significance of "alternative facts" and the anemic countermeasure of fact-checking.

To unpack the transmogrification of the deliberate lie into something more sinister, against which fact-checking is virtually helpless, we could start with Arendt's refusal to counter the modern lie by restoring the philosophical idea of objective truth, as did George Orwell and other intellectuals of her generation. This is the realist idea of truth indifferent to what humans think, say, or feel: the truth behind appearances that we examined in chapter 1. In "Truth and Politics," Arendt distinguishes between rational and factual truth. She argues that the Western philosophical tradition's attempt to hold the political realm to the standards of logical truth is both apolitical and antipolitical. In its search for what is Objective and devoid of anything subjective, the tradition's idea of rational truth is hostile to plurality and democratic politics. This idea of truth, which also governs our understanding of scientific, mathematical, and logical truths, finds its opposite not in deliberate falsehood or lie but in illusion, opinion, error, and ignorance.

Arendt has been received as denying the relevance of truth to politics tout court. I have found this to be a mischaracterization of her position.[24] She is concerned with the question of when and how truth can matter for politics and is accordingly critical of the assumptions, inherited from the Western philosophical tradition, that truth has intrinsic value for politics and, further, that all political thinking is, by definition, a search for truth. This way of conceptualizing the problem of truth and politics brings her remarkably close to the later work of Foucault, as we will see. Pace her critics, Arendt is deeply concerned with the fate of factual truths, which "constitute the very texture of the political realm" ("TP," 227). She writes:

> Factual truth . . . is always related to other people: it concerns events and circumstances in which many are involved; it is established by witnesses and depends upon testimony; *it exists only to the extent that it is spoken about*, even if it occurs in the domain of privacy. *It is political by nature. Facts and opinions, though they must be kept apart, are not antagonistic to each other; they belong to the same realm.* Facts inform opinions, and opinions, inspired by different interests and passions, can differ widely and still be legitimate as long as they respect factual truth. Freedom of opinion is a farce unless factual information is guaranteed and the facts themselves are not in dispute. In other words, factual truth informs political thought just as rational truth informs philosophical speculation. ("TP," 233–34, my emphasis)

"Political by nature," factual truths are also at risk. Related to human action, they "have no conclusive reason whatever for being what they are" ("TP," 238). That "Germany invaded Belgium in August 1914" is a factual and hence contingent truth and, in some important sense, one among those "brutally elementary data . . . whose indestructibility has been taken for granted even by the most extreme and most sophisticated believers in historicism," she remarks ("TP," 245, 234–35). But Arendt also gives many examples that belie this intrinsic resilience of factual truths: the complete erasure of a man named Trotsky from official Soviet history; the Nazis' successful use of anti-Semitic tales, such as the Protocols of the Elders of Zion, that had already been fact-checked as false by journalistic authorities of the time; and the whole web of conspiracy theories that sustained totalitarian rule by terror. What resilience factual truths have ultimately depends on the continual testimony of human beings, who affirm reality as shared in their ordinary speech and action. Infinitely fragile because of this dependency, "once they [factual truths] are lost, no rational effort will ever bring them back" ("TP," 227).

The transformation of fact into *mere* opinion destroys the common world about which to exchange opinions and form judgments. Yet Arendt, to the dismay of her cognitivist critics, refuses to oppose opinion to the truth. In her Socratic view, there is truth in opinion, and speaking and acting with plural others in the public realm is the practice of freedom that factual truth needs to survive and to be acknowledged in the politically significant way mentioned earlier. Facts cut loose from this practice cannot survive and remain irreducibly intertwined with the opinions that can also displace them as facts, namely, the "it-seems-to-me" that is indifferent to how it seems to plural others.[25]

The "it-seems-to-me" can land in subjectivism, but that danger arises in contexts where how things seem to one person finds no exchange with how they seem to another. Because dokei moi always "varies according to the standpoint and the perspective of the spectators," this exchange yields a fuller picture of how things stand in the world. As Arendt told us in chapter 1: "Seeming—the it-seems-to-me, *dokei moi*—is the mode, perhaps the only possible one, in which an appearing world is acknowledged and perceived"; "it-seems-to-me" is thus the fundamental basis of any human conception of objectivity.[26] For Arendt, who thinks about objectivity not as the transcendence of human perspective (e.g., the God's-eye view) but in terms of engaging plural standpoints in the public space, dokei moi cannot be gotten around or left behind in the search for truth. The idea that it not only can but *must* be gotten around characterizes the rational or philosophic truth and form of thinking she characterized as antipolitical. Truth is not deduced (from first principles) but disclosed (with plural others). As argued previously, speech brings things into salience, allowing them to be seen and confirmed as real. Fact-checking that dismisses opinions as cognitively worthless does not disclose truth but leads, instead, right back into the jaws of positivism, the tenacious idea that facts speak for themselves, that they do not rest on opinion or "it-seems-to-me."

In "Lying and Politics," the problem Arendt identifies as of paramount importance is not the relativism or subjectivism of plural opinions that have been the sole focus of the philosophical tradition, in whose footsteps tread contemporary critics of "post-truth." Instead, it is "the deliberate falsehood and the outright lie used as a legitimate means to achieve political ends" ("LP," 4). Considering that "truthfulness has never been counted among the political virtues, and lies have always been regarded as justifiable tools in political dealings," Arendt goes on to register her surprise by "how little attention has been paid, in our tradition of philosophical and political thought, to their significance, on the one hand[,] for the nature of action and, on the other, for the nature of our ability to deny in thought and word whatever happens to be the case. This active, aggressive capability is clearly different from our passive susceptibility to falling prey to error, illusion, the distortions of memory, and to whatever else can be blamed on the failings of our sensual and mental apparatus" ("LP," 4–5).

The critical move here is to shift the problem from the traditional philosophical register of the antagonism between truth and opinion, where the latter is deficient and always fails to disclose the former, to the political register of an "active, aggressive capability" that attacks reality itself. Arendt refuses the problem as traditionally formulated, arguing that not opinion, as the Western tradition has held, but lies are the real threat to truth. Although post-truth critics, too, are concerned with the lie as their object of fact-checking, they target the subjectivism and relativism of opinion, for they find no truth-revealing capacity in the dokei moi. Arendt, by contrast, severs the lie from dokei moi, radically distinguishing between deliberately denying and being wrong about what is the case.

But that is not all. Arendt links the reality-denying and potentially reality-destroying capacity to lie to the reality-creating ability to act.

A characteristic of human action is that it always begins something new, and this does not mean that it is ever permitted to start *ab ovo*, to create *ex nihilio*. In order to make room for one's own action, something that was there before must be removed or destroyed, and things as they were before are changed. Such change would be impossible if we could not mentally remove ourselves from where we physically are located and *imagine* that things might well be different from what they actually are. In other words, the deliberate denial of factual truth—the ability to lie—and the capacity to change facts—the ability to act—are interconnected; they owe their existence to the same source: imagination. It is by no means a matter of course that we can *say*, "the sun shines," when it actually is raining . . . ; rather, it indicates that while we are well equipped for the world, sensually as well as mentally, we are not fitted or embedded into it as one of its inalienable parts. We are *free* to change the world and to start something new in it. ("LP," 5)

The ability to lie, then, is the ability to begin, to act. The most significant consequences for the political realm arise from this feature of lying. As an action, the liar's denial of reality starts something new; to have the capacity to begin, however, is not to control the consequences of what one inaugurated. On the contrary, writes Arendt, the

> consequences [of action] are boundless, because action, though it may proceed from nowhere, so to speak, acts into a medium where every reaction becomes a chain reaction and where every process is the cause of new processes. Since action acts upon beings who are capable of their own actions, reaction, apart from being a response, is always a new action that strikes out on its own and affects others. Thus action and reaction among men never move in a closed circle and can never be reliably confined to two partners . . . ; the smallest act in the most limited circumstances bears the seed of the same boundlessness, because one deed, and sometimes one word, suffices to change every constellation.[27]

The reality-destroying capacity of lying as action is tied less to the intention or abilities of the exceptional liar. Important though these might be for establishing a charismatic public presence, a following of true believers, or access to the highest and most secretive workings of government, we will misjudge the problem of lying in politics if we remain focused on the liar. Enthralled by the virtuosity of the liar, we lose track of the lie: it is the lie as a "boundless" action that "has an inherent tendency to force open all limitations and cut across all boundaries."[28] Returning to our opening example, it is not Donald J. Trump the masterful liar, but the Trump lies "act[ing] into a medium where every reaction becomes a chain reaction and where every process is the cause of new processes."

In its capacity as boundless action cut loose from the intentions and the control of the liar, the deliberate lie takes on the "active, aggressive capability" Arendt described as having been wholly neglected by the tradition. At this point, the intentional lie becomes far more sinister; it has what Cathy Caruth calls "its own political and historical unfolding."[29] The Pentagon Papers revealed the lie in service to what Arendt called an "image of omnipotence" entirely disconnected from even the "aim of world conquest" and any pragmatic question of resources; the lie took on a life of its own, wholly disconnected from factual reality ("LP," 39). Although

Arendt first described the lie as concerning particular facts and serving specific political ends, writes Caruth, "over time a fundamental change takes place. The lie is now aimed at facts everyone knows; it deceives not only particular individuals but also everyone in society (including the liars themselves); and it is aimed not at particular facts but at the entire framework of factuality as such. The lie moves out of its subordinate position, in other words, to become an absolute framework in which nothing but the creation of the lie acts in the world."[30]

In the case of the "professional 'problem-solvers'" (i.e., the individuals like Ellsberg who were recruited from "think tanks" and "universities" and are central characters in Arendt's critical reading), the reality-destroying lie begins in their use of "game theories and systems analyses ... [with which they proposed] to solve all the 'problems' of foreign policy" ("LP," 10).[31] The problem-solvers, she observes, were "in love with 'theory' ... [and] eager to find formulas, preferably expressed in a pseudo-mathematical language, that would unify the most disparate phenomena with which reality presented them; that is, they were eager to discover *laws* by which to explain and predict political and historical facts as though they were as necessary, and thus as reliable, as the physicists once believed natural phenomena to be" ("LP," 11). By contrast with "natural scientist[s]" who cannot escape the non-human-made reality that is their object of study, the problem-solver is the person of action who has not "the patience to wait until his theories and hypothetical explanations are verified or denied by facts" ("LP," 12). Instead, as people of action, problem-solvers "will be tempted to fit their reality—which was, after all, man-made to begin with and thus could have been otherwise—into their theory, thereby mentally getting rid of its disconcerting *contingency*" ("LP," 12). Living in the alternate reality composed of the alternative facts created by their theories, the problem-solvers become entangled in the reality-denying "image of omnipotence." This image, comments Caruth, "has, in fact, no relation to actual power or any other interest to which it might be subordinated, but rather becomes the principle *in itself* that subordinates all other realities to it."[32]

The rational problem-solvers do not start as liars. Still, they serve and further animate the boundless movement of the modern lie insofar as their "aversion to contingency" and love of theory leads them to refuse any possibility that does not follow the neat pattern of "logical conclusions." They had "an utterly irrational confidence in the calculability of reality" ("LP," 39). Indeed, in their view, if reality presents us with many possibilities that cannot be forced into "mutually exclusive dilemmas," all the worse for reality. "They needed no facts, no information; they had a 'theory,' and all data that did not fit were denied or ignored" ("LP," 39). Arendt comments: "What these problem-solvers have in common with down-to-earth liars is the attempt to get rid of facts and the confidence that this should be possible because of the inherent contingency of facts" ("LP," 12).

Not all deliberate lies have the power to destroy: "Under normal circumstances the liar is defeated by reality," Arendt reminds us ("LP," 7). No matter how "experienced" the liar may be or how "large the tissue of falsehood" created, the liar, even with "the help of computers," can never "cover the immensity of factuality" ("LP," 7). Not even reality-destroying totalitarianism could, finally, withstand resilient factual reality. Arendt's reassurance that no matter how bad things get, we will always find our way back to the facts might ring hollow, considering her devastating account of the damage done by the modern lie. The valuable point here, however, is that the attempt to get rid of facts "can never be done by either theory or opinion manipulation—as though a fact is safely removed from the world if only enough people believe in its non-existence. It can be done only through radical destruction—as in the case of the murderer who *says* that Mrs. Smith has died and then goes and kills her" ("LP," 13). As argued in the introduction, this is what Arendt called "lying the truth."[33] This kind of lying is not purely mental or epiphenomenal (classically ideological) but material: it changes reality (Mrs. Smith is now dead). In politics, this kind of destruction would have to be total, and even where the will to it has existed (e.g., Hitler and Stalin), "the power to achieve it would have to amount to omnipotence" ("LP," 13). For example, one would have to destroy every trace in every library and archive worldwide to eliminate Trotsky from Soviet history. And yet, stressing the contingency of factual truths, Arendt is aware that totalitarianism could have achieved world domination and that a "fearful number of war crimes [were] committed in the course of the Vietnam war" before the truth came out ("LP," 13). It is of small solace to know the dream of political omnipotence has yet to be achieved.

Arendt's account of the reality-destroying modern lie provides critical tools that run against the grain of received understandings of "post-truth," our age of alternative facts. Her central teaching is that an "aversion to contingency" drives the animus against facts, the desire to drive them out of the world.[34] "The lie did not creep into politics by some accident of human sinfulness," she observes. "Moral outrage [in no short supply in the post-truth debate], for this reason alone, is not likely to make it disappear. The deliberate falsehood deals with *contingent* facts; that is, with matters that carry no inherent truth within themselves, no necessity to be as they are" ("LP," 6), Arendt reminds us. "Factual truths are never compellingly true. . . . Facts need testimony to be remembered and trustworthy witnesses to be established in order to find a secure dwelling place in the domain of human affairs. From this, it follows that no factual statement can ever be beyond doubt—as secure and shielded against attack as, for instance, the statement that two and two make four" ("LP," 6). Thinking that factual truth *can* be beyond doubt animates a practice of fact-checking that treats factual truth like logical truth and eliminates contingency. But then we find ourselves in the company of the very liars our fact-checking was meant to challenge, not to mention the philosophers who seek eternal truth behind appearances.

Alternative facts are not just more or better lies (or falsehoods); they speak to some significant shift in the shared factual reality we take for granted in politics. Part of their corrosive force consists in turning fact into *mere* opinion, that is, an opinion in the merely subjective sense: an "it-seems-to-me" that remains indifferent to how it seems to plural others. Accordingly, the alternative fact that more people attended Trump's inauguration than Obama's is another "mere" opinion in the wholly subjective sense of what is true *for* me. It can be mere opinion, just as the number that attended Obama's inauguration is held to be mere opinion, because there is no shared reality or object—a fact—on which to have an opinion. We are debating not why more (or fewer) people attended one or the other inauguration; we are discussing not what was said or done in the public space. We are not debating *anything*. We are simply registering "merely subjective" opinions, no different from the avowal that I like coffee and you like tea. What could there be to dispute?[35]

The absence of a shared object concerns altering what we count as real. The problem of alternative facts is more than the "falsehood" that Chuck Todd named in his rejoinder to Conway. Whether or not it began as a deliberate lie consciously deployed as a tool of political power, an alternative fact is the child of action: it is the destruction of one reality (e.g., the crowd size at Obama's inauguration) and the creation of another (Spicer: the "largest audience to ever witness an inauguration [Trump's], period, both in person and around the globe"). Granted, the factual truth of Obama's inauguration did not share the fate of Mrs. Smith—though for 41 percent of Trump voters, it did. Those who bought the lie believed in a reality created less by Sean Spicer's alternative fact utterance at his January 21 press conference than by the wide circulation of, and commentary on, intentionally altered photographs (at Trump's request) of the inauguration and the entire "chain reaction" of events that followed the lie as a form of action.[36] As a "boundless" action, the lie sets an unpredictable set of potentially reality-destroying and reality-creating processes in motion. Once in place, this new reality can withstand fact-checking—perhaps not indefinitely or unanimously—as we typically understand it. Establishing the truth of the matter must confront more than a liar and a statement aimed at manipulating opinion; instead, it faces a new reality no longer tethered to the liar's intention or will. Consequently, I will now argue we need to refigure the problem of truth, indeed the whole issue of post-truth politics, from a problem of fact-checking to a problem of truth-telling.

Truth-Telling

What could this be? Isn't the truth-teller a fact-checker? Characteristically figured as the courageous individual who speaks truth to power and sees through the delusions that captivate his or her fellow citizens, the truth-teller stands at the center of Michel Foucault's late work on the Greek notion of parrhesia, or frank speech.[37] As discussed in the introduction, the study of parrhesia brings to light a crucial distinction between what Foucault called "the analytics of truth" and the "tradition of the question." Whereas the former concerns being able to determine whether a statement is true and centers on correct reasoning, the latter involves the ability to discern "who is able to tell the truth and why [we] should . . . tell the truth" (DT, 224). Although these related but different abilities represent the "two sides, two major aspects" of what Foucault calls the "problematization of truth" as it originated in ancient Greek society (DT, 224), it is the "the tradition of the question" that he identifies as being "at the root, at the foundation of what we could call the critical tradition of philosophy in our society" (DT, 224).

What idea of truth is at stake in truth-telling, and how is it like or unlike that of fact-checking? According to Foucault, "the existence of a true discourse, of a veridical discourse, of a discourse with the function of veridiction . . . is never entailed by the reality of the things of which it speaks."[38] When it comes to "games of truth," Foucault explains, we cannot be "content with saying: If such a truth has been said, it is because that truth was real. One must say rather: Reality being what it is, what were the improbable conditions, the singular conditions that meant that a game of truth could appear in relation to that reality, certainly a game of truth with its reasons, its necessities, but reasons and necessities that are not simply the fact that the things in question existed?"[39]

Although the epistemic legitimacy of a game of truth depends on the reality of which we speak (e.g., the statement, "the sky is blue" is valid only if the sky is blue), truth is not reducible to that reality. Foucault calls attention to "the game of truth [as] . . . a singular historical event, an ultimately improbable event in relation to that of which it speaks."[40] In Foucault's view, Daniele Lorenzini comments, "it is precisely this singular historical event that we must strive to reconstruct." Foucault's "insight that reality alone is not enough to account for the historical emergence" and "continuing existence" of games of truth, he continues, "explains why Foucault's history of truth is also, at the same time, a history of truth-*telling*: its aim is to genealogically trace the emergence of true discourses, not in the abstract, nor by considering them simply entailed by the reality of which they speak, but by construing them as singular events in human history. Thus, it is clear that a history of truth must also ask the question of *who* can and actually does utter them, in what circumstances, and at what cost."[41] This is another way of saying that the facts do not speak for themselves but require individuals who recognize the truth obligations that such facts place on them: to tell the truth, sometimes under conditions where the facts are unwelcome or outright denied. These obligations cannot be derived from the intrinsic veridical structure of facts themselves.

Starting in 1980, Foucault turned his attention to the role that the subject plays in truth.[42] In *On the Government of the Living*, he moves beyond an earlier discussion of truth as truth demonstration, or truth as knowledge (*connaissance*), which belongs to "science, objective knowledge," to describe other forms of what he calls "'alethurgy,' the manifestation of truth" (GL, 7).[43] In the introduction I discussed the distinction between a "game of truth" and a "regime of truth" that Lorenzini helped us draw out of Foucault's "history of truth." The former concerns the criteria of truth and falsity that belong to the "autonomous" logic of a specific "game of truth." The latter concerns "that which determines the obligations of individuals with regard to the procedures of manifestation of truth" (GL, 93). This distinction between a game and a regime, we recall, is more analytic than real. Foucault shows that any game of truth always entails a regime.[44] Truth must be manifested, and the "truth act (*acte de verité*)," writes Foucault, is "the part that falls to the subject in the procedures of alethurgy.... In other words, in the procedure of manifestation of the truth, the subject may be the active agent thanks to which truth comes to light" (GL, 81).

Introducing the idea of "obligations" that attend "manifestation" of truth, Foucault challenges a deeply held idea of truth as entirely distinct from power. Foucault does not deny the existence of truth or reduce it to power, as critics aver. Instead, he challenges the sedimented notion that the truth is intrinsically valuable and "sufficient unto itself for making its own law," as if it obliges the subject to submit to what is true because it is true, as if truth "has no need of a regime, of a regime of obligation" (GL, 95).[45] Indeed, according to the received idea of truth that belongs to the "analytic [Greek philosophical] tradition," characterizes our own concept of truth, and persists in post-truth critics' pleas to track and restore objective truth, "the coercive force [and value] of truth resides within truth itself" (*GL*, 95). And yet this coercive power is freely recognized by the subject, for truth "can only emancipate, it never subjugates."[46]

By contrast with the received idea of truth, Foucault shows that "it is not true that the truth constrains only by truth" (*GL*, 96). What binds or constrains us "does not arise from the truth itself in its structure and content"; it does not inhere in the formal structure of the game of truth. Instead, "the 'you have to' internal to the truth, immanent to the manifestation of the truth," writes Foucault, entails "an assertion that does not belong exactly to the realm of the true or false, that is, a sort of commitment, a sort of profession": "If it is true, then I will submit; it is true, *therefore* I submit" (*GL*, 97, 96–97). In the "you have to" of the truth, Foucault argues, "there is something that does not arise from the truth itself in its structure and content," that is, in the game of truth itself (*GL*, 97). Giving a genealogy of regimes of truth, observes Lorenzini, Foucault seeks to make visible what is occluded in our received conception of truth: "*making us see* the (often imperceptible) 'therefore' on which they [regimes of truth] rely." It is *we* who bind and oblige ourselves to truth and manifest truth by expressing an obligation toward it.[47] The *force* of truth is what we give to truth, not an inherent property of truth itself.[48]

Separating the "it is true" from "therefore I submit," Foucault calls attention to the part each of us plays in sustaining—or contesting—received truths. His nuanced account of the subject's relationship to truth, writes Sergei Prozorov, "is reducible neither to the domination of the subject by discourses of truth nor to the production of the subject in these discourses."[49] The subject constitutes itself in relation to discourses of truth, accepting or refusing, defending or contesting them in ways neither wholly voluntary nor wholly determined. We might say that with the supplement of truth, the subject *orients* itself in relation to reality, not because true discourse reflects reality but because it adds something essential to reality: "truth."[50] For Foucault, then, the nonnecessary character of "true discourses," the fact that "their emergence can never be justified by the way things are in reality and that their effects go beyond merely reflecting what is already the case," as Prozorov argues, opens the possibility of their contestation.[51]

Foucault's intervention allows us to rethink what Arendt describes as "the compelling force of truth" ("TP," 236). For her, we recall, truth is indifferent if not hostile to opinion and therefore antipolitical, even "tyrannical." In her view, "all truths [be they rational or factual] are opposed to opinion in their mode of asserting validity. Truth carries within itself an element of coercion," she argues, that can be reflected in the "frequently tyrannical tendencies so deplorably obvious among of professional truth-tellers" ("TP," 235). Paradoxically, the compelling force of logical truth can also lead to the denial of factual truth, as it did in the theories of the "problem-solvers" and the "ideologies" of totalitarian leaders (discussed in the next chapter): both denied factual truth less for the sake of power than for "the consistency of a lying world order" and its reality-proof image of omnipotence.[52] And, though factual truths are essential for the existence of the political realm, she argued, when stated in the form of logical truths (as if they could not have been otherwise), even factual truths can undermine rather than sustain the public space.[53]

Like Foucault, Arendt criticizes the received idea that truth "is intrinsically valuable and belongs to the realm of freedom—it can only emancipate, it never subjugates," as Lorenzini puts it.[54] By contrast with Foucault, the force of truth for Arendt seems to need nothing more than truth itself. Does it not need the contribution of the subject who, by way of the "therefore," links the "it is true" to the "I submit"? And yet by speaking of *compulsion* and *coercion* rather than freedom as the characteristic feature of truth, Arendt relies on—without fully thinking through—the idea of submission and the role of the subject that are essential to Foucault's "force of truth."

Notwithstanding her tendency to speak about truth as that which compels by a force all its own, Arendt is perfectly aware that what Foucault calls a game of truth is always played within a particular regime of truth: this is the basis, as argued in the next chapter, of her stunning critique of "logicality" as the totalitarian regime of "truth." She is also aware that not everyone is compelled by what goes by the name of truth in a particular regime. As we saw in chapter 1, she recognizes that "thinking" can facilitate a critical relation to reality that men like Eichmann mindlessly accept, especially when "the chips are down."[55] Yet the part played by the subject when it comes to factual truth, such as "Germany invaded Belgium in August 1914," remains underarticulated—perhaps unthought—in her work. However, she recognizes that the epistemic status of factual truth alone cannot guarantee its survival. Following Foucault, I have argued that each citizen-subject must produce that fact as a truth to which it submits in more than an epistemic sense, namely, to which it gives political significance and finds meaning for its own public existence. The "therefore" that links "it is true" to "I submit," in other words, is never a purely epistemological but always an ethical and political problem. It stretches beyond the knowledge that "x" is true—the checked fact—to a decision as to how one will now act. Therein lies the force of truth.

If it is not truth as such but whether those who play the game link the "it's true" to the "I submit"—their part in the game as constituted—then we cannot say with Arendt that *truth* compels. No game of truth compels based on an internal logic and formal structure that is wholly autonomous, separate from a regime of truth (be it liberal democracy or totalitarianism) and the subjects who play the game. "On the contrary," observes Lorenzini, "every game of truth is part of a broader regime of truth that determines the obligations of the individuals who—either explicitly or implicitly, consciously or unconsciously, willingly or unwillingly—utter the 'therefore' that links the 'it is true' (defined by the game of truth) to the 'I submit.'"[56] The mutual imbrication of games of truth and regimes of truth—of a formal (epistemic) structure that establishes the distinction between true and false, on the one hand, and of the "It is true" and "I submit," on the other—has consequences for how we think about the possibility of truth-telling not only in totalitarian regimes but in nontotalitarian regimes of truth such as liberal democracy in an age of alternative facts.

Distinguishing between a game of truth and a regime of truth with a focus on the subject and the procedures of "alethurgy" that manifest truth beyond scientific truth demonstration, or truth as knowledge-connaissance, Foucault allows us to problematize truth in ways that deepen and complicate Arendt's fraught problematization of the "compelling force of truth" ("TP," 236). The process of "problematization," he explains, concerns "how and why certain things, conducts, phenomena, processes, become a problem. Why some conducts were for a long time, for instance, characterized as 'madness,' while others were completely neglected, and why those different things, different conducts were at a certain moment problematized as mental illness? Same question for crime and delinquency, same question for sexuality" (*DT*, 224).[57]

Following Foucault, truth is not already given as a problem; truth must be formulated as a problem. Like Arendt, Foucault argues that truth is not intrinsically a problem for politics; truth must be developed as a problem for politics. *How* we formulate the problem of truth for politics matters—matters for politics. To critics of post-truth politics, we should ask: How are you problematizing truth? If you think of the problem of truth as a problem of correct reasoning, you will likely focus on fact-checking practices. As a game of truth played within a particular regime of truth, fact-checking may produce compelling evidence at the level of the game, that is, demonstrate what is epistemically valid. However, citizens might accept the validity of the facts and yet find them of no political significance or meaning for shared public life.

The Downing Street memos, recall, did not appear in the US context as they did in the British; to the extent that they appeared at all, the memos were dismissed not as truth-telling but as mere fact-checking: facts that everyone already knows and accepts, simply old news. Foucault helps us understand why. From acceptance of the checked fact that President George W. Bush lied, I either do or do not connect by way of the "therefore" consequences for my actions. That he lied can result from a fact-checking process that I accept. But acceptance of a fact does not have the *"force* of truth" in Foucault's sense; it does not have what, with Arendt, I've called political significance.

To have force, the "it is true" must be linked to the "therefore I submit." No one can make that link but the citizen-subject to whom fact-checking is addressed. Like the scientific regime of truth within which "this 'therefore' is masked by the structure of evidence, or obviousness," to cite Lorenzini,[58] so too does a positivist practice of fact-checking assume what Foucault calls "the exact coincidence of the manifestation of truth and my obligation to recognize and posit it as true" (*GL*, 95–96). Diligent fact-checkers assume that a checked fact is a truth that rational subjects *must* accept; to refuse is to act irrationally. But facts have no "force" in themselves; they have no intrinsic political significance. The force of truth is different from a merely tracked truth.

Parrhesia and Isegoria

Foucault's account of parrhesia raises the problem of truth as different from the ability to assess the correctness of statements (e.g., through epistemic practices such as fact-checking). Offering a genealogical account of the deep skepticism about the possibility of truth-telling in democracies, Foucault traces it back to the complex entanglement of parrhesia and democracy. He also hints at why we have come to identify truth-telling with fact-checking, thereby reducing truth to a purely epistemic concern best handled by experts.

In *The Government of Self and Others*, Foucault focuses on the relationship between parrhesia ("saying all," "speaking frankly") and isegoria ("equal [right to] speech in public") granted to all Athenian citizens, regardless of rank, origin, or wealth.[59] The right of every citizen to speak, which was essential to democracy, was not dependent on one's ability to speak truthfully. He argues that the critical turning point for the Western tradition occurred with the Greek recognition that, though every citizen has the right to speak, not everyone speaking frankly will tell the truth. As argued in the introduction, there can be "bad *parrhesia*," "false-truth-telling," speech, for example, that aims to "flatter" rather than challenge an interlocutor with the unwelcome shock of truth, or mindless speech, "chattering," "saying anything one has in mind" (*GS*, 182; *DT*, 41).⁶⁰

> We could say that Athens, at the end of the fifth century, experienced this *parrhesia*-crisis at the intersection between an interrogation about democracy and an interrogation about truth. On the one hand, democracy as an institutional system of equality is not able by itself to determine who should have the right and the aptitude for telling the truth. [On the other hand], *parrhesia* as a verbal activity through which one says frankly and courageously what he has in mind, this *parrhesia* as pure frankness is not sufficient to disclose truth. That is, I think, the new problematization of the *parrhesia*. (*DT*, 114)

The difference between parrhesia and isegoria "introduces a difference" in democracy, whereby those capable of true discourse gain "ascendancy" over others, notwithstanding everyone's equal right to speak in public (*GS*, 183, 184.) "True discourse and the emergence of true discourse underpins the process of governmentality. If democracy can be governed, it is because there is true discourse" (*GS*, 184). On the one hand, although any such ascendancy is at odds with the principle of isegoria, "true discourse is what will enable democracy to exist, and to continue to exist. . . . But on the other hand, insofar as true discourse only comes to light in the joust, in conflict, in confrontation, and rivalry, it is always threatened by democracy" (*GS*, 184). Parrhesia requires "courage, courage in the struggle" to "deliver a discourse of truth" that the demos may not want to hear and may violently refuse. Foucault summarizes: "No true discourse without democracy, but true discourse introduces differences into democracy. No democracy without true discourse, but democracy threatens the very existence of true discourse. These are . . . the two great paradoxes at the center of the relations between democracy and true discourse, at the center of the relations between *parrhesia* and *politiea*: a *dunasteia* indexed to true discourse and a *politeia* indexed to the exact and equal distribution of power" (*GS*, 184). The paradoxical relationship of democracy and true discourse is, in his view, a problem to be confronted, not avoided by eliminating one or the other.

The "deterioration of the relations between *parrhesia* and democracy" gives rise to a "new kind of *parrhesia*," namely, "philosophical *parrhesia*." Its "target . . . is not to persuade the city or the Assembly or the fellow citizens to make the best possible decisions for themselves and for the city, . . . but to convince someone that he must care for himself and change his life" (*GS* 173; *DT*, 156). By contrast with political parrhesia, then, this philosophical form has the quality of a "conversion": "it is not only a question of changing one's opinions, but of changing completely one's life, one's style of life, one's relations to others, and one's relations to oneself" (*DT*, 136). Based on "care for the self" and modeled for Foucault by Socrates, this new parrhesia takes its distance from the political realm in pursuing truth as an ethical good (*GS*, 320).

For Foucault, this philosophical idea of parrhesia as care for the self holds the most interest. It has certainly been deeply attractive for most of his readers, who find the possibilities for loosening modern biopolitical rule in the new form of parrhesia. Freedom of speech and the right to speak frankly (parrhesia) across hierarchies as friends rather than citizens with the equal right to speak in public leaves subjects alone to care for themselves and pursue truth undisturbed by politics—but at a cost. The philosopher's complete withdrawal from the political realm, as Foucault himself recognizes in his reading of the empire of Cyrus in Plato's *Laws*, is bought at the price of collaboration in autocracy.[61] Lida Maxwell argues that the imbrication of parrhesia with power and thus with politics in Foucault's account throws into doubt readings that celebrate truth-telling as a strictly ethical practice of freedom.[62]

I agree with Maxwell that Foucault's account is more nuanced on the relationship between politics and ethics than this reception suggests. Nevertheless, because he was deeply attracted to the ancient philosophical idea of parrhesia as care of the self and fascinated by how discourses of truth intervene and transform the relationship of subjects to themselves (subjectivation)—in a way that remains foreign to Arendt—it is easier to see the ethical relevance than the political importance of parrhesia for Foucault. Can there be enduring *philosophical parrhesia* (even for the few) in the absence of equal rights to speak (isegoria), as in an autocracy? Can democracy survive in the absence of *political parrhesia*: that is, a *public* practice of speaking frankly about common affairs? As in chapter 2, I ask these questions to draw out the prior political worldly conditions—what must already exist—for Foucault's ethical "subject" and critical relation to true discourse to get off the ground.

"For there to be democracy there must be *parrhesia*; for there to be *parrhesia* there must be democracy," writes Foucault (*GS*, 155). As the imbrication of parrhesia and democracy is irreducible, one must "disentangle" a relationship characterized by a "fundamental circularity," he remarks (*GS*, 155). To blame democracy for "bad *parrhesia*" represents a failure to think through the complex and fraught relationship of democratic societies to their truth-tellers—a problem Arendt will also address. That there can be frank and equal speech, but no truth-telling might lead us—when we fail to think it through—to a deep distrust of democracy and the opinions of the many. It leads Plato to the pursuit of truth and care of the self in the company of the few and to the disdain for plural opinion as the radical other of truth. And it leads us today to find in "post-truth" our relativist "postmodern" condition and liberal-democratic pluralism's necessary fate.

Captivated by the philosophical tradition's first problematization of truth as correct reasoning, we have lost track of the critical "tradition of the question" and its problematization of truth as truth-telling. Truth-telling can never involve a single individual engaged in correct reasoning alone; it depends on speech directed at others who may or may not link the "it is true" to the "I submit." For Foucault, observes Lorenzini, "parrhesiastic alethurgy can only take place in the encounter between two or more individuals, and never in the solitary, 'intimate' experience of the discovery of an inner truth. The truth that *parrhesia* manifests is an ethical and political *force* that challenges the way the parrhesiast's interlocutor lives, while also expressing and reinforcing the speaker's own mode of being."[63] Crucial as the subjectivizing force of truth is for Foucault, we should not lose sight of its political effects. Parrhesia, be it political or philosophical, is speech directed at others. It is a distinctive (courageous and unpredictable) speech act—Lorenzini calls it "perlocutionary"[64]—addressed to someone or some group with reason to be challenged. Parrhesiastic speech is never without risk. Foucault is clear: "*parrhesia* refers to the dangerous game of telling the truth in the political and ethical field."[65]

The Risk of Truth-Telling

"The mere telling of facts," writes Arendt, "leads to no action whatever; it even tends, under normal circumstances, toward an acceptance of things as they are. . . . Truthfulness has never been counted among the political virtues, because it has little indeed to contribute to that change of the world and of circumstances which is among the most legitimate political activities."[66] To state what is the case, as she sees it, is to utter words that are mostly invisible and powerless in their ordinariness, merely a confirmation of the status quo.

When is telling the truth more than stating a fact in this ordinary sense? When is it parrhesia? Arendt well knew that not all historical times are characterized by normal circumstances. "Only where a community has embarked upon organized lying on principle, and not only with respect to particulars, can truthfulness as such, unsupported by the distorting forces of power and interest, become a political factor of the first order. Where everybody lies about everything of importance, the truth-teller, whether he knows it or not, has begun to act; he, too, has engaged himself in political business, for, in the unlikely event that he survives, he has made a start toward changing the world" ("TP," 247).

The force of truth that belongs to truth-telling as action does not rest on the accurate stating or checking of factual truths. Indeed, as Lorenzini clarifies, "the truth(s) manifested by the parrhesiast should not be assessed in light of the 'truth value' of her statements, even though the latter can *also* be true from a constitutive, logical, or epistemological perspective. It was not the (constative or scientific) truth value of Galileo's claim according to which the earth revolves around the sun that made his utterance a parrhesiastic one: Galileo was a parrhesiast because of the risk he took by courageously making his views public, even while knowing that the Catholic Church would deem them heretical."[67] Likewise, Daniel Ellsberg was aware that making public government-documented facts on the Vietnam War carried tremendous risk. Tried under the 1917 Espionage Act, he knew he would spend much of his life in prison if convicted.[68]

Although Foucault does not deny its potentially veridical aspects, then, the measure of truth for him is not epistemic validity but the risk to the parrhesiast. Nor, for that matter, is the measure of parrhesiastic truth its persuasiveness, as Foucault's distinction between rhetoric and parrhesia makes clear.

> Rhetoric does not entail any bond between the person speaking and what is said, but aims to establish a constraining bond, a bond of power between what is said and the person to whom it is said. *Parrhesia*, on the other hand, involves a strong, constitutive bond between the person speaking and what he says, and, through the effect of the truth, of the injuries of truth, it opens up the possibility of the bond between the person speaking and the person to whom he has spoken being broken. Let's say, very schematically, that the rhetorician is, or at any rate may well be an effective liar who constrains others. The parrhesiast, on the contrary, is the courageous teller of a truth by which she puts herself and her relationship with the other at risk.[69]

"Puts herself at risk to what end?," we might ask. The parrhesiast's own ethical integrity is one of those ends, to be sure. Beyond that, why does truth-telling matter for democratic politics?

The distinction Foucault draws between rhetoric and parrhesia, argues Lorenzini, "should give pause to all scholars who have criticized him [Foucault] for his alleged reduction of truth claims to the power effects they have on the audience [i.e., their rhetorical effects]." Nevertheless, the question remains as to the relevance of truthful philosophical parrhesia for democracy, whose fate is entangled, on Foucault's own account, with the ability to tell the truth and to recognize those who can.[70] How does the truth-teller recognize truth in the first place? Since Foucault, like Arendt, rejects the two-world theory and its philosophical ideal of speechless contemplation as the way to truth, we are left to wonder how appearances can be world giving for the parrhesiast philosopher. We will revisit the opposition Foucault draws between persuasion and rhetoric in chapter 6. Here, we are concerned with the difference between the truth in appearances and the epistemic idea of truth that both Foucault and Arendt treat as secondary to the truth at stake in truth-telling.

The Truth of Socrates

As argued in chapter 1, at stake for Arendt is the meaning of appearances for the common world. Truth is to be found in opinion, that is, in how the world "appears to me," *dokei moi*. This truth is not just given—how things appear to me is not necessarily how things are—but must be discovered through the comparative and critical process of imagining how they appear to others and through exchanging opinions in the public space.[71] This political approach to truth shapes Arendt's significantly different reading of Socrates, a philosopher who appears in her work as a parrhesiast, but not as the *philosophical* parrhesiast that he is for Foucault.

Arendt would grant that Socrates does not practice what Foucault calls "political parrhesia" and (partly) defines as speaking truth to the demos and trying "to persuade the Assembly of the truth of what he was saying" (*DT*, 139). Socrates is not actively engaged in the official political life of the polis—on that point, they agree.[72] In Foucault's reading, however, the "new [form of philosophical] *parrhesia* [represented by Socrates]" not only no longer takes place in the Assembly or Ecclesia (*Ekklesia*), the official meeting place where citizens could speak freely and try to influence their peers; "*parrhesia* is no longer linked to the agora as the public place where political discussions and decisions take place" (*DT*, 157). Arendt's Socrates, by contrast, "refused public office and honor, never retired into . . . private life, but on the contrary moved in the marketplace [*agora*], in the very midst of these *doxai*, these opinions [of the many]" ("PP," 81). Socrates's practice of critical thinking, then, neither private nor (officially) political, is not "philosophical" either. As we saw in chapter 2, he does not retreat, as Plato (after Socrates's death) did, from the opinions of the many into the company of the few (the Academy), and though his "parrhesiastic role" involved what Foucault calls "the personal-face-to-face-relation," this too mostly takes place, according to Arendt, in the public space (*DT*, 142). Socrates is a "philosopher," she writes, but "the role of the [Socratic] philosopher is not to rule the city but to be its 'gadfly'; not to tell philosophical truths, but to make citizens more truthful" ("PP," 81).

The point here is not to debate who places the historical Socrates "right"—in the *agora* or not—but instead to think through the implications of Foucault's versus Arendt's "Socrates" for their related but different understandings of truth-telling. For Arendt, Socrates teaches others how to find the truth in their doxa by asking questions and engaging with others in the public though not officially political space. Arendt explains: "He [Socrates] cannot know beforehand what kind of *dokei moi*, of it-appears-to-me, the other possesses. He must make sure of the other's position in the common world. Yet, just as nobody can know beforehand the other's *doxa*, so nobody can know without further effort the inherent truth of his own opinion" ("PP," 81). This latter point includes Socrates himself, who was the first to admit his ignorance of truth. "On this level, the Socratic 'I know that I do not know' means no more than: I know that I do not have the truth for everybody, I cannot know the other fellow's truth except by asking him and thereby learning his *doxa*, which reveals itself to him in distinction from all others" ("PP," 85).

Indeed, Socrates's willingness to allow himself, in the public space of the *agora* speaking to others, to be challenged by how the world appeared to his interlocutors is crucial to Arendt's reading of his "decisive" difference with Plato: "Socrates did not want to educate the citizens [with his truths] so much as he wanted to improve their *doxai* [and his own], which constituted the political life in which he too took part [which was not restricted to the Assembly or Ecclesia]. To Socrates, maieutic [the art of midwifery] was a political activity, a give and take, fundamentally on the basis of strict equality, the fruits of which could not be measured by the result of arriving at this or that general truth" ("PP," 81). He accepted "the limitations of truth for mortals, its limitations through *dokein*, appearances," but he also held, "in opposition to the Sophists . . . that *doxa* was neither subjective illusion nor arbitrary distortion but, on the contrary, that to which truth invariably adhered" ("PP," 85).

Foucault's interest in truth, too, clearly rejects the Platonic idea of truth and any education of the citizens. Still, it leaves unremarked how a parrhesiast like Socrates could arrive at the truths he eventually staked his life on to tell. Surely, the political give-and-take of the "it-seems-to-me" must play some role in our ability to recognize the truth and those who tell it, which is essential to Foucault's account of the critical tradition's reproblematization of truth. "The parrhesiast," writes Foucault, "says what is true because he thinks that it is true, and he thinks that it is true because it really is true. Not only is the parrhesiast sincere, not only does he state his opinion frankly, but his opinion is also the truth. He says what he knows to be true. In parrhesia, there is a coincidence, an exact coincidence, between belief and truth" (*DT*, 41–42). Rejecting the idea that what the parrhesiast *thinks* is true *is* true (true belief) because it can be substantiated by "the modern notion of Cartesian evidence," Foucault insists that the truth of parrhesia refers instead to "a kind of relation between subject and truth" (*DT*, 42). "The coincidence between belief in truth takes place, not through a cognitive experience like evidence, but through verbal activity—and this verbal activity is *parrhesia*" (*DT*, 42).

Following "the Greek conception of language," Foucault argues that the truth of parrhesiastic speech lies in its lack of "embellishment'" or artifice of any kind and in the speaker's belief that what he says is true (*GS*, 314). Whereas "rhetorical language is a language chosen, fabricated, and constructed in such a way as to produce its effect on the other person," writes Foucault, "the mode of being of philosophical language is to be *etumos*, that is to say, so bare and simple, so in keeping with the movement of thought that, just as it is without embellishment, in its truth, it will be appropriate to what it refers to and it will also be true to what the person who uses it thinks and believes" (*GS*, 314–15). "Language, words, and phrases bring with them what is essential (*ousia*), the truth of the reality to which they refer" (*GS*, 314). The "false" gets hold of the mind not because of language as such but because the speaker has lost touch with this original form of language, "*etumos* language," language in the "naked state" (*GS*, 314).

In many respects, Foucault's reading of the Greek conception of language is compatible with what Heidegger, in his return to the ancient texts, said about true beliefs and assertions being true because they make possible a perceiving that, as Heidegger put it above, "lets what is itself be encountered as it is."[73] In Foucault's account, the received idea of "correspondence" becomes a matter of "orientation" to things that let them show up for us "just as they are." Arendt, we recall, agrees with this view of language, but she refuses the idea that one could—Heidegger would say *must*—access the truth of appearance without engaging the doxai of others. For Foucault, "Socrates, speaking everyday language, saying what comes to mind, and affirming what one thinks is right absolutely go together" (*GS*, 313). Arendt would say that is not only because Socrates uses everyday language, the language of "the public square, the market" (*GS*, 313), but because his activity of thinking is public: it manifests, through public verbal activity, how things appear to him in relation to how they appear to others (*GS*, 313).

Furthermore, there is always the risk of "bad *parrhesia*": "saying anything one has in mind, without any distinction, without taking care of what he says," which is a form of unreflective or careless speech, "chattering" (*DT*, 41). If Socrates the parrhesiast is to speak language that is more than whatever comes into his mind, more than *merely* subjective, his "verbal activity," Arendt would argue, must engage with the doxai of others—*must* engage because, as Arendt moving from the example of Socrates to Kant explains, "to think critically applies not only to doctrines and concepts one receives from others, to the prejudices and traditions one inherits; it is precisely by applying critical standards to one's own thought that one learns the art of critical thought. . . . And this application one cannot learn without publicity, without the testing that arises from contact with other peoples' thinking."[74]

The point of the Socratic or (as we will see in chapter 6) Kantian exchange of opinions with others is not to reach an agreement or consensus about truth. On the contrary—as the Socratic dialogues show—no such consensus is needed; in any case, it is rarely forthcoming. Nevertheless, the public character of the parrhesiast's verbal activity is crucial for developing the *political* significance of Foucault's central claim: what connects the relation between the subject and truth in democracy is the function— the essential function—of parrhesia as "criticism." Criticism, or the art of critical thinking needs publicity. That is the difference, as we saw in chapter 1, between the search for eternal truth that is contemplation and the critical relation to truth that Arendt called "thinking." It is the difference between Plato and Socrates and Plato and Kant, whose work plays a crucial role in Foucault's later thought, as it did in Arendt's. By contrast with "his great work of critique," Kant's writings on the Enlightenment and the French Revolution are credited by both Arendt and Foucault with the further development of the critical tradition and departure from the "analytic of truth," whose preoccupation is with defining the "conditions under which true knowledge is possible."[75]

This criticism, writes Foucault, goes beyond any straightforward "demonstration of truth, and it is not a discussion or contest about truth with somebody else. *Parrhesia* has always the function of criticism, the speaker himself, or criticism of the interlocutor," but "always in situations where the speaker is in a position of inferiority to the interlocutor. *Parrhesia* comes from 'below' and is oriented towards those 'above'" (*DT*, 43, 44).[76] Put otherwise, parrhesia is criticism of the political relations of "rule," an expression, as we saw in chapter 2, of not wanting to be "governed *like this*, by these people, in the name of these principles" ("WC," 23). As Foucault sees it, "If governmentalization is a movement that subjugates individuals through the reality of a social practice with mechanisms of power that claim to be based on truth, well, I would say that critique is the movement that enables the subject to take up the right to question on its effects of power and to question power about its discourses of truth" ("WC," 26). This interrogation, I argued, needs to involve the "to-and-fro" of engaging doxai in the public space. This space is not identical to the official political space, just as the agora (marketplace) is not the Ekklesia (Assembly). Nevertheless, it allows "each citizen . . . to show his opinion in its truthfulness" and to engage the variety of realities that belong to "fellow citizens," writes Arendt, "so that the common-ness of this world becomes apparent" ("PP," 84).

Albeit "philosophical *parrhesia*," Socratic truth-telling goes beyond the risk involved in self-criticism and criticism of one's interlocutor, which is its defining feature, according to Foucault. To be *world building*, parrhesia must link the ethical transformation of the subject's own relation to truth (subjectivation) through the equal exchange of doxai to the possible emergence of no-rule and the common world, the "space in which things become public."[77] "Socrates seems to have believed that the political function of the philosopher was to establish this kind of common world," writes Arendt, in which "each citizen" could "show his opinion in its truthfulness" and "in which no rulership is needed" ("PP," 84).

Conclusion

I have argued that our relation to facts must remain alert both to the truth denialism that is the sole object of fact-checkers *and* to how we resist it. Too often, the mode of asserting the validity of facts reproduces the disdain for plural opinions and their reduction to "mere" opinion (i.e., their relativization) that gave rise to authoritative claims to Truth and denialism in the first place. Post-truth cynicism, or what Arendt called the "fundamental attitude that excludes the very distinction between truth and falsehood," can never be overcome by restoring the authority of Truth.[78] Such efforts are bound to fail, for they assume that truth is intrinsically valuable and that it compels by a force intrinsic to it. We have seen that the force of truth lies not in the game but in the regime of truth, and so in the "truth act," that is the part played by the subject in bringing truth to light. It belongs to truth in a plural democracy to be the object of ongoing contestation and debate.

Thinking about truth-telling under the nonnormal circumstances that post-truth critics take to be our own is to view it with Arendt as a form of action and thus of politics. Arendt invites us to refigure what it would mean to affirm factual truth: to check a fact is not to point—not simply—to what already exists, to what is past, but to what could have been otherwise and so to what could be otherwise, to the future. That revisionism lurks as a danger in every reference to the contingency of factual truths is, for Arendt, the price of freedom. As a practice of freedom through which we are reminded of the contingency of what has happened and cannot be changed, truth-telling in dark times is crucial to what can be changed. That is what most current forms of fact-checking tend to conceal or deny.

If we should be more cautious in our approach to fact-checking, the same goes for truth-telling. When understood as a nonidealized form of action, truth-telling outruns the will and intention of the truth-teller, just as lying outruns those of the liar, carrying unforeseen risks. The Pentagon Papers, for example, precipitated a chain of events that led to the end of the Vietnam War and brought down the presidency of Richard Nixon. Still, their publication also accelerated and intensified citizens' distrust in politics and cynicism toward every expression of opinion.[79] Ironically, truth-telling played some part in bringing about the situation we now call "post-truth."

Where does this leave us? Less with a definitive answer to critics of post-truth politics than with a cautionary note: specific ways of problematizing truth and politics can lead us to chase after an ideal of correct reasoning and factual truth without understanding why we, democratic citizens, should care about truth. Pace his critics, Foucault convincingly shows that truth matters; it shapes how we relate to ourselves and others as subjects and citizens. Nevertheless, he rejects all calls to "restore" truth, as if truth, once restored, could or should tell us what to do or how to act. This is the objectivist fantasy of the "force of truth" that animates the critique of post-truth. Just because something is true and accepted as such does not mean we should or must submit to its consequences for our actions. Truth, Foucault teaches, does not always emancipate and, in any case, carries no "force" in itself. Whether we submit or resist is an ethical and political question for each citizen-subject and can never be decided by the mere fact of truth.

Furthermore, there are ways of caring for truth that lose track of the only reason for democratic citizens to care about truth, namely, what Arendt calls "care for the world." Parrhesia as an ethos or "care for the self," which defines philosophical parrhesia for Foucault, does not automatically translate into care for the world. "Since philosophical truth concerns man in his singularity," writes Arendt, "it is unpolitical in nature" ("TP," 241). Consequently, she warns, ethical propositions, such as the Socratic "ethical proposition about doing and suffering wrong," may have the force of truth for the subject ("TP," 241). "But to man insofar as he is a citizen, an acting being concerned with the world and the public welfare rather than his own wellbeing [e.g., care for the self,] . . . the Socratic statement is not true at all. The disastrous consequences for any community that began in all earnest to follow ethical precepts derived from man in the singular—be they Socratic or Platonic or Christian—have frequently been pointed out [e.g., by "Machiavelli" and, before him, "Aristotle"]" ("TP," 241).

"What concerns philosophy is not politics, it is not even justice and injustice in the city, but justice and injustice inasmuch as they are committed by someone who is an acting subject; acting as a citizen, or as a subject, or possibly as a sovereign. Philosophy's question is not the question of politics; it is the question of the subject in politics," writes Foucault (GS, 319). Arendt would agree. For her, however, what concerns politics is not philosophy. Democracy's question is not the question of philosophy: it can never be about the subject alone, in or out of politics, for politics begins not with the subject or "Man in the singular," but "men in the plural." In her view, philosophical parrhesia and care for the self that loses track of care for the world can never survive. Convinced that the truth-teller would be killed, Plato abandoned the common world and the critical function of parrhesia exemplified by his mentor (Arendt's) Socrates's verbal activity amid plural doxai. But philosophers and citizens who retreat from the political world and pursue truth and ethical well-being are not secure: they inevitably find themselves, in autocracy, beholden to the all-powerful politicians who seek only council that flatters or, in democracy, and at the mercy of the demos, the many whose opinions have been discarded as cognitively worthless from the standpoint of philosophical truth.[80]

Notwithstanding his fascination with philosophical parrhesia, Foucault's description of the "crisis of *parrhesia*" in democratic Athens does not endorse, as did Plato, parrhesia as a solitary affair or deny the possibilities for truth-telling in a democracy. But Foucault's primary interest in the subject's "manifestation of truth" (GL, 10), though it rightly reminds us of our part in the "force of truth," risks losing sight of "men in the plural" and the common world, without which, Arendt argued, the truths relevant to politics could never survive.

Perhaps this is why Foucault neglects a question posed by his genealogical account of the relationship between the subject and truth: why are some people accepted as truth-tellers while others are not? Central to Foucault's story of the birth of the critical tradition and the second great problematization of truth, after all, is the importance for society in truth-telling and our ability to recognize those who can tell the truth.

Any plausible answer must account for the uneven reception that different people and groups receive as speakers of truth. Defining the new problem discovered by the Greeks as general skepticism toward democratic citizens and political parrhesia as such—however correct that may be—Foucault does not go on to attend, as he might have, to what Maxwell calls "the problem of the hierarchy of truth in which some people (usually white, heterosexual, cisgender men) are assumed to be truthful while others (usually women, people of color, and queer/non-gender-conforming individuals) are not."[81] A shift in our focus from truth as a problem of correct reasoning to truth as a problem of truth-telling, as Foucault has made, must come to terms with the social hierarchies that authorize received understandings of who counts as a truth-teller.[82]

Finally, in answer to the "not minor problem" raised by parrhesia for Foucault—namely, "How can democracy withstand the truth?"—we might say that it all depends on *how* and *by whom* truth is told (*GS*, 174).

❋ 4 ❋
Ideology and the Ordinary

Social life is essentially practical. All mysteries which mislead theory into mysticism find their rational solution in human practice and in the comprehension of this practice.

MARX, "THESES ON FEUERBACH"

Did "thousands and thousands" of people cheer in Jersey City when the New York World Trade Center towers fell on September 11, 2001?[1] Does the COVID-19 vaccine cause autism? Is climate change a hoax perpetrated by advocates of big government? Did President Obama plan to sign an executive order to take away Americans' guns? Do the 2015 Planned Parenthood videos released by an anti-abortion group show "a fully formed fetus on the table, its heart beating, its legs kicking while someone says we have to keep it alive to harvest its brain"?[2] Hint: "no"; yet such claims barely capture the range of what is declared and defended in the public contexts of our so-called post-truth era.

In the view of many critics, this era seems wholly defined by the classic problem of ideology and its aggressive obfuscation of truth.[3] "The central puzzle of a theory of ideology is this: why is our behavior so often guided by states that do not seem to be sensitive to available evidence?" asks Jason Stanley.[4] Even our perceptual beliefs are not immune to ideological distortion. Consider Cara Carleton ("Carly") Fiorina's misrepresentation of a Planned Parenthood "sting" video in a 2016 GOP presidential primary debate hosted by CNN. When asked to retract her grisly description of "fetal-brain harvesting" by Planned Parenthood, when reminded by *Good Morning America* anchor George Stephanopoulos that no such video existed, and when asked by *Fox News Sunday* anchor Chris Wallace to acknowledge "what every fact-checker has found" (that the video contains no such scene), Fiorina replied: "No, I don't accept that at all. I've seen the footage. And I find it amazing, actually, that all these supposed fact-checkers in the mainstream media claim this doesn't exist. They're trying to attack the authenticity of the videotape," declared Fiorina. To those who say "that I am mistaken" and "the images aren't real," she later told a conservative audience in South Carolina, "[I say,] 'Well, yes, they are real.'"[5]

Widely discredited by fact-checkers, the videotape, made by the anti-abortion group inaptly named "The Center for Medical Progress," was deceptively edited to show that Planned Parenthood sought to profit from the sale of fetal tissue.[6] But let's be clear: what Fiorina claims to have seen is not even the already distorted "reality" portrayed in that video. Instead, she claims to have seen actual fetal brain harvesting. Leaving aside brazen mendacity and political opportunism, how might we account for the tenacity of the claim to "reality," clung to by Fiorina and repeated on conservative social media and websites, long after the videos were released for public viewing and fact-checking?[7] How are we to explain the powerlessness of facts to call into question the presentation of "reality" in her anti-abortion ideology? The answer depends partly on how one defines ideology.

According to Stanley, "a belief is ideological insofar as it is connected with one's various identities. And connection with, for example, one's social identity comes in degree. It is possible but hard to resist the conclusion that whether or not a belief is ideological also depends upon degree. Some beliefs are more ideological than others: those that are more closely connected with one of the agent's identities."[8] The closer a belief relates to one's identity, the harder it will be to revise it.

Connection with an identity, however, cannot be the whole of what makes an ideological belief resistant to revision. At issue is less the tenacity of an identity than, as Stanley himself recognizes, the worldly status of the belief.[9] As I argue below, the powerlessness of facts to correct a flawed ideological belief reflects the status of ideologies as ideas that traffic a world apart from facts; they appear to have their own reality and logic created out of our ordinary activity; they present reality and the true discourses that supplement it as if they could not have been otherwise. Ideologies are not errors that can be corrected but worldviews that seem to contain all reality. There is an objectivity to ideology.

Just this objectivity is highlighted by Sally Haslanger in her essay "'But Mom, Crop-Tops *Are* Cute!'"[10] Focusing more on social practices than on beliefs, Haslanger argues that the role played by ideology "in constituting and reinforcing social structures" is not mere mystification, the illusion of beliefs wrapped around a material core that exists apart from ideology.[11] "An ideology is not just a set of beliefs, and ideology critique is not just a matter of showing that the beliefs in question are false or unwarranted," writes Haslanger.[12] Instead, ideology is a material practice that constitutes what is real: "Ideology functions to create social reality."[13] Ideology critique faces the challenge of criticizing something that seems to be always already there insofar as "once we constitute our social world, descriptions of it not only appear true, but are true," writes Haslanger.[14] "Under conditions of male dominance, for example, women are, in fact, more submissive than men. This is a true generalization, and those who live under male dominance are justified in believing it. But again, if male dominance is hegemonic, this seems not only to describe how women happen to be but more than this: how women *are*."[15] Socially constructed gender relations are naturalized. Ideology critique would expose the contingency of male dominance and contest such naturalization. Still, too often, it treats gender relations as mere illusions concealing a "hidden" reality of power that critique would unmask.

For Haslanger, "'ideology' is the background cognitive and affective frame that gives actions and reactions meaning within a social system and contributes to its survival."[16] It is not just "a set of beliefs, understood as discrete and determinate propositional attitudes," but it "must include more primitive dispositions, habits, and a broader range of attitudes than just belief."[17] Notwithstanding their differences on the centrality of belief for a theory of ideology, Haslanger agrees with Stanley that the central question raised by ideology is this: "How do we explain our ongoing and yet unintended participation in structures of domination and subordination?"[18] Put otherwise, remarks Haslanger, "there is an important sense in which social structures are not imposed upon us, for they are constituted by our everyday choices and behaviors. We are not simply cogs in structures of subordination, we enact them."[19]

Althusserian Ideology Critique

The subject's "voluntary" participation in its own subjection is the puzzle behind Louis Althusser's famous claim that ideology makes subjects "'go.' They 'go all by themselves,' without a cop behind them," without the explicit threat of force.[20] Althusser's 1969 account of interpellation and "ideological state apparatuses" redefined ideology from a problem of "false" ideas lodged in consciousness to an everyday matter of constituting subjects who "willingly" reproduce an oppressive social order, the order of capitalist society. Ideology exists materially in "ideological state apparatuses" (e.g., the family, the church, the school, the army), which, in contrast to "repressive state apparatuses" (e.g., police, courts, military, government), employ noncoercive measures to dominate the working class and sustain capitalist order.[21] The function of ideology in capitalism is first and foremost to constitute individuals *as* obedient subjects.[22]

"The category of the subject is constitutive of all ideology only insofar as every ideology has the function (which defines it) of 'constituting' concrete individuals as subjects (such as you and me)" writes Althusser.[23] Ideology constitutes the subject through everyday material practices that belong to specific ideological apparatuses. It is not reducible to an illusory "world of ideas."[24] A religious ideology such as Christianity, for example, is not a set of abstract ideas or beliefs in the minds of subjects that exist before or outside their engagement with "an apparatus and its practices" but involves, instead, concrete material actions such as bowing one's head, attending Mass, kneeling, praying, or taking confession. As Pascale Gillot explains, the epistemological model here is not one of "causal consequentiality—between body and mind—but the Spinozistic model of strict simultaneity between mental events and bodily events." She continues: "Thus the materialism of the imaginary, which Althusser borrows from Spinoza, does not seem to imply the secondary or epiphenomenal character of mental states, "representations" and subjective life. Rather . . . this non-mechanistic materialism, far from being reductionist or even 'behaviourist,' admits the effectivity of mental activity and subjectivity, while asserting its always-already social and public existence. What this *habitus* model refutes, rather, is the traditional mentalist framework according to which representations, ideas, beliefs, and so on first exist in the individual mind, in an inner and private realm, and are then expressed and 'externalised' in the social-public world."[25]

Arguing that ideology is materialist and "profoundly unconscious," Althusser's critique of the mentalism associated with the (Cartesian) inner/outer and mind/world distinction has been crucial for rethinking the traditional inscription of ideology in the region of consciousness. Though the Frankfurt School's *Ideologiekritik* drew on Freud to show how ideology satisfies unconscious desires to sustain social order, Althusser's turn to Jacques Lacan radicalizes the place of the unconscious such that distortion and misrecognition are the sine qua non of subjectivation qua ideological "interpellation." Althusser argues that specific ideologies have a history, but "*ideology is eternal*, just like the unconscious," pervasive, and fundamentally distorting.[26]

Furthermore, "since ideology is eternal," it "has always-already interpellated individuals as subjects," writes Althusser. "An individual is always-already a subject, even before she is born."²⁷ There is a symbolic web of meanings and imperatives already in place where the unborn child has been inscribed.²⁸ Misrecognizing itself as self-constituting, autonomous, and freely choosing, the subject takes for granted that whatever he or she experiences is just the way things are. The subject does not question what is given through common sense.

Ideology has no outside, and no class or subject that escapes ideological distortion. Geoff Pfeifer clarifies Althusser's view: "As ideological, consciousness is distorted because 'consciousness' knowledge (and its world) appears to it as natural, static, and nonhistorical. This ideological mode of awareness is only ever partially overcome in that ideology is never something that we can be rid of and new modes of ideology arise as old modes are overcome. There is, then, a kind of symbiotic relationship between one's subjectivity and ideology: it is in ideology that the subject is constituted but at the same time it is the constituted subject that sustains (or reproduces) ideology."²⁹

A set of material practices in which we are always already enmeshed rather than a corrigible false belief or cognitive error, ideology cannot be exposed by pointing to the actual world hidden by ideology (e.g., the economic base), as the early Marx held, argues Althusser. Rejecting the epistemological realism of *The German Ideology*, Althusser breaks with what he claims to be the "positivist-historicist" character of the "humanist" Marx's theory of ideology, according to which ideology is the (false) ideas of the ruling class.³⁰ So portrayed, writes Althusser, "ideology is sheer illusion, sheer dream, in other words, nothingness. All its reality lies outside it."³¹ It is "an imaginary assemblage, a pure dream, empty and vain, constituted by the 'diurnal residues' of the only full, positive reality, that of the concrete history of concrete, material individuals materially producing their existence."³²

Althusser's critique of the philosophy of consciousness and its subject has freed the discussion of ideology from the mentalist understanding of error or false belief. But critics argue that his assimilation of ideology to subject constitution (understood as misrecognition) all but foreclosed political transformation.³³ "Ideology represents individuals' imaginary relation to their real conditions of existence," writes Althusser in his most famous restatement of the Marxian concept.³⁴ If ideology does not "reflect" the real world but "represents" the "imaginary relationship of individuals" to the real world, the thing ideology (mis)represents is itself already at one remove from the real.³⁵

Althusser's refusal of the prevailing Marxian theory of ideology as the reflection of the "conditions of existence of men, i.e., their real world," fundamentally alters the relationship of ideology to the material contradictions that constitute capitalism. Isabelle Garo explains:

> In defining ideology as the representation of individuals "to their real conditions of existence," and not as the representation of these conditions themselves, Althusser may seem to be indulging in a Byzantine taste for nuance. But the remark is in fact crucial, for it disconnects . . . representation from its object, it stretches to the breaking point the relationship between ideology and the real contradictions that constitute its stakes, it imposes its limits upon it while also granting it its relative validity and its determined social function. Instead of being shot through by the real contradictions of the real, ideology is situated entirely on the side of the functions of preservation and reproduction, thus authorizing the splendid autonomy of class struggle in theory, but also automatically depriving itself of social and political effects beyond it.[36]

Garo does not endorse a naive representationalism but calls attention to how Althusserian ideology has lost any relation to material practice and class struggle. Notwithstanding Althusser's valuable idea of ideology as a material practice embedded in received social institutions, ideology is foremost the distorted relation that subjects always already have with themselves as subjects and to a social world they misrecognize as given, necessary, and real. It is no surprise, then, that ideology is described, save in his very late writings, as the other of (Marxist) science (discussed below), for only science can attenuate the irremediably distorting character of human subjectivity, ordinary life, and common sense.[37] By contrast, writes Garo, "for Marx, ideology, understood as an inverted and partial representation [e.g., *The German Ideology* and its famous image of the camera obscura, discussed later], could still be examined in terms of relative adequacy, of a partial grasping of its object. Marx could consequently conceive ideological struggle as the dialectical moment of the formation of consciousness, individual as well as collective, through which individuals fought out their struggles to the end."[38] I will take up Garo's insightful reading when I turn to Marx's view.

Althusser's account of ideology is an account of the *reproduction* of oppressive social institutions and practices. As human subjects, we cannot transcend our perspective, but that perspective is irremediably distorting; it can never attain knowledge of the way reality is versus what we, imprisoned in ideological common sense, take it to be. All our knowledge is merely subjective, premised on the misrecognition of the conditions of our own existence and reduction of the real to the given. Accordingly, objective knowledge of the world must involve knowledge of properties of the world that in no way depend on the effects such properties have on the cognizing subject.[39] Only (Marxist) science (aided by materialist philosophy) can break with ordinary ideological "knowledge" and produce true discourse.

Scientific practice is distinguished from ideological practice by its rule-following procedures, which can be made explicit and are subject to revision, holds Althusser. These procedures minimize the necessarily distorting effects of subjectivity and thus of ideology in knowledge production. Following the idea of science advanced by Gaston Bachelard, Althusser argues that Marxism's break with ideology is facilitated through the relative autonomy of its scientific rationality and modeled in the "epistemological break" of the later Marx.[40] Internal to science, an epistemological break carves out the difference between science and ideology. Ideology becomes visible only from the standpoint of science. Althusser writes: "Ideology never says, 'I am ideological.' One has to be outside ideology, in other words, in scientific knowledge, to be able to say, 'I am in ideology.' . . . Ideology *has no outside* (for itself), but, at the same time . . . *it is nothing but outside* (for science), within scientific discourse itself."[41]

For Althusser, pace empiricism, the "real object" is unreachable (i.e., cannot be known) save by means of science's "theoretical object."[42] In *Reading Capital*, for example, we learn that, whereas the object of a nonscientific (ideological) discourse is given and can only be recognized, science formulates its own theoretical object and creates knowledge on the basis of strictly internal criteria.[43] The theoretical object is not a mere reflection but an enrichment of the real object. Science works on different theoretical objects (e.g., T_1, T_2, T_3) as it progresses, throwing off layers of ideological distortion.[44] Hristos Verikukis explains: "The theoretical object is not a result of a process of abstraction, of getting rid of essential features of the real object, but is an addition to the real object producing new realities; it does not describe what already exists," nor does it in any way "alter the real object."[45] The relation between the real and the theoretical object is constructed strictly in the "problematic" of science; it is wholly internal to scientific practice and takes place entirely within thought.

"The rationale for conceiving this relation [between the real and the theoretical object] as internal to scientific practice was, for Althusser, to avoid the counterposition of a subject and an object independent from each other, and the problems associated with this structure—that is empiricism . . . guarantees subject-centeredness (knowledge as an effect of the subject)," explains a sympathetic Verikukis.[46] This may well have been Althusser's reasoning. Still, in my view, it is symptomatic of the problem described above: namely, that, for him, the attainment of objectivity, the move out of ideology into the true discourse of Marxist science, "requires the pruning away of every admixture of subjectivity," to borrow James Conant's apt formulation.[47]

Not even science, however, can escape the endless imperative to prune, as scientists themselves import into their research the (ideological) assumptions of the wider culture. Some of what the scientists import will be subject to criticism because their "spontaneous materialism" calls them to attend to the materially real world, argues the later Althusser, but there is no point at which ideology can be fully excised from scientific practice.[48]

This (impossible) task then falls to (Marxist materialist) philosophy, which the later Althusser, critical of his earlier "theoreticism" and "positivism," frees from the initial epistemological task of providing the foundations (extrascientific criteria) with which to separate science from ideology in terms of the way the object of knowledge is constructed. No longer a science, as positivism conceived it, philosophy's role changes from providing guarantees for scientific knowledge to clarifying which of its concepts are ideological for science. William Lewis writes, "Philosophy still works on concepts, but it does not guarantee their veracity. Instead, philosophy is theory that intervenes in theory, marking divisions within it and producing theses. This intervention [writes Althusser] 'draw[s] . . . a line of demarcation that separates, in each case, the scientific from the ideological.'"[49]

Althusser recognizes that this new nonpositivist form of philosophy cannot ensure science's clean break from ideology—philosophers like scientists are only human. Having relinquished the epistemological absolutism with which the theoretical production of science was credited in *For Marx* and *Reading Capital*, the later Althusser describes ideology as something like the necessary condition of science. Science is not outside ideology but rather in a continuous struggle against ideology. "Every recognized science," he writes, "not only has emerged from its own prehistory [in ideology], but continues endlessly to do so (its prehistory remains always contemporary: something like its *Alter-Ego*) by *rejecting* what it considers to be *error*, according to the process which Bachelard called 'the epistemological break [rupture].'"[50] In other words, there is never a final break with ideology tout court, only with specific ideologies. The progress of science is the story of this ongoing struggle.[51]

Even with this concession to the tenacity of ideology, Althusser always supported the initial and all-important distinction between scientific and ideological discourses. Althusser's failure to redefine the scientific nature of Marxism in the wake of his self-criticism (1976), however, left his project open to the charge that this distinction is bankrupt and, with it, the entire structural Marxist project. Subsequent debates have circled the question of whether the science/ideology distinction can be upheld on nonrationalist grounds.[52] Althusser clearly thought it could but never coherently explained how.

What concerns us here is not the possibility, let alone desirability, of upholding the science/ideology distinction on whatever grounds but the political and theoretical consequences of positing such a distinction in the first place.[53] And if the difference cannot be defended, what becomes of the concept and critique of ideology? Admitting that science could never free itself once and for all from ideology, Althusser nonetheless clings—as do those intent on advancing his unfinished project—to a conception of true discourse that excludes the contribution of the subject to the production of objective knowledge. It does not deny that there is no such thing as a cognitive perspective on the object that is unmediated by any structure of human subjectivity but, rather, laments this irreducible fact. Everything in Althusser's account of Marxist science is devised to get around what it defines as the unfortunate limitation of human subjectivity.

Recognizing that such a science can never achieve its full "pruning away" without falling back into the positivism of his earlier work, Althusser could have generated a form of self-criticism that rethinks what counts as objective knowledge and true discourse from the ground up. Instead, he and his followers hold to the received philosophical opposition of subjectivity and objectivity: an opposition, to speak with Conant, that "precludes a feature of our experience from being subjective (in the sense of depending on our perceptual or evaluative perspective) and at the same time objective (in the sense of affording true estimation of how things are)."[54] For Althusser, whatever is "subjective" is rooted in the illusions of an ideologically constituted subjectivity.

This rejection of the subjective in the objective, of the constitutive role of the subject in the creation of knowledge and true discourse, vastly limits the significance of Althusserian criticism and places it in a kind of permanent antagonism to what I have called the realistic spirit of critique. Qualifying his rationalist view of science, Althusser argued that science must be understood as a historical practice that contains its internal criteria of truth and error but no epistemological guarantee for scientific knowledge, no independent philosophical certitude. This concession, as the sympathetic critic Robert Paul Resch argues, was part of an attempt to eliminate the tension between conventionalism and realism in Althusser's work, which arose as a consequence of his conventionalist idea of science as constituting and working on its theoretical objects, on the one hand,

and his location of that idea in a realist and materialist ontology.⁵⁵ In *Reading Capital*, he insisted on the difference between things in themselves (the real) and concepts of things (science), arguing that the former had logical priority over the latter. In other words: "The real is one thing. . . . Thought about the real is another."⁵⁶ And again in *Essays in Self-Criticism*, he restates "both the thesis of the *primacy of the real object over the object of knowledge*, and . . . *the distinction between the real object and the object of knowledge*."⁵⁷ And, perhaps most tellingly: "The principle of all existence is *materiality*; and all existence is *objective*, that is, 'prior' to the 'subjectivity' which knows it, and independent of that subjectivity," wrote the later Althusser.⁵⁸

Althusser's stating and restating of his materialist thesis—though it hardly reduces the tension between conventionalism and realism—can be read, with Resch, as an attempt to define science in a way that avoids falling into idealism and the reduction of science to a discourse that merely reflects on the real. But it can also be read as an expression of the "absolute conception of the world" that animates Althusser's earlier and later ideas of Marxist science. In Althusser's materialist account of the priority of the real, the world is on one side, the subject on the other. Access to the real world is barred by the eternally ideological nature of human consciousness, its materially constituted state of misrecognition and self-delusion. Ubiquitous and eternal, ideology is fully generative of what reality can be for human beings. It is as if we were cognitively confined within our forms of human subjectivity so that knowledge of how things are would have to be free of any admixture of human subjectivity. But this complete elimination of the subjective from the objective is, on Althusser's own account, impossible: even scientists following procedures and rules cannot thoroughly prune it away, nor can the philosophers whose job is to alert scientists to ideology's corrosive presence in their theories. Despite his critique of empiricism, Althusser posits the world as an object to be known by a subject that always already stands in its own way to objective knowledge.

A realistic democratic theory of "ideology"—should one wish to retain the term—must insist on the possibility of critique rooted not in scientific practice but in ordinary life and as the purview not of specialists but of citizens. For that, it needs a theory of true discourse that does not deny but recognizes the essential contribution of the subject to any game of truth in a particular regime of truth, such as liberal-democratic capitalism. It needs a theory of true discourse that does not assume, as Althusser's theory of Marxist science did, that truth will free us and that we should never resist the force of truth. And it needs an understanding of that force as something that inheres not in truth itself but in us, subjects who manifest (or refuse to manifest) truth. Let us turn, then, to Althusser's onetime student Foucault.

Foucault's Truth Alternative

The puzzle of the subject's complicity in its subjection is also a central concern of Foucault. Like Althusser, he is critical of humanist conceptions of the subject and explores the construction of subjectivity as entangled with power. Furthermore, Althusser's attempt to combine an account of repressive state apparatuses with ideological state apparatuses finds echoes in Foucault's recognition that "pure violence or strict coercion" cannot account for the modern power relations that rely on the idea of a free subject. In his shift from a theory of biopower (*History of Sexuality*, vol. 1) and disciplinary power (*Madness and Civilization*) to a theory of governmentality, Foucault conceives of power as an intricate network of relations that "involve a set of rational techniques" that bring together "coercion technologies and self-technologies."[59]

Notwithstanding these critical points of overlap, Foucault was adamant in rejecting the language of ideology and refused the idealized view of science and truth that captivated Althusser. Relying on a conception of science fully distinguished from ideology, argues Foucault in a 1977 interview, the theory of ideology reproduces a metaphysical account according to which ideology is mere appearance.[60] According to this distinction, ideology "always stands in virtual opposition to something else which is supposed to count as truth."[61] He explains: "Basically, ideological discourse always appears as alienated discourse in relation to the right discourse, the discourse that speaks the truth," and that discourse is "science."[62] As discourses, science and ideology are merely inverse sides of the same coin of "truth." Whether they obscure and distort or reflect and reveal truth, both science and ideology are measured according to a reality external to them. Each fails to grasp discourses of truth as supplements to reality with "truth effects" that are not reducible to reality.

In contrast with this approach, explains Foucault, "I believe that the problem does not consist in drawing a line between that in a discourse which falls under the category of scientificity or truth, and that which comes under some other category [ideology], but in seeing historically how effects of truth are produced within discourses which in themselves are neither true nor false."[63] For Foucault, discourses have no meaning beyond what they say. He denies the general categories of illusion and misrecognition, which figure prominently in Althusser's theory of ideology. "However," as Mark Cousins and Athar Hussain observe, "for Foucault, if things are not hidden nor masked, they are not transparent either. They may not be visible. And he would attribute that non-visibility to the fact that the field of coverage of discourses—what they say and how they say it—is limited by their very conditions of existence. Moreover, no discourse is self-subsistent; they are nodes in a network of discursive practices. Non-visibility is simply a result of this fact that discourses are 'partial and limited.' And an analysis such as Foucault's . . . brings the non-visible to light by a grouping of discursive and non-discursive practices and tracing their ramifications [their "truth" effects]."[64]

Thinking about how things can be nontransparent and yet not hidden or masked is a productive way to reframe the problem of ideology and the task of critique. Yet, surely, the ability to light up or make visible what has gone unnoticed cannot be restricted to the prodigious intellectual skills of a philosopher like Foucault (as Foucault would be the first to say). Ideology presents a political problem that, in the introduction, following Cora Diamond, I called "the difficulty of reality," a problem that ordinary citizens often manage through "deflection," a refusal or inability to "fac[e] up to . . . reality," as Arendt put it (*OT*, 478). By now, it should be clear that to face reality is not to unmask it as "false" but to recognize (one's part in) the effects of its game of truth within a specific regime of truth. To do that, we need not science but an ordinary idea of human affective propensities (i.e., as world giving and corrigible) as the basis not for discovering "what is concealed," writes Foucault, "but rather to make visible what precisely is visible, which is to say to make appear what is so close, so immediate, so intimately connected with ourselves that we cannot perceive it."[65]

This alternative idea of the subject dependence of objective thought can be teased out of Foucault's later work on truth, which articulates his stance on ideology. I said earlier that Foucault was adamant in his opposition to speaking in terms of ideology, but a more accurate description would be to say that he was tenaciously searching, continually trying to find a more precise formulation of the problem that ideology posed. In a January 30, 1980, lecture at the Collège de France and published in *On the Government of the Living*, Foucault tells his audience:

> I come back once again to what I am constantly returning to, that is to say, the rejection of analysis in terms of ideology, the rejections of the analysis of men's thought, behavior, and knowledge in terms of ideology. I have insisted on this rejection of ideological analysis many times. I have returned to it, I think, in practically all of the annual courses I have given . . . , and even so I would like to return to it again, for a very simple reason. This is

that each time I return to it I think, . . . I hope to have carried out a very slight displacement. (GL, 76)

Before elaborating what this "slight displacement" might be, it is worth noting that the lecture raised the question, "how is it that, in our type of society, power cannot be exercised without truth having to manifest itself, and manifest itself in the form of subjectivity" (GL, 75)? The "new line" on ideology, the "rejection of analysis in terms of ideology," originates in this question of the relationship of the subject to truth and power. The question allows Foucault to radically restate "a traditional . . . way of posing the philosophical-political question," according to which "when the subject voluntarily submits to the bond of the truth, in a relationship of knowledge (*connaissance*), that is to say, when, after providing himself with its foundations, instruments, and justification, the subject claims to deliver a discourse of truth, what can he say about, or for, or against the power to which he is involuntarily subject? . . . What can the voluntary bond with the truth say about the involuntary bond that ties us and subjects us to power?" (GL, 76–77). There is, however, another way of stating the problem:

> Not by positing first of all the right of access to the truth, not by establishing first of all this voluntary and as it were contractual bond with the truth, but by posing first of all the question of power in the following way: what does the systematic, voluntary, theoretical and practical questioning of power have to say about the subject of knowledge and about the bond with the truth by which, involuntarily, this subject is held? In other words, it is no longer a matter of saying: given the bond tying me voluntarily to the truth, what can I say about power? But, given my desire, decision, and effort to break the bond that binds me to power, what then is the situation with regard to the subject of knowledge and the truth? It is not the critique of representations in terms of truth or error, truth or falsity, ideology or science, rationality or irrationality that should serve as indicator for defining legitimacy or denouncing the illegitimacy of power. It is the movement of freeing oneself from power that should serve as revealer in the transformations of the subject and the relation the subject maintains with the truth. (GL, 77)

Turning the problem around, prioritizing not the desire for truth but the wish to free oneself from power, the desire to be governed differently (see chapter 2), Foucault challenges the (Althusserian) idea that what stands between the oppressed and freedom is access to truth: "knowledge/

connaissance," that is, the scientific understanding of knowledge based on "foundations, instruments, and justification" (*GL*, 77). Although the later Althusser recognized that such access could never achieve a perspective on power free of any admixture of (ideologically constituted) subjectivity—even scientists and materialist philosophers never wholly escape the delusions of ideology—he nevertheless took for granted that the subject's quest for and submission to truth (as given by Marxist science) was the only means for liberation. For Althusser, then, the goal was to distinguish, as best one can, ideological discourse from the true discourse of Marxist science. Whatever is revealed to be ideological should be resisted; whatever is nonideological should be embraced as freeing truth.

For Foucault, the (Althusserian) focus on unmasking ideology as the linchpin in the struggle against power must be upended. When we begin with the desire to transform existing relations of rule, we alter our relation to truth: We should resist—where we should—even when something is true. Otherwise, we are still treating truth as if it had a force in itself, as if truth decided what we should do, as Daniele Lorenzini described Foucault's teaching.[66] Accordingly, Foucault shifts the axis of the problem he shared with Althusser—namely, the creation of subjects who "'go all by themselves,' without a cop behind them," without the explicit use of force.[67] For Althusser, the problem opened a radical rethinking of ideology as subject constitution, whose aspirational political horizon is freeing oneself using Marxist science qua true discourse. In his view, it is not only that truth frees us but, to use Foucault's terms, that freeing truth just is knowledge-connaissance, the scientific conception of truth governed by specific rules and procedures. In this way, Althusser reproduces what Foucault argues to be the concealment of the status of truth as knowledge-connaissance, that is, the concealment of the conceit that scientific truth is the only game of truth in town that remains (relatively) untainted by power: it escapes given regimes of truth.[68]

For Foucault, who calls out the mechanisms of power that permeate truth as knowledge-connaissance, the scientific standpoint of truth, the problem of power takes a radically different form: "Why and how does the exercise of power in our society, the exercise of power as government of men, demand not only acts of obedience and submission, but truth acts in which individuals who are subjects in the power relationship are also actors, spectator witnesses, or objects in manifestation of truth procedures? Why in this great system of relations of power has a regime of truth developed indexed to subjectivity?" (*GL*, 82). Examining power in terms of what Foucault calls the problem of "the government of human beings by the truth," Lorenzini explains that, for Foucault, "there is a 'ring of truth' or an 'alethurgic circle' that revolves around the exercise of government, because to conduct the conduct of others (and of oneself) one must always carry out 'operations in the domain of truth'—operations that, however, 'are always in excess of what is useful and necessary to govern in any effective way.' No government, then, without alethurgy."[69]

Starting from the question of power or—more precisely—from "an attitude," namely, the "non-necessity of all power," Foucault advances a different critical approach to the problem he shared with Althusser (*GL*, 78). As noted earlier, ideology is an infelicitous way of talking about the noncoercive bases of power because things are not hidden or masked—but they are not transparent either. A better way to put the problem for realistic critique is this: how to make visible that which is already in plain view but remains unseen because, as Foucault told us, it "is so close, so immediate, so intimately linked to ourselves that, as a consequence, we do not perceive it."[70] This is the problem of the ordinary, as Foucault, recognizing the contribution of ordinary language philosophy, understood it. Power is in plain view—it is everywhere, in fact—but we do not see it for what it is because we are enmeshed in power relations: not as the Althusserian subject, without Marxist science, who is hopelessly deluded, but relatively unaware that we could act differently, that things as they now are could be different because they are nonnecessary, that they could have been otherwise.

The problem of critique in Foucault's view is not one of ideological false belief but of our captivation by a perspective in which things appear to us as how they must be. The critical task is to make that captivation visible, not by turning to (Marxist) science and its putatively objective view of how power works, but by showing that there are other perspectives from which power can be seen as contingent: "no power whatsoever is acceptable by right and absolutely and definitely inevitable" (*GL*, 78). In *On the Government of the Living*, this discussion of the nonnecessity of power follows directly on the previous discussion of inverting the traditional philosophical-political question regarding truth, the subject, and power. Foucault's order of argumentation is unsurprising because getting us to see what is in plain sight, that "power has no intrinsic legitimacy," is the main task of critique (*GL*, 77). That we fail to see the contingency, the "it could have been otherwise," of power is due not to our being hopelessly mired in ideology but, in no small part, to our status as "alethurgic" subjects, subjects who, captive to a perspective, manifest truth and, in this way, repeatedly testify to the reality and the necessity of power, of things as they are given in a particular regime of truth.

Out of this critical "attitude" toward power, Foucault develops his "approach," which "consists in wondering, that being the case [the non-necessity of power], what of the subject and relations of knowledge do we dispense with when we consider no power to be founded either by right or necessity, that all power only rests on the contingency and fragility of a history . . . and that there is no universal, immediate, and obvious right that can everywhere and always support any kind of relation of power" (GL, 77–78). The aim is to bring into play in a systematic way, not the suspension of every certainty, but the "nonnecessity of all power of whatever kind" (GL, 78). Anticipating his audience objecting that "this is anarchy; it's anarchism," Foucault playfully calls his approach, the methodology informed by his critical "attitude," not "science" but "anarcheology" (GL, 78, 79).

Refusing the specialized language of science to study power and the ordinary makes sense when one's objective is not to speak in universals and generalizations, that is, in a nomothetic tongue where every explanation is a prediction. The scientific standpoint of truth is entangled in relations of power that certify those individuals deemed capable of its form of "truth-demonstration." As argued previously, science marks what Foucault calls the "transition from a technology of truth-event to truth-demonstration."[71] Although "truth is everywhere and awaits us everywhere," the "universal subject of this universal truth . . . will be an abstract subject because, concretely, the universal subject able to grasp this truth is rare, since it must be a subject qualified by procedures on pedagogy and selection."[72] In other words, the scientific standpoint of truth demonstration relies—as does any other truth event—on the "rarefaction of those who can know a truth that is now present everywhere and at every moment."[73]

Beholden to science and its knowing subjects, the "ideological study" of "madness," Foucault explains, begins with two givens: the universal reality of madness and the nature of human beings as nonalienated, free beings. "On the basis of these universalist and humanist positions, [it then asks,] what are the grounds and conditions governing the system of representation that has led to a practice of confinement with its well-known alienating effects and need for reform." Foucault continues:

> The anarcheological type of study, on the other hand, consist[s] in taking the practice of confinement in its historical singularity, that is to say in its contingency, in the sense of its fragility, its essential non-necessity, which obviously doesn't mean (quite the opposite!) that there was no reason for it and is to be accepted as a brute fact. That the practice of confinement is intelligible implies that we understand the at once perfectly intelligible

but fragile fabric within which this practice came about. In other words, it was not a matter of starting from a universal that says: this is madness. It did not involve starting from a humanist position saying: this is human nature, the human essence, human freedom. Madness had to be taken as an x and the practice alone grasped, as if one did not know, and proceeding without knowing, what madness is. And from there it was a matter of seeing what types of relations of knowledge (*connaissance*) were founded by this practice itself, with their structuring and determining effects in the field of knowledge (*savoir*), of theory, medicine, and psychiatry, but also with their effects and the experience of the subject regarding the division of reason and unreason. (*GL*, 79–80)

Describing his approach as a "refusal of universals," Foucault brings into view the nonnecessary origin, the "historical singularity," of the psychiatric asylum, the penal system, schools, churches, the military—the entire panoply of what Althusser called the repressive and the ideological state apparatuses (*GL*, 80, 79). In them, something that is already "given in reality" (e.g., the suffering of a mentally unstable person) is transformed into the site of true discourse. This is the process of "problematization" that we examined in previous chapters. Is there a "relation between the things that are problematized and the problematization," or is the latter a "theoretical object" that has no relation to the "real object," as an idealist might claim (*DT*, 225)?

Addressing the charge directly, Foucault states: "When I say that I am studying the problematization of madness, or of sexuality, or of crime, it's not a way to deny the reality of those things—crime, sexuality, madness" (*DT*, 225). How is this defense different from that of Althusser who, responding to the same charge, repeatedly stated both "the thesis of the *primacy of the real object over the object of knowledge*, and . . . the distinction between the real object and the object of knowledge"?[74]

For Althusser, we recall that the object of a nonscientific (ideological) discourse can be only "recognized" by common sense, not cognized and developed like the theoretical object of scientific discourse. The "real object" is unreachable (i.e., cannot be known) save through science's theoretical object. The latter is not a mere reflection of the former but an enrichment, creating new theoretical objects as science progresses. Nevertheless, the purpose of the theoretical object is to gain knowledge of the real object, on which the entire project of structural Marxism as a politically relevant science rests: it is a true discourse that tells us how the world is, whereas ideological discourse tells us only how it appears to us. In the wake of Althusser's self-criticism, the fate of structural Marxism hung on developing the nonrational grounds of science, freeing science from its positivist past and making it politically relevant, related to class struggle. Yet he never questioned that such a science must affirm the prior reality of the real object, make it "knowable" and subject to critique through the construction, entirely in thought, of the "theoretical object." This project was haunted by the irremediably distorting nature of subjectivity, which even scientists and philosophers could not entirely escape.

However, there is another problem with Althusser's critical practice of Marxist science, which Foucault's critical practice of problematization illuminates. Problematization of madness proceeds through a discourse of truth that adds something to the reality of "suffering, anxiety, deviant behaviors, and all those types of reactions and feelings due to brain damage and other [such causes]" (*DT*, 225). It combines all these things, characterizes, treats, and describes them as "mental diseases," explains Foucault (*DT*, 225). The supplement of truth internal to the process of problematization does not take place merely in thought, however, as does the enrichment of the "real" object by the "theoretical object" in Marxist science. On the contrary, this supplement alters reality: altering the material practices through which mental disease is identified, treated, and experienced, it alters the experience of suffering, anxiety, and so on, the subject's relation to him- or herself as mentally ill. Indeed, material reality changes could not occur without the subject's manifestation of truth, the truth of (his or her) mental illness.

"The problematization is an answer to something which is real," affirms Foucault (*DT*, 225). This relationship cannot be "analyzed in terms of a direct relation of representation to that which is represented" (*DT*, 225), not only because the material practices and discourses of the science(s) of mental illness are a supplement that organizes reality in new ways or even because a given problematization goes on to create new realities. Instead, it is because, like the "real object," any problematization of it, too, is nonnecessary, radically contingent: it did not have to arise; it could have been otherwise. "The problematization is in a way always a kind of creation, but it is a creation in that sense that, given a certain situation, you can never infer that *this* kind of problematization will follow" (*DT*, 226). For Foucault to see this reality already in plain view, we need not unmask it as ideological and show the necessity (e.g., the economic logic of capitalism) that underwrites it. We need, instead, to recognize that it could have been otherwise. He calls problematization "this kind of original, specific and singular relation between thought and reality" (*DT*, 226).

An "original, specific and singular relation between thought and reality" is a claim not about the general relation of the theoretical to the real object, to use Althusser's terms. It is a claim about creating a new reality in its "historical singularity, that is to say, in its contingency, in the sense of its fragility, its essential non-necessity." Here, realistic critique is no longer a question of the "primacy of the real object over the object of knowledge" nor of "the primacy of . . . the distinction between the real object and the object of knowledge," as it was for Althusser.[75] These distinctions fall away not because everything is discourse but because the return to the ordinary has come back to "the rough ground" (*PI*, §107), as Wittgenstein referred to the terrain of critical thinking, where we can glimpse the nonnecessity of what is, the "it could have been otherwise."

Recognition of the "otherwise," we will now see, is more appropriate to what Marx understood by ideology critique than anything cooked up in the scientific laboratories of structural Marxism.

Rethinking Marx's Ideologiekritik

"Marx, who borrowed the term 'ideology' from the Ideologues while considerably altering its original meaning, basically always conceived of it as something related to the consciousness-form, as an 'object' of consciousness. He conceived consciousness, in turn, in very traditional fashion, as the subject's capacity to be present to sense perceptions, emotions and ideas that come to it from without or within," writes Althusser.[76] To this conventional account of consciousness, Marx nevertheless added something important "by considering the possibility that the ideologies are *systems of ideas and representations* in which the reality of the subject itself is represented, although it is distorted and usually inverted; and also by defending the thesis that ideologies are social . . . and have a function in the class struggle."[77] However, comments Althusser, "Marx basically never abandoned the conviction that *ideology consists of ideas*" as distinguished from "the real," and that the task of critique is to show that the real has "primacy" over ideas.[78] In other words, "the real was real and the ideas of ideology were *merely ideas*."[79]

Missing in Marx's theory of ideology, argues Althusser, was a theory of "the material existence of ideology," the very thing that his theory of "ideological state apparatuses" was intended to elaborate.[80] But it is Marx, not Althusser, I argue, who theorizes the *materiality* of ideology and does so without holding to a positivist conception of the real, confining *Ideologiekritik* to the truth-demonstration powers of science, and turning the whole realm of the ordinary into ideology.

Althusser's account of the Marxian concept of ideology is just one in a long line of criticisms. *The German Ideology* is considered the classic

Marxist statement on ideology, though what Marx means by ideology is far from clear. Riddled with aporias, argue even sympathetic critics, the Marxian concept of ideology can be understood in at least one of the following three ways: (1) as encompassing all the ideational productions by which a ruling class justifies its rule; (2) as a theory of social consciousness according to which the latter is seen as arising from real relations of production; (3) as a rhetorical weapon in the polemic against the Young Hegelians. Although the concept of ideology, primarily when understood in terms of (1) and (2), is too unstable and contradictory to offer much in the way of a theory, I would agree with Laurence Gayot that (3) provides a way of getting at what is crucial in the Marxian concept, namely a kind of idealism about social reality, the belief in the independence or autonomy of ideas and their internal logic or necessity that Marx identified with the Young Hegelians.[81] Criticizing this idealism, however, Marx does not simply assert the primacy of the "real" over "ideas" but reveals how an idealist conception of ideas (i.e., an idea of ideas as the real "real") takes on material reality.[82]

We can approach this autonomy of ideas by looking at the famous metaphor of *The German Ideology*, the camera obscura. "If in all ideology men and their circumstances appear upside-down as in a *camera obscura*, this phenomenon arises just as much from their historical life-process as the inversion of objects on the retina does from their physical life-process."[83] According to Isabelle Garo: "Ideology, as we've known since Marx, is first and foremost a question of perspective, that is to say, the construction of a representation from the point of view of a subject who, far from being a passive spectator of what unfolds before him, is an actor in its elaboration."[84] Describing inverted social relations as ideological and as the products of the actual activity of men, Marx establishes an internal relation between objective and subjective moments in a perceptual encounter between a perceiving subject and the object(s) of his or her perception. This relation, crucial to attaining critical knowledge of the historical life process, is always in danger of falling apart, such that human beings lose track of their activity in constructing the perspective from which ideas appear to have an independent reality. In other words, the Marxian critical concept of ideology identifies not just the inversion of reality, expressed by the famous camera obscura metaphor, but the creation of a *perspective* from which ideas appear to precede material activity and to create that reality.

The perspective from which ideas appear to have a life and logic of their own is perhaps best expressed in the famous section on commodity fetishism from volume 1 of *Capital*, often taken by sympathetic critics to be a significant advance on Marx's theory of ideology.[85] "There is a definite social relation between men, that assumes, in their eyes, the fantastic form of a relation between things," writes Marx. But this relation between things is not just how things appear: To the producers, he clarifies, "the relation of the producers to the sum total of their own labour is presented to them as a social relation, existing not between themselves, but between the products of their labour.... This I call the Fetishism which attaches to the products of labour, so soon as they are produced as commodities, and which is inseparable from the production of commodities."[86]

But while the term "fetishism" implies that the relation is wholly illusory, Marx makes clear that relations between things can at once be "fantastic" and yet "what they are" under capitalism. Marx writes: "To [the producers], therefore, the relations connecting the labour of one individual with that of the rest appear, not as direct social relations between individuals at work, but as what they really are, material relations between persons and social relations between things."[87]

Under the conditions of capitalism and wage labor, comments David Andrews, "commodity fetishism [according to Marx] . . . is not simply an error such that people believe in something as if it were real when in fact it is only an illusion. It is a feature of how things actually are in commodity production," just as women's submissiveness, as Haslanger argued, is a feature of how things are under conditions of male dominance.[88] Fetishistic illusion is a misleading appearance but also a necessary appearance resulting from a particular structuring of reality. As I. I. Rubin concurs, "fetishism is not only a phenomenon of social consciousness, but of social being."[89] It cannot be reduced to mystification, ideological distortion.

Although conceptualized by what Althusser calls the later Marx (the "scientist"), the fetishism of commodities has echoes in the writings of the early Marx (the "humanist"). In the *Economic and Philosophical Manuscripts of 1844*, for example, Marx argues that the products of the worker's labor confront him as something alien and coercive; this is not just in his head but a structuring feature of material reality.[90]

> The worker puts his life into the object; but now his life no longer belongs to him but to the object. Hence, the greater this activity, the greater is the worker's lack of objects, whatever the products of his labor is, he is not. Therefore the greater this product, the less is he himself. The *alienation* of the worker in his product does not only mean that his labor becomes an object, an *external* existence, but that it exists *outside* him, independently as something alien to him, and that it becomes a power of its own confronting him; it means that the life which he has conferred on the object confronts him as something hostile and alien.[91]

As an objective illusion (not a lie or an error), commodity fetishism does not lose its power even after it is shown to be wrong, criticized, and denounced. With the fetish concept, Marx provides a materialist theory of illusion that radically departs from the philosophical criticism of illusion, argues Garo.[92] In *The German Ideology*, he mocked the Young Hegelians for believing that simply recognizing that people allow their own ideas to rule over them is sufficient to overcome those ideas. "The phantoms of their brains have got out of their hands. They, the creators, have bowed down before their creations. Let us liberate them from the chimeras, the ideas, dogmas, imaginary beings under the yoke of which they are pining away. Let us revolt against the rule of thoughts. Let us teach men, says one, to exchange these imaginations for thoughts which correspond to the essence of man; says the second, to take a critical attitude toward them; says the third, to knock them out of their heads; and—existing reality will collapse."[93] In so far as commodity fetishism is part of an activity, a material practice and not just ideas about a material practice, if one wants to overcome commodity fetishism, one must change the way people live, their form of life.

Rooted in the commodity form, fetishistic illusion cannot be combated at the level of the traditional notion of critique, "as it had been charged by the entire rationalist tradition with distinguishing the false from the true, with delivering the true from the false (from errors, 'prejudices' and illusions); or again, and more boldly still, with denouncing error... in the name of Truth, whenever Truth was ridiculed or assailed by error," writes Althusser.[94] Consequently, he continues, "critique is not, for Marx, the judgement which the (true) Idea pronounces on the defective or contradictory real; critique is critique of existing reality by existing reality (either by another reality, or by the contradiction internal to reality). *For Marx, critique is the real criticizing itself*, casting off its own detritus itself, in order to liberate and laboriously realize its dominant tendency, which is active within it. It is in this materialist sense that Marx's critique could, as early as 1845, treat communism as the very opposite of the 'ideal,' the deepest tendency of the 'real' movement."[95] Most importantly, Marx tied critique not to himself, the author, but to the working-class struggle itself: "For it was the real—the worker's class struggle—which acted as the true author (the agent) of the real's critique of itself," writes Althusser.[96]

I agree with Althusser that Marx radicalized critique by seeing it not as an individual mental act but as a collective activity, the class struggle, that transforms reality. Pace Althusserian science, however, Marx proposed

Ideologiekritik as a register of political struggle that involved the continuous interplay of subjective and objective moments in workers' attempts to gain critical purchase on worldly reality. The only way to make sense of this radical materialist conception of critique as an activity of people engaged in collective political struggle is to recognize that the object of critique (i.e., the autonomy of ideas) is already embedded in existing practice.

For Marx, ideology does not "consist of ideas" (as opposed to the real).[97] Althusser's criticism assumes Marx thinks that objective knowledge (of commodity relations) is possible only from a perspective that is free of any admixture of human subjectivity, namely, the objectivity of science. It assumes that for Marx objective knowledge of the world must involve knowledge of properties of the world that in no way depend on the effects such properties have on the cognizing subject and, accordingly, that objective knowledge of how things stand in commodity production will be possible only for those who are able to construct a view of how things are wholly independent of subjective response. As Foucault showed us, this is the scientific conceit of "truth demonstration," the system of ordered procedures and rules and qualification mechanisms, which minimizes the part played by the subject and determines who can practice science and manifest (its form of) truth. These assumptions are necessary only for a thinker for whom human perspective is irremediably distorting, not corrigible using other human perspectives. But that thinker is Althusser, not Karl Marx.

In Marx's account, ideology does not amount to cognitive confinement in our human forms of subjectivity. It is possible to gain a critical perspective on power in a capitalist society, and such gains are understood not on the philosophical model of truth and the critique of illusion but as a materialist political practice of an ongoing class struggle. Understanding how critique operates from within the ordinary for Marx requires a better grasp of the central feature of his account of ideology, namely the belief in the autonomy of ideas, their begetting each other from within the ideational sphere and according to their own logic. To be in the grip of an ideology is to be captive to a certain perspective: to assume ideas give themselves their own laws; they evolve as an inner necessity, obeying a purely ideational logic that could not have been otherwise. So understood, ideology is not the other of truth (false belief) but a particular manifestation of a game of truth in a specific regime of truth that cannot be adequately challenged through critique as unmasking. This concept of ideology as the necessary logic of an idea in a regime of truth was central to Hannah Arendt's analysis of totalitarianism.

The Logic of an Idea

For Arendt, "an ideology is quite literally what its name indicates: it is the *logic* of an idea" (*OT*, 469). She continues:

> The "idea" of an ideology is neither Plato's eternal essence grasped by the eyes of the mind nor Kant's regulative principle of reason but has become an instrument of explanation. To an ideology, history does not appear in the light of an idea . . . but as something which can be calculated by it. What fits the "idea" into this new role is its own "logic," that is a movement which is the consequence of the "idea" itself and needs no outside factor to set it into motion. Racism is the belief that there is motion inherent in the very idea of race, just as deism is the belief that a motion is inherent in the very notion of God. (*OT*, 469)

Ideologies generally, and totalitarian ideologies especially, argues Arendt, claim "the total explanation of the past, the total knowledge of the present, and the reliable prediction of the future" (*OT*, 470). Concerned strictly with "the element of motion [that inheres in ideas]," they eliminate the contingent: the "it could have been otherwise" of the past and the "it can be otherwise" of the future (*OT*, 470). Furthermore, "in this capacity ideological thinking becomes independent of all experience from which it cannot learn anything new. . . . Hence ideological thinking becomes emancipated from the reality that we perceive with our five senses, and insists on a 'truer' reality concealed behind all perceptible things, dominating them from this place of concealment and requiring a sixth sense that enables us to become aware of it. The sixth sense is provided by precisely the ideology" (*OT*, 470–71).

Within the totalitarian metaphysical game of truth, ideology is a "supersense" that discovers the hidden "laws" behind mere appearances. Substituting itself for the world-giving "sixth sense" of "common sense," ideological supersense "serves to emancipate thought from experience and reality" (*OT*, 471). Although all ideology has nothing but "contempt for factuality" and the world of appearances, it nevertheless retained the assumption of "human mastery over the world" (*OT*, 458), comments Arendt. Totalitarian ideology, in contrast, destroys even this "element of [human] pride," substituting for it "the supersense which gives the contempt for reality its cogency, logicality, and consistency" (*OT*, 458). Subjects obey the order of an ideological "supersense" that "knows" what must be done following the demand of "stringent logicality" (*OT*, 472).[98] "Common sense trained in utilitarian thinking is helpless against this ideological supersense, since totalitarian regimes establish a functioning world of no-sense" (*OT*, 458).

Carried to its extreme in totalitarian societies, "ideological thinking orders facts into an absolutely logical procedure which starts from an axiomatically accepted premise, deducing everything else from it; that is, it proceeds with a consistency that exists nowhere in the realm of reality" (*OT*, 471). And "once it has established its premise, its point of departure, experiences no longer interfere with ideological thinking, nor can it be taught by reality" (*OT*, 471). Reality is whatever ideology says it is. This is not mere mystification, as if ideology concealed or masked reality. For Arendt, the received idea of ideology does not begin to capture the "aggressiveness of totalitarianism," which inaugurates the reality-destroying-and-creating power of "the modern lie." Ideological thinking does not just falsify but violently destroys reality. Like "Mrs. Smith" in the previous chapter, whose murder postdates the statement "Mrs. Smith is dead" to verify the statement, reality that does not conform to the "supersense" is changed for the sake of "ideological reasons: to make the world consistent, to prove that the respective supersense is right" (*OT*, 458).

On the one hand, like Marx, Arendt argues that ideologies are not composed of lies that can be rationally exposed but are, instead, realities created through human practices. On the other hand, her account of totalitarian ideologies departs from this materialist understanding to argue for the cognitive attractions of relentless logic. What distinguishes totalitarian ideologists from their predecessors, argues Arendt, is less their attachment to a particular idea (e.g., "the struggle of races") than "the logical process which could be developed from it" (*OT*, 472). They were spellbound by what Stalin called "the irresistible force of logic." Both Stalin and Hitler were "fond" of saying, as Arendt put it, "You can't say A without saying B and C and so on, down to the end of the murderous alphabet. Here, the coercive force of logicality seems to have its source; it springs from our fear of contradicting ourselves" (*OT*, 472–73).

For Arendt, logic is inexorable. Though deeply critical of the totalitarian ideologists, Arendt appears to share their view of "the coercive force of logicality." Even when the topic is not totalitarian ideology but logical thought itself, Arendt seems to take for granted, to use Foucault's terms, that the "force" of truth belongs to logic as a game of truth. In *The Human Condition*, for example, she tells us that the laws of logical reasoning "can be discovered like other laws of nature because they are ultimately rooted in the structure of the human brain, and they possess, for the normal healthy individual, the same force of compulsion as the driving necessity which regulates the other functions of our bodies. It is in the structure of the human brain to admit that two and two equal four."[99]

Although such passages smack of cognitive determinism, Arendt's theory of human freedom and critique of determinisms of all kinds should temper the haste with which some readers have reached this conclusion.[100] In the previous chapter, I suggested that Arendt's account of logic could better be criticized from the perspective on truth offered by Foucault. Distinguishing between a game of truth and a regime of truth, Foucault provides an example of a game that, as Lorenzini writes, "we would be tempted to consider 'pure' and isolated from any 'regime.'"[101] This is the game of logic.

In *On the Government of the Living*, Foucault asks us to imagine a game of two logicians agreeing on the truth of a proposition that one had initially denied. At that point, he says, "explicitly or implicitly: it is true, therefore I submit. What happens when he says "it is true, therefore I submit"? If he says "it is true," it is not insofar as he is a logician, well, I mean it is not because he is a logician that the proposition is true" (*GL*, 97). The truth of the proposition relies not on him but on the "symbols, rules of construction, axioms, and grammar" of logic as a game of truth (*GL*, 97).

> But when he says "it is true, therefore I submit," he does not utter this "therefore" because it is part of the logic. It is not part of the logic, for it is not the truth of the proposition that, in fact, actually constrains him, it is not because it is logical, it is because he is a logician, or rather it is insofar as he *is doing* logic [he need not be a logician] . . . that is to say, because he constitutes himself, or has been invited to constitute himself as operator in a certain number of practices or as a partner in a certain type of game. (*GL*, 97–98)

In this game of logic, Foucault concludes, "the whole effect of truth will be to constrain any person playing the game and following the regulated procedure to acknowledge it as true. We can say with logic that we have a regime of truth in which the fact that it is a regime disappears, or at any rate does not appear, because it is a regime of truth in which the demonstration as self-indexation of truth is accepted as having absolute power of constraint. In logic, regime of truth and self-indexation of truth are identified, so that the regime of truth does not appear as such" (*GL*, 98).

Tracking the disappearance of logic as a regime of truth in logic as a game of truth is crucial to both grasping the subject's genuine experience of cognitive determinism that Foucault never doubts and that Arendt describes as "the coercive force of logicality," on the one hand, and questioning its origin in "the structure of the human brain" or in the game of logic itself, on the other. In "shifting the accent from the 'it is true' to the force we accord truth," Foucault foregrounds the regime of truth and the role played by the subject in any game of logic, including, by extension, what Arendt describes as totalitarian ideologies (*GL*, 101).

However, the regime of truth in which the game of logical truth is played in Arendt's account of ideology and the modern lie is not just any regime of logic in which subjects who play it constitute themselves and are constituted by the constraints and procedures of logical truth. They play the game of truth in a *totalitarian* regime of truth in which logical thinking has displaced all other games of truth. Indeed, for Arendt, the question would arise as to why political subjects—not logicians but ordinary individuals—constitute themselves as bound to the rules of the game in the way Foucault describes. It is not just that they find themselves in a game of logic or even seek it out but that, under totalitarianism, logic is the only game of truth in town.

For Arendt, the question is once again one of the prior worldly conditions that must exist for logic to gain traction to the exclusion of all other games of truth. Focused more on the constitution of the subject in the manifestation of truth, this is not the primary question of a regime of truth for Foucault, though he would not deny its importance.[102] For Arendt, the answer lies not in the human brain but in the destruction of the public and the private realm, the spaces in which we are "together with other men" and rely "upon our *common sense*, which regulates and controls all other senses and without which each of us would be enclosed in his own particularity of sense data which in themselves are unreliable and treacherous. Only because we have common sense, that is, only because not one man, but men in the plural inhabit the earth, can we trust our immediate sensual experience" (*OT*, 475–76).

Arendt emphasizes the connection between the hegemonic status of the game of logical truth and the loss of the shared world. The "law of movement" that defines ideology for her has its realization in "terror, whose chief aim is to make it possible for the force of nature or of history to race freely through mankind, unhindered by any spontaneous human action" (*OT*, 465). Terror, "the essence of totalitarian domination," she argues, "substitutes for the boundaries and channels of communication between individual men a band of iron which holds them so tightly together that it is as though their plurality had disappeared into One Man of gigantic dimensions" (*OT*, 465–66). "By pressing men against each other, total terror destroys the space between them" (*OT* 466). "Totalitarian government . . . certainly could not exist without destroying the public realm of life, that is, without destroying, by isolating men, their political capacities. But totalitarian domination . . . destroys private life as well. It bases itself on loneliness, on the experience of not belonging to the world at all, which is among the most radical and desperate experiences of man" (*OT*, 475).

Totalitarian ideologies take root in a soil from which individuals have been uprooted and become "superfluous": "To be uprooted means to have no place in the world, recognized and guaranteed by others; to be superfluous means not to belong to the world at all" (*OT*, 475). The loss of common sense that results from the destruction of both the public and the private realms and the substitution of common sense by the "supersense" of ideology creates mass "loneliness." Different both from "solitude" (in which, as we saw in chapter 1, we still engage in the two-in-one of thinking modeled by Socrates) and from "isolation" (in which we remain in contact with the world of things but apart from the public world where we act with others), loneliness is characterized by the complete loss of the shared world and thus the "capacity for thought and experience" (*OT*, 474, 476, 477). Loneliness is the "basic experience in the living together of men," which "permeates a form of government and whose principle of action is the logicality of ideological thinking" (*OT*, 474).

Logical reasoning becomes hegemonic under a totalitarian regime of truth:

> The only capacity of the human mind which needs neither self nor the other nor the world in order to function safely and which is as independent of experience as it is of thinking is the ability of logical reasoning whose premise is the self-evident. The elementary rules of cogent evidence, the truism that two and two equals four cannot be perverted even under the conditions of absolute loneliness. It is the only reliable "truth" human beings can fall back upon once they have lost the mutual guarantee, the common sense, men need to experience and live and know their way in a common world. (*OT*, 477)

One can quarrel with Arendt's reliance on the idea of logic as having its own "force" of truth, as if that force did not need a subject who says, "It is true; therefore, I submit." This quarrel is the legitimate criticism raised not by her critics (i.e., as a naive acceptance of cognitive determinism) but by my reading of Foucault (i.e., as a problem of the subject's constitution in the manifestation of truth). Nevertheless, Arendt provokes a form of questioning that focuses on the subject's fate in a world whose public and shared features have been lost. She shows how logic's game of truth comes to be hegemonic in a specific political regime, not unlike how the "truth-demonstration" of science became hegemonic in Althusser's Marxism and, more generally, in Western society (according to Foucault).

Given Arendt's description of ideology as reality destroying and creating rather than simply denying or masking, critique cannot take its conventional form. As we saw in the introduction: "The ideal subject of totalitarianism is not the convinced Nazi or the convinced Communist, but people for whom the distinction between fact and fiction (*i.e.*, the reality of experience) and the distinction between true and false (*i.e.*, the standards of thought) no longer exist" (*OT*, 474). The problem is not belief in the "false ideas" of a particular ideology (Nazism or communism). Instead, it is the loss of a shared reality in which games of truth provide criteria for judgment. For her, the "truth" of logic, already contained in the premise, "is empty or rather no truth at all, because it does not reveal anything. (To define consistency as truth as some modern logicians do means to deny the existence of truth.)" (*OT*, 477). One reading suggests that "the distinction between true and false" no longer exists for the subject engaged in the hegemonic game of truth under totalitarianism, according to Arendt, because logical truth is meaningless.

However, this hermeneutic-phenomenological objection to what we call "truth" does not answer to the relation between logic as both a game of truth and a regime of truth, which stands at the center of Foucault's account. Disputing the received idea that "the absolute power of constraint" is always already given in the game of truth, Foucault distinguished the "regime" from the "game" and argued that the former contains "an assertion ['It is true; therefore, I submit'] that does not belong exactly to the realm of the true or false," that is, to the game (*GL*, 96). We have seen that Foucault's initial use of the distinction is analytic; he goes on to show that there is no "realm of the true and false," no pure game of truth, apart from the regime of truth in which the subject accepts (or rejects) the terms and outcome of the game. The criteria of truth, in other words, belong to the game only because the subject plays the game, that is, because there is a regime of truth. He told us that, in the game of logic, "we have a regime of truth in which the fact that it is a regime disappears ... because it is a regime of truth in which the demonstration as self-indexation of truth is accepted as having an absolute power of constraint" (*GL*, 98). In other words, the game seems to determine how it will be played independently from the subject.

But what if this absolute power of constraint that is logic's regime of truth is not just one the subject gives him- or herself by choosing to play the game of logic? What if it is a power the subject is *forced* to accept under conditions of terror and radical loneliness in which there is no other game to play? In that case, it is less the game that has swallowed the regime than the regime (the totalitarian logical regime of truth) that has swallowed the game.

In Arendt's view, the criteria of true and false no longer exist in totalitarianism, but not only because logical truth is "empty," as the hermeneutic-phenomenological reading suggests. Instead, for the "ideal subject" of totalitarian rule, the criteria no longer exist because there is no worldly space in which a game of truth could be played by a subject constituting him- or herself in anything other than a regime of truth restricted to strict logicality and its "absolute power of constraint." One enters the power relations of the regime of truth not because "one will be obliged to posit it as true, although one knows that it may be false," or one is unsure, as Foucault described the standard objection to associating "truth" with a "regime" (*GL*, 95). Although it is undoubtedly the case that some subjects asserted the "therefore" because they felt they had no choice, Arendt describes a problem in which the possibility of refusing the absolute constraint of logic has, in the ideal case, disappeared. The "ideal subject of totalitarianism" has been constituted by its regime of truth. It can no longer meaningfully be said to play even the game of logic, the only game in town; instead, the game plays it. In the regime/game of logic, where the "supersense" of ideology leads, "the ideal subject of totalitarian rule" follows.

Consequently, criticism of ideologies as false ideas is, as Marx argued, mere movement in thought. In contrast, ideology acts at the level of reality, bypassing the part played by the subject and starting from "the only possible movement in the realm of logic [, which] is the process of deduction from a premise" (*OT*, 469). This premise (e.g., the "idea of race") cannot be "interrupted by a new idea" (proposed by a subject), Arendt argues, for the latter would be "another premise with a different set of consequences" (*OT*, 470). But neither can one critique ideological thinking by playing another game of truth—there is none—or the game of logic and refusing its regime of truth. Once in the game that the regime has swallowed up, there is no alternative to the assertion "It is true; therefore, I submit," save designation as mad. More precisely, the "therefore" that links the subject to a game of truth and affirms the ideal subject's "consent" to truth (which sustains the game of truth) practically disappears. What remains is: "Whatever the 'supersense' says is true, is true."

For Arendt, the coercive force of logicality cannot be resisted by a different claim to truth but only by free action:

> Totalitarian rulers rely on the compulsion with which we can compel ourselves . . . : this inner compulsion is the tyranny of logicality against which

nothing stands but the great capacity of men to start something new. The tyranny of logicality begins with the mind's submission to logic as a never-ending process, on which man relies in order to engender his thoughts. By this submission, he surrenders his inner freedom as he surrenders his freedom of movement when he bows down to outward tyranny. Freedom as an inner capacity of man is identical with the capacity to begin.... Over the beginning, no logic, no cogent deduction can have any power, because its chain presupposes, in the form of a premise, the beginning. (*OT*, 473)

The impossibility of fighting totalitarianism at the level of ideology critique helps explain the surprising final paragraph of *Origins*. Arendt tells us that "the crisis of our time and its central experience have brought forth an entirely new form of government which as a potentiality and an ever-present danger is only too likely to stay with us from now on," while reassuring us that "there remains also the truth that every end in history necessarily contains a new beginning; this beginning is a promise" (*OT*, 478). The promise lies in "the supreme capacity of man" to begin anew. Before it is realized politically in action, this capacity for beginning, writes Arendt—citing Augustine: "*Initium ut esset homo creates est*"—"is guaranteed by each new birth; it is indeed every man" (*OT*, 479).

If this conclusion strikes an odd note of optimism after close to five hundred pages describing absolute rule by terror and the total loss of reality and truth, it also highlights Arendt's conviction, shared with Foucault and Marx, that political things can be otherwise because they were initiated by human action and could have been otherwise. The past of totalitarianism looms as a threat to the present, but it does not determine the future. Totalitarianism did not have to happen. Just because it happened does not mean it will happen again. What will stop it, however, will be not the scientific critique of false ideas (Althusser) or the demand to restore objective Truth, but maintenance of the public world in which political action remains possible.

In the next chapter, we will see how contemporary debates over the future of critique remain entangled in objectivist conceptions of reality and truth as they address the relationship between critical thought and sociopolitical transformation.

* 5 *
Feminism, Critique, and the Realistic Spirit

Anyone who goes beyond procedural questions of a discourse theory of morality and ethics and, in a normative attitude . . . embarks on a theory of the well-ordered, or even emancipated, society will quickly run up against the limits of his own historical situation.

HABERMAS, JUSTIFICATION AND APPLICATION

For some time now, a particular strand of contemporary critical theory has understood its task in terms not of providing a substantive critique of power relations, let alone an alternative normative conception of what social relations might be, but of how to justify critique as such: how to justify those elements that critique owes to its philosophical origins, albeit in a nonfoundationalist manner.[1] This focus on—if not obsession with—the theoretical problem of how to ground critique arose primarily as an intervention into the long-standing debate over positivism and scientism in figurations of the relation between theory and practice. And though it came to define the work of thinkers associated with the third- (and to a lesser extent the fourth-) generation Frankfurt School of critical theory, the demand for a philosophical ground animated a wide array of debates, from postmodernism and deconstruction to cultural studies and feminism, if only in the form of emphatic denials and assertions regarding its impossibility. As crucial as this intervention has been for exposing the dangers of social and political philosophy's implication in a purely technocratic order, it has not been without cost to the very idea of critique itself: the crucial connection between critique and social/political transformation.

Seyla Benhabib usefully characterizes the two tasks (or "dimensions") of critical theory as "explanatory-diagnostic" and "anticipatory-utopian."[2] It is not enough to analyze existing social relations; one must also put forward viable alternatives. She asserts that any genuinely critical social and political theory needs to address "the lived needs and experiences of social agents in order to interpret them and render them meaningful in light of a future normative ideal."³ Echoing Max Horkheimer's 1937 account of the difference between "traditional and critical theory," Benhabib continues: "If it [critical theory] excludes the dimension of anticipatory-utopian critique, . . . it cannot be distinguished from other mainstream social [and political] theories that attempt to gain value-free knowledge of the world."⁴ A critical theory does not feign neutrality but inspires a creative, world-building practice. Change is the aim of critique.⁵

If the anticipatory and value-laden dimension of critique guards against positivism, what will guard against an unrealistic and potentially dangerous utopianism? A genuinely critical theory must navigate between the Scylla of false neutrality, indifferent to the values of the audience to whom it is addressed, and the Charybdis of false idealism, indifferent to the material and historical context in which change is pursued. Such a theory, I argued in the introduction, should refuse the choices offered in current debates on post-truth and the future of critique: it should be neither *realist* nor *antirealist* but *realistic* in spirit, to borrow Frank Ramsey's phrase.⁶

First, aspiring to a critical, realistic theory is becoming aware of certain temptations that arise whenever we engage in theory-producing critique. There is the temptation to think—even though we late (post)moderns "know better"—that we can stand outside our practices and take stock of what they are; we can unmask, for example, the mystifications of ideology (discussed in the previous chapter), reveal that social identities are "socially constructed," or show that all knowledge and values are historically contingent: there is no such thing as Truth. And there is the temptation to slide from the arrogance of the external standpoint from which such claims are often made into the despair of seeing that standpoint to be an illusion; there is nothing we can say, judgments we can make, with any certainty whatsoever, certainly not beyond the confines of our location in time and space. Objective knowledge seems impossible since attaining the transcendent perspective that Alice Crary called the "abstraction requirement" required by this idealized, "narrow conception of objectivity" is foreclosed for us.⁷ We may deny but cannot finally escape the use of our affective propensities and what James Conant called "the subject dependence" of all objective thought.⁸ In Western philosophy, this is the familiar drama of dogmatism and skepticism, of realism and antirealism. However, that drama is far from its final curtain call when it comes to critical theory.

The tenacity of this way of understanding the practice of critique does not represent a failure on our part, as if it were a matter of being convinced, for example, that the "absolute conception of the world" is a scientific myth. It may well be, but if we hold fast to a frame of reference that does not reflect what we claim to know, it is not always for lack of knowledge. Often, we already know all we need to know, but we do not acknowledge it (to riff off Stanley Cavell's well-known distinction).[9] But neither is our attachment to frames of reference that we know to be illusory just a comment on the necessarily delusional features of our psychic apparatus, as many neurobiologists and cognitive scientists argue, or on the "eternal" nature of ideology and subjective misrecognition, as Althusser and the strand of critical theory that follows him holds.[10]

Wittgenstein presses us to see how this view of ordinary critical thought underwrites scientism in knowledge production. Still, it is easy to miss his contribution in what appears to be a refusal to accord theory any role in critical thinking, save science. "We may not advance any theory. There must not be anything hypothetical in our considerations. We must do away with all *explanation*, and description alone must take its place," he declares in that rare passage of *Philosophical Investigations* where he declares anything (*PI*, §109). Should we interpret this declaration as a taboo? After all, left with description, the first task of critical theory, the explanatory-diagnostic task, must be immediately thrown overboard. Any social-scientific approach expresses what he calls our "craving for generality," whose "source" lies in the "method of science," that is, "the method of reducing the explanation of natural law phenomena to the smallest possible number of primitive natural laws."[11]

The taboo on theory, however, is not what I take from Wittgenstein. Instead, his work uncovers the impossible philosophical demands to which the realist and antirealist remain hostage: there must be *something* behind appearances that guarantees their reality and validity; there is *nothing* behind appearances that guarantees their existence and validity, as Cora Diamond showed us in the introduction.[12] When we theorize, we are confronted with a choice: what we call "real" or "valid" is either independent of what we say or "merely" a construct of language and the mind. Both realist and antirealist positions believe that the choice is necessary if critical theory is to perform its tasks. This is an assumption I will dispute.

The tenacious demand for a philosophical justification of our critical practices, on one side, or the adamant denial of its possibility, on the other side, leads to various (albeit) postfoundationalist iterations of the realist/antirealist debate and, with it, to a situation in which both tasks of critical theory remain within the grip of philosophy and its "mode of necessity," to speak with Nancy Streuver.[13] Few, if any, contemporary critical theorists would agree with the basic tenets of metaphysical realism or antirealist skepticism as they have been formulated in the Western philosophical tradition.[14] Arguments about the socially constructed nature of identities, for example, inevitably come under pressure to affirm that constructs too are "real," but the intellectual gymnastics performed should give us pause. Notwithstanding significant modifications, the fundamental concern that drove philosophical realism and its critics continues to haunt critical theory in its postfoundationalist mode: namely, the worry that ordinary human practices cannot be the source of their reality, validity, and critique and, further, that everyday language is not up to the dual task of critical inquiry.[15]

On the contrary, either the ordinary is taken to be the register of unreflective opinion and irreconcilable value conflict in need of a transcontextual metric of adjudication (e.g., Habermas), or, for those suspicious of such a metric, the ordinary is the register of the taken for granted, where common sense must be exposed as the normalizing crucible of power/knowledge (e.g., Butler). Consequently, thinkers who insist on the priority of validity in a critical theory demand normative standards that will validate in advance of locally contingent experience which anticipatory-utopian visions are truly liberatory and which are not. Those who refuse the demand for normative criteria also decline to provide any such visions, for these are held to be presumptuous extensions of the "taken-for-granted," often in the form of ideal theory.[16] As we will see, this fraught relationship of critique to the ordinary and ordinary language has significant consequences for thinking about what counts as a critical theory and its tasks. I will now explore them by turning to feminist theory as a paradigmatic practice of politically motivated critique that is openly concerned with challenging received modes of human comportment and thought.

Feminist Critical Theory

For a feminist critical theory, the stakes of this fraught relationship with the ordinary are high. After all, feminist critique, in all its variety, aims not merely to explain but to change the world. Consequently, feminist critical theory should be animated less by epistemological imperatives than by the urgency of practical change. This demand for change has led some feminists to rethink and reimagine sex/gender difference, its putative basis in unchanging biology, and the whole gambit of sexual/gender dimorphism. Although certain aspects of feminist critique have gotten entangled in questions of whether gender is objectively real or socially constructed, deciding this question, I argue, should not be the primary aim of a feminist critical theory that is focused on the realization of both explanatory-diagnostic and anticipatory-utopian tasks. Instead, endless debates over identity and the metaphysics of gender lead feminists away from the public character of feminism as a nonsovereign world-building practice of freedom, which is how I have advocated for feminism in the recent past and imagine critical feminist theory today.[17]

I recognize that there are feminist forms of critique for which questions of metaphysics, epistemology, and ontology seem crucial—feminism is a diverse and heterogeneous cluster of practices—and what drives, say, a feminist struggling with intellectual questions of moral realism in an academic department dominated by analytic philosophy will be different from what animates a reproductive justice activist trying to decide whether to continue support for the Affordable Care Act if it does not include the costs of contraception. My point is not to pit "the intellectual" against "the activist" but rather to say that we should guard against the easy assimilation of a second-order practice to a first-order practice (their differences are examined in detail later). Such assimilation can make it seem as if the future of feminist politics hangs on the state of feminist theory. It gave rise to the sense of crisis in third-wave feminist theory.

Indeed, notwithstanding the assumed shared identity of first- and second-order practices, the connection between feminist theory and social and political change has been deeply fraught. Third-wave feminist theory incited widespread consternation about the presumed debilitating effects of certain (postmodern) forms of social constructivist thought on the possibilities of transformative politics. The "category of women" debates, which consumed the energies of many third-wave thinkers, called into question the unity of the subject of feminism, namely "women," and in this way generated (what for some was) a sense of political crisis. If we could not speak of "women," in whose name was feminism to be fought? Though no skeptic of "women as the subject of feminism" would have denied that change was the aim of theory, it nonetheless appeared to many critics that third-wave feminist theory had become the gravedigger of feminist politics: it either (1) undermined the ontological and epistemological ground from which to authorize its critical political claims and now needed to reconstruct those grounds anew or (2) focused on denying the need for such grounding and, in the process, became fully untethered from the pragmatic aims of feminist politics and mired in an acrimonious philosophical war of position on the necessity of foundational categories for feminism.[18] With the rise of US academic feminist theory in the late 1980s and 1990s, the emerging consensus was that theory had lost its footing in the ordinary experiences of gender power and the connection to practice and social change.

Regardless of how one parses the theoretical obsessions of the third wave, the "category of women" debates gave acute voice to a problem that has bedeviled feminism since its inception, namely, the relationship of theory to practice. To some feminists, these debates exemplify the loss of what was once a more symbiotic relationship between theory and practice, which is taken to have characterized the first and the second waves with their shared objective of social and political transformation. Furthermore, these earlier forms of feminist critique, it is argued, were not exercises in writing abstract theory, which in turn guides transformative political action, but were themselves generated out of a wide array of feminist practices (e.g., consciousness-raising, institution building, and political protest).

Whatever one may think of this recounting of the past, we do better to resist nostalgia for past "waves" of feminism and to reflect instead on what we, contemporary feminists, want from a critical theory. And what does it mean to think about feminism as a mode of critique in the first place?

The Problem with Critique

To pose the question of feminism and critique today is to encounter a wide-ranging debate, both within and outside feminism, about the future of critique. Overall, it is a debate about what critique can be once it is no longer understood, in supposedly Kantian terms, as a practice of unmasking the limits to knowledge or, in presumably Marxian terms, as exposing ideological mystifications. Increasingly, critics of critique worry that the antirealist tendencies of social constructivist approaches have generated a deep and corrosive skepticism toward not only the objects of critique but also the idea of any shared reality whatsoever, thereby undermining our political grasp of the genuine effects of power that these approaches were meant to reveal.

In the view of Bruno Latour, for example, antirealist practices of critique have undermined scientific research on existential matters such as climate change, leaving in their wake a general distrust toward any claims to scientific evidence or factual truth—with potentially devastating ecological consequences of course but also deeply corrosive ramifications for democracies. It is now time for "the critically minded" to reject this inherited skeptical posture and adopt a *"stubbornly realist attitude,"* he declares.[19] And Latour is far from alone. Charles Taylor and Hubert Dreyfus articulate their joint philosophical project as "retrieving realism" in the face of a tenacious Cartesianism, which also has adverse social effects.[20] Likewise, the feminist turn to "affect" and to the "new materialism" claims to restore a shared sense of the real in the wake of poststructuralist accounts of gender identity and the sexed body as socially constructed all the way down.[21] The same goes for those humanities scholars and literary theorists who speak of "the limits of critique," to borrow Rita Felski's phrase, for grasping what is valuable and enduring in human cultural artifacts and works of art.[22]

What appears to be a politically motivated "return to realism" in contemporary critical thought demonstrates not only a wariness toward specific iterations of the "linguistic turn" but also an acute awareness of what S. J. Methven calls "the beguiling simplicity of the realist outlook."[23] This is the Western metaphysical tradition's view that what is real is entirely independent of and indifferent to human minds (our linguistic practices, epistemic limitations, and so forth). Nevertheless, crucial questions can be raised about the extent to which critics of critique remain hostage to the metaphysical framework they claim to reject. I have pursued this suspicion elsewhere concerning affect theory.[24] Here, I am interested in how the turn to realism cannot quite shake the justification demand mentioned previously: *something* outside our practices must guarantee their validity (or, from the antirealist perspective, if nothing can be found, then the historical conditions and limits of our practices and knowledge should be exposed and their validity questioned). More importantly, it is not clear that this second-order quarrel about the need for an epistemological/ontological basis for critique responds adequately to the distinctly *political* anticipatory-utopian task of critical theory: to bring into view new forms of being in common, to posit "new forms/figures of the thinkable," to speak with Cornelius Castoriadis.[25]

Latour's worry about the destructive force of critique and the need to affirm the reality of its objects is instructive. Striking in his well-known essay "Why Has Critique Run Out of Steam?" is not only a distorted understanding of the relationship of second- to first-order practices (what Didier Fassin aptly calls Latour's outsized "confidence in the impact of social sciences on people") but also how the problem of critique itself is figured in exclusively epistemological terms.[26] Although a specific practice of critique has had devastating *political* effects, we are told the solution lies in adopting the proper epistemology or what Latour calls a "second empiricism."[27] I recognize that this form of empiricism, by contrast with the traditional form associated with Locke and Hume, sees facts as always already infused with values. I understand (though I would not endorse) the appeal of developing pragmatic and ontological realism in the spirit of William James and Alfred North Whitehead, respectively.[28] What concerns me, however, is the implicit assumption that political problems can be adequately understood, let alone effectively addressed, if we remain within the grip of philosophy and focus our understanding of critique on what are essentially philosophical problems of developing the proper epistemology (or ontology).

The widespread skepticism described by many critics of critique is not just an intellectual position created by constructivism (or Cartesianism) to which a "stubborn [albeit modified philosophical] realism" might be a credible response.[29] It expresses far more profoundly what Arendt describes as the absence of the common world, a condition of radical world alienation that was not caused and cannot be solved by refusing or adopting a specific epistemology.[30] The loss of a shared reality, which characterizes modern democratic mass societies in her view, expresses not the corrosive effects of (academic) critique that are held responsible for our post-truth condition but the shrinkage of a shared public world, a space in which our sense of the reality of an object is generated through exposure to perspectives not our own. If "the attitude of alienation from the world and from the community is not just a theory," as Hilary Putnam likewise asserts, then the challenge for critical theory, feminist or otherwise, is not to be a realist in the newfangled manner advocated by many critics of critique but rather to reanimate those ordinary world-building practices that yield a sense of a shared reality and bring new objects of public concern into view.[31] And just that is what we can gain from what I argue to be the theory-producing activity of first-order discourses such as feminist politics.

What Justifies Feminist Critique?

Feminist theory has not been immune to the idea that political claims require some epistemological apparatus to authorize them. We can recognize in Latour's diagnosis of what ails contemporary critical theory the all-consuming second-wave and (if only in a negative antirealist sense) third-wave quest to provide an epistemological basis for feminist politics and the assumed devastating consequences for feminism if such a project were to fail. So understood, the whole task of critique is to "justify the truth of the feminist claim that women have been and are oppressed," as Susan Hekman succinctly puts it.[32] Like Latour's worry that the lack of realism in social constructivism had produced a fatal relativism about the claims of science, Hekman worries that absent such epistemic justification, feminist political claims would be no better than the "merely" subjective claims to what is agreeable: the claim "women are oppressed" has no more truth-value than the claim "I like red wine." The task of feminist critical theory, then, is to avoid the reduction of feminist claims to subjective avowals: "Feminist standpoint theorists have recognized that feminist politics demand a justification for the truth claims of feminist theory, that is, that feminist politics are necessarily epistemological," declares Hekman.[33]

Hekman grapples with the problem that has driven so much of contemporary critical theory: What authorizes critique? What justifies it? I have argued elsewhere that feminist and democratic politics, though engaged in *quotidian* ordinary language games of justification, neither demand nor require the philosophical machinery of justification that Hekman's wholly epistemic version of standpoint theory was charged with providing.[34] We need a philosophical answer because no ordinary justification will do.

I wish to explore the animating assumptions behind the argument that the first-order practice of feminist politics requires redescription in the second-order conceptual language of feminist theory or risks the charge of subjectivism. It has been an abiding assumption of the Frankfurt School and its strand of feminist theory that any critical theory requires the normative and analytic categories of philosophy to underwrite it. In this way, Benhabib, speaking for others in the acrimonious third-wave debates over foundationalism, could declare: "Social criticism without philosophy is not possible, and without social criticism the project of feminist theory, which is committed at once to knowledge and to the emancipatory interests of women[,] is inconceivable."[35] Feminist politics is triply indentured: first to feminist theory, second to social criticism, and third to philosophy. If this idea of critical theory dies hard, perhaps that is not because feminist politics needs feminist theory, as Hekman and Benhabib presume, but because feminist theory needs feminist politics.

The point here is not to reverse the direction of need and thus indebtedness but to recognize how we misunderstand the explanatory-diagnostic task of a realistic feminist critical theory (which in turn will bear on its anticipatory-utopian task) when we imagine it as providing the normative criteria and arsenal of proof that first-order political claims supposedly require. This will involve clarifying the relationship of first-order practices/discourses to metapractices/metadiscourses (i.e., second- and third-order practices and discourses).

First-Order and Metapractices/Metadiscourses

Metapractices and metadiscourses (including second-order practices/discourses such as feminist theory, philosophy, social science, etc.), writes John Gunnell, "gain their primary identity in terms of the fact that they have another conventional activity as their subject matter. They are essentially *supervenient*, since they are predicated on the existence of other practices and discourses and since they are not, in a primary sense or the typical course of events, constitutive of their object."[36] A second-order discourse such as feminist theory takes as its "object" feminist politics (and aspects of politics generally that are relevant to feminism). Although we could imagine a world in which there was feminist politics but no feminist theory, it is impossible to conceive of a world in which there could be feminist theory without feminist politics. This does not indicate that one is more "authentic" than the other or that the world would be "better" (or worse) without feminist theory.[37] It indicates that without a critical awareness of the relationship between first- and second-order discourses/practices, we might well misunderstand the practice of a critical feminist theory and its tasks.

"This relationship [between first-order practices and metapractices]," observes Gunnell, "has often, and traditionally, been referred to as that of theory and practice, but this typology is often both prejudicial and rhetorically motivated. It suggests, first, either that a metapractice possesses some sort of inherent authority over its object or that it can make a claim to some sort of identity with it [i.e., feminist theory just *is* feminist politics]. Second, it implies that [a first-order] practice [such as feminist politics] is either devoid of theory or deficient and that theory is the province of another activity."[38] This does not mean "that second-order discourses cannot critically examine first-order claims or even in some respects to substitute their judgment," he qualifies, only that it is in the register of first-order discourses that the "world" that is at once taken for granted and subject to critique is created.[39] For example, "the facts of social science are, in the first instance, preconstituted by the theories of a first-order discourse and are discursively distinct from social scientific theories, that is, theories *about* those facts or what social science takes to be the reality of its subject matter."[40]

How does Gunnell's account reflect the relationship between feminist theory and feminist politics? Historically speaking, this relationship has been increasingly fraught, with theory claiming cognitive and epistemic authority over feminist politics in the manner asserted by Benhabib and Hekman. But their view is possible only on the assumption that feminist theory is somehow the theoretical dimension of feminist practice (politics), as if the practice of feminist politics itself were devoid of theory. And that assumption depends on how you define "theory."

"The idea of theory as a potentially unified or unifiable concept is chimerical. The variable senses of theory can only be located pragmatically, as contingent and historically positioned practices," observes D. N.

Rodowick.⁴¹ My aim here is not to provide a comprehensive guide to feminist senses of the term, let alone to define what "theory" is in some unitary sense. I am trying to open a space in which feminists might rethink the contingent relationship between theory and practice and, with it, the two tasks of critique. After all, it is not as if there were a singular and accepted idea of theory within feminism, certainly not that of a scientific theory based on a nomothetic rather than idiographic approach to social and natural phenomena. Instead, we might think of "theory" with Rodowick as an ongoing "activity wherein experience is converted into thought, and so made expressible and communicable to others."⁴²

Likewise, Cornelius Castoriadis, challenging the tenacious and pervasive idea that theory begins with skeptical doubt issued from an external standpoint, explains that theory is a creative practice of "positing a new imaginary figure/model of intelligibility," as Freud did, for example, with his radical concept of the unconscious.⁴³ And Gunnell, drawing on the Greek word for theory (*Theoria*) and its meaning of "seeing" and on Nelson Goodman's idea of "worldmaking," invites us to think about theory as creative ordinary acts of world disclosing. "In the case of first-order discourses . . . the 'world' that they articulate, or their object of knowledge, is theoretically or conceptually produced and constituted in the language of the activity."⁴⁴ What we call "theory" is here not yet sundered from "fact," as it is in empiricism and scientific realism: that which is "abstract" by contrast with that which is "concrete." Gunnell explains:

> By returning to this [Greek] idea of the identification of theory with what is seen or . . . with those claims that are constitutive of or conceptualize facts, we have an account of theory that I will call *theoretical realism* as opposed to scientific realism. . . . Theories are that species of claim that we call *empirical ontology*. They are generic or universal claims about what kinds of things exist and the basic manner of their existence no matter how or in what form particulars may be contingently manifest. Theories are that class of claim that constitutes and defines facticity and specifies the stuff identified as the object of inquiry. Theories need not or may only sometimes be reflectively explicitly or formalized.⁴⁵

Gunnell's reference to "theoretical realism" should not be read as synonymous with the realism in the realist/antirealist debate. Instead, he highlights how ordinary but theoretical first-order practices constitute a "world," what reality is for us, and thus how it is disclosed. Gunnell and Rodowick offer a more elastic and accurate account of theory, according to which there is no a priori sharp distinction between first-order practices and metapractices. Second-order (meta)practices such as feminist theory create their theories, of course, but the theories they make take as their object the facts "theorized" by first-order practices. Should we fail to see this theory-creating power of first-order practices, we will continue to think of theory as a metatheoretical term and accordingly misconstrue the so-called theory/practice problem as one of two distinctly and hierarchically ordered registers of feminist practice, with feminist theory providing the conceptual tools of critical analysis and the epistemic guarantees of feminist critique to an otherwise lively but theoretically and conceptually impoverished practice of feminist politics.

Returning to Hekman, we can see how such a scenario unfolds. Standpoint theory, she rightly argues, represents an alternative to the tenacious idea that there is an Objective truth of women's oppression. Nevertheless, jettisoning metaphysical realism for the notion that all knowledge is situated and perspectival, standpoint theory (and much of the feminist postpositivist thought described by Hekman) does not necessarily lead to a refusal of the justification demand that *something* must authorize the truth of feminist political claims, *something* must underwrite their objectivity. As Gunnell writes of social theory generally, the feminist rejection of positivism led not always to rejecting the realist demand but to embracing or developing "an alternative epistemology."[46] In this case, that alternative was the idea of standpoint and an extension of what was taken (wrongly, in my view) to be Marx's account of the epistemic privilege of oppressed groups.[47]

Accordingly, a feminist political claim about how sexual harassment works in any specific context must be "backed up" by something that goes philosophically and methodologically "deeper" (and thus *authorizes* as "objective" rather than "merely" subjective) than the claim itself. That is perhaps one reason why Catharine MacKinnon has been keen on grounding her theory of sexual harassment in an epistemology of sex/gender.[48] This "something" is not the standard criteria of ordinary evidence, but the epistemic guarantee presumably provided by the philosophical idea of standpoint. It can then appear that any political claim about the exercise of power is only as good as the epistemology/ontology on which it is based.

Second-Order Distortions

Consider the bewilderment and frustration expressed by the four giants of standpoint theory (Nancy Hartsock, Sandra Harding, Patricia Hill Collins, and Dorothy Smith), who responded to Hekman's account in a 1977 issue of *Signs*. "Where's the Power?"; "Whose Standpoint Needs Truth and Reality?"; "Truth or Justice?"—these response titles expressed clearly the difference between the political reality that standpoint theorists set out to describe and Hekman's reframing of their work as exercises in feminist epistemology.[49] "Standpoint theory never was designed to be argued as a theory of truth or method," objected Collins. Instead, it was designed to account for "knowledge/power."[50]

I am sympathetic to this objection, but it does not rule out the possibility that standpoint theory—and its modern version, intersectionality—might invite such a misreading.[51] The problem is how to think about that which lies at the heart of standpoint theory, namely, the first-order claim made by someone regularly subjected to illegitimate power such as sexual harassment. This claim describes or—more precisely—redescribes, say, the free-market workplace as a site rife with illegitimate, masculinist, and heteronormative forms of power, fear, and intimidation and so discloses features of that world to which many may well be blind (and indeed were blind before the growing feminist organization around sexual harassment in the 1970s). When politically articulated with many other such redescriptions, a phenomenon (sexual harassment) attains the "reality" that I am associating with the theory-creating disclosive power of first-order discourses. In this sense, feminist theory creation is about "lighting up" certain features of our everyday existence, to speak with Nancy Bauer, such that we now see what was always there, only under a different aspect, namely, unjust relations of power as objects of common concern, which can and should be changed.[52]

The history of sexual harassment case law was built, first, out of the experiences of women and their political articulation and, second, out of the arguments made in the 1970s by Lin Farley, Catharine MacKinnon, and many other lawyers and activists who represented women in and out of court. And settling on the term *sexual harassment* (instead of, say, *sexual coercion* or *sexual intimidation*), as the group of young feminist activists did in a now famous 1974 consciousness-raising meeting in Farley's Cornell University office, was itself a theory-creating activity that produced a "new for[m]/figure[e] of the thinkable" (Castoriadis) not in an aspirational utopian sense of course but as a way of critically naming and collectively organizing what had been individual experiences of illegitimate power.[53] The second-order concept of epistemic privilege associated with standpoint theory arrives late to this political happening, if it arrives at all.

My point is not to discount the potentially critical function of the various second-order discourses of feminist theory. It is to query why we think that claims of sexual harassment require a theory of epistemic privilege (or any other second-order theory) to underwrite them. Second-order theories are post hoc attempts to redescribe what has already been redescribed and given meaning in the world-creating and theory-producing first-order discourses that are their object. As post hoc, they surely can add another dimension of critique. Still, they can also distort what it means to practice critique, especially when first-order discourses are seen as wholly devoid of theory and in need of justification.

When the relationship is not distorted, the second-order theory neither reproduces nor justifies what happens at the first-order level; it is instead potentially productive of new ways of disclosing the world. Consider, for example, women reading Betty Friedan's *The Feminine Mystique*, Simone de Beauvoir's *The Second Sex*, or Angela Davis's *If They Come in the Morning* at some of the earliest second-wave consciousness-raising sessions and being mobilized to act. The same goes for the work on sexual harassment written by MacKinnon, Farley, Andrea Dworkin, and other feminists. Further, second-order theories of sexual harassment may well be helpful if not necessary for clarifying what might be at stake in specific contexts (e.g., in actual legal or administrative proceedings where such theories provide a way to make sense of a complex reality, as MacKinnon's work has been pragmatically deployed).

The dynamic relationship between first- and second-order discourses can be intensely creative and politically generative. At its best, this can involve inaugurating relationships among terms that had none. For example, as Reva B. Siegel observes, Farley and MacKinnon "understood the sexual coercion women encountered at work as part of a larger political economy of heterosexuality, a social order that situates sexual relations between men and women in relations of economic dependency between men and women . . . and reproduce[es] women's social subordination as a class." In other words, they brilliantly "read the sexual advances constituting harassment within a semiotics of status inequality," the latter being a legal grammar that the courts already understood.[54] Theory creation, at a first- or second-order level, brings about something new, not by turning its back on ordinary experience, ordinary language, or ordinary concepts, but by connecting them in new and unexpected ways. Toril Moi describes it as the "revolution of the ordinary."[55]

Furthermore, the theory-producing capacity of first-order discourses is crucial to tempering what Gunnell portrays as two historical tendencies of second-order discourses: (1) the tendency to assert mastery over their subject matter (first-order discourses) and (2) the tendency to formulate theories that no longer reflect or speak to the reality they claim to explain/diagnose—and to explain/diagnose *better* than what are often taken to be wholly unreflective first-order discourses, with the idea of what it would mean to be reflective construed in strict intellectualist terms.[56]

The arguments for the reality of the phenomenon of sexual harassment developed by feminist legal theorists such as MacKinnon, for example, were made under a specific legal regime, Title VII of the Civil Rights Act of 1964. To make the claim that harassment was employment discrimination on the basis of sex (and not just something that can happen to anyone, man or woman, or on the basis of anything, be it hair color, wardrobe, or mannerisms, or "sex" in addition to one of these characteristics), however, came to involve constructing *all* women as a sex class whose rights could be violated on the basis of their sex-class membership. This construction created a semblance of unity among women where there was none.[57]

Furthermore, the juridical notion of membership in a sex class refused the idea, advanced at the time by the women's movement that gave rise to the legal cases in the first place, that sex and gender difference were socially constituted categories of membership and identity. Instead, writes Siegel, judicial opinion clung to the "fiction" that it was "merely analyzing discrimination as the practice of sorting sexed bodies: sexual harassment involves 'a treatment differential allegedly predicated upon an immutable personal characteristic gender which subjected appellant to a marked disadvantage in comparison with men employed at the agency,'" to cite Judge Spottswood Robinson's description of sex-class-categorical discrimination in the famous 1977 case of *Barnes v. Costel*.[58] This is not merely a problem of how legal regimes reduce the heterogeneous reality of social membership, crucial as that is, but also a problem of how second-order feminist theory then takes up existing legal precedents (in this case, antidiscrimination law based in supposedly immutable racial difference) and employs it to create legally persuasive but also falsely unifying and potentially naturalizing theoretical frameworks for winning cases. Much of the feminist brouhaha around MacKinnon's academic work and its stark portrayal of all women as the sexualized objects of masculine fantasy is a case in point.

Theory and Event

The problem of losing track of complex phenomena also applies to second-order theories that only sometimes respond to the categorical difficulties of legal reasoning. Here, I would like to turn to the other side of the feminist debate, namely, the thinkers for whom standpoint theory was just another expression of the metaphysical realism about gender that, in their view, characterized second-wave feminist theory.

Consider the transformative performative theory of gender developed by Judith Butler. *Gender Trouble* was received as a powerful antirealist intervention into what Butler described as a tradition of feminist theory whose sex/gender distinction remained beholden to what Butler called "the metaphysics of substance."[59] "The challenge for rethinking gender categories outside the metaphysics of substance," Butler asserted, will require the relinquishment of gender as a state of "being" and the reconceptualization of gender as a "doing."[60]

In the view of critic Linda Martín Alcoff, Butler's performative theory of gender does not radically depart from the metaphysics of gender but instead reinstates it in another form.[61] Alcoff accuses Butler of "creat[ing] new dilemmas of determinism" with their "process metaphysics," but that is not a debate that I wish to enter here. The crucial issue now is that even as acute a critic of metaphysical thinking as Butler may be was pulled into a logic of explanation that demands that "something" must underwrite their claims about how gender comes to appear as a substance that inheres in human beings from birth and the significance of this assumption of stable gender identity for relations of power (e.g., heteronormativity).

Unsurprisingly, Butler's redescription of gender as a doing, a performance, would be received as *the* Theory of how gender works—always and everywhere. What goes missing when we think of performativity as such a Theory is the very thing Butler brilliantly illuminated: the specific quality of *individual* performances of gender, particular enactments of gender identity that undercut the idea of gender identity as a generalized essence or stable core.

We might describe this problem of theory as the loss of what Foucault called—in "What Is Critique?," begging his audience forgiveness for his use of such a "dreadful word"—"eventalization [*événementialisation*]," in this case of gender ("WC," 40).[62] Foucault's critique was centered on standard historiographical practice, but his point can be extended. Objecting to the tendency to develop modes of explanation that lose track of their object of analysis, Foucault describes his work as an attempt to attend to "a *singularity* at places where there is a temptation to invoke a historical [or social or anthropological] constant . . . to show that things 'weren't as necessary as all that'; it wasn't as a matter of course that mad people came to be regarded as mentally ill; it wasn't self-evident that the only thing to be done with a criminal was to lock him up."[63] And so on. Furthermore, he adds, "eventalization means rediscovering the connections, encounters, supports, blockages, plays of forces, strategies and so on which, at a given moment establish what subsequently counts as being self-evident, universal and necessary. In this sense one is indeed effecting a sort of multiplication or pluralization of causes."[64]

Built into our received understanding of what constitutes an explanation, the first task of a critical theory bypasses "eventalization" and treats the first-order discourses that function as objects for second-order critical theory as always already meaningful and stable. This is not a new observation but worth pursuing because it bears on what feminists want from critique and from a feminist critical theory. Isn't the whole point of such an enterprise to produce theories of sex/gender, just as it was initiated by Beauvoir's 1949 claim that "one is not born, but rather becomes, a woman" and carried through Butler's 1990 performative theory of sex/gender and beyond?[65] Are we to be left with the first-order practice that tells us nothing about the general case? What, in short, is left of the explanatory-diagnostic aspect of a critical theory if we can say nothing of the larger structures of power in which the specific case is formed?

Again, Foucault's account of "eventalization" helps respond to these objections. Does attending to singularity "mean that one regards the singularity one is analyzing simply as a fact to be registered, a reasonless break in an inert continuum? Clearly not, since that would amount to treating continuity as a self-sufficient reality which carries its own *raison d'être* within itself."[66] Rather than treat the singular case as if it were a mere exception to the rule that confirms the rule, writes Foucault, "this procedure of causal multiplication means analyzing an event according to the multiple processes which constitute it. So to analyze the practice of penal incarceration as an 'event' (not as an institutional fact or ideological effect) means to determine the process of 'penalization' (that is, progressive insertion into the forms of legal punishment) of already existing practices of internment."[67]

"Eventalization," then, is not a failure to theorize. Instead, writes Foucault, it is "a way of lightening the weight of causality. . . . (In concrete terms: the more one analyses the process of 'carceralization' of penal practice down to its smallest details, the more one is led to relate them to such practices as schooling, military, discipline, etc.)"[68] We should focus on the first-order discourses and practices that created the social environment in which carceralization seemed necessary and was normalized. Of course, many metapractices and metadiscourses contributed to what eventually became a specific carceral worldview, which Foucault also described. However, focusing exclusively on their accounts of what was happening at a first-order level, we will lose track of how the "problematization" discussed in the previous chapter works, that is, how it transforms the "real object" such that it appears to be always already given: "there are criminals; they must be locked up." We will be left with "theories" of punishment that have lost track of the origin of their object in first-order discourses/practices. Foucault shows that problematization is neither determined by nor unrelated to its "real object." Instead, it takes account of the object in ways not given by the object itself but also not thinkable apart from the thing.

Put otherwise, attending to "eventalization" facilitates a critical awareness of how true discourse (e.g., a theory of criminality) is produced as a supplement to reality. As argued in previous chapters, Foucault shows that "reality will never account for that particular, singular, and improbable reality of the game of truth in reality."[69] The historical emergence of discourses of carceralization, for example, cannot be accounted for merely by locating their origins in reality (e.g., actions we call crimes) but instead create criteria of judgment, truth and falsity, that in turn set the terms of how we think about the problem of "crime" and the fate of the "criminal."

Toward a Realistic Feminist Critical Theory

I have suggested that a feminist critical theory should be "realistic" in spirit and that this stance would avoid entanglement in questions about the "metaphysics of gender," regardless of whether one takes a realist or antirealist position, in the qualified postfoundationalist sense that I gave to those terms. This realistic stance in no way involves abandoning theory; on the contrary, it is an invitation to imagine a more robust and diverse practice of theoretical creation. Debates in feminist theory are peppered with pointed laments about what counts as theory. Still, some have accepted the basic framework within which our dominant philosophical idea of theory as a second-order discourse has been formed. The problem is not to show that excluded forms of theorizing meet the criteria of a second-discourse theory; it is to reveal the restrictive character of this idea of theory and its generative possibilities in other forms. It is not a matter of being more "inclusive" by calling first-order practices and discourses "theory" (too), as if they were now admitted to a special club. We need, instead, to recognize what our received conception of theory suppresses or denies. I take that to be at stake in these critical laments.[70]

"While epistemology [and ontology] might provide a critical explication of a practice of theoretically grounded inquiry or even a defense of a particular theory," observes Gunnell, "there has been a tendency to make truncated theoretical claims in the course of elaborating and defending metatheoretical constructions about the nature of social scientific [or, in this case, feminist] explanation."[71] These truncated theoretical claims are the world-disclosing claims that belong to critical theory. They are occluded when we assume that feminist reality claims (such as sexual harassment) need a metatheoretical (philosophical) discourse to underwrite them. That is one reason why the refusal of the hypothetical-deductive model of scientific explanation in postpositivist social and feminist theory, as in most of the human sciences, has led to a "crisis" of theory, where theory creation remains haunted by the specter of abstraction and generalization to which the only alternative appears to be an impossible particularism.

What Gunnell calls the pervasive "inversion of theory and epistemology" has had significant and constraining consequences for the development of feminist theory and its increasing alienation from feminist politics.[72] Recognizing the theory-creating (or world-building) power of first-order discourses is crucial to freeing second-order theories to critically redescribe what has *already* been redescribed (and theorized) at a first-order level, but without performing this second-order act as if it were all that was standing between first-order practices and theoretical irrelevance. Once again, the boundaries between the two orders are fluid, not fixed. I deploy them here as analytic or heuristic devices to better understand what we want from (feminist) critique and what we count as critique and theory. They should not be taken as definitions or categories into which we must slot one practice or another. There are, for example, many feminist texts that originated in political protest but were later distributed and perhaps collected in anthologies that are read as works of theory in academic, public, or private contexts. In this sense, nothing in a particular text determines its first- or second-order status, but rather how a text emerges and is put into use in various contexts.

Suppose the boundary between first- and second-order discourses/practices is flexible. As I have argued, the same can be said about the relationship between a critical theory's first and second tasks. In Benhabib's formulation, the first (explanatory-diagnostic) task may be charged with the "truth-tracking" or validity function. In contrast, the second (anticipatory-utopian) task is charged with the "possibility-disclosing" function, to borrow Nikolas Kompridis's terms. In this way, the two tasks would appear to stand in some temporal order, as "first" does to "second," with the first performing a kind of "reality and truth check." Accordingly, the first task entails exposing how things are—it tracks truth, which, contra Foucault, it conflates with reality—and the second task involves putting forward a normatively inflected alternative, which remains subject to the reality/truth check performed by the first task. But if the possibility of "imagining a utopia with [substantive] content is a necessary condition of critique," as Kompridis asserts, then the anticipatory-utopian task of critique is the condition of its explanatory-diagnostic task, and vice versa.[73]

To see the two tasks of critique as mutually imbricated, we need to rethink critique as reflective disclosure rather than as reality/truth-tracking and see that true discourse is a supplement added to reality. This does not mean that we cannot better understand how things are or how power works and dispute so-called alternative facts qua facts. But this view is won by disclosing different ways of seeing the same object and not, as the traditional conception of critique would have it, "absolute critical distance from its object."[74]

The misunderstanding of critique expressed in the temporal ordering of tasks is symptomatic of a distorted theory-practice relation. "A change in perspective, a new interpretive language, and the disclosure of alternative possibility depend on the *practical* abilities, not theoretical knowledge, of agents," observes Kompridis.[75] Suppose we view first-order practices such as feminist politics as wholly devoid of these world-disclosing capacities. In that case, we risk seduction by a metapractical concept of critique for which what Crary called the "abstraction requirement," absolute distance from the object—however questionable in these postpositivist and postfoundationalist times—remains the impossible ideal to which critique should aspire. The ideal is impossible because it presupposes that, if only we *could* engage in some total unmasking, we *could* somehow rationally reconstruct the conditions of the existence of "x" quite apart from our standpoint and the background conditions of "x." In that case, we would attain objective knowledge of "x." But this standpoint and background, as Wittgenstein shows and even Habermas concedes, is not the limit but the very condition of anything we can claim to know.[76]

Finally, if what it means to be realistic in our practices of critique entails remaining true to the facts of our lives (our cognitive capacities, conceptual abilities, finitude, etc.), then we need to generate questions from within our form of life, not as if we were somehow standing outside it, looking down on ourselves, as it were, able to survey those practices from an external point of view. "Our questions are formed from notions of ordinary life, but the ways we usually ask and answer questions, our practices, our interests, the forms our reasoning and inquiries take," writes Cora Diamond, look from such a position to be concealing "some reality, some kind of fact or real possibility."[77] This is the place we occupy when we engage in the form of theory that disavows, explicitly or not, the sources of justification in that ordinary life. When engaged in this theory, I want to know what justifies a woman's claim of sexual harassment apart from anything that could be supported with ordinary evidence. What will count as doing gender right (or not) apart from any modes of bodily comportment in a specific context? And so on.

Thinking of first-order discourses as wholly devoid of theory, we are inclined to assume that second-order practices must "do all the theorizing" and provide all the tools for critique, understood in the temporal order described. This assumption, in turn, produces not only a misunderstanding of what first-order discourse already does and can do but also a highly restrictive image of what second-order discourses do and can do. The former occupies what amounts to a theoretical desert, while the latter becomes a theoretical justification (or antijustification) machine; in both cases, the inaugural and world-building power of theory creation is left undone, and at that point, feminist critique does indeed, to borrow Latour's phrase, seem to have "run out of steam."

✳ 6 ✳

The Problem of Democratic Persuasion

What is the problem of democratic persuasion today? The possibility of persuading someone who aligns with political beliefs different from one's own is becoming increasingly more remote. Warring opinions appear to be irrationally entrenched and, when publicly voiced, frequently amount to little more than divisive partisan posturing.[1] Indeed, at times we seem to find ourselves in what Corey Brettschneider aptly describes as "The Hateful Society": this society has formally legitimate laws, but a vast majority of its citizens reject the values on which these laws are based and cling tenaciously to their most antidemocratic beliefs.[2]

In *When the State Speaks, What Should It Say?* Brettschneider challenges the neutrality imperative that characterizes liberalism's ideal of the state/society relation. Liberal-democratic states, he argues, should attempt to transform citizens' inegalitarian beliefs when they oppose the core values of liberal democracy. The state should speak to hate groups and the larger society in value-laden terms. It should attempt to convince citizens to respect the core values of free and equal citizenship through what he calls "democratic persuasion."[3] Insofar as "giving reasons" is an alternative to state coercion, persuasion falls within the liberal state's expressive function.[4]

Brettschneider's "democratic persuasion," comments feminist legal theorist Robin West, is "unrealistic, and a bit naïve-sounding about the nature of hate speech."[5] It neglects the vast terrain of hate speech not based on a well-formed ideology (e.g., male superiority or white supremacy) with explicit beliefs that could be identified and potentially transformed but of "hate, pure and simple." Furthermore, argues West, "it is hard to even know how to respond to Brettschneider's apparent insistence that it is morally incumbent upon people who hold these noxious views to change them so that they accord with the minimal decency required by liberal principles, and that the state should be engaged in the project of exhorting them to do so."⁶ The people who engage in hateful speech and action also hate the liberal state, argues West, and are not available for moral exhortation. "The foundational incompatibility of values and worldviews of antagonists" in current debates over free speech, abortion, affirmative action, gun control, or intelligent design creationism, she writes, reveals persuasion based on "shared premises and sound logic" to be illusory.⁷

Although I share West's skepticism, we should not exclude from the start the possibility of persuading other citizens to change their point of view. The question is not whether persuasion under challenging cases is possible but how it might *become* possible. This possibility involves rethinking what persuasion entails. Persuasion is typically understood as requiring an ideal argument that works from shared premises to alter beliefs. This argument might appeal not to truth but to what is reasonable, as in Brettschneider's political liberalism.⁸ It might assemble truth claims that can be openly debated and adjudicated according to argumentative norms, as in Jürgen Habermas's deliberative democracy. The ideal argument is the "picture"—to speak with Wittgenstein—that holds us "captive." Enthralled by the unadorned force of reason (or reasonableness) to expose false beliefs, we miss the problem posed by "deep disagreements," namely, their apparent immunity to facts, evidence, and logic—the tools of rational argumentation (*PI*, §115).⁹

In Robert Fogelin's classic formulation, deep disagreements differ fundamentally from ordinary disputes. They are disagreements in which "the conditions for argument do not exist. The language of argument may persist [i.e., may *sound* like an argument], but it becomes pointless since it makes an appeal to something that does not exist: a shared background of beliefs and preferences," which gives facts their meaning.¹⁰ "When we inquire into the source of a deep disagreement, we do not simply find isolated propositions ('The fetus is a person'), but instead a whole system of mutually supporting propositions (and paradigms, models, styles of acting and thinking) that constitute . . . [what Wittgenstein calls] a form of life." But "the notion of form of life is dangerous, especially when used in the singular." In fact, comments Fogelin, "a person participates in a variety of forms of life that overlap and crisscross in a variety of ways," making it possible for us to speak with people who believe some things we might find absolutely "mad." Deep disagreements are not "common," but when they occur, they are intractable. So argues Fogelin.¹¹

A striking feature of deep disagreements is that they are "immune to appeals to facts," not (necessarily) because antagonists do not believe what their interlocutor claims to be fact but because the facts themselves are powerless to alter the opinion at stake in the disagreement.[12] Parties may agree on various facts and disagree on the fundamental issue. In the abortion debate, for example, there may be an agreement between antagonists on both sides as to when a fetal heartbeat can be detected and brain development can be observed, and even on a broad moral principle such as the sanctity of human life. Nevertheless, the critical moral issue between them, the moral status of the fetus, cannot be settled by appeal to these facts or decided based on proof, where "proof" means the analysis of the meaning and implications of the relevant concepts.[13]

Deep disagreements are distinguished by an absence of shared background commitments, a web of unquestioned and unarticulated beliefs that structure what counts as a reason in any argument.[14] The invisible framework of these commitments provides the fixed context in which argument can occur, and differences of opinion can be clarified and resolved. Drawing on Wittgenstein, Fogelin points to the idea of a "*Weltbild*" (world picture), a systematic framework for making sense of and giving meaning to reality. A world picture is not acquired through reasoning processes. We adopt it by learning our mother tongue and being enculturated into a form of life through training and habits.[15] Rather than the product of evidence and facts, a world picture underwrites what we count as evidence and facts, what we count as true or false. Wittgenstein remarks in *On Certainty*: "I did not get my picture of the world by satisfying myself of its correctness; nor do I have it because I am satisfied of its correctness. No: it is the inherited background against which I distinguish between true and false" (*OC*, §94).

Deep disagreement arises when two world pictures collide. Fogelin calls attention to key passages from *On Certainty*:

§608. Is it wrong for me to be guided in my actions by the propositions of physics? Am I to say I have no good ground for doing so? Isn't precisely this what we call a "good ground"?

§609. Supposing we met people who did not regard that as a telling reason. Now, how do we imagine this? Instead of the physicist, they consult an oracle. (And for that we consider them primitive.) Is it wrong for them to consult an oracle and be guided by it?—If we call this "wrong" aren't we using our language game as a base from which to *combat* theirs?

§610. And are we right or wrong to combat it? Of course there are all sorts of slogans which will be used to support our proceedings.

§611. Where two principles really do meet which cannot be reconciled with one another, then each man declares the other a fool and heretic.

§612. I said I would "combat" the other man,—but wouldn't I give him *reasons*?

Certainly; but how far do they go? At the end of reasons comes *persuasion*. (Think what happens when missionaries convert natives.)

On the face of it, Wittgenstein's idea of persuasion looks nothing like the rational practice of democratic persuasion described by Brettschneider. Where reasons run out is where persuasion for Wittgenstein begins: "At the end of reasons comes persuasion," he tells us. However, that sentence can be misleading when taken out of the larger context of Wittgenstein's thought. It can be—and has been—misunderstood as a leap into irrationality. Without reasons, we seek *merely* to persuade, using rhetorical deception or, if necessary, force. In this view, persuasion is an inferior form of communication; it is what we are left with when reasons run out, and *this* is what *we* do. Richard Rorty, for example, has made quite a lot of this idea of reasons running out with his notion of "epistemological ethnocentrism," which I've discussed in previous work.[16] And Fogelin, answering what rational procedures exist to resolve deep disagreements, takes Wittgenstein to say: "NONE."[17]

For Fogelin (and Rorty), deep disagreements are conflicts of world pictures intractable to rational resolution. If we were honest, we would admit as much and embrace the nonrational "technique" of persuasion from the start. Our reluctance to do so, says Fogelin, reflects worries about the loss of normativity and the demands on ourselves and others that it entails. Whereas "in the context of a normal argument, people claim to be invoking mutually acceptable grounds, and they can be held responsible for this claim," in deep disagreements, we give up all such hope and risk falling into irrationality. And so, we live in denial of the limits of reason that characterize our most fundamental beliefs, our world picture, and persist in the delusional "assumption that earnest clear thinking can resolve fundamental issues," concludes Fogelin.[18]

Does the idea that rational argumentation comes up against the hard kernel of deep disagreement rooted in different worldviews find unequivocal support in Wittgenstein? And is this a helpful way of thinking about how these disputes arise in the first place? The received reading distorts Wittgenstein's views and how reasons work. For example, it can lead us to think that when reasons are working correctly—when they have not (yet) run out—we would not need persuasion. It might lead us to believe that reason and rational speech are devoid of the doxastic and symbolic elements that the Western philosophical tradition attributes to rhetorical speech and its corrupting epistemic tendency to create the illusion of truth. It might lead us to think that deep disagreements are of an altogether different order of language and logic than the ordinary disagreements expressed in the political realm.[19]

The focus on deep disagreements as irrational and intractable can lead us to misunderstand what ordinary political debate requires and how we might persuade other citizens on matters of common concern. In Arendt's considered view, to speak politically is always to persuade. Political speech is, by its very nature, persuasive. Does this mean that, for Arendt, all political discourse happens "at the end of reasons" or that persuasion marks the move into rhetorical deception or force? Surely not. I will argue that shared premises are, for Arendt as for Wittgenstein, less the necessary condition than the novel creation of persuasive speech. The ability to persuade is a quotidian skill in speaking to others that rests on the public practice of what Arendt calls learning to see politically and Wittgenstein calls seeing an aspect.

Arendtian Seeing Politically

To see politically is to view the world from standpoints other than one's own and, in this way, to alter what Arendt, following the Greeks, calls *dokei moi*, "it seems/appears to me," whose formulation in speech is doxa or opinion. That dokei moi (and with it, doxa or opinion) can be altered, as we will see, shifts the question of how things first appear from a fully nonconceptual and unjudged phenomenal register, where how the world seems to each of us remains an intractable worldview, to a political and normative register, where persuasion as Arendt understands it can occur. In her account, the democratic problem of persuasion is not foremost one of convincing argumentation. Indeed, "skill in argumentation," she writes, "is of secondary importance to the first successful creation by the polis of the public realm." "The crucial factor is not that one could turn arguments around and stand propositions on their heads [a skill in which the Sophists excelled], but rather that one gained an ability to truly *see* topics from various sides—that is, politically—with the result that people understood how to assume the many possible perspectives provided by the real world, from which one and the same topic can be regarded and in which each topic, despite its oneness, appears in a great diversity of views" ("IP," 167).

To see politically is not to strive for "the God's eye view," the traditional ideal of objectivity that, in Arendt's account, "runs the danger of losing our ties to the world" ("IP," 168). By contrast, she writes, "The ability to see the same thing from various standpoints stays in the human world; it is simply the exchange of the standpoint given us by nature for that of someone else, with whom we share the same world, resulting in a true freedom of movement in the mental world that parallels our freedom of movement in the physical one" ("IP," 168). Furthermore, the ability to argue and to persuade rests on this more fundamental discovery of "the realm in which all things can first be recognized in their many-sidedness" ("IP," 167). This is the political realm that first emerged in ancient Greece. "Being able to persuade and influence others, which was how the citizens of the polis interacted politically, presumed a kind of freedom that was not irrevocably bound, either mentally or physically, to one's own standpoint or point of view" ("IP," 168). Put otherwise, one cannot begin to persuade democratically until one has learned to see politically, that is, from standpoints not one's own. And where deep disagreements about matters of common concern arise, one cannot persuade in the absence of the public space in which seeing politically is learned and practiced.

The resistance of deep disagreements to the force of the better argument is significant for Arendt's account of political speech: it is a reminder that in the registers of evaluative judgment in which they tend to arise (politics, morality, and aesthetics), the appeal to logic, evidence, and proof often fails us in the search for agreement. As Wittgenstein shows, a "picture" rather than a reason underwrites how the world first appears to us. This picture is not intractable to change but is open to persuasion. Persuasion seeks to alter the ungrounded picture (i.e., the worldview that is neither true nor false but, rather, the framework for what can count as true or false) that makes reasons meaningful. "The difficulty is to realize the groundlessness of our believing" (*OC*, §166). Wittgenstein speaks here of what we have difficulty doing, not what we *must* do to free ourselves of the pictures that hold us captive: "Realize the groundlessness of your believing!" This is how Fogelin misunderstood him. Rather than being an imperative for delusional foundationalists, Wittgenstein's remark suggests not that persuasion is possible because beliefs are *merely* contingent and groundless, which is more likely to incite the despair of radically skeptical doubt than critical and curious questioning. Instead, to persuade is to bring someone to see that those beliefs, though stable (i.e., rooted in habit and training, not just up for grabs), may be unnecessary and open to change. We can form a different picture of things and how they might be otherwise.

Wittgensteinian "Pictures"

Understanding the place of pictures in Wittgenstein's philosophical critique of inherited ideas of rationality and the resolution of disagreement requires keeping two ideas in view at once: pictures can imprison us in a certain way of thinking, and no way of thinking is free of pictures. Peter Winch comments: "A large part of Wittgenstein's philosophical practice consists in attempting to break the hold of certain 'pictures' [e.g., the logical "must"] on our thinking, pictures to which we may obsessively be attached and which in a real sense imprison us."[20] At the same time, to think and grasp reality, we require a picture, a figure of some sort. As Wittgenstein puts it: "A picture that is firmly rooted in us may indeed be compared to superstition, but it may be said too that we always have to reach some sort of firm ground, be it a picture, or not, so that a picture at the root of all our thinking is to be respected & not treated as a superstition."[21]

Basic to the inherited view of rationality, Wittgenstein questions the idea that we could discover general criteria that would allow us to discern, as he put it, which pictures are "at the root of all our thinking" and which are mere "superstitions," argues Winch.[22] This view is illusory—itself a *picture* of how rationality *must* function. "Whether a particular picture is superstitious or not is not an inherent character of the picture, but a matter of how we are tempted to use it. We shall just have to investigate, in the particular case, whether the way we are using a picture is leading to confusions," Winch concludes.[23]

If there is no such thing as finding a place outside all pictures from which to assess them apodictically, a critical engagement with the world pictures of others with whom we deeply disagree would proceed in the same way that Wittgenstein invites us to question our own world picture, which, too, is "after reasons." Assuming that "persuasion" is not a euphemism for force or deception but an attempt to get free of the very specific pictures that hold different parties to a dispute captive, what would persuasion entail? I have suggested that Wittgenstein's understanding of persuasion as coming at the end of reasons is not some general statement about the end of reason tout court. He calls our attention not to the absolute limits of reason—an idea dear to skeptics—but to the contingent end of the persuasiveness of reasons we have given to someone in a particular time or place. At that point and in that place where reasons run out, we do not look beyond reason, as the leap into irrationality suggests; rather, we recalibrate the *appeal* of the reasons we now give. Assuming we want to go on, reasons must be found anew. More exactly, reasons need to be *renewed*, that is, they need to become part of a new picture that persuades. Are such persuasive pictures mere rhetorical devices indifferent to truth?

Rhetoric and the Figurative "Ground" of Truth

In chapter 3, we discussed the distinction Foucault draws between rhetoric and persuasion. Daniele Lorenzini showed us that in 1984 Foucault, having sharpened the difference between the two, "claim[ed] that *parrhesia* 'is opposed to the art of rhetoric in every respect.'"[24] Foucault writes:

> Rhetoric does not entail any bond between the person speaking and what is said, but aims to establish a constraining bond, a bond of power between what is said and the person to whom it is said. *Parrhesia*, on the other hand, involves a strong and constitutive bond between the person speaking and what he says, and, through the effect of the truth, the injuries of truth, it opens up the possibility of the bond between the person speaking and the person to whom he has spoken being broken. Let's say, very schematically, that the rhetorician is, or at any rate may well be an effective liar who constrains others. The parrhesiast, on the contrary, is the courageous teller of a truth by which he puts himself and his relationship with the other at risk.[25]

I agree with Lorenzini that Foucault's emphasis in the 1984 lecture is less on rhetoric's indifference to truth than on the relation established in parrhesia between the speaker and his or her words. And I agree that Foucault's effort to distinguish parrhesia from rhetoric in this way should "give pause" to all those who accuse him of reducing truth to power.[26] Although Foucault came to rearticulate the relationship of rhetoric to parrhesia, however, he never questions what Ernesto Grassi argues to be the reductive traditional philosophical understanding of rhetoric as the mere technique of persuasion, and often a deceptive one at that.[27] Foucault rightly sees that philosophy itself cannot wholly escape using rhetoric as a persuasion technique. He also argues that to establish as normative its own form of truth (knowledge-connaissance), philosophy created the figure of the Sophist as the "outside" that had to be "elimin[ated]."[28] Nevertheless, when describing parrhesia Foucault accepts the received philosophical view of rhetoric as opposed to truth. "Rhetoric is first of all defined as a technique whose methods obviously do not aim to establish a truth; rhetoric is defined as an art of persuading those to whom one is speaking, whether one wishes to convince them of a truth or a lie, a nontruth," he wrote in 1982.[29] Albeit "very schematically," therefore, "the rhetorician is, or at any rate may well be an effective liar who constrains others," he writes again in 1984.[30]

The point is not to deny that rhetorical speech can be used to deceive. Instead, it is to say that the wholesale view of rhetoric as a "technique [of persuasion that] does not aim at truth" is inextricable from the philosophical conception of truth in the sense of phainetai: "truth is only truth when it describes what appears as it *is*, independently from singular appearance [i.e., under "aspects" and "*doxai*"]," writes Guido Niccolò Barbi.[31] Foucault himself argues that this is not the truth at stake in parrhesia but rather the conception of truth as knowledge-connaissance, which philosophy establishes as normative partly by constituting Sophistry and rhetorical speech as the "outside" of truth. And yet he seems to accept what Nancy Streuver calls "its initial definition by philosophy— primarily in the Platonic dialogues (Gorgias, Sophist)—as a Sophistic practice (professionally political?): defined pejoratively, it is true, by a 'Sophist.'" This received view of "rhetoric as relativist, an argumentative competence in finding possible arguments on either side, . . . confronting philosophy's search for necessary truths," writes Streuver, has endured in ways that block our understanding of rhetoric's peculiar civil capacities, "especially its reinvention of civil strategies in response to novel civil affairs."[32] "Rhetorical interests, tasks, performances—all are informed by the press of possibility, the discrimination of the actual, the response to necessity and contingency."[33] It is these qualities, recognized by Arendt, that make rhetoric "of the utmost importance to issues of political capacity and action."[34]

Pace the philosophical tradition, deception or indifference to truth is not the whole of rhetoric. On the contrary, rational speech, true discourse, could not get off the ground without the essential tool of rhetorical figuration. Ernesto Grassi brilliantly explains:

> To prove {apo-deiknumi} means to *show* something to be something, on the basis of something. To have something through which something is shown and explained definitively is the foundation of our knowledge. Apodictic, demonstrative speech is the kind of speech which establishes the definition of the phenomenon by tracing it back to ultimate principles, or *archai*. It is clear that the first *archai* of any proof and hence of knowledge cannot be proved themselves because they cannot be the object of apodictic, demonstrative, logical speech; otherwise they would not be the first assertions. Their nonderivable, primary character is evident from the fact that we neither can speak nor comport ourselves without them, for both speech and human activity simply presuppose them. But if the original assertions are not demonstrable, what is the character of the speech in which we express them? Obviously this type of speech cannot have a rational-theoretical character.[35]

According to Grassi, then, "the rational process and consequently rational speech must move from the formulation of primary assertions."[36] However, these "basic premises" themselves "cannot have an apodictic, demonstrative character and structure but are thoroughly *indicative*."[37] In that case, he argues, "the indicative or allusive {*semeinein*} speech [that characterizes first assertions] provides the framework within which the proof can come into existence.... Such speech is immediately a 'showing'—and for this reason 'figurative' or 'imaginative,' and thus in the original sense 'theoretical' {*theorein*—i.e., to see}. It is metaphorical, i.e., it shows something which has a sense, and this means that to the figure, to that which is shown, the speech transfers {*metapherein*} a signification. Such speech 'leads before the eyes' {phainesthai} a significance."[38] The basis of rational speech, then, "is and must be in its structure an imaginative language."[39] Grassi's conclusion radically alters the relationship of rational speech and rhetorical speech: "The term 'rhetoric' assumes a fundamentally new significance; 'rhetoric' is not ... the technique of an exterior persuasion; it is rather the speech which is the basis of rational thought."[40]

If Grassi is right, any argument from shared premises or first principles (archai) is parasitic on figurative (metaphorical) speech that "in its indicative structure has an 'evangelic' character, in the original Greek sense of the word, i.e., noticing."[41] To "notice" is to call attention to something and to see similarities between unlike things, as expressed through metaphorical language, through the activity of "ingenium." Recognized by Cicero, it is through this "ingenious activity that we surpass what lies before us in our sensory awareness," writes Grassi, "catching sight of relationships, of similitudes among things."[42] A metaphor makes "visible a 'common' quality between fields. It presupposes a 'vision' of something hitherto concealed; it 'shows' to the reader or to the spectator a common quality which is not rationally deducible." But this form of noticing similarities, he rightly insists, goes beyond "the 'literary' plane. The metaphor lies at the root of our human world. Insofar as the metaphor has its roots in the analogy between different things and makes this analogy immediately spring into 'sight,' it makes a fundamental contribution to the structure of our world."[43]

Grassi's materialist emphasis on the imaginative, creative, and figurative character of human linguistic activity foregrounds the nonrational but not irrational basis of first principles (archai) and thus of every attempt to persuade or convince that works from them.[44] "The first principles—all or some—must necessarily be lent *more belief* than what is deduced [from them]," writes Grassi quoting Aristotle.[45] Consequently, any alteration in what we come to believe or claim to know on the basis of the principles (though the process of deduction) relies for its force of truth on the grip that such principles exert on our thinking. And that grip is no mere effect of the deductive rational process but belongs instead to the figurative character of the first assertions. Put otherwise, if one wishes to alter belief, one must work on the figures—what Wittgenstein calls pictures—that "ground" the first principles or archai of rational thought. We have shared premises—when we do—because we share a (world) picture and can reach an agreement on that basis. The picture is not incidental but essential to what we are willing to count as true or false.

Furthermore, if Grassi is right about the irreducibly figurative character of rational speech, then even the parrhesiast employs rhetoric. The parrhesiast employs it not necessarily because the aim of parrhesiastic speech is to persuade in the received view of rhetoric as a mere technique of persuasion—though Foucault does not exclude that possibility—but because there is no true discourse, hence no parrhesia, without rhetorical figuration.

Accordingly, I would qualify my agreement in chapter 3 with Foucault's endorsement of the Greek conception of language as "etumos," "which is found in Plato but goes way beyond the framework of Platonic philosophy" (GS, 314). He accepts the Greek idea of "philosophical discourse as opposed to rhetorical [discourse]." Whereas "rhetorical language is a language chosen, fabricated, and constructed in such a way as to produce its effect on the other person," he writes, "the mode of being of philosophical language is to be *etumos*, that is to say, so bare and simple, so in keeping with the very movement of thought that, just as it is without embellishment, in its truth, it will be appropriate to what it refers to and ... to what the person who uses it thinks and believes" (GS, 314, 314–15).[46] But this familiar contrast of rhetorical and philosophical (rational) speech, as Grassi showed, loses track of the imaginative and figurative basis of true discourse. What Foucault calls "an original relationship with truth" is, for Grassi, enabled through rhetorical figuration, which by no means distances the speaker from the truth but makes it available in the first place. The same goes for "the soul of the person who utters it" (GS, 314, 315).[47]

Furthermore, Foucault's acceptance of the philosophical view of rhetoric is even more puzzling considering his powerful objection to what Streuver calls "philosophy's allegiance to systemic necessity ... [and] its modal commitment to necessitarian truth."[48] In the spirit of Grassi's claim to "rhetoric as philosophy," my point here is not to revalue rhetoric over philosophy, any more than Arendt's was to revalue appearance over Being (see chapter 1). Instead, I wish to call into question the binary opposition, rhetoric versus philosophy, that is an artifact of Platonic thought that continues to influence our view of opinion and political speech. If we wish to disentangle ourselves from the necessitarian view of (world) pictures that sees them as fixed and unavailable for democratic persuasion, then we do well to question "the negative definitions of the human discursive capacity" that characterize the received view of rhetoric.[49]

Though his focus was not rhetoric as such, Wittgenstein shares Grassi's view that all rational speech finds its basis in figuration and imagination (a picture), without which no proof could exist. He agrees that with these picture-forming persuasion resources, we can move others, if not to adopt, at least to appreciate the potentially transformative possibilities of our view of "x" for their own lives. In his remarks on religious belief, for example, Wittgenstein questions the idea that such faith rests on a "proof of God."[50] Although believers—especially under the weight of the dominant scientific worldview—often feel called on to "give their 'belief' an intellectual analysis and foundation," he writes, "it appears to me as though a religious belief could only be (something like) passionately committing oneself to a system of reference [*Bezugssystem*]. Hence, although it's *belief*, it is really a way of living, or a way of judging life. Passionately taking up *this* interpretation. And so instructing in a religious belief would have to be portraying, describing that system of reference & at the same time appealing to the conscience. And these together would have to result finally in the one under instruction himself, of his own accord, passionately taking up that system of reference."[51]

Not all fundamental beliefs are religious, of course. Still, all share this meaning-making quality of the pictures at the bottom of our language games, the ungrounded ground of certainty, which "is not *true*, nor yet false" (*OC*, §205)[52] to which one forms a passionate (nonrational but not irrational) attachment. A picture can "[hold] us captive," but it can also illuminate worldly reality, and, most importantly, a picture can change. Such change generates a specific sense of realness (e.g., God exists, Nature is benevolent, women are evil) and might involve something akin to a conversion, a new "system of reference" for making sense of what was there all along. When it comes to getting the world in view, there are better and worse "pictures." These are not given in some transcendent order of ideal thought but arise as part of ordinary practice and in response to human problems and needs as they appear in everyday life, just as Grassi suggests. On what basis can we persuade someone to relinquish attachment to one picture and take passionate hold of another system of reference? This is the real question at stake in democratic persuasion.

Seeing Politically

For Arendt, to admit that the archai cannot themselves be proven leaves open the question of what it means to persuade in the political realm, whose basis is learning to see politically, that is, from the standpoint of others. Though first discovered by the Greeks, writes Arendt, seeing politically was rediscovered by Kant, who calls it "'the enlarged mentality' and explicitly defines it as the ability 'to think from the position of every other person'" ("IP," 168). Kant invoked this ability as the basis for moving beyond impasses of rational argumentation in deep disagreements about judgments of taste: "There can be no rule by which someone could be compelled to acknowledge that something is beautiful. No one can use reasons or principles to talk us into a judgment on whether some garment, house, or flower is beautiful."[53] Although Kant agreed with the inherited view that one could not "dispute" (*disputieren*) taste using concepts or rules (*degusto non est disputandum*), he held one could certainly "quarrel" (*streiten*) about it, and rightly so. By contrast with the merely subjective judgments of the agreeable ("I like canary wine"), aesthetic judgments ("This rose is beautiful") are normative. It would be "ridiculous," quips Kant, to say, this rose is "beautiful *for me*"; a judgment of beauty takes for granted that others, too, ought to agree.[54] Yet, we cannot compel such assent logically, which would involve cognition of the object through shared concepts or criteria of beauty. Just this absence of shared concepts led classic emotivists (Ayer, Stevenson) or value noncognitivists (Hume, Mackie, Blackburn) to declare all evaluative judgments (aesthetic, moral, political) to be noncognitive and nonrational; wholly outside the realm of reasoned debate, they were at best objects of the most deceptive form of persuasion or brute force. Their prejudices resurface in the idea of deep disagreement as beyond the reach of the rational, rooted in beliefs that we not only do not doubt but *cannot* doubt, as they have no "objective" grounds.[55]

For Kant, however, to leave matters there would be to concede that where disputing based on proofs fails, there can be only a garrulous idle talk (*Geschwätz*). Kant thinks we can resolve quarrels rationally, argues Joseph Tinguely, "although the grounds for doing so will have more to do with traditional rhetoric than with logic, appealing as they do to a shared affective sensibility."[56] Notwithstanding his critique of rhetoric, Kant sees that we quarrel because it is rational to expect "agreement in the way we sense," that is, how the object strikes us.[57] Tinguely observes that Kant already recognizes in the first *Critique* "that there is a surplus of perceptual material that individuates any given object over and above the characteristics captured in its generic name," a determinate concept.

Still, it is not until the *Critique of Judgment* that this insight is extensively thought through.[58] "What each holds the other responsible for in aesthetic experience is the mode of receptivity within which the object appears, the general mental economy or frame of mind which orients how the object happens to look, as it were *to me*. If one were to declare, 'That object doesn't look beautiful to me,' it is not nonsensical to reply, 'Then you are not looking at it in the right way; you are not seeing it as it is supposed to look.'"[59] Getting you to look "in the right way" is the task of persuasion in the absence of shared criteria that Kant called aesthetic "quarreling" (*streiten*).

In Kant's view, the objective question of what one perceives cannot be considered independently of the subjective question of how one ought to be struck, that is, how one *should* "take up" or be oriented toward an object or scene. For Kant, as argued in chapter 1, the way the world "seems to me" is the kind of thing about which we can make claims on one another; it is normative and thus a legitimate topic for debate. We do not relinquish normativity when we quarrel without mutually acceptable grounds, as Fogelin's idea of deep disagreements would have it. Instead, Kant insists that we can be held responsible for how things appear, even without shared concepts for ordering experience and judging reflectively. And Arendt will agree.

Arendt defends the value of Kantian quarreling in the absence of determinate concepts and standards of proof. For her, quarreling is the locution that best describes differences of opinion, disagreements, and attempts to persuade others in the political realm. As Habermas sees it, political disagreement must remain interminable in Arendt's account, as it does in Kant's account of aesthetic judgment. Accordingly, she does not provide the truth criteria by which disagreements could be rationally adjudicated, just as Kant refused to grant standards in quarrels of taste.[60] But Habermas and like-minded critics are working with a binary concept of truth—either a proposition corresponds to reality, or it does not—that is foreign to Arendt's distinctively political idea of truth. As we saw in chapter 3, she accepts the relevance of truth to politics—contrary to how she is typically read—but insists that the validity of any publicly relevant truth depends on opinion, with which the binary concept of truth is at odds. This is because opinion, whose original expression Arendt traced back to the Greek *dokei moi*, "it seems to me," is neither subjective nor arbitrary but the basis for knowledge of the shared world and any rational debate about it.

As Guido Niccolò Barbi argues and I discussed in the introduction, "conceiving truth as something needing support from opinion runs counter any conventional wisdom about the nature of truth itself, which is rooted in a *binary* understanding of truth from Plato onwards."⁶¹ This binary concept conceives of truth as an expression of phainetai ("it shows itself") of the world, in distinction to dokei moi ("it seems/appears to me"). That is, truth should describe only phenomena as such and should ignore any relation between phenomenon and observer. Truth should describe only what appears as it is, independently from its singular appearance in the dokei moi—how "it seems/appears to me." I have no say in how the world appears in this binary concept of truth. Arendt comments in her *Denktagebuch* that Plato inserted an "abyss" between phainetai and dokei moi, making the former a "showing itself that was absolute," not partial. "Politically," she writes, this turns "the aspect" under which something appears into something "universally valid" and "absolutized." How things show themselves becomes how things *are*, about which there can be no debate; it is a matter not of plural aspects and opinions but singular truth.⁶²

Although modern philosophy departs from Plato in crucial ways, it retains the idea that truth always refers to phenomena as they are, independently of dokei moi, that is, how they appear to any individual subject. In short, modern thought remains in the grip of the binary concept of truth and so of Platonic phainetai. In her *Denktagebuch* Arendt explains:

> The doubt of modern philosophy arises when one becomes aware that the Platonic *logos* is a tyrant, who claims that the aspect already shows the phenomenon in its entirety. Since one lived in the illusion that human senses could show more than aspects, one started to distrust first sense perceptions and then "reason truths." Modern relativism could be the redissolution of all universal unconditional "truths" into justified "*doxai*," aspects, if one had not discredited these aspects once and for all so that everybody believes whatever he thinks up [*was er sich irgend ausdenkt*] (but not his "aspect" which is "objectively" verifiable!) is just as true as everything else.⁶³

The discrediting of aspects is a refusal to see anything but subjective arbitrariness in dokei moi such that the aspect can never be world giving. It is a refusal to grant the subject dependence of all objective thought that keeps the post-truth debate captive to an impossible objectivist picture of truth. Indeed, according to the binary conception of truth, which modern philosophy inherits, and modern relativism expresses, plural aspects are equally illusory. As Barbi parses Arendt: "Instead of bringing us closer to things, the continuous search for the 'entirety of the phenomenon' [phainetai] perennially ignores the world and the diversity of its appearance under different aspects."⁶⁴ In the binary conception of truth that carries over to modern political and philosophical thought, plural aspects are discredited as defective truth statements, and their exchange is rendered pointless. The exchange of opinions is haunted by a deep lingering doubt that human perspective can be world giving at all.

Against this Platonic inheritance, which places truth outside the public sphere as a nondebatable fact, Arendt reminds us again of the plurality of aspects in which the shared world appears to us. In her *Denktagebuch* she notes:

> On the Sophists' doctrine of two sides [λόγοι]: This is the real philosophical-political discovery of the polis: that in its togetherness, it becomes apparent that plurality essentially implies the plurality of aspects signified by πολιτεύειν: matters enduringly prove to have many sides (not just two; that is already a logical distortion). To assert [*durchsetzen*] one's aspect [*Aspekt*] ... means to be able be able to persuade [*überreden*]. Therefore, Peitho became an Athenian goddess with a temple. The corresponding τέχνη, i.e., the art of convincingly presenting one's aspect, was the art of oratory [die *Rednerkunst*]. This is the original connection between rhetoric and politics. The actual τέχνη πολιτική [political art] is not the art of ruling but of "persuading" ["überreden"]. This is where δόξ [*doxa*] shows itself in its true form: it is not a non-binding, unfounded opinion—which is what Plato first made it into, but the expression of *dokei moi*: In contrast to *phainesthai*, only an *aspect* [*Aspekt*] shows itself here, not the whole; but this aspect is no mere *appearance* [*Schein*].⁶⁵

Arendt's thinking about aspects refuses at once the skeptical and the dogmatic view: both reduce aspects to "mere appearance" and sow perennial doubt about the possibility of human perspective yielding knowledge of the shared world. In the introduction, Arendt told us that doxa is not "subjective fantasy and arbitrariness, but also not something absolute and valid for all" ("PP," 80). Put otherwise, doxa expresses something about how things are (it is not "mere" opinion), but how they *are* can be first grasped only by how they appear *to* me (which can never be universally valid). By contrast with Plato, for Arendt, phainetai and dokei (or *phainesthai* and *dokeō*) are not opposed but complementary. To say that doxa shows itself or appears in "its true form," that is, as only an aspect, is precisely to affirm that there is a sense of phainetai that is irreducible to the Platonic notion of self-showing Being *opposed* to the supposedly "mere" appearance of dokei.⁶⁶

Arendt reclaims opinion as world giving rather than "merely subjective" by rooting it in appearance and putting dokei moi into dialogue with how it looks to others through learning to "see politically." For her, *dokei moi* is not "subjectivist," an untranscendable form of subjectivity that limits knowledge of a shared world; it is the political basis from which our sense of the shared world can arise at all. To bring others to see that "aspect" (*Aspekt*) of a thing that I see is to persuade (*Überzeugen*), and it belongs to the oratory (*die Rednerkunst*) that was prized in the polis, and that is the "political form of speech" *überhaupt*.[67] By contrast with Plato's claim about *phainetai* as that which shows itself as it is independent of the subject to whom it appears, Arendt holds that *dokei moi* always involves the subject to whom something appears under a particular aspect. This aspect is no "*mere* appearance [*Schein*]," as a subjectivist idea of the receiving subject would have it, nor is belief based on it an "unfounded" perspective on the world, as the binary concept of truth inherited from Plato holds.

We have seen that under the spell of *phainetai*, the primary and immediate perception of the world is wholly independent of any singular appearance or standpoint on the world. Accordingly, I have no say in how something appears. Arendt's view is different. For her, as for Kant, objects in the world never appear in the abstract but always to someone from a specific standpoint or perspective. We have seen that appearance in the *dokei moi* is never merely subjective but normative. I am not passive in how the world appears to me but active in how I receive it. The world does not just appear in *dokei moi*; *it* appears *to me*. Arendt agrees with Kant that how it appears to *me* has as much to do with me as it does with the world. I am at least partly responsible for how the world appears to me and can be held accountable in a disagreement that cannot be settled by appeal to shared criteria. The possibility of persuasion rests on the fact that every object is seen under an aspect and, in the cases that concern the evaluative judgments of the political realm, can be seen under a different aspect.

If persuasion rests on bringing someone to see an object under another aspect, lighting it up so that it can be seen anew, how might that proceed? How does one alter the aspect under which to see an object without the already shared background commitments or web of unquestioned and unarticulated beliefs that make up the competing world pictures I described earlier? A critic might argue that Arendt takes these shared premises for granted and must take them for granted to get the game of persuasive political speech off the ground. This would mean, as Fogelin's "Wittgensteinian" account of deep disagreements held, we can only persuade people who already share our world picture. Pushing back on that charge, I will now draw on Wittgenstein to argue that persuasion, rooted in the Arendtian practice of seeing politically, creates rather than takes for granted shared premises where they are not already given in a particular worldview. It entails the capacity to bring others who do not share my beliefs to change their opinion, with opinion understood as how the world appears and is first encountered or seen.

For persuasion to be world giving, to generate our sense of a shared or common world in the political manner Arendt suggests, it must also be world opening—not just to you but to me. Persuasion based on seeing from other standpoints is more than the art of bringing others around to *my* view as if that view itself were not at stake in change. Persuasion also alters how the world initially appears to me (dokei moi) and how I perceive the world—what is real—by changing how I receive it. Persuasion opens the possibility that I, too, might see differently.

Persuasion as Seeing Aspects

Wittgenstein was fascinated with the question of what it would mean to bring others to relinquish attachment to a particular way in which the world appears or seems to them. This fascination, though populated with examples of people radically other (e.g., the man who believes he has no body, the king who believes the earth began at his birth, etc.), also stayed closer to home (*OC*, §258). Consider the following example from his Cambridge lectures on the foundations of mathematics, which is nicely summarized in Peter Winch's essay, "Persuasion."

> In one of his Cambridge lectures on "the foundations of mathematics" Wittgenstein had tried to bring out the difference between mathematical calculations and experiments. Alan Turing, who was in the audience, resisted Wittgenstein's arguments and, at one point in discussion of the lecture, said that the difference between Wittgenstein and himself lay in the fact that they were using the word "experiment" in two different ways. Wittgenstein opens Lecture XI by taking up and rejecting this interpretation of the disagreement. The way in which he characterizes the argument that follows is itself revealing. He does not say he is going to prove Turning wrong. Rather, he insists on the *persuasive* character of what he is about to attempt. [Winch quoting Wittgenstein:]
>
> > ... I think that if I could make myself quite clear, then Turing would give up saying that in mathematics we make experiments.
>
> He [Wittgenstein] then asks how it is that the misunderstanding between him and Turing is so difficult to clear up and compares the issue between

them to the way in which he, Wittgenstein, would respond to a remark of [the mathematician, David] Hilbert's:

"No one is going to turn us out of the paradise which [Georg] Cantor [the inventor of transfinite numbers] created."

I [Wittgenstein] would say: "I wouldn't dream of trying to drive anyone out of this paradise." I would try to do something quite different: I would try to show you that it is not a paradise—so that you'll leave of your own accord. I would say, "You're welcome to this: just look about you."[68]

What would such an investigation on Turing's part yield? Not a different definition of "experiment," the one Wittgenstein supposedly favors. The change is not in concepts but in the aspect or picture under which a concept such as "experiment" is seen and grasped. Turing would walk freely through the doors out of his former Cantorian mathematical paradise because it had lost its air of perfection, its beauty. This change of orientation, then, is not brought about through argument in the sense of a Kantian dispute but through a quarrel. Wittgenstein is not searching for agreement through agreement in definitions (of what an experiment is). He is trying to alter the picture or aspect to which Turing is attached and in which his definition of experiment is meaningful and can serve as a reason in his form of argumentation.[69]

Persuasion for Wittgenstein, observes Stanley Cavell, turns not on bringing forward more evidence but on "producing or deepening an example, which shows him [one's interlocutor] that he would not say what he says 'we' say."[70] Persuasion alters a style of thinking, and this altered style does not necessarily introduce new facts; it makes meaningful the facts we already know. Relating what Wittgenstein said of persuasion in judgments of taste, G. E. Moore relates: "*Reasons*, he [Wittgenstein] said, in Aesthetics are 'of the nature of further descriptions': *e.g.*, you can make a person see what Brahms was driving at by showing him lots of different pieces by Brahms, or by comparing him with a contemporary author; and all that Aesthetics does is 'to draw your attention to a thing,' to 'place things side by side.'"[71] Reasoning here involves the act of comparing and finding similarities between things. Rather than deducing from given premises, we create them anew, as Grassi also argued. One tries to light up the object in such a way that it appears differently, though the object itself has not changed.

How might one light up an object such that it appears differently, under a different aspect, though the thing itself has not changed? Wittgenstein addresses this central question in his discussion of "seeing aspects" in part 2, section xi, of *Philosophical Investigations*.[72] Among the most striking examples of what he calls "noticing an aspect" (*PI*, 193) and the "'dawning' of an aspect" (194) are the figures of a "double cross" that we might first see as a black figure on a white foreground, then as a white figure on a black background (207); the picture of the "duck-rabbit" that appears, now as a duck, now as a rabbit (194); and, less striking but significant, suddenly seeing the "likeness" in two different faces (e.g., the father's face in the son's) (210).

Characteristic of aspect seeing is our sense that something has changed, yet we know that no such empirical change has occurred. As Stephen Mulhall observes, aspect change has an "inherent paradoxicality."[73] When I see the difference of aspect, writes Wittgenstein, "I *describe* the alteration like a perception; quite as if the object had altered before my eyes" (*PI*, 195). How, then, is such change—such a paradox—to be explained?

In Mulhall's view, Wittgenstein's discussion of "seeing an aspect" is part of a broader critique of the metaphysical, philosophical tradition, whose explanations for the paradox Wittgenstein shows to be empty but tenacious. Yet Wittgenstein's primary concern, he argues, is not with the unique experience of aspect change itself but with the ordinary character of perception: we *always* see things under an aspect; no phenomenon shows itself as it is (phainetai), independently of a singular point of view. In other words, the (phenomenological/hermeneutic) "as-structure" of understanding (discussed in chapter 3) is operative in every encounter with objects in the world. On the one hand, this seems correct as far as it goes and aligns with Arendt's insistence on the irreducibility of dokei moi, that is, that we always see things under aspects and that aspects are not "merely subjective" ways of receiving the appearing world. On the other hand, Mulhall's interpretation of aspect seeing as a ubiquitous feature of ordinary perception and language use tends to rob aspect seeing of its potential for novelty, seeing things anew.

Wittgenstein's discussion of aspects, Avner Baz objects, is not only about continuous aspect perception, how we usually see things, but also a discussion of how things can appear differently to us, how our routinized ways of seeing and meaning can be disrupted, and how new concepts can be formed about changes in our experience of the world.[74] "The point of seeing aspects," he writes, "lies in its being the place where we expand our experience of the ordinary and the familiar without, as it were, turning our backs on it; the place where we strengthen our bonds with the world by renewing them; and the place where we go beyond habitual ways and established routines without giving up intelligibility."[75] Agreeing with Baz, I argue that this potential for novelty, for seeing anew, is central to the experience of a shared world and crucial to democratic persuasion.

Nevertheless, we should not lose track of the ubiquitous character of aspect seeing (described by Mulhall), which reminds us of the presence of a picture in ordinary judging, both in the broadest sense of a *Weltbild* and in the specific sense of whatever picture is operative in a particular language game.

Like Arendt, Wittgenstein discusses aspects in terms that run against the grain of the Western philosophical tradition. Neither objective nor subjective in the tradition's use of those terms, aspects (like beauty) point to something that I can try to get you to see because it is there, but not in the way you would not have to see it for yourself: beauty must appear *to* you. We have objective criteria for establishing that something exists, even in your absence, but aspects require your presence. I can say, "I saw his face in the crowd." Assuming you find me trustworthy and the conditions for such a siting plausible, you would likely accept my statement as a perceptual report. But if I say, "I saw his father's face in his own," you might believe that is what I think I saw but not necessarily what is there to be seen. To be persuaded of such resemblance, you would have to see for yourself—just like you must see for yourself that the duck-rabbit can now be a duck, now a rabbit, or, for that matter, that the painting not only is hanging on the dining-room wall, for which my word might suffice, but is "beautiful."

Persuasion is the practice of seeing aspects anew for oneself. It concerns not the existence of things but your relationship to what you see, the part you play in what can appear to you and attain reality in a shared world. In showing you the image of the duck-rabbit, I am not trying to teach you that there are rabbits and there are ducks—to recognize either would, after all, assume prior knowledge of what both are (*PI*, 207). I am trying to get you to see that what you took to be the one could also be seen as the other if viewed in a certain way. Hence, there is an element of surprise: "It's a duck!" What dawns on you is not just the reality of another object (a rabbit or a duck) but *your* ability to see differently.

When we find ourselves in interminable disagreement, are we like those Wittgenstein calls the "aspect-blind"? The aspect-blind, he explains, are not those who cannot see the facts of any given matter; for example, the double cross contains both a black and a white figure. Instead, they are blind to something else: "The aspect-blind man is supposed not to see the aspects A change. But is he also supposed not to recognize that the double cross contains both a black and a white cross? So if told 'Shew me figures containing a black cross among these examples' will he be unable to manage it? No, he should be able to do that; but he will not be supposed to say: 'Now it's a black cross on a white ground!'" (*PI*, 213). He will not experience the change of aspect as a surprise, as something he is now capable of seeing.

Although the aspect-blind can see that there is a black cross and a white cross in the same figure, they are blind to aspects, that is, to their *capacity* to see differently and its importance for being with others in the world. To be aspect-blind is to remain in the grip of phainetai and the binary concept of truth: it is to insist that what one sees (be it the black cross or the white cross) is all there is to see and that one has no fundamental part in perception, the "me" to which something appears in dokei moi. It is to be held captive to a picture not as false—the black or white cross one sees is objectively there—but as the only picture or perspective available.

Put otherwise, aspect blindness is not, in the first place, a problem of what David Owen calls "ideological captivity," an epistemic state of "holding beliefs that are both false and compose a world picture."[76] Instead, aspect blindness is a form of "aspectival captivity," that is, the condition of being captive to a picture, "where picture refers to a system of judgments" that serve as principles for making other judgments for making the world "intelligible."[77] When in such a state of captivity, we still see things under aspects (the cross is black or it is white) but are fully unaware that how we see is just one aspect under which to see the object at hand. "Such systems [of judgment]," writes Owen, "govern what is intelligibly up for grabs as true-or-false. They do not determine what *is* true or false, but rather what statements *can count as* true-or-false."[78] Hence in *On Certainty*, Wittgenstein described a world picture as "the inherited background against which I distinguish between true and false" (*OC*, §94). Neither true nor false itself, a picture is "the frame of reference" to which belongs "the truth [or falsity] of certain empirical propositions," he wrote (*OC*, §83).

The problem with such captivity, argues Owen, is that it "prevents us from making sense of ourselves as subjects or agents in ways that matter to us" (e.g., our part in the truth of what appears) and that ultimately matters to our "capacity for self-government."[79] The aspect-blind may well see what we want them to see based on the evidence—the fact of the black and the white cross—but not see how their ability to see it—now as black or now as white—holds any consequence for their lives (with others). As a result, they will never experience the change in aspect as a surprise: a new picture, a "conversion," a different "system" or "frame of reference" with which to view the shared world. This may be why, in the abortion debate mentioned earlier, my opponents might agree on all the same facts regarding when a fetal heartbeat can be detected, brain development can be observed, and so on, and still refuse to be persuaded that abortion should be legal. My opponents accept the facts (much like the aspect-blind can recognize the black or the white cross) but see no consequence for their position. It is not the factual evidence that they cannot see but the change in perspective that could be their own. The aspect-blind can neither persuade others when reasons run out nor be persuaded by them, for persuasion involves recognizing one's own capacity to see anew.

More than the ability to change someone's mind when reasons run out, persuasion entails recognizing one's capacity to see anew. This capacity may well be the real object of democratic persuasion. At stake is less my ability to bring you to accept my doxa (opinion) by adopting my dokei moi than getting both you and me to see that our world pictures are partial and that there are other ways to see the same thing: recognize that plurality gives us the world as shared. The aim of persuasion is not to convince you (or me) of the truth of my (or your) perspective but to free you (and me) from the thought that there is no other perspective or way the world appears but one's own, which one then confuses with how things objectively are.

If we think about this as a problem of "ideological capture," we will likely focus on altering a false belief, thereby missing the frame of reference in which that belief remains resistant to the evidence. "What stands fast does so," writes Wittgenstein, "not because it is intrinsically obvious or convincing; it is rather held fast by what lies around it" (*OC*, §144). The received idea of the art of persuading as the act of convincing bypasses this irreducible feature of belief. Owen writes, "If you think of yourself as correcting an ideological mistake [false belief], then you see yourself as presenting something like an undistorted view, that is, something like the truth of the matter."[80] According to the inherited idea of truth as having "force" in itself, which Foucault critically interrogated, persuasion is nothing other than what Habermas famously calls the force of "the better argument," coming to an agreement based on reasons working from shared premises.[81]

There is another way of describing the dialogue called democratic persuasion. "If you think of yourself as freeing a person from the limitations of a picture [rather than a false belief] and of presenting another one (also limited), which does this freeing by juxtaposition [think of Wittgenstein and Turing], then one's attitude to the dialogue that follows is completely different," writes Owen.[82] "One actually needs others to present rival pictures in order to see the limitations of one's own picture and the ways in which it inhibits self-government. We are dependent on the dialogue [democratic persuasion] for enlightenment just because pictures are partial but we are never completely self-aware of their partiality (or they wouldn't be pictures)."[83]

The object of democratic persuasion, then, is not false belief with the aim of "presenting something like an undistorted view, that is, something like the truth of the matter."[84] That would assume that my belief is not also based on a partial picture of how the world "seems to me." Instead, democratic persuasion is a dialogue in which "the exchange of pictures or perspectives is the condition of our getting clear about the partialities of our picture and the pictures of others."[85] There is no one picture that captures things as they are in some absolute sense but only better and worse pictures for making sense of ourselves as free beings and remaining connected to a shared world.

Conclusion

Recognition of the shared world and of meaningful differences is the real aim of Brettschneider's "value democracy."[86] Unfortunately, his state-centered idea of democratic persuasion cannot quite arrive at that insight because it has lost track of the background conditions for what Arendt described as seeing politically: "the public political space [that] is common to all (*koinon*), the space where the citizens assemble, . . . the realm in which all things can first be recognized in their many-sidedness" ("IP," 167). Consequently, Brettschneider's art of democratic persuasion, though it subordinates truth to reasonableness, is restricted to the act of convincing based on shared premises (e.g., the free and equal standing of citizens) already accepted. In "The Hateful Society,"[87] however, these premises are refused or denied.

Following Wittgenstein, we might consider dogmatic worldviews a form of Owen's "aspectival captivity" characterized by aspect blindness. In that case, persuasion is not a matter of convincing based on shared premises but of getting two people in a dialogue to recognize their respective captivation by a picture, that is, by the absolute demand of one aspect under which to see the matter at hand. Owen explains: "This is why we value dialogue as 'reciprocal elucidation.' In such a dialogue . . . the question is not 'Who is Right?' or 'Who has the truth?' Rather, the question is: 'What difference does it make to look at the problem this way rather than that? What difference does it make to look at the problem under this picture rather than that?'"[88]

The need for "rival pictures" or perspectives animates Arendt's claim that persuasion is the political form of speech überhaupt.[89] Opinions become intractable and persuasion impossible because those who hold them rarely encounter other ways of seeing the world in the public space. As cultural beings, we are all vulnerable to aspectival capture. But politically speaking, aspect blindness is learned—and it can be unlearned. I've argued that "The Hateful Society" arises not because worldviews are inherently fixed, as if this were an intrinsic feature of language use, but because the space for exchanging perspectives is radically attenuated, distorted, or nonexistent. It arises where there is no meaningful exchange or where such exchange is reduced to convincing based on premises already shared. This is a problem to which the liberal idea of freedom as sovereignty and freedom from politics has made no small contribution. What exists instead are spaces in which like-minded citizens find their opinions—hateful or not—repeated and confirmed. These echo chambers, where all voices are the same, reproduce a state of doxastic solipsism, and facts lose their evidentiary force to alter belief.

I argued in chapter 3 that facts do not speak for themselves but require a public frame of reference that makes them meaningful. Following Kant, Arendt argues that "the very faculty of thinking depends on its public use; without [what Kant called] 'the test of free and open examination,' no thinking and no opinion-formation are possible. Reason is not made 'to isolate itself but to get into community with others.'"[90] "Critical thinking implies communicability."[91] This "factor of publicity" is essential for critical thought and the possibility of democratic persuasion.[92] Without a robust public realm, opinions—hateful or not—are not critically formed in communication with other opinions but merely voiced. The free expression of such opinions accords with the anemic liberal conception of freedom of speech that Arendt questions:

> Free speech has always come in many different forms and with many meanings. . . . The key thing, however, . . . is not that a person can say whatever he pleases, or that each of us has an inherent right to express himself just as he is. The point is, rather, that . . . no one can adequately grasp the objective world in its full reality all on his own, because the world always shows and reveals itself to him from only one perspective, which corresponds to his standpoint in the world and is determined by it. If someone wants to see and experience the world as it "really" is, he can do so only by understanding it as something that is shared by many people, lies between them, separates and links them, showing itself differently to each and comprehensible only to the extent that many people can talk *about* it and exchange their opinions and perspectives with one another, over against one another. Only in the freedom of our speaking with one another does the world, as that about which we speak, emerge in its objectivity and visibility from all sides. ("IP," 128–29)

If we want to alter how the world looks to some people, Arendt teaches, it is there, in the freedom of speaking with one another, that we must begin. We should refuse the binary conception of truth that inserts a sharp distinction between phainetai ("it shows itself") and dokei moi ("it seems to me"), which Arendt showed to be an artifact of Platonic philosophy.[93] In other words, we need to reconceive truth not as something we "track" because it exists independently of any singular point of view, independently of us, but as something needing support from each of us (as Foucault says) and from plural opinion (as Arendt says). It should be clear by now that the truth of "opinion" is not "merely subjective" but "subject dependent": it always involves knowledge of properties that depend on the effects that such properties have on cognizing subjects, as James Conant told us. For Arendt, we reach how things are only through the exchange of doxai, for each dokei moi is only one standpoint on the world. There is no truth without the "factor of publicity."

What place does parrhesia have in democratic persuasion, especially in the cases of deep disagreement that concern us here? After all, as we saw in the previous chapter, Foucault, too, is concerned not with ideological captivity, focused on altering false belief, but on aspectival captivity, focused on altering a perspective that blinds the subject to what lies in plain view: the contingent relations of power that keep it in a state of unfreedom. For Foucault, however, persuasion, though it may be the outcome of parrhesiastic speech, is not its essential goal. Whereas rhetoric aims only to persuade and is therefore "an art capable of lying," he writes, "there can only be truth in *parrhesia*. Where there is no truth, there can be no speaking freely. *Parrhesia* is the naked transmission, as it were, of truth itself. *Parrhesia* ensures in the most direct way . . . this transfer of true discourse from the person who already possesses it to the person who must receive it, must be impregnated by it, and who must be able to use it and subjectivize it."[94] It takes "courage" to be persuaded, to accept a truth that is hurtful because it challenges one's worldview or self-conception and the untruths on which it is based. But what makes telling the truth parrhesia is not its uptake, argues Foucault. Instead, it is "the courage of truth in the person who speaks and who, regardless of everything, takes the risk of telling the whole truth that he thinks, but it is also the interlocutor's courage in agreeing to accept the hurtful truth that he hears."[95] Nevertheless, it is not persuasion, but "transparency," rightly comments Lorenzini, that is the necessary condition of parrhesia for Foucault: "*parrhesia* always conveys the speaker's thoughts as clearly and openly as possible, and exactly as they are," free from the embellishments and "oratorical tricks" of rhetoric.[96]

Invoking Grassi's critique of this philosophical idea of rhetoric, I suggested that Foucault accepts—or at least does not question—the Western tradition's view of rhetoric as a mere technique of persuasion unconcerned with truth. This view fails to account for the figurative and imaginative character of indicative speech, without which the archai or first principles could not be expressed—since they cannot be demonstrated or proved—and, consequently, the true discourse spoken by the parrhesiast could not come into existence at all.

More importantly, the problem of *democratic* persuasion is not the problem of truth as it was defined in Foucault's account of parrhesia. Whereas parrhesia concerns "the strong and constitutive bond between the person speaking and what he says [the truth]," persuasive rhetoric concerns, in the first instance, the bond between the person speaking and his or her interlocutor and their rival pictures or perspectives that bring the shared world into view.[97] This latter bond, however, is not (necessarily) "a bond of power between what is said and the person to whom it is said," as Foucault would have it.[98] That bond of power is based on a narrow view of rhetoric as a technique of persuasion and the idea that persuasion is indifferent to truth. I've argued that "persuasion comes after reasons," as Wittgenstein put it, but not because persuasion is just a grab bag of oratorical tricks required in the abyss of truth opened by irreconcilable "world pictures." On the contrary, persuasion employs the imaginative power of words to alter the pictures or figures (according to Grassi) that grounds what we will count as part of the shared world, the basis of what we will accept as true.

Political speech is persuasive—when it is—not because it will do anything (e.g., lie, dissemble, or distort) to gain agreement. In Arendt's counterintuitive view, agreement is not even the essential object or aim of persuasive speech.[99] Democratic persuasion is the problem of getting the shared world in view in the first place through the exchange of how the world appears to each of us. Dokei moi is not whatever anyone just happens to believe to be the case but expresses how things are. Arendt's claim that doxai (aspects) are "objectively verifiable," that they are not "subjective fantasy and arbitrariness, but also not something absolute and valid for all," sounds strange because received understandings of "democratic persuasion" remain in aspectual captivity: hostage to the binary conception of truth ("PP," 80).

CONCLUSION

A Realistic Picture of Democracy and Truth

> *Call me a truth-seeker and I will be satisfied.*
> WITTGENSTEIN, COMPLETE CORRESPONDENCE

In this book, I've described "post-truth" as a picture that holds us captive.[1] It is a picture to which we remain "obsessively attached and which in a real sense imprisons us," blocking alternative ways to understand and transform our current predicament.[2] Within its frame, democratic citizens have lost contact with a suprahistorical concept of Truth that deftly bypasses contemporary dilemmas of radical relativism, corrosive historicism, and "bad *parrhesia*" because it has nothing to do with us. The only task that falls to us now is to recommit to tracking Truth as best we can, reaffirm it as the essential ground of democracy, and follow wherever it leads. Truth always sets us free.

Those who question this picture are accused of denying that truth exists and lending support, consciously or not, to "alternative facts," fake news, brazen lies, and the whole arsenal of post-truth. These traitors to Truth include a motley group of "MAGA" Republicans, "woke" Democrats, and social constructionists of all stripes (e.g., postmodernists, critical race theorists, feminists, etc.), depending on your political point of view. Whatever their disagreements, all defenders of democracy are now called on to take a stand against its further erosion by defending objective Truth.

But what if the "crisis of truth" were symptomatic of problems internal to the received understanding of truth? What if Truth were imbricated in the very erosion of the public realm that it is now called on to restore? How might we break the spell of "post-truth" and form a different picture?

The lesson I drew from Wittgenstein is that we cannot free ourselves from all pictures. "It is true that we can compare a picture that is firmly rooted in us to a superstition, but it is equally true that we always eventually have to reach some firm ground, either a picture or something else, so that a picture which is at the root of all our thinking is to be respected and not treated as a superstition," he told us.[3] Rejecting the foundationalist idea that our "world picture" is either true or false and, if true, must be based on convincing reasons, he urged us "to realize the groundlessness of our thinking" as the condition of a realistic attitude toward the shared world. "Giving grounds," he writes, "justifying the evidence, comes to an end:—but the end is not certain propositions' striking us as true, i.e. it is not a kind of seeing on our part; it is our acting, which lies at the bottom of the language game" (*OC*, 204). It is not knowledge but acting based on "certainty" (*Gewissheit*) that lies at the bottom of our "world picture" and the diverse pictures that lie at the bottom of any language game.

Wittgenstein invites us to face the difficulty of acknowledging this groundlessness without falling into the despair of skeptical doubt. To say that something is groundless is not to say it is up for grabs. On the contrary, the certainties on which our form of life rests are contingent *and* stable ways of acting and speaking learned and sedimented through training and habit. "Certainties . . . express the agreement and constancy in our judgments [e.g., about measurement, color, arithmetic, etc.] which is necessary in order to have language at all," writes Andreas Krebs.[4] Without them, rule following and claims to knowledge and truth would not be possible. Certainties are presupposed without question; they have normative power. And they are expressed through the various "pictures" that give meaning to our ordinary lives.

What "stands fast" for us at any moment is experienced as simply given. Certainty is a doing, not a knowing: "Why do I not satisfy myself that I have two feet when I want to get up from a chair? There is no why. I simply don't. This is how I act," declares Wittgenstein (*OC*, §148). Having two feet is not an empirical proposition; it is neither doubted nor known. But certainties, as Wittgenstein's many examples make clear, can and do change.[5] It is essential to his view of the role played by certainties in our language games that we keep this possibility of change in view. In *On Certainty*, he explains:

> It might be imagined that some propositions, of the form of empirical propositions, were hardened and functioned as channels for such empirical propositions as were not hardened but fluid; and that this relation altered with time, in that fluid propositions hardened, and hard ones became fluid.
>
> The mythology may change back into a state of flux, the river-bed of thoughts may shift. But I distinguish between the movement of the waters on the river-bed and the shift of the bed itself; though there is not a sharp division of the one from the other. . . .

And the bank of the river consists partly of hard rock, subject to no alteration or only to an imperceptible one, partly of sand, which now in one place now in another gets washed away, or deposited. (*OC*, §§96–97, 99)

Where does the "is not true nor yet false" of certainty fit in forming a new picture of truth for democratic citizens and, with it, a better understanding of our current predicament (*OC*, 205)? That truth is not given in the existence of a given reality, as Foucault argued, could be understood as an effect of certainty. The question of the true and the false does not arise in the register of the unquestioned given. A game of truth rests on certainty: it rests on something that never takes the form of an empirical proposition to whose epistemic validity one could or could not submit. We can doubt some things because others stand fast for us. Certainty falls outside the game of truth and the regime of truth. But discourses of truth also arise where "the river-bed of thoughts . . . shift." True discourse marks not only where a given practice gets codified and stabilized but also where questions initially arise and what was "certain" takes the form of an empirical proposition subject to the true and the false. Games and regimes of truth, in other words, arise where once there was certainty. This again indicates that truth is nonnecessary and a potential site of critique.

My reading of the relationship between certainty and true discourse invites a synergistic understanding of Foucault and Wittgenstein. In the introduction, I argued that Foucault's critical approach to truth exemplifies what Cora Diamond called the "realistic spirit." Foucault agrees with ordinary language philosophy that "the role of philosophy is not to discover what is concealed [hidden], but rather to make visible what precisely is visible, which is to say to make appear what is so close, so immediate, so intimately connected with ourselves that we cannot perceive it."[6] It is a matter neither of getting behind appearances nor of denying that there is anything to be seen, as the realist and the antirealist assume. Instead, it is learning to notice and attend to what is "in plain view."

Foucault's account resonates with Wittgenstein's famous claim in sections 126 and 129 of *Philosophical Investigations*:

Philosophy simply puts everything before us, and neither explains nor deduces anything.—Since everything lies open to view there is nothing to explain. For what is hidden, for example, is of no interest to us.

The aspects of things that are most important for us are hidden because of their simplicity and familiarity. (One is unable to notice something—because it is always before one's eyes.) (*PI*, §§126, 129)[7]

Comparing these passages, Daniele Lorenzini also argues for a significant relationship between ordinary language philosophy and Foucault's methodological approach, but with one crucial difference: "Foucault imbues this task with a critical, ethico-political value that we do not (explicitly) find in Wittgenstein." Whereas Wittgenstein's understanding of philosophy "leaves everything as it is," writes Lorenzini, Foucault would have us unmask the operations of power. In other words, "while drawing from ordinary language philosophy, Foucault explicitly *politicizes* its insights."[8] Foucault might then appear as a necessary supplement to Wittgenstein for an ordinary language approach to political questions of truth and power.

I agree that Foucault works within the ordinary language tradition, and it seems fitting to say that Wittgenstein did not "politicize" his philosophical findings. However, I question this familiar image of Wittgenstein's philosophical quietism, "leav[ing] everything as it is," versus doing something in the world (contesting power) with critical philosophy. This quietism has implications for my understanding of what I have called a realistic spirit of democratic critique and a new picture of truth.

Taking up the charge of quietism, John McDowell invokes Wittgenstein's claim, in *Philosophical Investigations*, that "the work of the philosopher consists in assembling reminders" (§127) and his famous refusal to "advance *theses* in philosophy" (§128) to query what philosophical practice could then be.[9] Anticipating that question, Wittgenstein writes in section 118: "Where does our investigation get its importance from, since it seems only to destroy everything interesting, that is, all that is great and important? (As it were all the buildings, leaving behind only bits of stone and rubble.) What we are destroying is nothing but houses of cards and we are clearing up the ground of language on which they stand."

The charge that Wittgenstein is a quietist, writes McDowell, assumes that "there are only two things for philosophy to be, either succumbing to an illusion of producing important structures of thought [e.g., theories of truth] or else assembling reminders as therapy for intellectual pathologies involved in falling into such illusions [houses of cards]." But "that idea," he continues, "seems seriously questionable in connection with much of what we call 'philosophy.'"

> Think, for instance, of reflection about the requirements of justice or the proper shape for a political community. I know no reason to suppose Wittgenstein would have insisted that everything that happens in political philosophy, to stay with that example, falls under that "either/or." . . .

In those remarks [cited above] he is talking about a particular mode of philosophical activity. We do best not to take him to be making pronouncements about just anything that counts as philosophy.[10]

The point is not to defend the critical potential of a nonquietistic philosophy that builds "important structures," argues McDowell. "Wittgensteinian quietism involves being suspicious of philosopher' questions, before we start interesting ourselves in the specifics of how they are answered." It "is absolutely not a recommendation of a kind of idleness, a practice of leaving necessary tasks [of critical thought] to others."[11] Before engaging in "substantive philosophy" and building any such structures, then, we should first make sure that we are dealing with *actual* problems and not just "a variety of fantastications one can be tempted into" when doing philosophy or, for our purposes, political theory.[12] Wittgenstein's quietism does not leave the hard work of necessary tasks to others like the more "political" Foucault. His "quietism does indeed urge us not to engage in certain supposed tasks, but precisely because it requires us to work at showing that they are not necessary [where they are not]."[13] This, I would argue, is the hard work of showing that we are held captive to a picture rather than the more familiar idea of our captivation by an ideology or false belief that guides the debate over post-truth. It is the work done by every practitioner of realistic critique, including Foucault.

Foucault questions the received idea that the "essential vocation of philosophy is to address the truth, or to question being; and that by digressing into these empirical domains like the issue of politics and power, philosophy cannot but get compromised."[14] Suggesting that the issue is not the topic but the approach, the method of critique, he poses the possibility of "another path." If "philosophy stops thinking of itself as prophesy, . . . as pedagogy, or as legislation," it might abandon its role as either the "foundation . . . [or] renewal of power" and refuse to build those important structures in which to house its fantastical problems. Instead, "it gives itself the task to analyze, clarify, and make visible and thus intensify the struggles that develop around power, the strategies of the antagonists within relations of power, the tactics employed, the *foyers* of resistance."[15] Rather than take for granted that there already is a problem of power that we all understand, Foucault asks a "naive question, which has not been posed so often . . . : what do power relations fundamentally consist in?"[16]

Asking his naive question, Foucault then turns to the ordinary language tradition. It offers a new way of doing philosophy that is not afraid of compromising itself by abandoning its traditional vocation to address truth. Instead of rejecting truth as a worthy topic, let alone denying truth exists, this new philosophy would approach truth as it approaches power: not as a problem we already understand but as a question we have yet adequately to pose. Such a project first exposes great structures (e.g., the inherited theories of truth and power) as "houses of cards"; it shows that the problem we thought we needed to address is no genuine problem at all but a perspective or picture of how things must be. Examples include the idea of (all) power as "sovereignty," the "repressive hypothesis" of sexuality, and the suprahistorical idea of truth as "force." Philosophical pictures should not be dismissed as "false," for pictures are neither true nor false (according to Wittgenstein), but the frame within which things can count as true or false and we can make judgments. Instead, they should be treated as serious objects of philosophical therapy (e.g., by means of other perspectives and pictures) aimed at enhancing our ability to think and act otherwise. "The philosopher's treatment of a question is like the treatment of an illness," wrote Wittgenstein (*PI*, §255). The new task of philosophy is to release us from the thought that "*this*" is the problem that needs to be solved, which, in turn, "gives philosophy peace" by redirecting it to actual problems that can be solved (*PI*, §133).

Although she does not mention ordinary language philosophy, Arendt is also concerned with the problem of what David Owen called "aspectival capture": the state in which citizen-subjects remain hostage to a "picture or perspective as the *only* possible picture or perspective open to them."[17] For her, the problem is the "unmediated, attentive facing up to, and resisting of, reality—whatever it may be or might have been" (*OT*, viii).[18] Arendt, too, sees her project as "clearing up the ground of language" (Wittgenstein) so that the problem that lies in plain view can first be perceived. To see what is novel—or, in the case of totalitarianism, unprecedented—we should resist employing familiar concepts (e.g., authoritarianism) that remain alien to the new reality. As we saw in chapter 1, the essential task of "thinking" for Arendt is to identify the exhaustion of a concept for describing the appearing world. Far from building important structures (grand theories) or any structure at all, thinking reduces first to "bits of rubble" the concepts that had become empty slogans and cliches in the mouths of men like Adolf Eichmann. Thinking from standpoints not our own and publicly exchanging points of view is Arendt's answer to our captivation by a picture of truth as phainetai in which we lose track of the plural ways the world appears/seems to each of us (dokei moi).

Reframing the Problem of Truth

How might a new picture of (the democratic problem of) truth be developed from the realistic critique practiced by Arendt, Foucault, and Wittgenstein? Thus far, I have argued that the first step is to see whether what everyone accepts as a genuine problem is not just a captivating picture of how things *must* be. Wittgenstein called this "clearing up the ground of language on which they [the problems] stand" (PI, §118). Post-truth is not an actual or genuine problem but one that arises within a way of thinking about truth (as Truth). It should be clear by now that this is in no way to say fake news, lies, and "alternative facts" are not real problems for democracy. However, we will misrecognize the sources of and solutions to these dangerous and perhaps novel forms of deception if we remain within the picture of post-truth. Rather than lead back to what is already "open to view" with Arendt (e.g., the worldlessness, loneliness, and attenuated public realm that characterize democratic mass society) or with Foucault (e.g., the part that each of us plays in sustaining the force of games and regimes of truth), this picture tempts us to look for the real causes elsewhere: in ideological discourse that conceals and distorts Truth, in the subjectivism of citizen opinion, or in the easygoing relativism of democratic pluralism. To break the hold of this picture, I invite us again to ask: What concept of "truth" is presupposed in the post-truth debate?

This debate, I've argued, is rooted in the suprahistorical idea of truth as presently concealed but omnipresent and waiting to be rediscovered by us. Although post-truth is our contemporary way of problematizing truth, it is continuous with what Foucault associated with "one side" of the problematization of truth in Greek society, namely the "analytics of truth": a purely logical, epistemological concept of truth whose (re)discovery rests on honing the skills of correct reasoning (*DT*, 224).[19] Understood in terms of the problem of false belief, post-truth arises where our ability to tell truth from falsity has been lost to a failure in our reasoning capacities. Although attributed to sociocultural causes (e.g., the decline of authoritative sources, the development of new technologies, the proliferation of social media, the instrumental mendacity of politicians, etc.), this failure is seen as strictly epistemic: we no longer know how to make sure that a statement is correct.

Such a diagnosis leads unsurprisingly to calls for restoring truth by recovering facts, which has spawned a vast machinery of fact-checking to respond to our deformed cognitive state of post-truth. To tell the truth is to state a fact, give evidence. But if we continually fail to recognize checked facts *as* facts with political consequences for our lives as citizens, that is because facts do not speak for themselves but rely on a meaning-making picture for their significance and force. Consequently, no mere accumulation of facts will alter the picture in which facts alone gain meaning.

What, then, might truth-telling be for us today if it is more than the mere stating of a fact or correct reasoning? We recall that "the other side" or aspect of the great problematization of truth was what Foucault called "the importance of telling the truth and of having people telling the truth and of recognizing which people are able to tell the truth." He identified this way of problematizing truth as being "at the root, at the foundation of what we would call the critical tradition of philosophy in our society" (*DT*, 224).

Truth-telling, Foucault implies, begins with the counterintuitive idea that truth does not always set us free. Correct reasoning guarantees nothing. Showing that truth can be a force of freedom but also subjection, he distinguished between a game and a regime of truth to illuminate the "truth obligations" of the latter: "how the individual is constituted as subject in the relation to self and the relationship to others" (*GS*, 42). Furthermore, the "therefore" that links "it is true" to "I submit" binds the subject to the truth obligations of a historically specific regime of truth. Acceptance of a game of veridiction and the ability to reason correctly does not automatically entail submission to the regime, that is, to the pragmatic consequences that follow from one's epistemic acceptance of the game ("It is true"). The force of truth rests on subjects binding themselves to various obligations not given in the veridicality of the game itself. This binding is crucial to Foucault's analysis of modern power, that is, the "government of human beings by truth."

That truth can lead to subjection and not freedom is crucial to seeing the blind spots in approaches to post-truth that associate truth-telling with democracy and its emphasis on liberating oneself from false beliefs whose causes remain hidden. The truth-teller here is the one who exposes and assess the rationality of systems of power from an observer position outside power. Notwithstanding their differences, this search for the hidden defines the (first generation) Frankfurt School's use of *Ideologiekritik* to unmask false rationalizations of social domination and, later, Habermas's implicit redefinition of ideology as "distorted communication,"[20] Althusser's turn to science to falsify ideological common sense, and contemporary theories of ideology that extend Althusser's account of subjective misrecognition.

Rejecting the "critique of representations in terms of truth or error, truth or falsity, ideology or science, rationality or irrationality" as the method for criticizing power, Foucault also rejects the assumption about the freeing nature of truth on which the game of ideology critique is based (*GL*, 77). Taking "the contemporary medical and psychiatric game of truth that defines the condition of 'gender dysphoria'" as his example, Lorenzini explains Foucault's complex stance:

> Thus, he [Foucault] does not want to say: This game of truth is wrong, you do not really suffer from gender dysphoria, and that's why you should resist. Indeed, the risk would be to suggest that one should resist because (and *only insofar as*) the exercise of medical power relies on errors and false conclusions [or is based on *ideological* heteronormative notions of sexual dimorphism]—and conversely that, when it relies on the truth, one must *never* resist. By contrast, Foucault argues that the "movement of freeing oneself from power" should not depend on whether the truth that accompanies a given exercise of power is "really" true or not, but should instead target the "therefore," which gives *force* to that truth, allowing a governmental apparatus to say: "It is true, therefore, you must submit." Indeed, this "therefore" is not necessary and can be rejected.... Ultimately, the aim of Foucault's critical anarchaeology is to make us perceive all the "therefores" that silently govern our conduct.[21]

These "therefores" are an object of what I've called an ordinary or realistic critique of truth. They belong to what is "so intimately connected with ourselves that we cannot perceive it," as Foucault told us.[22] The first task, then, is not to discover the hidden but to make visible what, being familiar, remains unseen: the "therefores" that give force to truth as a mechanism of power, perhaps of freedom, and that have everything to do with us. Realistic critique is a form of truth-telling that aims to light up the unseen visible such that we recognize our part in the relationship of truth to power. Critique does not reduce truth to power but alerts us to how power can seem to operate *on* us without any contribution *from* us. Truth appears necessary when how we react seems decided by the truth itself.[23] Accordingly, if I accept that it is true (i.e., epistemically valid), I must do "x." But this illusion is spawned by the received idea of Truth.

Lorenzini explains that there are, for example, at least three options open to me in the game of gender dysphoria: I could accept the diagnosis of gender dysphoria as true and submit to the treatment, I could accept the diagnosis and refuse the treatment, and I could refuse the diagnosis (because I refuse being categorized as mentally ill) but accept the treatment (because I desire bodily change).[24] In any game of truth, there is no one necessary outcome. I could resist and refuse to be governed "like that," as Foucault showed us in chapter 2.

In the post-truth debate, it is assumed that truth is valuable—it is Truth, after all—and once recognized, Truth will lead the way to freedom. That is why, as discussed in the introduction, adherents of "epistemic democracy," though many refuse epistocracy and argue for the possible sharpening of the ordinary citizen's cognitive skills, nevertheless believe it is the job of citizens to "track truth." Once properly tracked, the truth will secure its own acceptance. The problem, however, is not always a failure of correct reasoning or inability of citizens to track truth. I could recognize and accept the epistemic validity of "x" and still refuse to "manifest" the truth of "x" and bind myself to its regime. Within the picture of post-truth, such behavior is "irrational": either a cognitive failure to grasp truth or a refusal to accept truth. But this judgment assumes that truth will make us free.

What if instead of dutifully tracking truth and following where it leads, I began to imagine pathways not already trodden by other truth seekers but possible, nonetheless?

The "Otherwise" in Plain View

If the first task of realistic critique as a practice of truth-telling is an activity of "clearing up the ground of language" on which stand "houses of cards" (*PI*, §118), what would we see if we could make appear what lies in plain view, and how might it facilitate transformative social change?

Here, I return to the point made by both Arendt and Foucault that the tenacious idea of "politics as rule" roots itself in power's supposedly intrinsic legitimacy and the inevitability of rule in the political realm. This necessity of power is entangled with what Foucault called "the government of men by the truth" (*GL*, 11). Of making the visible (power) "appear," lighting it up so we can direct out attention to it, Foucault argued: "It is not a question of having in view, at the end of a project, a society without power relations [call it the anticipatory-utopic view]. It is rather a matter of putting nonpower or the non-acceptability of power, not at the end of the [critical] enterprise, but rather at the beginning of the work, in the form of a questioning of all the ways in which power is in actual fact accepted" (*GL*, 78).

To put nonpower at the beginning rather than the end of critical inquiry, we are "clearing the ground" and working to dispel the illusion that power's past and present are evidence of its future necessity. "If politics is defined in its usual sense, as a relationship between the rulers and the ruled," writes Arendt, then any "hope [for a different future] is, of course, purely utopian" ("IP," 97). The problem for both thinkers is seeing what exists as contingent, what could have been otherwise. The task of realistic critique is not to build future structures but to identify the opening for political imagination and action in contingency, to shine a light on the "otherwise."

Locating the "otherwise" that exists in every claim to truth as the basis of power and rule is the first step to developing "the art of not being governed," which is how Foucault (in chapter 2) described the task of "critique" ("WC," 24). It involves recognizing that by binding ourselves to truth, we can accept or reject different forms of being governed or not being governed at all (*isonomia*). Arendt, too, argued that the question of governance has historically been entangled with specific conceptions of truth. The picture that holds us captive is the tenacious idea of politics as rule. In her genealogical account, "the commonplace notion already to be found in Plato and Aristotle that every political community consists of those who rule and those who are ruled" explicitly "rests on a suspicion of action," the capacity of citizens to govern themselves and to begin anew.[25]

In his "escape from action into rule," writes Arendt, "Plato was the first to introduce the division between those who know and do not act and those who act and do not know.... [He] identified the dividing line between thought and action with the gulf that separates the rulers from those over whom they rule.... He who knows does not have to do and he who does needs no thought or knowledge."[26] For Plato, this "relationship between ruling and being ruled," Arendt explains, was legitimated by the philosopher's superior ability to "rule oneself": control one's passions and achieve the inner stillness required to contemplate the eternal nature of things.[27] Applying "the doctrine of ideas [forms] to politics," to the merely appearing world of the "cave," Plato sought their "guidance as standards and rules by which to measure and under which to subsume the varied multitude of human deeds and words with ... absolute, 'objective' certainty."[28]

The "isolated mastership" of the ruler rests on beginning a series whose outcome he seeks to control. Arendt explains:

> The problem, as Plato saw it, was to make sure that the beginner would remain the complete master of what he had begun, not needing the help of others to carry it through. In the realm of [contingent and unpredictable] action, this isolated mastership can be achieved only if the others were no longer needed to join of their own accord, with their own motives and aims, but are used to execute orders, and if, on the other hand, the beginner who took the initiative does not permit himself to get involved in the action itself. To begin (*archein*) and to act (*prattein*) thus can become two altogether different activities, and the beginner has become a ruler

(an archōn in the twofold sense of the word) who does not have to act at all (*prattein*) but rule (*archein*) over those who are capable of execution.[29]

Plato's restriction of the prerogative to begin to the one who knows, and ultimately his "substitution of rulership [and the execution of orders] for [inaugural] action," had decisive consequences for Occidental conceptions of political life.[30] "The Platonic identification of knowledge with command and rulership and of action with obedience and execution overruled all earlier experiences and articulations in the political realm and became authoritative for the whole tradition of political thought," Arendt concludes.[31]

No mere aberration in an otherwise enlightening and freeing history of Truth, "the Platonic separation of knowing and doing has remained at the root of all theories of domination which are not mere justifications of an irreducible and irresponsible will to power," declares Arendt.[32] I have argued that to make sense of our current predicament, Arendt's genealogical examination of truth and politics can be productively read in tandem with what Foucault called "the government of men by truth" (*GL*, 11). Indeed, the "Platonic separation of knowing and doing" and the "substitution of rulership for action" persist in defenses of epistocracy and carry over to the only apparently less troubling idea of "epistemic democrats" that cognitive competence should be the measure of any right to full participation in public affairs.[33] Once started by "those who know," all that remains for the rest of us is to continue the series, execute the order, and follow the rule.

In *Philosophical Investigations*, Wittgenstein famously describes the Platonic idea of rule following, its orderly quest for knowledge and truth, as captive to an arresting picture of what it means to "obey a rule" presumably dictated from above. To obey a rule is to follow a "series" started by the one who knows the fixed path, which, Wittgenstein suggests, we might "imagine as rails"; and "the beginning of a series is a visible section of rails invisibly laid out [for us] to infinity": "'All the steps are really already taken' means: I no longer have any choice. The rule, once stamped with a particular meaning, traces the lines along which it is to be followed through the whole of space.—But if something of this sort really were the case, how would it help?" (§219).

The Platonic picture ironically voiced by Wittgenstein can be transposed to post-truth. In both cases, we are left with no choice but to follow the rails to infinity, to "track" truth. We can, of course, deny truth, but then we risk exclusion as epistemically incompetent, perhaps "irrational." Outside the games and regimes of democratic politics and truth, we have nothing political to say.

This received understanding of democracy and truth "traces the lines along which it is to be followed." I hope to have shown that it really has not helped. There is, however, another option: we could refuse both to track truth and to deny truth. Rather than trace the line, continue the series, or exit all democratic games and regimes of truth, we could instead assert our capacity to seek an ordinary, realistic idea of truth and begin anew. We could recognize that we do have a choice: democratic truths and their consequences depend on us.

Acknowledgments

I have benefited from many friends' and colleagues' personal and intellectual generosity. Thanks to my political theory colleagues in the Department of Political Science at Chicago, Chiara Cordelli, Adom Getachew, Deme Kasimis, Matthew Landauer, John McCormick, Sankar Muthu, Jennifer Pitts, Nathan Tarcov, Lisa Wedeen, and James Wilson, who have supported my work and created an exciting and productive intellectual community in which to thrive.

Heartfelt thanks to my colleagues at the Center for the Study of Gender and Sexuality, especially faculty director Daisy Delogu, former faculty directors Kristen Schilt and Jane Daily, executive director Gina Olson, assistant director for programming and operations Tate Brazas, and assistant director for student affairs and curriculum Bonnie Kanter. The center has been a lifeline for me and many others in gender and sexuality studies. Thanks to Geoff Stone, who has supported the center's work through the years. Thanks to Lauren Berlant, whose shining and singular presence at the center and the university will outlive their untimely death. Thanks to Chantal Mouffe and to the late Ernesto Laclau for their friendship, support, and enduring contributions to radical democratic theory.

I thank my cherished friends and former Northwestern colleagues Ann Orloff, Mary G. Dietz, and James Farr. They have provided invaluable and brilliant intellectual and emotional sustenance over the years, for which I am most grateful. Thanks to my dear friend George Shulman, who has read more first drafts than anyone I know, patiently finding the germ of the argument and helping me to develop it. Thanks to John G. Gunnell, whose superb work on Wittgenstein has been a fundamental resource. Thanks to Nicholas Dunn for the conversations about Arendt and Kant at the Arendt Center for Politics and Humanities. Thanks to former members of my feminism and ordinary language philosophy group Nancy Bauer, Sarah Beckwith, Alice Crary, Sandra Laugier, and Toril Moi, whose writings inspire me. Special thanks to my colleague and dear friend Lisa Wedeen, who has always supported me, fostering my work through her brilliant directorship of the Chicago Center for Contemporary Theory.

Generous research leaves from the University of Chicago supported this book. Thanks to former department chair William Howell and the dean of the Social Sciences Division, Amanda Woodward, for securing a crucial year's leave to complete the project. Many thanks to the Institute for Advanced Study in Princeton, where I was fortunate to spend a second term as a visiting member and begin work on this manuscript. I owe a debt of gratitude to Bernard E. Harcourt and Didier Fassin for inviting me, and to Joan Scott for engaging my work.

I am deeply grateful for the many talented graduate students I have had the pleasure of teaching over the years this book was written. Exceptional thanks to Guido Niccolò Barbi, Nicolae Biea, Aylon Cohen, Elaine Colligan, Daniel Epstein, Silvia Fedi, Dana Glaser, Annie Heffernan, Dalaina Heiberg, Emily Katzenstein, Carlos Morado Vazquez, Rose Owen, Marshall Pierce, Niklas Plaetzer, Helen Galvin Ross, Omar Safadi, Agatha Slupek, Burak Tan, and Ismene Vedder.

I want to give special thanks to my research assistant Marshall Pierce, who helped prepare the final manuscript, to Kathleen Kageff for her careful copy editing, and to Derek Gottlieb for his excellent book indexing.

I was very fortunate to have Daniele Lorenzini and Patchen Markell, two superb scholars of Foucault and Arendt, respectively, as readers of the manuscript. They provided invaluable suggestions for revision, for which I am most grateful. Patchen Markell also helped with some problematic translation issues.

Thanks to Kyle Wagner and Kristin Rawlings at the University of Chicago Press for their assistance with the publication process. I especially thank Kyle for encouraging me to pursue the project in its early stages.

Thanks to my spirited sister, Amanda Zerilli, who shares precious memories of our recently deceased mother, Marie Antoinette Stillitano Zerilli.

Finally, and once again, *mille grazie* to Gregor Gnädig, whose kindness, sense of humor, and attentiveness have been crucial to this project and my life. Apart from reading drafts and correcting translations, he has supported my work in every way and convinced me that the manuscript was "book worthy" when I had my doubts.

An earlier version of chapter 2 was previously published as "Critique as a Practice of Freedom," in *A Time for Critique*, ed. Didier Fassin and Bernard Harcourt (Columbia University Press, 2019), 36–51. Copyright © 2019 Columbia University Press. Reprinted with permission of Columbia University Press. An earlier version of chapter 5 was previously published as "Feminist Critique and the Realistic Spirit" in *Philosophy and Rhetoric* 50, no. 4 (2017): 589–611, https://doi.org/10.5325/philrhet.50.4.0589. Used with permission from Penn State University Press.

Notes

Preface

1. Hannah Arendt, *The Promise of Politics*, ed. Jerome Kohn (New York: Schocken, 2005), 201. The epigraph for the present book is from Ludwig Wittgenstein, *Culture and Value*, ed. Georg Henrik von Wright in collaboration with Heikki Nyman, rev. ed. of the text by Alois Pinchler, trans. Peter Winch (London: Blackwell, 1998), 44.

2. Arendt, *Promise of Politics*, 201, 202.

3. Hannah Arendt, *The Origins of Totalitarianism* (1966; New York: Harcourt Brace Jovanovich, 1975), 476 (hereafter cited as *OT*).

4. Michel Foucault, *On the Government of the Living: Lectures at the Collège de France 1979–1980*, ed. Michel Senellart, trans. Graham Burchell (New York: Palgrave Macmillan, 2014), 95 (hereafter cited as *GL* with page numbers).

Introduction

1. Lee McIntyre, *Post-Truth* (Cambridge, MA: MIT Press, 2018); James Ball, *Post-Truth: How Bullshit Conquered the World* (London: Biteback, 2018); Ralph Keyes, *The Post-Truth Era: Dishonestly and Deception in Contemporary Life* (New York: St. Martin's, 2004); Jeffrey Dudiak, *Post-Truth: Facts and Faithfulness* (Eugene, OR: Wipf and Stock, 2022); Matthew D'Ankona, *Post-Truth: The New War on Truth and How to Fight Back* (London: Ebery, 2017); Julian Baggini, *A Short History of Truth: Consolations for a Post-Truth World* (London: Quercus, 2017); Abdu Murray, *Saving Truth: Finding Meaning and Clarity in a Post-Truth World* (Grand Rapids, MI: Zondervan, 2018); Daniel J. Levitan, *Weaponized Lies: How to Think Critically in a Post-Truth Era* (New York: Dutton, 2017); Ken Wilburm, *Trump and a Post-Truth World* (Boulder, CO: Shambhala, 2018); Arpad Szakolczai, *Post-Truth Society: A Political Anthology of Trickster Logic* (New York: Routledge, 2021); Donald A. Barclay, *Disinformation: The Nature of Facts and Lies in a Post-Truth World* (New York: Rowman and Littlefield, 2022); Bruce McComisky, *Post-Truth Rhetoric and Composition* (Logan: Utah State University Press, 2017). For more sober accounts of truth and politics, see Steve Fuller, *Post-Truth: Knowledge as a Power Game* (London: Anthem, 2018); Frank Fischer, *Truth and Post-Truth in Public Policy* (New York: Cambridge University Press, 2021); H. Kavanagh and M. Rich, *Truth Decay: An Initial Exploration of the Diminishing Role of Facts and Analysis in American Public Life* (Santa Monica, CA: Rand, 2020); Teresa Man Lin Lee, *Politics and Truth: Political Theory and the Postmodern*

Challenge (Albany: State University of New York Press, 1997); Maximilian Conrad et al., *Europe in the Age of Post-Truth Politics: Populism, Disinformation, and the Public Sphere* (London: Palgrave Macmillan, 2022); Sophie Rosenfeld, *Democracy and Truth: A Short History* (Philadelphia: University of Pennsylvania Press, 2019); Jason Stanley, *How Propaganda Works* (Princeton, NJ: Princeton University Press, 2015); Ari-Elmeri Hyvönen, "Defining Post-Truth: Structures, Agents, and Styles," October 22, 2018, https://www.e-ir.info/2018/10/22/defining-post-truth-structures-agents-and-style; Gerald Posselt and Sergej Seitz, "Truth and Its Political Forms: An Explorative Cartography," *Contemporary Political Theory* (2023), https://doi.org/10.1057/s41296-023-00669-7.

2. Political speeches are regularly fact-checked by major newspapers such as *The New York Times* and *The Washington Post* and by organizations like "FactCheck.org." On fact-checking as a strategy against post-truth, see Kavanagh and Rich, *Truth Decay*. I discuss the vast machinery of fact-checking in chap. 3. In *An Epistemic Theory of Democracy*, Robert E. Goodin and Kai Spiekermann argue that democracies are better than other forms of government at truth tracking. Building on Condorcet's jury theorem, they offer a nuanced defense of the epistemic advantages of democracy. However, these advantages are severely constrained under conditions of post-truth. Taking up the example of Brexit and Trump's election, both based on brazen lies, they qualify the truth-tracking potential of democracy: "The argument for the epistemic authority of the majority is conditional on favorable epistemic circumstances." Robert E. Goodin and Kai Spiekermann, *An Epistemic Theory of Democracy* (Oxford: Oxford University Press, 2019), 311. Although they attend to plural opinion, this qualification follows from a binary idea of truth (discussed below), which can be either confirmed or denied. As Camilo Ardila argues, "this crucial assumption seems to give a truth-confirming role to democratic institutions rather than a truth-constitutive one." In that case, however, it is unclear as to why we need democracy to reach answers to a political question that is in given in advance of democratic deliberation by the truth itself. Camilo Ardila, "Book Review: *An Epistemic Theory of Democracy* by Robert E. Goodin and Kai Spiekermann," *LSE Review of Books* blog, February 10, 2020, https://blogs.lse.ac.uk/lsereviewofbooks/2020/02/10/book-review-an-epistemic-theory-of-democracy-by-robert-e-goodin-and-kai-spiekermann/.

3. As discussed below, this "realist" idea of truth as suprahistorical is the other face of the "antirealist" idea of truth as "warranted assertability." Both concepts of truth presuppose the bivalence principle (i.e., a proposition corresponds to how things are, or it does not). Both assume that there must be something that grounds our knowledge practices beyond what we think, say, or do. For antirealists, there is nothing; truth is a purely epistemic concept that does not entitle us to speak of "reality." The procedures and mechanisms for ascertaining truth, however, share with the realist view the idea that the subject dependence of all world-directed thought makes it impossible to speak of truly objective knowledge. In the post-truth debate, the realist idea of truth generally takes priority over any antirealist purely epistemic notion.

4. Distinguishing a "game of truth" from a "regime of truth," Foucault addresses the objection that a "regime" is foreign to the received conception as truth, for it implies an exercise of power that can arise only where one is obliged to posit something as true even though one knows it is false or one is unsure whether it is true or false. Accordingly, the force of truth has no need of a regime but is intrinsic to the game, a formal structure that regulates truth claims and is fully distinct from the individuals who play it. For example, the scientific game of truth as "truth demonstration" is based on strict rules and procedures for ascertaining the truth of specific theories.

Truth is always there, but one needs to employ the correct method to find it, and this method is devised to minimize if not ideally eliminate the distorting effects of human subjectivity. I discuss Foucault's argument in chaps. 3 and 4.

5. "The truth is not the creator and holder of the rights it exercises over human beings of the obligations the latter have towards it" (Foucault, *GL*, 96).

6. Daniele Lorenzini, *The Force of Truth: Critique, Genealogy, and Truth-Telling in Michel Foucault* (Chicago: University of Chicago Press, 2023). My argument about the "force of truth" is deeply indebted to Lorenzini's brilliant reading of Foucault. I discuss his argument in the following chapters.

7. Lorenzini, 35.

8. I can admit that according to the criteria of the game, "x" is true, while refusing the consequences of that truth for my own life, among other options. Lorenzini provides clarifying examples: "Franz Fanon's discussion of medico-legal practices in Algeria during the 1950s" under a colonial regime of truth and "gender dysphoria" in contemporary society. I discuss the latter example in the conclusion. Lorenzini, 38–40.

9. Michel Foucault, *Subjectivity and Truth: Lectures at the Collège de France 1980–1981*, ed. Frédéric Gros, trans. Graham Burchell (New York: Picador, 2017), 12–13.

10. Foucault, 13.

11. Lorenzini, *Force of Truth*, 38.

12. Foucault, *Subjectivity and Truth*, 38.

13. I discuss Foucault's view of power in chap. 4.

14. Nancy Luxon deftly draws out what she calls "the psychodynamics of authoritarian political interactions." Although Foucault had dual degrees in psychology and philosophy, his readers have rarely seen him as engaged with psychoanalytic theory, save for criticizing it as a normalization technique. Luxon's novel move is to recognize in Foucault's image of the "truth-teller" a kindred spirit to Freud's "psychoanalyst": both were interested in bringing subjects to acknowledge the psychic investments that bound them to illegitimate forms of authority and in creating the space in which to refashion themselves as capable of self-governance. Although I do not focus on the psychoanalytic dimensions of truth-telling, I draw out the idea of "submitting" oneself to the practical consequences of the "it is true" as it bears on the practical problem of political rule. Nancy Luxon, *The Crisis of Authority: Trust and Truth-Telling in Freud and Foucault* (Cambridge, MA: Cambridge University Press, 2013).

15. Hannah Arendt, "Truth and Politics," in *Between Past and Future: Eight Exercises in Political Thought* (1954; New York: Penguin, 2006), 227–64, at 229 (hereafter cited as "TP").

16. Arendt, "TP," 254; Hannah Arendt, "On the Nature of Totalitarianism: An Essay in Understanding" in *Essays in Understanding 1930–1954*, ed. Jerome Kohn (New York: Harcourt Brace, 1994), 328–60, at 354.

17. Arendt, "On the Nature of Totalitarianism," 146–47.

18. Peg Birmingham, "A Lying World Order: Political Deception and the Threat of Totalitarianism," in *Thinking in Dark Times: Hannah Arendt on Ethics and Politics*, ed. Rogers Berkowitz, Jeffrey Katz, and Thomas Keenan (New York: Fordham University Press, 2007), 73–78, at 74. Cathy Caruth explains: "The violence of the modern lie consists in the absolute loss of the reality that it denies." Caruth, "Lying and History," in Berkowitz, Katz, and Keenan, *Thinking in Dark Times*, 79–92, at 83.

19. Hannah Arendt, "Approaches to the 'German Problem,'" in *Essays in Understanding*, 106–20, at 111. Discussed in Birmingham, "Lying World Order," 74.

20. Hannah Arendt, "Hannah Arendt: From an Interview," *New York Review of Books*, October 26, 1978, at 18. This is a selection from a 1974 interview with the French writer Roger Errera.

21. Anna-Karin Selberg observes: "What she [Arendt] sees totalitarianism replacing, and thereby destroying, is not a set of truths that constitute the transcendental ground of politics, but the space of appearances where truth, in a plurality of ways, introduces both a tension and an outside with respect to politics." Anna-Karin Selberg, *Politics and Truth: Heidegger, Arendt, and the Modern Political Lie* (Stockholm: Elanders, 2021), 234.

22. See Samir Okasha, "Verificationism, Realism, and Skepticism," *Erkenntnis* 55, no. 2 (2001): 371–85, at 375. John McDowell's argument for "disjunctivism" offers a critical refutation of the skeptic's claim that the mental states in the "good case" of veridical perception are indistinguishable from the "bad case" of hallucination or dreams. John McDowell, "Criteria, Defeasability and Knowledge," *Proceedings of the British Academy* 68 (1982): 455–79; see also John McDowell, *Perception as a Capacity for Knowledge* (Milwaukee, WI: Marquette University Press, 2001); John McDowell, "Knowledge and the Internal," *Philosophy and Phenomenological Research* 55 (1995): 877–93.

23. Descartes famously calls into question knowledge based on the testimony of the senses. In the *Meditations on First Philosophy*, he invokes three arguments: first, I could be imaging things to be the case; second, I could be hallucinating; and third, it is possible that "some evil genius not less powerful [than God] and deceitful, has employed his whole energies in deceiving me." Rene Descartes, *Philosophical Works of Descartes*, vol. 1, trans. Elizabeth S. Haldane and G. R. T. Ross (Cambridge: Cambridge University Press, 1967), 145, 146, 183.

24. The "brains in a vat" thought experiment is a modern rendition of Cartesian skepticism. See "The Brain in a Vat Argument," *Internet Encyclopedia of Philosophy*, accessed June 8, 2024, https://iep.utm.edu/brain-in-a-vat-argument/. For a critical refutation of the idea that we could all be "brains in a vat," see Hilary Putnam, "Brains in a Vat," in *Skepticism: a Contemporary Reader*, ed. K. DeRose and T. A. Warfield (Oxford: Oxford University Press, 1992), 27–42.

25. Okasha, "Verificationism, Realism, and Skepticism," 375, 373. There is another way in which our beliefs can be underdetermined by the evidence, which gives rise to a different form of skepticism: when they are underdetermined not by all *possible* data (Descartes) but by *actual* data. This form of skepticism is dramatized by Hume's critique of induction, the belief that we can infer from the observed to the unobserved, we can make predictions based on what we have already experienced, and the future will resemble the past. Here the skeptical claim concerns not underdetermination by all possible data but actual data. Verificationism has been attractive because it is assumed to deliver us from skepticism. Okasha argues that verificationism helps with skepticism of the Cartesian but not the Humean sort. Both types are relevant to post-truth politics. My argument addresses skepticism not as a philosophical problem of knowledge but, with Wittgenstein and Stanley Cavell, as a temptation that arises as a response to human finitude, a refusal of the ordinary, and with Arendt, as an expression of modern subjectivism and worldlessness.

26. First espoused by philosopher Nick Bostrom, simulation theory is the idea that our entire existence is a computer simulation. Outrageous as that seems, it has been the subject of popular films (*The Matrix*, *A Glitch in the Matrix*) watched

by millions of people, espoused by celebrities (e.g., Elon Musk), and believed by many Americans. Preston Greene, "Are We Living in a Computer Simulation? Let's Not Find Out," *New York Times*, August 10, 2019, https://www.nytimes.com/2019/08/10/opinion/sunday/are-we-living-in-a-computer-simulation-lets-not-find-out.html; Elon Musk interview on *The Joe Rogin Experience*, episode 1169, accessed June 8, 2024, https://www.youtube.com/watch?v=ycPr5-27vSI. For the latest film on simulation theory, Rodney Asher's *A Glitch in the Matrix*, see Charles Bramesco, "Are We All Living in the Matrix? Behind a Documentary on Simulation Theory," *Guardian*, February 4, 2021, https://www.theguardian.com/film/2021/feb/04/a-glitch-in-the-matrix-documentary-rodney-acher. For a discussion of Bostrom's ideas, see Anil Anathaswamy, "Do We Live in a Simulation? Chances Are about 50-50," *Scientific American*, October 13, 2020, https://www.scientificamerican.com/article/do-we-live-in-a-simulation-chances-are-about-50-50/; Nathan Hohipuha, "The Simulation Argument," *AbsurdBeing*, October 20, 2019, https://absurdbeingblog.wordpress.com/2019/10/20/the-simulation-argument/.

27. Conspiracy theories in the United States include 9/11 Truthers, QAnon, the Great Reset Theory, the Big Lie, PizzaGate, and UFOs. Such theories have become more normalized, widespread, and extreme. See Annie Kelly, "Even Conspiracy Theorists Are Alarmed by What They've Seen," *New York Times*, August 4, 2023, https://www.nytimes.com/2023/08/04/opinion/conspiracy-theory-qanon.html.

28. Okasha, "Verificationism," 375.

29. As noted previously, contemporary verificationism (i.e., the idea that the content of a statement is closely tied to what would count as evidence for its truth), as espoused by antirealist philosophers such as Michael Dummett, claims to hold this form of skepticism (underdetermination by *all* possible data) at bay. Okasha argues that it does not and that another form of skepticism, namely, underdetermination by *actual* data (e.g., Hume's problem of induction), is not touched by verificationism and the wholly epistemic conception of truth advocated by antirealists, i.e., truth as "justified or warranted assertion." Okasha, 371. Departing from these purely philosophical accounts of skepticism, I follow Arendt's lead and argue that both forms have significant *political* consequences only in contexts characterized by worldlessness, mass loneliness, disdain for opinion, and an attenuated public realm.

30. On the loss of common sense, see Hannah Arendt, *The Human Condition*, 2nd ed., introduction by Margaret Canovan (1958; Chicago: University of Chicago Press, 1998), 283. Arendt is clear: modern subjectivism and Cartesian doubt arose as a response not to debates in philosophy but to changes wrought by capitalism, science, and technology. For example, heliocentric theories predate Galileo's discovery, but it was the telescope that transformed our view of the world and inspired suspicion toward the senses (274).

31. Arendt, 275–76.
32. Arendt, 276.
33. Arendt, 282.
34. Arendt, 282.
35. Arendt, 284.
36. Arendt, 283.
37. Arendt, 282.
38. "What prepares men for totalitarian domination in the non-totalitarian world is the fact that loneliness, once a borderline experience usually suffered in certain

marginal social conditions like old age, has become an everyday experience of the evergrowing masses of our century." Arendt, *OT*, 478.

39. Guido Niccolò Barbi, "No Truth without Opinion: The Root of Post-Truth in a Binary Conception of Truth," unpublished paper, 2022, 13. See also Guido Niccolò Barbi, "Technocracy and Political Truth: An Inquiry into the Singularity of Political Judgment" (PhD diss., Katholische Universität Leuven, 2022).

40. James Conant, "Subjective Thought," in *Cahiers Parisiens / Parisian Notebooks*, vol. 3 (Paris: University of Chicago Center, 2007), 234–58, at 237. This idea of "subjective" as the opposite of "objective" is what we understand by one meaning of "subjective," namely subjectivism ("what is true *for* me"). This is to be distinguished from the Kantian idea of "subjective" as "subject dependent." The latter, argues Conant, refers to "a property whose very conception involves essential reference to how a thing which possesses the property affects the subject" (240).

41. Conant, 241.

42. Conant, 241–42. For a similar critique, see Alice Crary, *Beyond Moral Judgment* (Cambridge, MA: Harvard University Press, 2007), esp. 15–19. I discuss Crary below.

43. Hannah Arendt, "Philosophy and Politics," *Social Research* 57, no. 1 (1990): 73–103, at 80 (hereafter cited as "PP").

44. Foucault, *Subjectivity and Truth*, 221.

45. Foucault, 222.

46. Lorenzini, *Force of Truth*, 6.

47. Lorenzini, 7.

48. Lorenzini, 6.

49. "In short, any analysis that refers 'the game of truth' to reality by saying: 'The game of truth is explained because the real is such' is, according to Foucault, 'absolutely untenable and insufficient,' because 'reality will never account of that particular, singular, and improbable reality of the game of truth in reality.'" Lorenzini, 7. See also Sergei Prozorov, "Why Is There Truth? Foucault in the Age of Post-Truth Politics," *Constellations* 26 (2019): 18–30, esp. 19–21. I discuss this distinction between truth and reality in chap. 3.

50. Bradford Vivian, "On the Erosion of Democracy by Truth," *Philosophy and Rhetoric* 51, no. 4 (2018): 416–40, at 419.

51. Michel Foucault, *Discourse and Truth and Parrhesia*, ed. Henri-Paul Fruchaud and Daniele Lorenzini (Chicago: University of Chicago Press, 2019), 114 (hereafter cited as *DT*).

52. Jacques Rancière makes a similar this point. "At the people's assembly, any mere shoemaker or smithie can get up and have his say on how to steer the ships and how to build the fortifications and, more to the point, on the just and unjust way to use these for the common good. The problem is not the *always more* but the *anyone at all*, the sudden revelation of the ultimate *anarchy* on which any hierarchy rests." Jacques Rancière, *Disagreement: Politics and Philosophy* (Minneapolis: University of Minnesota Press, 1999), 16.

53. As we will see in chap. 3, this new form of parrhesia has as its concern not politics as such but "the complex relationship between truth and the self" (Foucault, *DT*, 157).

54. In Foucault's telling, this new philosophical parrhesia involves the "care" of the self (Foucault, *DT*, 156). I argue in chap. 3 that Foucault's account of the truth-teller does not turn away from politics but reveals the dangers of such a turn, while

also remaining true to the truth-teller's own interest in the ethical reformulation of parrhesia.

55. Michel Foucault, "The Concern for Truth," in *Politics, Philosophy, Culture: Interviews and Other Writings 1977–1984*, trans. Alan Sheridan et al., ed. Lawrence D. Kritzman (New York: Routledge, 1990), 255–67, at 267.

56. The difference between what we take to be epistemically valid, on the one hand, and its political significance, on the other, is exemplified in my reading of the Downing Street memo (which related the secret meeting between the Bush administration and Tony Blair's government in the lead-up to the Iraq War). The American press first ignored and then later dismissed the memo as a set of facts that everyone already knew—old news. Linda M. G. Zerilli, *A Democratic Theory of Judgment* (Chicago: University of Chicago Press, 2016), chap. 4. I return to this example in chap. 3 of the present work.

57. María Pía Méndez writes: "Roughly, epistocracy amounts to distributing political power in accordance with each citizen's competence for political decision-making.... The problem, epistocrats hold, is that most voters in democracies are *incompetent* to vote," let alone to have any meaningful say in public policy. Mendez contests this claim, arguing that restricting the electorate would create an information gap between the lay citizen and elites. María Pía Méndez, "An Epistemic Problem for Epistocracy," *Social Epistemology* 36, no. 2 (2022): 153–66, at 153, https://doi.org/10.1080/02691728.2021.1992531. For a defense of epistocracy, see Jason Brennan, *Against Democracy* (Princeton, NJ: Princeton University Press, 2017); Jason Brennan, "The Right to a Competent Electorate," *Philosophical Quarterly* 61, no. 245 (2011): 700–724; Kristoffer Ahlstrom-Vij, "Why Deliberative Democracy Is (Still) Untenable," *Public Affairs Quarterly* 26, no. 3 (2012): 1–12; Bryan Caplan, *The Myth of the Rational Voter* (Princeton, NJ: Princeton University Press, 2007). Caplan argues that voters' behavior reflects deeply biased beliefs and ignorance about basic economic concepts. See also Anne Jeffrey, "Limited Epistocracy and Political Inclusion," *Episteme* 15, no. 4 (December 2018): 1–21, https://doi.org/10.1017/epi.2017.8. According to Jeffrey, "limited epistocracies" avoid the usual objection that they violate political exclusion "if specialized institutions are confined to issuing directives that give citizens multiple actionable options."

Epistemic democrats, on the other hand, do not argue for the superiority of a certain political class. Their conception of politics disputes a purely proceduralist approach (e.g., John Rawls's "political liberalism") that brackets the question of truth. Hélène Landemore and David Estlund explain: "By 'correct or right decision' here, or 'the truth', can be meant an array of things, from objective truth of the matter (about facts or morality) to a more intersubjective, culturally dependent, and temporary construct (about more socially constructed facts or moral questions). What epistemic democrats emphasize ... is merely the Habermasian (and commonsensical enough) point that we wouldn't be exchanging reasons in the first place if we did not believe that there was something to figure out, whether we call this something the truth, the right, or the correct, just or socially useful answer." David Estlund and Hélène Landemore, "The Epistemic Value of Democratic Deliberation," in *The Oxford Handbook of Deliberative Democracy*, ed. André Bächtiger, John Dryzek, Jane J. Mansbridge, and Mark Warren (Oxford: Oxford University Press, 2018), 113–31, at 113. See also Joshua Cohen's foundational argument, "An Epistemic Conception of Democracy," *Ethics* 97:6–25. I agree that the question of truth cannot be bracketed in the way

Rawls assumed and Habermas contested. However, their idea of public deliberation is rooted in the binary conception of truth questioned in this book. Although Landemore rightly disputes the claim, dear to epistocrats, that there are reliable measures for linking political competence directly to levels of knowledge, she accepts the basic criterion of cognitive competence that animates the entire epistocratic debate: the ability to track truth. Presupposing what I argue to be the impossible distinction between the factual basis of judgment and normative evaluation, epistemic democrats take cognitive competence to be essential to the formation of a legitimate opinion, where informed opinion tracks truth. Consequently, it is hard to see how they can avoid the conclusion reached by Walter Lippmann in his debate with John Dewey, namely, that ordinary citizens will never demonstrate the level of such competence to justify their role in making the relevant decisions in public affairs. Dewey thought they could but eventually abandoned that argument and supplemented the "great society" with the "great community," which avoids an epistemic division of labor between citizens and experts. John Dewey, *The Public and Its Problems*, ed. Melvin Rogers (University Park: Pennsylvania State University Press, 2012), 141. Habermas himself recognizes the danger to citizen participation but nevertheless ends up conceding too much to cognitive competence. Opinion remains tethered to unwarranted cognitivism that leaves citizens and the process of deliberation hostage to the demands of binary truth. In my reading, this is precisely the compelling force of truth that worried Arendt. Her response is to reject the binary conception of truth and pursue the idea that there is no truth without opinion. I discuss these issues in chaps. 3 and 4 and return to them in the conclusion.

58. The debate between John Dewey and Walter Lippmann followed on the publication of the latter's *Public Opinion* (1922) and *The Phantom Public* (1925). Reviewing both books for the *New Republic*, Dewey advocated democratic collective problem-solving to counter Lipmann's claim that public opinion was unreasonable and democratic citizens incompetent. John Dewey, "Practical Democracy: Review of Walter Lippmann's *The Phantom Public*," in Dewey, *The Later Works, 1925–1953*, vol. 2, *1925–1927* (Carbondale: Southern Illinois University Press, 1984), 213–20. Guido Niccolò Barbi argues: "If one takes Lippmann's critique seriously, then one must realize that by accepting the premise that cognitive competence and instrumental rationality are unavailable to the public at large, but are necessary for democratic decision-making, the door is opened to the possibility of curtailing the public sphere in favor of the administrative one," favoring technocrats over citizens, truth over opinion. Barbi, "Technocracy and Political Truth," 138.

59. Michel Foucault, *The Government of Self and Others: Lectures at the Collège de France, 1982–1983*, ed. Frédéric Gros, trans. Graham Burchell (New York: Picador, 2011), 155 (hereafter cited as *GS*).

60. In chap. 5, I distinguish "realistic" from "realist" and extend but also depart from the idea of realism in existing debates over realism in contemporary philosophy and political theory. My concern is less with the realist criticism of politics as a form of "applied ethics," an "instrument for the application and realization of some antecedent moral values, principles, or ideals," as Matt Sleat puts it. Matt Sleat, "Introduction: Politics Recovered—on the Revival of Realism in Contemporary Political Theory," in *Politics Recovered: Realist Thought in Theory and Practice*, ed. Sleat (New York: Columbia University Press, 2018), 1–25, at 3. For Sleat, "it is misleading to think that realism is set against normative theorizing per se but rather [it] is critical of a particular way

of doing normative 'political' theory that, it turns out, is actually deeply unpolitical. Realism seeks a way of thinking normatively about politics that is suitably sensitive to the conditions and features of the political sphere" (8). Such normative thinking will turn on what those distinctive conditions of politics are. I also do not address the debate in international relations, be it the work of classical realists such as Hans Morgenthau and E. H. Carr or of contemporary structural realists such as Kenneth Waltz and John Mearsheimer. For an excellent account of the connections between classical realists and realist political theorists, see Alison McQueen, "The Case for Kinship: Classical Realism and Political Realism," in Sleat, *Politics Recovered*, 243–69.

61. Cora Diamond, *The Realistic Spirit: Wittgenstein, Philosophy, and the Mind* (Cambridge, MA: MIT Press, 1995). By "ordinary language philosophy" I follow Toril Moi's definition of it as "the philosophical tradition after Ludwig Wittgenstein, J. L. Austin, as constituted and extended by Stanley Cavell, specifically through his reading of Wittgenstein's *Philosophical Investigations*." Toril Moi, *Revolution of the Ordinary: Literary Studies after Wittgenstein, Austin, and Cavell* (Chicago: University of Chicago Press, 2017), 1.

62. Cora Diamond, "Realism and the Realistic Spirit," in *The Realistic Spirit: Wittgenstein, Philosophy, and the Mind* (Cambridge, MA: MIT Press, 1995), chapter 1, 39–72, at 39. See Ludwig Wittgenstein, *Remarks on the Foundations of Mathematics*, ed. G. H. von Wright, R. Rhees, and G. E. M. Anscombe (Oxford: Oxford University Press, 1978), 325. Diamond addresses herself to an enigmatic remark by Wittgenstein to Frank Ramsey, who defended empiricism against realism: "*Not empiricism and yet realism in philosophy, that is the hardest thing.*" Diamond, "Realism and the Realistic Spirit," 39. The problem with Ramsey's empiricism, as with all empiricism, writes Diamond, is that he "takes us to understand, or to be capable of understanding, *more* than we could in the ordinary sense explain" (65). Jettisoning an idea of the real as the cause of our experience and independent of it, observes Craig Taylor parsing Diamond, empiricists like Ramsey assume "that there must still be some underlining regularity—for Ramsey the known psychological laws of our inductive reasoning—that leads us to accept a causal generalization if we are to make useful judgments about particulars." Craig Taylor, "Diamond on Realism in Moral Philosophy," in *Morality in a Realistic Spirit: Essays for Cora Diamond* (New York: Routledge, 2020), 242–52, at 244. Following Wittgenstein, Diamond rejects the idea that sound judgment and claims to truth must be underwritten by features of reality that transcend any responses or reactions on the part of human beings engaged in rule-governed practices. "As Wittgenstein told Ramsey: "You do not yourself understand any more of the rule than you can explain" (Wittgenstein 1978 [*Remarks on the Foundations of Mathematics*, ed. G. H. von Wright, R. Rhees, and G. E. M. Anscombe], 325)." The claim to regularities of rule-following that transcend specific human practices shape not only realism but modern antirealism and verificationism. They also play a prominent role in the post-truth debate.

63. The realistic spirit of Diamond's Wittgenstein fits uneasily in the received literature, which, since the 1970s, reads his questioning of metaphysical realism as advancing a positive theory of antirealism. Drawing on Wittgenstein's account of "meaning as use," Michael Dummett spearheaded this interpretation by reformulating the standard contrast between realism and antirealism as a debate about the existence of distinct categories of *entities* into one about opposed theories of *meaning*. Dummett associated (metaphysical) realism with the claim that truth is a radically nonepistemic notion without connection to justification or warranted assertion. For

the realist, truth exists independently of our ability to recognize it: there can, in principle, be "evidence transcendent" or "investigation-independent" truth conditions. Contrasting the realist with the antirealist view that he—and later, others—ascribed to Wittgenstein, Dummett argued that meaning should be explained in terms of not truth conditions but verification conditions, which cannot transcend our ability to detect them. True is what can be verified. Michael Dummett, *Truth and Other Enigmas* (London: Duckworth, 1978), esp. 146. For an account of Dummett's foundational contribution to the debate over realism, see Michael J. Loux, "Realism and Antirealism: Dummett's Challenge," in *The Oxford Handbook of Metaphysics*, ed. Dean W. Zimmerman and Michael J. Loux (Oxford: Oxford University Press, 2005), 633–64. For a discussion of Diamond's foundational intervention into this appropriation of Wittgenstein as antirealist and verificationist, see Alice Crary, "Introduction," in *Wittgenstein and the Moral Life: Essays in Honor of Cora Diamond*, ed. Alice Crary (Cambridge, MA: MIT Press, 2007), 1–26.

64. Cora Diamond, "What Does a Concept-Script Do?," in *Realistic Spirit*, chap. 4, 115–44, 142.

65. Diamond, 142. Among political philosophers, the antirealist idea that moral truth claims could be considered arbitrary led Jürgen Habermas to radically alter his position. In *Truth and Justification*, he moves away from his former antirealist idea of truth as warranted assertability to affirm that truth is not an epistemic concept but an absolute property "that cannot be lost." Truth transcends every context of justification, including ideal ones. Habermas endorses a suprahistorical conception of truth, which is wholly external to situated games and regimes of truth. Jürgen Habermas, *Truth and Justification*, trans. Barbara Fultner (1999; New York: Polity, 2003), 250. Steven Levine argues that Habermas's departure from truth as what can be rationally warranted is rooted in his ongoing fear of contextualism, the indexing of what is true, right, and valuable to specific forms of life. Habermas's concern to defend the universality of moral claims, argues Levine, leads him to betray the pragmatism of his pragmatic theory of truth by denying that our background beliefs have anything to contribute to "moral rightness." Steven Levine, "Truth and Moral Validity: On Habermas's Domesticated Pragmatism," *Constellations* 18, no. 2 (2011): 244–59. I discuss Habermas's idea of truth and Levine's critique in *A Democratic Theory of Judgment*, 132–35.

66. Diamond, "What Does a Concept-Script Do?," 142–43.

67. In the realist truth-conditional account of meaning, every statement is either true or false, and this principle of bivalence holds regardless of the speaker's ability to verify the truth (or falsity) of what she says. There could be truths about the world that we will never know, and what is true (or false) has nothing to do with us but with how things objectively are. In this truth-conditional account of meaning, truth is an epistemically unconstrained notion. The antirealist claims that meaning must be explained in terms of verification conditions, which can never transcend our ability to detect them. Defending nonmetaphysical realism, John McDowell argues that a theory of meaning in terms of verification-transcendent truth conditions could do without bivalence if it were to employ an intuitionistic proof theory in the derivation of T-sentences. John McDowell, "Truth Conditions, Bivalence, and Verificationism," in *Truth and Meaning: Essays in Semantics*, ed. Garreth Evans and John McDowell (Oxford: Oxford University Press, 1976), 42–67.

68. Diamond, "Introduction II: Wittgenstein and Metaphysics," in *Realistic Spirit*, 13–38, at 20. This reading holds true for all of Wittgenstein's writings, including the

Tractatus, typically read as containing the metaphysical account of reality he would later reject.

69. Diamond, "Realism and the Realistic Spirit," 45.

70. Diamond, 69.

71. Diamond, "What Does a Concept-Script Do?," 143. For Diamond, this antimetaphysical position toward reality is likewise present in the *Tractatus*.

> What I am suggesting is that the criticism of the *Tractatus* may be viewed as a criticism of the *laying down of philosophical requirements*. . . .
>
> The laying down of philosophical requirements, the characteristic activity of the metaphysical spirit, may be contrasted with looking at the use, looking at what we do. . . . The philosophical theory lays down, without looking, what must be present in following a rule, while Wittgenstein's talk of what is possible is entirely different. Imagine such-and-such a change, he will say; and with the face of the activity thus altered, do you still want to call this following a rule? The important thing then is not what answer you give, but your willingness to look, i.e., your not laying down general philosophical conditions. (Diamond, "Introduction II: Wittgenstein and Metaphysics," 20–21)

For Diamond, this includes Wittgenstein's so-called requirements for something to count as the meaningful use of words: e.g., that language is not private but public, that agreement in judgment must be presupposed, etc. It extends as well to the antirealist demand for verification, which antirealists like Dummett claim to find in Wittgenstein's critique of metaphysics.

72. See Crary, "Introduction," 12.

73. Conant, "Subjective Thought," 250.

74. "A *picture* held us captive. And we could not get outside it, for it lay in our language and language seemed to repeat it to us inexorably." Ludwig Wittgenstein, *Philosophical Investigations*, 2nd ed., trans. G. E. M. Anscombe (1953; Malden, MA: Blackwell, 1977), §115 (hereafter cited as *PI*, with page nos. unless section nos. are specified).

75. John G. Gunnell, *Conventional Realism and Political Inquiry: Channeling Wittgenstein* (Chicago: University of Chicago Press, 2020), 3. Gunnell argues that the search for criteria of truth and objectivity continues to define the landscape of social science. His book brilliantly exposes "the imprint of realism and mentalism" in a wide array of fields, including international relations, philosophy of science, and political theory. In his view, social science, including political theory, has indentured itself to philosophy in the search for an "authoritative external philosophical basis for judging the validity of claims about what is real and true" (3). He criticizes Cora Diamond for betraying what she claimed to be "the realistic spirit" and seeking what she called "responsibility to reality" on external philosophical grounds (163). I agree with Gunnell's critique of Diamond. Here, I want only to take up and extend her general idea of "the realistic spirit" to the debate about post-truth and the "difficulty of reality." I discuss Gunnell's critique of Diamond in "What on Earth Is a 'Form of Life'?," in *Democratic Theory of Judgment*, 208–38, at 223–27.

76. Crary, *Beyond Moral Judgment*, 20, 21.

77. Crary, 18–19. The irreducibility of human affective propensities in claims to objectivity and truth makes all knowledge subject dependent, corrigible, and worldgiving, not merely subjective. All knowledge is created through what James Conant

calls "an internal relation between objective and subjective moments in a perceptual encounter between a perceiving subject and the objects of his [or her] perception." Quoted and discussed in Zerilli, *Democratic Theory of Judgment*, 5.

78. Cora Diamond, "The Difficulty of Reality, and the Difficulty of Philosophy," *Partial Answers: Journal of Literature and the History of Ideas* 1, no. 2 (June 2023): 10–26, at 2–3.

79. Diamond, 11.

80. Stanley Cavell, *The Claim of Reason: Wittgenstein, Skepticism, Morality, and Tragedy* (Oxford: Oxford University Press, 1982), esp. part 4.

81. Cavell, 12.

82. Diamond, "Difficulty of Reality," 20.

83. Diamond, 14.

84. Diamond, "Riddles and Anselm's Riddle," in *Realistic Spirit*, chap. 10, 267–90, at 279–80. Diamond considers here Descartes's *Meditations* III proof.

85. Deborah Nelson, *Tough Enough: Arbus, Arendt, Didion, McCarthy, Sontag, Weil* (Chicago: University of Chicago Press, 2017), 48.

86. Crary, *Beyond Moral Judgment*, 20.

87. See Michael Loux, "Realism and Anti-realism," 656. My point here is not to affirm the idea that skepticism lurks in every corner because of the underdetermination of the data, as someone writing wholly within the philosophical debate on skepticism understood as a problem of knowledge might. The skepticism that concerns me is the political problem of the erosion of the common world in which plural perspectives on reality can be exchanged.

88. By "picture," Wittgenstein does not mean to suggest that our view is necessarily distorted. We should look to see what kind of work a picture is doing in any particular case. I discuss the critical role of pictures in our lives with words in chap. 6.

89. Nancy Bauer, *How to Do Things with Pornography* (Cambridge, MA: Harvard University Press, 2015), 28–29, 31.

90. Hanna Fenichel Pitkin, *Wittgenstein and Justice: On the Significance of Ludwig Wittgenstein for Social and Political Thought* (1972; Berkeley: University of California Press, 1993), 1.

91. Moi, *Revolution of the Ordinary*, 6.

92. Michel Foucault, "The Analytic Philosophy of Politics" (1978), trans. Giovanni Mascaretti, *Foucault Studies* 24 (2018): 188–200, at 192. See also Michel Foucault, *Dits et écrits*, vol. 3 (Paris: Éditions Gallimard, 1994), 540–41. Sandra Laugier, Arnold Davidson, Daniele Lorenzini, and David Owen are four philosophers who have made important connections between Foucault and ordinary language philosophy.

93. Foucault, "Analytic Philosophy of Politics" 192–93.

94. Foucault, 193; Michel Foucault, "Kant on Enlightenment and Revolution," trans. C. Gordon, *Economy and Society* 15, no. 1 (February 1986): 88–96, at 96.

95. David Owen, "Criticism and Captivity: On Genealogy and Critical Theory," *European Journal of Philosophy* 10, no. 2 (August 2002): 216–30, 217. I discuss Owen's argument in chap. 6.

Chapter One

1. In the text and notes, I cite the critical edition of the writings of Hannah Arendt but give page references for both the critical edition and the published edition of Arendt's text. The texts of these respective editions are not identical. The first page

numbers of two sets of page numbers in references are for the critical edition: Hannah Arendt, "Thinking," in *The Life of the Mind*, part 1, Complete Works, Critical Edition 14.1, ed. Wout Cornellissen, Thomas Bartscherer, and Anne Eusterschulte (Göttingen: Wallstein Verlag, 2024), 13–200, https://hannah-arendt-edition.net/home?lang=en (the chapter epigraph is from p. 30 of this version); and the second page numbers are for the published edition, in this case, Hannah Arendt, *The Life of the Mind*, ed. Mary McCarthy (New York: Harvest, 1978) (the chapter epigraph will be found on p. 23 of this version).

2. Ronald Beiner, "Interpretive Essay," in Hannah Arendt, *Lectures on Kant's Political Philosophy*, ed. Ronald Beiner (Chicago: Chicago University Press, 1989), esp. 92.

3. Linda M. G. Zerilli, *A Democratic Theory of Judgment* (Chicago: University of Chicago Press, 2016).

4. Arendt explains: "What interested me in the Vita Activa was that this notion of complete quietness in contemplating was so overwhelming that compared with this stillness all other differences between the various activities in the Vita Activa disappeared. Compared to this quiet, it was no longer important whether you labored and tilled the soil, or worked and produced use-objects, or acted together with others in certain enterprises" ("Thinking," 18–19; 7).

5. Arendt, *Lectures on Kant's Political Philosophy*, 28.

6. Arendt, *OT*, viii; Deborah Nelson, *Tough Enough: Arbus, Arendt, Didion, McCarthy, Sontag, Weil* (Chicago: University of Chicago Press, 2017), 48. I discussed Nelson's reading in the introduction.

7. Thinking has intentional features; it is directed at or toward something in the world, even when that to which it is directed is absent. Whenever one thinks about something, one thinks in relation to a specific context and in a meaningful way. This is what Heidegger understood to be the intentional "as-structure" instantiated by both thoughts and perceptions. We do not encounter the world as a random collection of sights and sounds. What has been disclosed in understanding the world, writes Heidegger,

> has the structure of something as something. . . . What is disclosed in understanding, what is understood is always already accessible in such a way that in it its "as what" can be explicitly delineated. The "as" constitutes the structure of the explicitness of what is understood; it constitutes the interpretation. The circumspect, interpretive association with what is at hand in the surrounding world which "sees" this *as* a table, a door, a car, a bridge does not necessarily have to analyze what is circumspectly interpreted in a particular *statement*. Any simple predicative seeing of what is at hand is itself already understanding and interpreting. . . . The articulation of what is understood in the interpreting approach being guided by the "something as something" lies before a thematic statement about it. (Martin Heidegger, *Being and Time: A Translation of "Sein and Zeit,"* trans. Joan Stambaugh [1953; State University of New York Press, 1996], 139–40)

Arendt agrees that the intentional structure of our predicative experience of worldly objects does not differ significantly from how the content of that experience is thought or expressed in predicative judgments. The as-structure of predicative experience belongs to the *Vorurteile* or prejudices/prejudgments that orient us in the world. The problem arises when predicative ways of grasping the world block our ability to recognize what is new (the shock of reality), what does not already have an "as-structure" but elicits critical reflective judgment (i.e., judgment without the mediation of a concept). At that point, the as-structure of prepredicative experience fails to make sense of lived experience and transforms into the rigid concepts that characterized Eichmann's inability to think.

8. Kant discovers "the 'scandal of reason,'" writes Arendt, "that is, the fact that our mind is not capable of certain and verifiable knowledge with regard to matters and questions which it nevertheless cannot help thinking about, . . . [such as] what we now often call the 'ultimate questions' of God, freedom and immortality" ("Thinking," 25; 14). What he called "'the urgent need' of reason is different from and 'more than mere quest and desire for knowledge.' Hence, the distinction of the two faculties, reason and intellect, coincides with a distinction between two altogether different mental activities, thinking and knowing, and two altogether different concerns, meaning and cognition" (25; 14).

9. Hannah Arendt, *Eichmann in Jerusalem: A Report on the Banality of Evil* (New York: Penguin, 1977), 279.

10. Cora Diamond, "Realism and the Realistic Spirit," in *The Realistic Spirit: Wittgenstein, Philosophy, and the Mind* (Cambridge, MA: MIT Press, 1995), chap. 1, 39–72, at 69.

11. Diamond, 50.

12. Moore writes: "I can prove now that . . . my two hands exist. How? By holding up my two hands, and saying, as I make a gesture with the right hand, 'Here is one hand,' and adding, as I make a certain gesture with the left, 'and here is another.' And if by doing this I have proved *ipso facto* the existence of external things, you will all see that I can do it in a number of other ways: there is no need to multiply examples." G. E. Moore, "Proof of an External World," *Selected Writings*, ed. Thomas Baldwin (Routledge: New York, 1993), 106–33, at 165–66. Wittgenstein responds: "If you do know that here is one hand, we'll grant you all the rest." Ludwig Wittgenstein, *Über Gewissheit / On Certainty*, ed. G. E. M. Anscombe and G. H. Wright, trans. Denis Paul and G. E. M. Anscombe (New York: Harper and Row, 1972), §1, and see also §§1–36 (hereafter cited as *OC*). I discuss Wittgenstein's response to Moore and the skeptic in Linda M. G. Zerilli, *Feminism and the Abyss of Freedom* (Chicago: University of Chicago Press, 2005), chap. 1. I return to the theme of certainty in chap. 6 and the conclusion.

13. I discussed Wittgenstein's idea of a picture in the introduction.

14. Arendt sees herself as having "clearly joined the ranks of those who for some time now attempt to dismantle metaphysics, and philosophy with all its categories as we have known them from their beginning in Greece until today." This is not an act of destructive will:

> Such dismantling is possible only on the assumption that the thread of tradition is broken and that we shall not be able to renew it. Historically speaking, what actually has broken down is the Roman trinity which united for thousands of years religion, authority, and tradition. As I see it, the loss of this trinity did not destroy the past; it only draws the consequences of this loss, which is a fact and as such no longer a part of the "history of ideas" but of our political history, the history of our world. What has been lost is the continuity of the past as it seemed to be handed down from generation to generation. . . . What you then are left with is still the past, but a *fragmented* past, which has lost its certainty of evaluation. ("Thinking," 193; 212)

15. Arendt clarifies what is at stake for "positivism" in losing the two-world theory.

All thinking in terms of two worlds implies that these two are inseparably connected with each other. Thus, all the elaborate modern arguments against positivism are anticipated by the unsurpassed simplicity of a little dialogue by Democritus between the mind, the organ for the supersensual, and the senses. Sense perceptions are illusions, he says, they change according to the conditions of our body; sweet, bitter, color and such exist only *nomō*, by convention among men, and not *physei*, according to true nature behind the appearances—thus speaks the mind. Whereupon the senses answer: "Ced mind! Do you overthrow us while you take from us your evidence [*pisteis*, everything you can trust]? Our overthrow will be your downfall." ("Thinking," 22; 11)

Likewise, in "Thinking and Moral Considerations," Arendt writes: "it is indeed true that once the suprasensual realm is discarded, its opposite, the world of appearances as understood for so many centuries, is also annihilated. The sensual, as still understood by the positivists, cannot survive the death of the supersensual." In the text and notes, I cite the forthcoming critical edition of the writings of Hannah Arendt but give page references for both the critical edition and the published edition of Arendt's text. These two editions are not identical. The first page reference is to the critical edition, and the second is to the published edition. Hannah Arendt, "Thinking and Moral Considerations," in *Life of the Mind*, 477; Hannah Arendt, "Thinking and Moral Considerations," in *Responsibility and Judgment*, ed. Jerome Kohn (New York: Schocken, 2003), 159–89, at 162.

16. James Conant, "Perspectivism, II," *Sats: Nordic Journal of Philosophy* 7, no. 1 (2006): 6–57, at 42. Conant brilliantly defends Nietzsche's "perspectivism" against claims of relativism, showing how Nietzsche retrieves the ordinary concept of perspective and appearances. I have discussed this ordinary idea of perspective in *A Democratic Theory of Judgment*, chap. 1.

17. Margaret Canovan, *Hannah Arendt: A Reinterpretation of Her Political Thought* (Cambridge, MA: Cambridge University Press, 1994), 253. Ronald Beiner also sees Arendt as returning to philosophy in her later work on Kant, which was the basis for the unwritten third volume of *The Life of the Mind*, namely, "Judging." See Ronald Beiner, "Hannah Arendt on Judging," in Arendt, *Lectures on Kant's Political Philosophy*, 89–156, esp. 89–92.

18. Hannah Arendt, "What Is Existenz Philosophy?," in *Sechs Essays: Die verborgene Tradition*, Complete Works, Critical Edition 3, ed. Barbara Hahn (Göttingen: Wallstein Verlag, 2019), 267–87, at 267; Hannah Arendt, "What Is Existential Philosophy?," in *Essays in Understanding, 1930–1954*, ed. Jerome Kohn (New York: Harcourt Brace, 1994), 163–87, at 164. In the text and notes, I cite the Wallstein Verlag critical edition of the writings of Hannah Arendt but give page references for both the critical edition and the published edition of Arendt's text. The first page reference is to the 2019 critical edition, and the second is to the 1994 edition. The texts of the two editions are not identical and at times vary significantly.

19. Arendt sees modern philosophy, including not only German idealism and Hegel but phenomenology (Husserl and Heidegger), as captive to the quest memorably formulated by Parmenides. In his great poem "The Way of Truth," Parmenides describes a path that guides the philosopher-thinker to the unity of thinking and Being "far away

from the wanderings of men." Parmenides, *The Way of Truth*, Fr. 1.27. For Heidegger, "In the beginning of Western thinking, the saying of Parmenides speaks to us for the first time of what is called thinking." Martin Heidegger, *What Is Called Thinking?*, trans. J. Glenn Gray (New York: Harper and Row 1968), 196.

20. Arendt, "What Is Existenz Philosophy?," 267, 269; 164, 165.

21. Arendt, 268; 165.

22. Arendt, 268; 165.

23. Arendt, 270; 166. Husserl's return to the unity of thinking and being, writes Arendt, "seeks to make us tranquil about a fact over which modern philosophy cannot become tranquil—that man is compelled to assent to a Being which he never created and to which he is essentially alien. With the transformation of alien Being into consciousness he seeks to make the world again human" (269; 166).

24. Arendt, 270; 167.

25. Conant, "Perspectivism, II," 42.

26. Arendt, "What Is Existenz Philosophy?," 273; 170. That unity "presupposed the pre-established coincidence of essence [the What] and existence [the That], that, namely, everything thinkable also exists and every existent, because it is knowable, must also be rational" (271; 168). However, Kant's demolition of the ancient unity "accomplished only half the job. . . . What he did not destroy, but implicitly held on to, was the concept . . . of Being as the given, to whose laws Man is in all cases subject" (273; 170).

27. Arendt, 271; 168.

28. "The only exception is an occasional remark by Aristotle in *On Interpretation* which, however, for Aristotle's later philosophy remained without significance" (Arendt, "Thinking," 61; 58).

29. The point is not that this choice is wholly free as if it were free-floating of any socially given context or world in which objects tend to be treated differently. Arendt works within the hermeneutical tradition for which, as Heidegger argued, the appearance of things is already meaningful; that is, we recognize what something is by what it means. And this meaning is not individual but social. Saying as much, however, does not equate to declaring meaning to be determined by context. It is what I do with an object of perception, my active reception of it, that lends any object (or event) specific meaning in a particular context.

30. Hannah Arendt, "Some Questions of Moral Philosophy," in *Responsibility and Judgment*, ed. Kohn, 49–146, at 94. "Thinking in its noncognitive, non-specialized sense as a natural need of human life . . . is not a prerogative of the few but an everpresent faculty of everybody; by the same token, inability to think is not the 'prerogative' of those many who lack brain power but the everpresent possibility for everybody—scientists, scholars, and other specialists in mental enterprises not excluded—to shun that intercourse with oneself whose possibility and importance Socrates first discovered." Arendt, "Thinking and Moral Considerations," 496; 187–88.

31. Immanuel Kant, "What Does It Mean to Orient Oneself in Thinking?," in *Religion and Rational Theology*, ed. Allen W. Wood, trans. George Di Giovanni (New York: Cambridge University Press, 1996), 1–18, at 16.

32. However important this two-in-one may be, Arendt is clear that, "looked upon from the standpoint of human plurality, it is like the last trace of company—even when being *one* by myself, I am or can become two—which becomes so very important only because we discover plurality where we would least expect it. But insofar as

being with others is concerned, it still must be regarded as a marginal phenomenon." "Some Questions of Moral Philosophy," 106. I discuss the difference with loneliness in chap. 4.

33. Jennifer Gaffney argues that Arendt's critique of Heidegger in *The Life of the Mind* is directed at his equation of meaning and truth. Gaffney takes up Richard Bernstein's criticism that because Arendt never specified what kind of thinking could prevent wrongdoing, she could not explain, though she condemned, Heidegger's Nazi past. Gaffney's answer to Bernstein points to the very different ways in which Arendt and Heidegger orient thinking to the world. "I argue that Arendt criticizes Heidegger not by focusing on whether his thinking is worldly or political enough; instead, she is concerned with the way in which he draws thinking into a dangerously submissive relation to the world by locating its end in the event of truth or disclosure." I agree with Gaffney that Heidegger's form of thinking fails to gain critical purchase on how things are. But I disagree that the problem lies in remaining in "proximate" relation to the things of the world. For Gaffney, Arendt's critical form of thinking is based on gaining distance from things, withdrawing wholly from appearances. In my reading, Socratic thinking remains proximate to what appears to me (dokei moi), bringing it into conversation with the way things appear to others. Arendt show that the feeling of withdrawal is subjectively real but a "delusion," rooted in the denial of the prior condition of an appearing world. Jennifer Gaffney, "Thinking, Meaning, and Truth: Arendt on Heidegger and the Possibility of Critique," *Constellations* 31, no. 1 (March 2024): 3–17, at 4, https://doi.org/10.1111/1467-8675.12647. See also Richard Bernstein, "Arendt on Thinking," in *Cambridge Companion to Hannah Arendt*, ed. Dana Villa (Cambridge, MA: Cambridge University Press, 2000), 277–92.

34. Ashley Biser connects Arendt's reflections on thinking to the problem of orientation that has concerned me here, though her focus is different. Like Gaffney, Biser responds to Richard Bernstein's critique of Arendt (discussed in the previous note) and defends the novelty of Arendt's conception of thinking. For Biser, Arendt builds certain "safeguards" into her account of thinking, which keep us from becoming disoriented and are missing in Heidegger's account. The key move, however, is Arendt's turn to representative thinking, which allows us to take our bearings in the world. I agree with Biser that this turn is crucial, but I argue that it has roots in the Socratic thinking that is for Arendt a model of critical thought. Ashley Biser, "Calibrating Our 'Inner Compass': Arendt on Thinking and the Dangers of Disorientation," *Political Theory* 42, no. 5 (2014): 519–42, esp. 533–37.

35. I am indebted to private correspondence with Patchen Markell for this point.

36. Valeria Pashkova and Mikhail Pashkov, "Truth and Truthfulness in Politics: Reading Hannah Arendt's Essay 'Socrates,'" *Philosophy Today* 62, no. 2 (Spring 2018): 447–70, at 449.

37. Arendt, "Thinking and Moral Considerations," 496; 188.

38. Speaking of the life of the mind (thinking, willing, and judging), Arendt writes: "And although this will never directly change reality—nothing indeed in our world is in clearer and more radical opposition to each other than thinking and doing—the principles according to which we act and the criteria according to which we judge and conduct our life depend ultimately on the life of our mind, that is, on the performance of such apparently profitless mental enterprises that are without results and do 'not endow us directly with the power to act' (Heidegger)" ("Thinking," 70–71; 71).

39. Arendt, "What Is Existenz Philosophy?," 270.

40. Arendt, "Thinking and Moral Considerations," 497; 189.

41. Cora Diamond, "The Difficulty of Reality, and the Difficulty of Philosophy," *Partial Answers: Journal of Literature and the History of Ideas* 1, no. 2 (June 2023): 10–26.

42. "Thinking, no doubt, plays an enormous role in every scientific enterprise, but it is the role of a means to an end; the end I determined by a decision about what is worthwhile knowing, and this decision itself cannot be scientific" (Arendt, "Thinking," 58; 54).

43. Hannah Arendt, "The Concept of History: Ancient and Modern," in *Between Past and Future: Eight Exercises in Political Thought*, ed. Jerome Kohn (1954; New York: Penguin, 2006), 41–90, at 54, 53, my emphasis.

44. "The questions . . . which thinking raises and which it is in the very nature of reason to raise, the questions of meaning, are all unanswerable by common sense and its refinement which we call science. The quest for meaning is 'meaningless' for common sense and common-sense reasoning because it is the function of this sixth sense to fit us into the world of appearances and to make us at home in the world given by our five senses: there we are and no questions asked" (Arendt, "Thinking," 62; 58–59).

45. Jennifer Gaffney argues that by contrast with Heidegger, Arendtian thinking can gain the critical purchase on reality that common sense lacks because it takes distance from that reality. My point, however, is that critique is enabled not by distance but by remaining attuned to the irreducible singularity of things in the world ("Thinking, Meaning, and Truth," 12).

46. Arendt, *Eichmann in Jerusalem*, 48–49.

47. Roger Berkowitz, "Did Eichmann Think? A Review of *Eichman before Jerusalem: The Unexamined Life of a Mass Murderer* by Bettina Stangneth," *Good Society* 23, no. 2 (2014): 193–205, at 203.

48. Berkowitz, 204.

49. Hannah Arendt, "At Table with Hitler," in *Essays in Understanding, 1930–1954*, ed. Jerome Kohn (New York: Harcourt Brace, 1994), 285–96, at 294.

Chapter Two

1. Michel Foucault, "What Is Critique?" (1978), in Michel Foucault, *What Is Critique?, and the Culture of the Self*, ed. Henri-Paul Fruchaud, Daniele Lorenzini, and Arnold Davidson, trans. Clare O'Farrell (Chicago: University of Chicago Press, 2024), 19–62, at 24 (hereafter cited as "WC" with page numbers).

2. Michel Foucault, "Kant on Enlightenment and Revolution," trans. C. Gordon, Economy and Society 15, no. 1 (February 1986): 88–96, at 96.

3. Judith Butler, "What Is Critique? An Essay on Foucault's Virtue," 1–14, at 3, http://eipcp.net/transversal/0806/butler/en.

4. John Rajchman, "Enlightenment Today: Introduction to *The Politics of Truth*," in Michel Foucault, *The Politics of Truth*, ed. Sylvère Lotringer, trans. Lysa Hochroth and Catherine Porter (Los Angeles: Semiotext[e], 2007), 9–27, at 19.

5. Rajchman, 21.

6. Rajchman, 21.

7. Rajchman, 19.

8. Rajchman, 23, 21.

9. Rajchman, 13.

10. Rudi Visker, Michael Foucault: *Genealogy as Critique*, trans. Chris Turner (New York: Verso, 1995), 103.
11. Butler, "What Is Critique?," 11.
12. Butler, 12.
13. Butler, 12.
14. Butler, 12.
15. Butler, 10.
16. Butler, 3.
17. Butler, 5.
18. Butler, 13, 6.
19. Butler, 12.
20. Butler, 1–2.
21. Butler, 2.
22. Hannah Arendt, "What Is Freedom?," in *Between Past and Future: Eight Exercises in Political Thought*, intro. Jermone Kohn (1954; New York: Penguin Books, 2006), 142–69, at 156.
23. Arendt, 159.
24. Arendt, 159.
25. Arendt, 159.
26. See James F. Depew, "Foucault among the Stoics: *Oikeiosis* and Counterconduct," *Foucault Studies* 21 (June 2016): 22–51; Brian Seitz, "Foucault and the Subject of Stoic Existence," *Human Studies* 35, no. 4 (Winter 2012): 539–54.
27. A different version of this lecture appeared as Michel Foucault, "Un cours inédit," *Magazine littéraire*, no. 207 (May 1984): 35–39, and was translated as Michel Foucault, "Kant on Enlightenment and Revolution," trans. C. Gordon, *Economy and Society* 15, no. 1 (February 1986): 88–96.
28. Foucault, "Kant on Enlightenment and Revolution," 95.
29. Foucault, 91.
30. Foucault, 91.
31. See also Foucault, "Kant on Enlightenment and Revolution," 93.
32. Foucault, "Kant on Enlightenment and Revolution," 93. See also Foucault, *GS*, 18.
33. Foucault, "Kant on Enlightenment and Revolution," 94.
34. Hannah Arendt, *Lectures on Kant's Political Philosophy*, ed. Ronald Beiner (Chicago: University of Chicago Press, 1989), 56. See also Foucault, *GS*, 19.
35. Arendt, *Lectures on Kant's Political Philosophy*, 61.
36. Arendt, 55.
37. Arendt, "Introduction into Politics," in *The Promise of Politics*, ed. Jerome Kohn (New York: Schocken, 2005), 133 (hereafter cited as "IP").
38. Arendt, *Lectures on Kant's Political Philosophy*, 55–56.
39. Arendt, 39.
40. Arendt and Foucault agree that the private use of reason obtains for Kant when man remains in his strictly social role and is (to cite Kant) a mere "a cog in a machine." See Arendt, *Lectures*, 39; Michel Foucault, "What Is Enlightenment?," in *Essential Works of Foucault*, vol. 1, *Ethics, Subjectivity, and Truth*, ed. Paul Rabinow (New York: New Press, 1977), 303–20, at 103.
41. Foucault, "What Is Enlightenment?," 308.

42. Foucault, 308, 312.

43. Foucault, 315.

44. Foucault, "Kant on Enlightenment and Revolution," 89.

45. Arendt, *Lectures*, 39.

46. Arendt, 43.

47. Arendt, 39–40.

48. Foucault, "What Is Enlightenment?," 307.

49. I discuss Arendt and Kant on public reason in *A Democratic Theory of Judgment* (Chicago: University of Chicago Press, 2016), chap. 1.

50. Foucault, "What Is Enlightenment?," 315, 316; Foucault, "Kant on Enlightenment and Revolution," 89.

51. Foucault, "What Is Enlightenment?," 316.

52. Reinhardt Koselleck, *Critique and Crisis: Enlightenment and the Pathogenesis of Modern Society* (Cambridge, MA: MIT Press, 1998), 11. Koselleck argues that the enlightenment idea of critique as the total rational power to put all into doubt begins from a place outside politics and develops in an increasingly utopian register. According to him, critique arose in the eighteenth century as an art of moral and cultural opposition to monarchy, but also to political society generally. "Politically powerless as a subject of his sovereign lord, the citizen conceived himself as moral, felt that the existing rule was overpowering, and condemned it proportionally as immoral since he could no longer perceive what is evident in the horizon of human finiteness" (11). Unable or unwilling to put forward practical alternatives to existing institutions, Enlightenment morality thinks it can "completely eliminate the political aporia" and comes to be wholly in the grip of an unrealistic and antipolitical conception of critique (11).

53. The moralization of critique and its utopian character go hand in hand, but their historical condition has been political exclusion. Koselleck argues that the Absolutist State banished morality to the private realm in its effort to restore political order in the wake of the destruction wrought by religious wars. But by excluding citizens from the official public realm, it also created the breeding ground for utopianism.

> Inevitably, citizens will come into conflict with a State that subordinates morality to politics, adopts a purely formal understanding of the political realm and thus reckons without developments peculiar to the emancipation of its subjects. For their goal will be to perfect themselves morally to an extent that will permit them to know, and let every man know himself, what is good and what is evil. Each one becomes a judge who knows, on grounds of his enlightenment, that he is authorized to try whatever heteronomous definitions contradict his moral autonomy. Once implemented by the State the separation of morality and politics hence turns against the State itself; it is forced into standing a moral trial for having achieved something, i.e., to have created a space in which it is possible (for the individual) to survive. (*Critique and Crisis*, 11)

Koselleck raises a problem that persists in contemporary liberal democratic society, namely, the tendency to exercise critique from a moral position that is both outside and hostile to politics and especially to the formal political realm.

54. Koselleck, 134–35. For a fascinating study of how this retreat led to the canon wars over the literary curriculum at the modern university, see John Guillory, *Cultural Capital: The Problem of Literary Canon Formation* (Chicago: University of Chicago Press, 1993).

55. Michel Foucault, *Psychiatric Power: Lectures at the Collège de France 1973–1974*, ed. Jacques Lagrange, trans. Graham Burchell (New York: Picador, 2006), 247. On this point, see Daniele Lorenzini, *The Force of Truth: Critique, Genealogy, and Truth-Telling in Michel Foucault* (Chicago: University of Chicago Press, 2023), 20. I discuss the scientific conception of truth in chap. 4.

56. Critical accounts of the politicization of the university, which have exploded in recent years, can be traced back to the acrimonious debate over multiculturalism in the 1980s, when the demand for fair representation in the curriculum on the part of women and racial and ethnic minorities was seen as the triumph of cultural identity and particularism over academic neutrality and universality. More recent accounts focus on the debate over free speech, microaggressions, rape culture, and so on. See Frank Furedi, *What's Happened to the University? A Sociological Exploration of Its Infantalisation* (New York: Routledge, 2016); Bradley Campbell, *The Rise of Victimhood Culture: Microaggressions, Safe-Spaces, and the New Culture Wars* (New York: Palgrave Macmillan, 2018); Laura Kipnis, *Unwanted Advances: Sexual Paranoia Comes to Campus* (New York: Harper, 2017).

Chapter Three

1. *Meet the Press*, interview with Chuck Todd, NBC, January 22, 2017, https://www.nbcnews.com/meet-the-press/meet-press-01-22-17-n710491. The chapter epigraph is from FactCheck.org: A Project of the Annenberg Policy Center, January 23, 2017, https://www.factcheck.org/2017/01/the-facts-on-crowd-size/.

2. Based on aerial photos taken by the National Park Service, the approximate numbers put Obama's inauguration at 1.8 million attendees and Trump's at roughly one-third of that, three hundred thousand to six hundred thousand.

3. David Leonhardt and Stuart A. Thompson, "Trump's Lies," *New York Times*, December 14, 2017, https://www.nytimes.com/interactive/2017/06/23/opinion/trumps-lies.html. For a list of Trump's lies in connection with his claim that 2020 presidential election of Joe Biden was fraudulent, see Linda Qiu, "Fact-checking the Breadth of Trump's Election Lies," *New York Times*, August 17, 2023, https://www.nytimes.com/2023/08/17/us/politics/trump-election-lies-fact-check.html?campaign_id=190&emc=edit_ufn_20230903&instance_id=101834&nl=from-the-times&regi_id=47071185&segment_id=143644&te=1&user_id=394fcc9fabdd41067c6de18ca4e9ef01. The *Washington Post* has kept a tally of his false or misleading claims while in office. See Glenn Kessler, Meg Kelly, Salvador Rizzo, and Michelle Yee Hee Lee, "In Four Years President Trump Made 30,573 False or Misleading Statements," updated January 20, 2021, *Washington Post*, https://www.washingtonpost.com/graphics/politics/trump-claims-database/?itid=lk_inline_manual_11.

4. Mary Dietz, "Lying as Politics in the Age of Trump: What Hannah Arendt Does, and Does Not, Anticipate under a Deeply Vicious Presidency," *Public Seminar: A Global Intellectual Commons*, October 23, 2018, http://www.publicseminar.org/2018/10/lying-as-politics-in-the-age-of-trump/.

5. Hannah Arendt, "On the Nature of Totalitarianism: An Essay in Understanding," in *Essays in Understanding 1930–1954*, ed. Jerome Kohn (New York: Harcourt Brace, 1994), 328–60, at 354.

6. Some Trump voters based their opinion on altered photos. "The photographer cropped out empty space 'where the crowd ended' for a new set of pictures requested by

Trump on the first morning of his presidency, after he was angered by images showing his audience was smaller than Barak Obama's in 2009." Spicer himself was involved in the "effort to obtain more favorable photographs." See John Swaine, "Trump Inauguration Crowd Photos Were Edited after He Intervened," *Guardian*, September 6, 2018, https://www.theguardian.com/world/2018/sep/06/donald-trump-inauguration-crowd-size-photos-edited. Furthermore, when asked which inauguration was larger based on looking at two Park Service (original and uncropped) photos, 41 percent of Trump voters exhibited confirmation bias, wrongly aligning Obama's inauguration with Trump's, certain that the latter's must have been bigger. Even when asked which photo shows more people, 15 percent of Trump voters said that the Trump inauguration photo did. Whether this is an example of so-called expressive responding (i.e., answering based not on what one sees but on political ideology) or a defective cognitive ability is of some debate. See Brian F. Schaffner and Samantha Luks, *Washington Post*, January 25, 2017, https://www.washingtonpost.com/news/monkey-cage/wp/2017/01/25/we-asked-people-which-inauguration-crowd-was-bigger-heres-what-they-said/.

7. Hannah Arendt, "Lying in Politics" (1972), in *Crises of the Republic* (New York: Harcourt Brace, 1969), 1–47, at 44 (hereafter cited as "LP").

8. The Pentagon Papers were excerpts of a secret report on classified documents commissioned by Secretary of Defense Robert S. McNamara and leaked to *The New York Times* by Daniel Ellsberg, an analyst on the study. As Clay Jenkinson explains:

> In 1967, Secretary McNamara instructed Ellsberg and 35 others to compile a comprehensive history of America's involvement in Vietnam. The final report ran to 47 volumes. Intended to be what McNamara called an "encyclopedic history of the Vietnam War," the report examined America's mission in Vietnam from 1945 to 1967. In essence, the report revealed more than two decades of mistakes, miscalculations, deception (including self-deception), systematic lying to Congress and the American people, fudged statistics, deliberately inflated death tolls, knowingly false assurances, and a conspiracy to cover up atrocities and war crimes. Among other things, the study revealed the ways in which the Kennedy administration, and to a certain degree President Kennedy himself, acquiesced in the overthrow and assassination of South Vietnamese President Ngo Dinh Diem in 1963. The secret report was never intended to be released to the public. McNamara later said (perhaps disingenuously) that it was meant to serve as a "cautionary tale" to prevent similar policy errors in future administrations.

Clay S. Jenkinson, "Daniel Ellsberg and the Greatest Leak of Secret Documents in American History," *Governing*, June 25, 2023, https://www.governing.com/context/daniel-ellsberg-and-the-greatest-leak-of-secret-documents-in-american-history. For a concise history of the papers and the extent of the lies, see Elizabeth Becker, "The Secrets and Lies of the Vietnam War, Exposed in One Epic Document," *New York Times*, June 9, 2021, https://www.nytimes.com/2021/06/09/us/pentagon-papers-vietnam-war.html.

9. Dietz, "Lying as Politics in the Age of Trump."

10. Cathy Caruth, "Lying and History," in *Thinking in Dark Times: Hannah Arendt on Ethics and Politics*, ed. Rogers Berkowitz, Jeffrey Katz, and Thomas Keenan (New York: Fordham University Press, 2007), 79–92, at 83.

11. Arendt, *Crises of the Republic*, 45.

12. Beginning in 1965, Gallup Poll asked the following question: "In view of the developments since we entered the fighting in Vietnam, do you think the United States made a mistake sending troops to fight in Vietnam?" In 1971, 61 percent thought it was a mistake, 28 percent thought it was not a mistake, and 11 percent had no opinion. "61% Assert Entry into the War Was US 'Mistake,'" *New York Times*, June 6, 1971, https://www.nytimes.com/1971/06/06/archives/61-in-poll-assert-entry-into-the-war-was-us-mistake.html.

13. The Pentagon Papers revealed that the United States had bombed Cambodia and Laos and misled the American public and Congress in secretly expanding the war. It revealed that the Truman, Eisenhower, Kennedy, and Johnson administrations had all intentionally kept their war operations confidential and misled the public.

14. In the Downing Street memos, the head of the British Secret Intelligence Service was quoted as saying that the George W. Bush administration wanted to depose Saddam Hussein "thorough military action, justified by the conjunction of terrorism and weapons of mass destruction. But the intelligence and facts were being fixed around the policy." I discuss the memos in Linda M. G. Zerilli, "Objectivity, Judgment, and Freedom: Rereading Hannah Arendt's 'Truth and Politics,'" in *A Democratic Theory of Judgment* (Chicago: University of Chicago Press, 2016), 117–42.

15. For a brilliant critique of this high-level mendacity and the indifference of the American media, politicians, and citizens, see Mark Danner, *The Secret Way to War* (New York: New York Review of Books, 2006). I discuss Danner's argument in *Democratic Theory of Judgment*, 138–40.

16. Marieke Borren, "Amor Mundi: Hannah Arendt's Political Phenomenology of World" (PhD thesis, University of Amsterdam, 2010), 47. Borren offers a persuasive account of Arendt's hermeneutic-phenomenological understanding of truth.

17. What Bernard Williams called "the absolute conception of reality" or the "world" distinguishes between the objective and the subjective, the world as it is independent of our experience and the world as it seems to us. Adherents to the absolute conception draw a sharp distinction between belief states with cognitive content, which can disclose the world as it is, and noncognitive affective states, which cannot. Bernard Williams, *Descartes: The Project of Pure Inquiry*, rev. ed. (New York: Routledge, 2025), 49–50. For a discussion of this distinction, see Zerilli, *Democratic Theory of Judgment*, 11.

18. Borren, "Amor Mundi," 48.

19. Quoted in Mark Wrathall, *Heidegger and Unconcealment: Truth, Language, and History* (Cambridge: Cambridge University Press, 2011), 18.

20. Wrathall, 19.

21. Wrathall, 19.

22. Wrathall, 19.

23. Dietz, "Lying as Politics."

24. See Zerilli, *Democratic Theory of Judgment*, chap. 4.

25. I discuss the relation of truth to opinion in chap. 1 and in Zerilli, *Democratic Theory of Judgment*, chap. 4.

26. Hannah Arendt, "Thinking," in *The Life of the Mind*, part 1, Complete Works, Critical Edition 14.1, ed. Wout Cornellissen, Thomas Bartscherer, and Anne Eusterschulte (Göttingen: Wallstein Verlag, 2024), 13–200, at 29; Hannah Arendt, "Thinking," in *The Life of the Mind*, vol. 1, 2-vol. ed., ed. Mary McCarthy (New York: Harvest, 1978), 21.

The two page numbers in citations refer to the former version and the latter version, respectively.

27. Hannah Arendt, *The Human Condition* (Chicago: University of Chicago Press, 1958), 190.

28. Arendt, 190.

29. Caruth, "Lying and History," 82.

30. Caruth, 82.

31. Borrowing "Neil Sheehan's felicitous phrase," Arendt distinguishes the "professional 'problem-solvers'" and their "art of lying" from that of the "image-makers," though the two were intertwined in the fiasco that was Vietnam ("LP," 9). The image makers were the "managers in governments who learned their trade from the inventiveness of Madison Avenue" (8). Their job was to create the images to sell the war. The "problem-solvers" (including Ellsberg) were "drawn into government from the universities and the various think tanks" (8, 10). Caruth summarizes the distinction: "If the public relations managers *make images to sell the war*, the problem solvers *make war to sustain the image*." This is the image of "omnipotence." Caruth, "Lying and History," 85.

32. Caruth, "Lying and History," 86.

33. Hannah Arendt, "Approaches to the 'German Problem,'" in *Essays in Understanding*, 106–20, at 111.

34. Furthermore, though both the truth-teller and the liar are appropriately characterized as acting in the context of pervasive lying, "the contingent character of facts, which could always have been otherwise," insists Arendt, invariably gives the liar the advantage in the game of truth: "Since the liar is free to fashion his 'facts' to fit the profit and pleasure, or even the mere expectations, of his audience, the chances are that he will be more persuasive than the truth-teller. Indeed, he will usually have plausibility on his side; his exposition will sound more logical, as it were, since the element of unexpectedness—one of the outstanding characteristics of all events—has mercifully disappeared" ("TP," 247).

35. But neither is the problem of alternative facts one of relativism, where all perspectives are equal, and no one view is any better than any other in its ability to reveal how things stand in the world. This would assume that there is a shared object about which to have different views, and what is missing is only the means of adjudication: Which view is correct? If that were the situation in which we now find ourselves, then checking the facts would bring these otherwise competing perspectives into relation with each other and a judgment could be made. Ordinary language can guide us here. We speak not of alternative *perspectives* but of alternative *facts*—this difference in phrasing should caution us against formulating our problem, as do many commentators on Trumpism, as a familiar one of relativism. Alternative facts are not incommensurable perspectives on a shared object; they remain in the absence of such an object and, thus, in the absence of the common world in which the object can appear as shared.

36. The history of the inauguration photos is discussed above.

37. Contrasting himself to "historians of ideas . . . interested in ideologies," Foucault describes as his primary concern "to outline a genealogy of what we could call the critical attitude in our society. Most of the time, the historians of ideas are interested in the problem of 'ideologies,' or in the problem of relationships between society and representation, in order to decipher how far social structures or social processes help or prevent the discovery of truth. I think there is another problem about the relationships between truth and society. This is not the problem of society's relation

to truth through ideologies, it is the problem of what we could call the truth-teller, the *Wahrsager*." Foucault, *DT*, 63.

38. Michel Foucault, *Subjectivity and Truth: Lectures at the Collège de France 1980–1981*, ed. Frédéric Gros, trans. Graham Burchell (New York: Picador, 2017), 221. In the second part of the course, Foucault examined the emergence of a new philosophical discourse on marriage in the Hellenistic period, especially in Stoic authors. He is struck by the emergence of a discourse that seems merely to inscribe in the prescriptive form of the judicial code an already existing social practice. "Why was it necessary to say it, and to say it in a prescriptive form? Why transform into a rule of conduct, why present as advice for living well something that would have effectively already been established at the level of real behaviour? Why would philosophers have been led to reproduce in the form of injunctions what was already given in reality?" (220). For a good discussion of this passage, see Sergei Prozorov, "Why Is There Truth? Foucault in the Age of Post-Truth Politics," *Constellations* 26 (2019): 18–30, esp. 19–21.

39. Foucault, *Subjectivity and Truth*, 221.

40. Foucault, 221.

41. Daniele Lorenzini, *The Force of Truth: Critique, Genealogy, and Truth-Telling in Michel Foucault* (Chicago: University of Chicago Press, 2023), 7.

42. The shift occurs in *On The Government of the Living*, in which Foucault turns his focus from governmentality and biopolitics to the techniques of the self and the aesthetics of existence. This focus continues in the course that soon followed, in *Subjectivity and Truth*. See Lorenzini, *Force of Truth*, 24; Prozorov, "Why Is There Truth?," 19.

43. "Looking for a word that corresponds, not to the knowledge useful for those who govern, but to that manifestation of truth correlative to the exercise of power," Foucault settles on the Greek word "*alēthourgēs* for someone who speaks the truth." From it, he "forges the fictional word *alēthourgia*, alethurgy," to describe "the set of possible verbal or non-verbal procedures by which one brings to light what is laid down as true as opposed to false, hidden, inexpressible, unforeseeable, or forgotten, and say that there is no exercise of power without something like an alethurgy" (*GL*, 6, 7). See also Lorenzini, *Force of Truth*, 23, 139n47.

44. Although Foucault "never denies that every game of truth possesses a logic and structure that autonomously establish the distinction between truth and falsity," comments Lorenzini, that autonomy requires a "standpoint *internal* to a game of truth itself, thus bracketing the sociopolitical, cultural, and historical context, as well as the flesh-and-blood individuals who concretely engage with a game of truth and bring it to life." For Foucault, however, no such absolute autonomy exists, for no game of truth can be considered apart from a regime of truth; consequently, the standpoint from which the distinction between truth and falsity is wholly internal to the game is more analytic than real: it can never account for the *force* of truth. Lorenzini, *Force of Truth*, 37.

45. See also Lorenzini, *Force of Truth*, 34; Prozorov, "Why Is There Truth?," 27.

46. Lorenzini, 34.

47. Lorenzini observes: "In 1980 Foucault entirely recenters his history of truth on the role that the subject plays in relation to the procedures for the manifestation of truth. Indeed, Foucault's aim is no longer exclusively that of writing an archaeology of knowledge-*savoir* and a genealogy of knowledge-*connaissance*: his history of truth now also functions as a genealogy of the modern subject" (*Force of Truth*, 24).

48. Daniele Lorenzini, private correspondence.

49. Prozorov, "Why Is There Truth?," 24.

50. "On the basis of this principle of [the] contingency [of truth discourses] Foucault proceeds to identify four characteristics of discourses of truth. The first is their supplementary character. While Foucault makes no reference to Jacques Derrida's notion of supplementarity, there is an evident resonance with Derrida's use of the notion to designate something that is at once essential and extraneous, constitutive and external to that which it supplements. Truth arises 'in the depths' of reality, yet it is not in any way necessary from the standpoint of this reality itself. Truth merely adds something to reality, but what it adds is something essential to this reality, which it nonetheless cannot formulate without being supplemented by a specific discourse" (Prozorov, 21).

51. Prozorov, 24. Foucault "introduces a gap between the subject and discourse that permits the former to make use of the latter without being entirely subsumed by it or experiencing its statements as a matter of necessity," observes Prozorov (24). This gap is the space occupied by the "therefore" that links "it is true" to "I submit."

52. Hannah Arendt, "On the Nature of Totalitarianism," 354.

53. Furthermore, as argued in the next chapter, it raises questions about Arendt's account of the compulsory character of totalitarian ideology as a form of logic and logical thinking.

54. Lorenzini, *Force of Truth*, 34.

55. In the text and notes, I cite the forthcoming critical edition of the writings of Hannah Arendt but give page references for both the critical edition and the published edition of Arendt's text. These two editions are not identical. The first page reference is to the critical edition, and the second is to the published edition. Hannah Arendt, "Thinking and Moral Considerations," in *The Life of the Mind*, Complete Works, Critical Edition 14.1, ed. Wout Cornellissen, Thomas Bartscherer, and Anne Eusterschulte (Göttingen: Wallstein Verlag, 2024), 474–97, at 497, https://hannah-arendt-edition.net/home?lang=en; Hannah Arendt, "Thinking and Moral Considerations," in *Responsibility and Judgment*, ed. Jerome Kohn (New York: Schocken, 2003), 159–89, at 162.

56. Lorenzini, *Force of Truth*, 39.

57. "When I say that I study the problematization of madness, or of sexuality, or of crime," protests Foucault, "it's not a way to deny the reality of those things—crime, sexuality, or madness." This is not "historical idealism": "There is a correspondence.... Well, there is a relation between the thing which is problematized and the problematization. Anyway, the problematization is an answer to something which is real, but the way the problematization organizes the thing which is problematized is not, most of the time—or at least sometimes—able to be analyzed in terms of a direct relation of representation to that which is represented" (*DT*, 225).

58. Lorenzini, *Force of Truth*, 36.

59. Foucault explains:

What is *isegoria*? *Isegoria* is the right to speak, the statutory right to speak. It is the fact that, in terms of the town's constitution (its *politeia*), everyone has the right to give his opinion, whether this be ... by defending himself before a tribunal, by voting, or possibly by voicing one's views. This right of speech is constitutive of citizenship, or again it is one of the elements of the city's constitution. As for *parrhesia*, it is linked both to the *politeia* (the city's constitution) and to *isegoria*. It is obvious that there cannot be *parrhesia* if citizens do not have this right to speak, give their opinion by voting, or testify in court, etcetera. So, for there to be *parrhesia* there must be this *politeia* which gives each individual the equal right to speak (*isegoria*). But parrhesia is something different. It is not just the constitutional right to speak. It is an element which, within this necessary framework of the democratic *politeia* giving everyone the equal right to speak, allows a certain ascendancy of some over others. It is what allows some individuals to be among the foremost, and, addressing themselves to the others, to tell them what they think, what they think is true, what they truly think is true . . . and thereby, by telling the truth, to persuade the people with good advice, and thus direct the city and take charge of it. *Isegoria* merely defines the constitutional and institutional framework in which *parrhesia* will function as the free and, consequently, courageous activity of some who come forward, speak, and try to persuade and direct the others, with all the attendant risks. (*GS*, 157–58)

60. The rise of "bad *parrhesia*" becomes an "obsession after the death of Pericles." Besides "false truth-telling," bad parrhesia comes about because there is a "refusal of truth-telling" by the demos. "The Athenians cannot stand any criticism in the form of a reproach addressed directly to the Assembly by an orator. They get rid of orators or politicians who play this game" (*GS*, 180, 182).

61. Commenting on Plato's description of the empire of Cyrus in *The Laws*, Foucault writes:

> Parrhesia is the most manifest form of an entire process which, according to Plato, guarantees the good functioning of the empire, namely that the hierarchical differences that may exist between the sovereign and the others, between his entourage and the rest of the citizens, between officers and soldiers, and between victors and vanquished, are in a way attenuated or compensated for by the formation of relationships which are designated throughout the text as relationships of friendship [*philia*]. . . . In this way, the text says, the entire empire will be able to function and work according to the principles of "*eleutheria*" (a freedom), not in the constitutional form of shared political rights, but in the form of freedom of speech. This freedom of speech will give rise to philia (friendship). . . . This freedom of speech, this *parrhesia* is therefore the concrete form of freedom in autocracy. It is a freedom which founds friendship—friendship between different hierarchical levels of the State—and the collaboration—the *koinonia* which ensures the unity of the entire empire. (*GS*, 203–4)

For a discussion of Foucault's reading of Plato, see Lida Maxwell, "The Politics and Gender of Truth-Telling in Foucault's Lectures on *Parrhesia*," *Contemporary Political Theory* 18, no. 1 (2018): 22–42, esp. 26–27. In Arendt's account, philosophical parrhesia is addressed to the tyrant as a desperate measure to gain a hearing for the truths that fail to resonate with the multitude. Interpreting this failure as evidence of the importance of truth in the political realm, the philosopher will try "to win the ear of some philosophically inclined tyrant, and in the fortunately highly unlikely case of success he might erect one of those tyrannies of 'truth' which we know chiefly from the political utopias . . . [and that] are as tyrannical as other forms of despotism" ("TP," 241). For a good account of parrhesia in nondemocratic regimes, see Matthew Landauer, "*Parrhesia* and the *Demos Tyrannos*: Frank Speech, Flattery and Accountability in Democratic Athens," *History of Political Thought* 33, no. 2 (Summer 2012): 185–208.

62. Maxwell, "Politics and Gender of Truth-Telling," 26. Examples of the ethical reading, as Maxwell argues, include Nancy Luxon, "Truth, Risk, and Trust in Foucault's Late Lectures," *Inquiry* 47 (2004): 464–89; and Nancy Luxon, "Ethics and Subjectivity," *Political Theory* 36, no. 3 (2008): 377–402; David Owen and Claire Woodford, "Foucault, Cavell, and the Government of Self and Others," *Iridie: Filosofia e discussion pubblica* 25, no. 2 (2012): 299–316; Sergie Prozorov, "Foucault's Affirmative Biopolitics: Cynic Parrhesia and the Biopower of the Powerless," *Political Theory* 45, no. 6:801–23, https//doi.org/10.1177/0090591715609171715609963.

63. Lorenzini, *Force of Truth*, 88.

64. Lorenzini, 10.

65. Michel Foucault, *Speaking the Truth about Oneself*, ed. Henri-Paul Fruchaud and Daniele Lorenzini, trans. Daniel Louis Wyche (Chicago: University of Chicago Press, 2021), 173.

66. Arendt adds, parenthetically: "This, of course, is not to deny that the disclosure of facts may be legitimately used by political organizations or that, under certain circumstances, factual matters brought to public attention will considerably encourage and strengthen the claims of ethnic and social groups" ("TP," 246).

67. Lorenzini, *Force of Truth*, 86.

68. The trial commenced in Los Angeles on January 3, 1973. Ellsberg held that the papers were "illegally classified," and that he had served "a higher law" of democracy in leaking them to the press and the American people. US District Court judge William Byrne refused to hear Ellsberg's defense. The only question, he ruled, was whether Ellsberg had violated the Espionage Act by leaking classified documents. Ellsberg's likely guilty sentence was avoided by astonishing evidence of the Nixon administration's serious misconduct in handling the case, which involved breaking into the office of Ellsberg's psychiatrist, Lewis Fielding; illegally wiretapping Ellsberg's conversations; and, not least, Nixon aid John Ehrlichman's attempt to bribe the judge with the offer of the directorship of the FBI. On May 11, 1973, Judge Byrne dismissed all charges. See Jenkinson, "Daniel Ellsberg and the Greatest Leak of Secret Documents." According to Cathy Caruth, Ellsberg foregoes straightforward truth-telling yet serves nevertheless as a political witness ("Lying and History," 92).

69. Michel Foucault, *The Courage of Truth: Lectures at the Collège de France, 1983–1984*, ed. F. Gros, trans. Graham Burchell (New York: Picador, 2008), 14; Lorenzini, *Force of Truth*, 79.

70. Lorenzini, *Force of Truth*, 79.

71. See also Arendt, "PP," 83.

72. In the *Apology*, writes Foucault, Socrates explains why he has never addressed the Assembly or given advice to the people. "Why have I never played the role of [public] advisor, why have I never been a political parrhesiast? Well, he says, if 'I had engaged in politics, my ruin would have been complete long ago'" (*GS*, 315).

73. Quoted in Wrathall, *Heidegger and Unconcealment*, 19.

74. Hannah Arendt, *Lectures on Kant's Political Philosophy*, ed. Ronald Beiner (Chicago: University of Chicago Press, 1989), 42.

75. In his writing on Kant and Enlightenment, Foucault describes a new form of philosophical reflection: "Philosophy as the problematization of a present-ness." Locating this new form of philosophy in Kant's writings on the French Revolution, Foucault distinguishes two critical traditions inaugurated by Kant: the first tradition, the "analytics of truth," "defines the conditions under which true knowledge is

possible" and is associated with Kant's first *Critique*. The second, the "ontology of the present, an ontology of ourselves," concerns itself with the question: "What is our present? What is the contemporary field of possible experience?" Michel Foucault, "Kant on Enlightenment and Revolution," trans. C. Gordon, *Economy and Society* 15, no. 1 (February 1986): 88–96, at 96. I discussed this essay in chap. 2.

76. "In parrhesia, the danger comes always from the fact that the truth you say is able to hurt or anger the interlocutor. Parrhesia is always a game between the one who speaks and the interlocutor" (*DT*, 43).

77. Hannah Arendt, "'What Remains? The Language Remains': An Interview with Gunther Gauss," in Hannah Arendt, *Essays in Understanding, 1930–1954*, ed. Jerome Kohn (New York: Harcourt Brace, 1994), 1–23, at 20.

78. Hannah Arendt, "On the Nature of Totalitarianism: An Essay in Understanding," in *Essays in Understanding 1930–1954*, 328–60, at 354.

79. The UK *Guardian*'s Michael Carlson wrote in the paper's obituary of Ellsberg, "It is not unreasonable to set Ellsberg's leak alongside President John F. Kennedy's assassination as the ground zero of today's distrust of politics." Michael Carlson, "Daniel Ellsberg Obituary," *Guardian*, June 17, 2023, https://www.theguardian.com/us-news/2023/jun/17/daniel-ellsberg-obituary.

80. As discussed in chap. 2, the disdain with which the Western philosophical tradition has regarded the realm of human affairs led Plato to seek truth wholly undisturbed by the contingency of politics. Preferring the enlightened company of the few over the opinions of the many, Plato would have the philosopher withdraw entirely into the Academy, which then becomes the model space for free speech. This "new concept of freedom," Arendt argued, is hostile to plurality as a feature of political life and, thus, intended as "a fully valid substitute for the marketplace, the agora, the central space for freedom in the polis." In her view, however, this new freedom is illusory, for the "few, wherever they isolated themselves from the many—be it in the form of academic indifference or oligarchic rule—have manifestly ended up depending on the many, particularly in all those matters of communal life requiring concrete action" ("IP," 131, 133).

81. Maxwell, "Politics and Gender of Truth-Telling," 23. Foucault offers a rereading of Sophocles's *Oedipus the King* in terms of truth and power, which foregrounds the role of the servants and the slaves who offer testimony based on the first person, "seeing with their own eyes and acting with their own hands" (*GL*, 37). Also, his account of those who have been historically viewed as truth-tellers ("prophets, seers, innocents, the blind, the mad, the wise, etc.") opens this question of who can be a truth-teller. Michel Foucault, *Psychiatric Power: Lectures at the Collège de France 1973–1974*, ed. Jacques Lagrange, trans. Graham Burchell (New York: Picador, 2006), 237. Furthermore, I argued in chap. 2 that Foucault's own criticism of the "rarefication" of those who are deemed qualified to discover the truth under the scientific standpoint of truth introduces just this question of selection and power.

82. The problem today is not that democratic citizens think that those who have walled themselves off in their modern version of the Platonic Academy are truth-tellers—on the contrary, they are viewed as elites who have nothing true to say. Instead, the problem is that we are far less likely to accord credibility to the speech of historically disenfranchised individuals and groups. The truth is being told (by some), but many of us are not listening. This is the irreducibly dialogic problem of parrhesia that both Arendt and Foucault bring to light. Any successful effort to relocate the

discussion of post-truth from the "analytics of truth," where it is a problem of correct reasoning, to the "critical tradition," where it is a problem of truth-telling, must confront the problem of the hierarchy of truth, lest it lose track of the central question of power that Foucault's analysis otherwise usefully tracks. Foucault, *DT*, 224.

Chapter Four

1. The chapter epigraph is from Karl Marx, "Theses on Feuerbach," in *The Marx-Engels Reader*, ed. Robert C. Tucker, 2nd ed. (New York: W. W. Norton, 1978), 143–45, at 145. A video clip of Donald Trump shows him making the following comments: "Hey, I watched when the World Trade Center came tumbling down. And I watched in Jersey City, New Jersey, where thousands and thousands of people were cheering as that building was coming down. Thousands of people were cheering." When questioned by George Stephanopoulos in a November 25, 2015, interview on ABC's *This Week* about the veracity of that claim, which Jersey City police called untrue, Trump replied: "It did happen. I saw it [on television]. There were people that were cheering on the other side of New Jersey, where you have large Arab populations. They were cheering as the World Trade Center came down. I know it might be not politically correct for you to talk about it, but there were people cheering as that building came down—as those buildings came down. And that tells you something. It was well covered at the time, George. Now, I know they don't like to talk about it, but it was well covered at the time. There were people over in New Jersey that were watching it, a heavy Arab population, that were cheering as the buildings came down. Not good." See Glenn Kessler, "Trump's Outrageous Claim That 'Thousands' of New Jersey Muslims Celebrated the 9/11 Attacks," *Washington Post*, November 22, 2015, https://www.washingtonpost.com/news/fact-checker/wp/2015/11/22/donald-trumps-outrageous-claim-that-thousands-of-new-jersey-muslims-celebrated-the-911-attacks/.

2. These comments (discussed below) were made by Republican presidential candidate Carly Fiorina. See David Weigel, "Planned Parenthood Tries in Vain to Get Carly Fiorina to Retract Video Claim," *Washington Post*, September 23, 2015, https://www.washingtonpost.com/news/post-politics/wp/2015/09/23/planned-parenthood-tries-in-vain-to-get-carly-fiorina-to-retract-video-claim/.

3. See Fredric Jameson, *The Political Unconscious: Narrative as a Socially Symbolic Act* (Ithaca, NY: Cornell University Press, 1981); Slavoj Žižek, *The Sublime Object of Ideology* (London: Verso, 1989); Terry Eagleton, *Ideology: An Introduction* (London: Verso, 1991); Jan Rehmann, *Theories of Ideology: The Powers of Alienation and Subjection* (Leiden: Brill, 2013). For a brilliant restatement of the classic concept of ideology to make sense of contemporary authoritarian politics, see Lisa Wedeen, *Authoritarian Apprehensions: Ideology, Judgment, and Mourning in Syria* (Chicago: University of Chicago Press, 2019).

4. Jason Stanley, *How Propaganda Works* (Princeton, NJ: Princeton University Press, 2015), 190.

5. Quotes are from Weigel, "Planned Parenthood Tries in Vain to Get Carly Fiorina to Retract Video Claim."

6. Lauren Carroll, "At CNN Debate, Carly Fiorina Urges Others to Watch Planned Parenthood Video," *Politifact: The Poynter Institute*, September 17, 2015, https://www.politifact.com/factchecks/2015/sep/17/carly-fiorina/cnn-debate-carly-fiorina-urges-others-watch-planne/.

7. According to the *Los Angeles Times*, "The Federalist, a conservative website, contends that Fiorina is right and it's the media that's lying about her statement. But the website's own analysis shows that it's Fiorina who is in the wrong. The Federalist acknowledges that neither of the two fetuses in the CMP video is the one referred to in CMP's voiceover—one is 'another baby of roughly the same gestational age,' it acknowledges—and that the Center for Bio-Ethical Reform, the source of the footage, doesn't identify it as coming from Planned Parenthood, but merely from 'an abortion clinic.'" Michael Hiltzik, "It's Time for Carly Fiorina to Apologize to Planned Parenthood," *Los Angeles Times*, September 18, 2015, https://www.latimes.com/business/hiltzik/la-fi-mh-it-s-time-for-fiorina-to-apologize-20150918-column.html.

8. Stanley, *How Propaganda Works*, 188.

9. According to Stanley, identity must be understood in social rather than psychological terms. Stanley distinguishes his understanding of intractable beliefs from that of philosophers such as David Hume. For Hume, Stanley argues, flawed (human) psychology is the source of flawed ideological beliefs. Hence, our erroneous belief that there are external things, argues Hume in "Of Skepticism with Regard to the Senses," is not something we can relinquish even when presented with compelling rational arguments against the existence of external things. For Stanley, however, the source of flawed ideological beliefs is not human psychology but "flawed social structures" (Stanley, *How Propaganda Works*, 179).

10. Sally Haslanger, "'But Mom, Crop Tops Are Cute!': Social Knowledge, Social Structures, and Ideology Critique," in *Resisting Reality: Social Construction and Social Critique* (New York: Oxford University Press, 2012), 406–28.

11. Haslanger, 413.

12. Haslanger, 412–13.

13. Haslanger, 412–13; Sally Haslanger, "Critical Theory and Practice: Ideology and Materiality," Spinoza lecture 1, April 9, 2015, 1–5, 2; lecture handout available at http://sallyhaslanger.weebly.com/research.html.

14. Sally Haslanger, "Ideology, Generics, and Common Ground," in *Resisting Reality*, 446–47, 449.

15. Haslanger, 449.

16. Haslanger, 447.

17. Haslanger, 447. Although Stanley focuses on belief, he agrees that ideological belief must be understood as "built out of regularities of convention" and thus about social practices, as they are emphasized in the work of Tommie Shelby and Sally Haslanger. Stanley, *How Propaganda Works*, 184.

18. Haslanger, "Critical Theory and Practice," 2.

19. Haslanger, "Ideology, Generics, and Common Ground," 447.

20. Louis Althusser, *On the Reproduction of Capitalism: Ideology and Ideological State Apparatuses* (1969), trans. G. M. Goshgarian (New York: Verso, 2014), 197.

21. Distinguishing repressive and ideological state apparatuses (ISAs), Althusser writes:

> Remember that in Marxist theory, the state apparatus contains: the government, the administration, the army, the police, the courts, the prisons, etc., which constitute what I shall in future call the Repressive State Apparatus. Repressive suggests that the state apparatus in question "functions by violence"—at least ultimately (since repression, e.g. administrative repression, may take non-physical forms).

I shall call Ideological State Apparatuses a certain number of realities which present themselves to the immediate observer in the form of distinct and specialized institutions. I propose an empirical list of these which will obviously have to be examined in detail, tested, corrected and reorganized . . . :

the religious ISA (the system of the different churches),
the educational ISA (the system of the different public and private "schools"),
the family ISA,
the legal ISA,
the political ISA (the political system, including the different parties),
the trade union ISA,
the communications ISA (press, radio and television, etc.),
the cultural ISA (literature, the arts, sport, etc.).

Louis Althusser, "Appendix 2: Ideology and Ideological State Apparatuses," in *On the Reproduction of Capitalism*, 232–72, at 242–43. See also Louis Althusser, "Ideology and Ideological State Apparatuses," in *Lenin and Philosophy, and Other Essays*, trans. Ben Brewster (New York: Monthly Review Press, 1971), 127–87, at 143.

22. Writes Althusser:

All ideology hails or interpellates concrete individuals as concrete subjects, through the functioning of the category of the subject. . . .

We shall go on to suggest that ideology "acts" or "functions" in such a way as to "recruit" subjects among individuals (it recruits them all) or "transforms" individuals into subjects (it transforms them all) through the very precise operation that we call *interpellation* or *hailing*. It can be imagined along the lines of the most commonplace, everyday hailing, by (or not by) the police: "Hey, you there!" (Althusser, *On the Reproduction of Capitalism*, 190)

Furthermore, "Experience shows that . . . hailing hardly ever misses its mark: verbal call or whistle, the one hailed always recognizes that *he* really was the one hailed" (191). "Thus ideology hails or interpellates individuals as subjects" (192). But this temporal structure, argues Althusser, deceives: "Since ideology is eternal, we must now suppress the temporal form in which we have represented the functioning of ideology and say: ideology has always-already interpellated individuals as subjects, which amounts to making it clear that individuals are always-already interpellated by ideology as subjects. This ineluctably leads to one last proposition: *individuals are always-already subjects*" (192). For an excellent discussion of the circularity in the Althusserian concept of interpretation, see Wedeen, *Authoritarian Apprehensions*, 9–10.

23. Althusser, *On the Reproduction of Capitalism*, 188.

24. Althusser writes: "Ideology does not exist in the 'world of ideas' conceived as a 'spiritual world.' Ideology exists in institutions and the practices specific to them" (*On the Reproduction of Capitalism*, 156). Further, Althusser claims that "individuals are always-already subjects" (192). Althusser invokes Lacan's understanding of the "Name of the Father to designate the socio-symbolic character of identity formation."

25. Pascale Gillot, "The Theory of Ideology and the Theory of the Unconscious," in *Encountering Althusser: Politics and Materialism in Contemporary Radical Thought*, ed. Katja Diefenbach, Sara R. Farris, Gal Kirn, and Peter D. Thomas (New York: Bloomsbury, 2013), 289–306, 293. Likewise, Warren Montag emphasizes the influence of Spinoza's materialism on Althusser's philosophy and his critical strategy. Warren Montag, "'The Soul Is the Prison of the Body': Althusser and Foucault, 1970–1975," *Yale French Studies* 88 (1995): 53–77, at 66.

26. Althusser, *On the Reproduction of Capitalism*, 176. "If eternal means, not transcendent to all (temporal) history, but omnipresent and therefore immutable in form throughout all of history, I will go so far as to adopt Freud's formulations word for word and write: ideology is eternal, just like the unconscious" (176).

27. Althusser, 192.

28. "It is certain in advance that it [the unborn child] will bear its father's name and so have an identity and be irreplaceable. Before its birth, then, the child is always-already a subject, marked out [*assigné*] as a subject in and by the particular familial ideological configuration in which it is 'expected' once it has been conceived (deliberately or by accident)" (Althusser, 192–93).

29. Geoff Pfeifer, *The New Materialism: Althusser, Badiou, and Žižek* (New York: Routledge, 2015), 36.

30. Pfeifer, 175, 173.

31. Althusser, *On the Reproduction of Capitalism*, 174.

32. Althusser, 175.

33. Mark Cousins and Athar Hussain argue that this reduction of psychic to normative social relations assumes the Other in Lacan's theory is equivalent to a set of social relations, whereas for Lacan it is in an eccentric if not antagonistic relation to it. Mark Cousins and Athar Hussain, "The Question of Ideology: Althusser, Pecheux, and Foucault," *Sociological Review* 32, no. 1 (May 1984): 158–79, 171.

34. Althusser, *On the Reproduction of Capitalism*, 181.

35. Althusser follows the Lacanian understanding of the imaginary order as being one step removed from the Lacanian Real. We are always within ideology because of our reliance on language to establish our "reality." Many thinkers, including Wittgenstein, share this idea of language as the basis for our conception of the real. However, for Althusser, the subject's constitution in language, which is to say, in ideology, creates a sense of reality that is always already distorted. I discuss the difference between the Althusserian idea of ideological distortion and the Wittgensteinian idea of being "held captive" by a picture in chap. 6.

36. Isabelle Garo, "The Impossible Break: Ideology in Movement between Philosophy and Politics," in Diefenbach, Farris, Kirn, and Thomas, *Encountering Althusser*, 284.

37. "One has to be outside ideology, in other words, in scientific knowledge, to be able to say 'I am in ideology' (a quite exceptional case) or (the general case) 'I was in ideology'" (Althusser, *On the Reproduction of Capitalism*, 191).

38. Garo, "Impossible Break," 283.

39. James Conant, "Subjective Thought," in *Cahiers Parisiens / Parisian Notebooks*, vol. 3 (2007), 234–58, at 242. Conant examines the conflation of "the subjective" with the "merely subjective" in Western philosophical thought. The basis for the received idea of objectivity, this reduction belongs to the idea of "the merely perspectival character of all human cognition," as if all human knowledge, being perspectival, were objectively deficient (237). Accordingly, "every cognitive achievement that exhibits the least admixture of subjectivity . . . amounts, in the end, to nothing but 'illusions'" (237). I discuss this ideal of objectivity in the introduction and in Linda M. G. Zerilli, *A Democratic Theory of Judgment* (Chicago: University of Chicago Press, 2016), chap. 1.

40. According to Althusser, the "realist" concern with life championed in *The German Ideology* is superseded by *Capital*'s critical reading strategy. Marx shows that "the production of knowledge which is peculiar to theoretical practice constitutes a process that takes place entirely in thought," and that knowledge "does not work on the real object but on the peculiar raw material, which constitutes . . . its 'object'

(of knowledge), and which . . . is distinct from the real object." Louis Althusser and Étienne Balibar, *Reading "Capital,"* trans. Ben Brewster (London: New Left Books, 1970), 42, 43. Pointing to these passages, Andrew Ryder argues that there are crucial similarities between Althusser and Foucault on the nature of reading and knowledge. Andrew Ryder, "Foucault and Althusser: Epistemological Differences with Political Effects," *Foucault Studies* 16 (September 2013): 134–53. I agree, but Althusser's use of the concept "real object" and its difference from the "object of knowledge" loses track of the world in which knowledge practices and true discourses are produced. Foucault's focus on discourse and epistemes never loses sight of an extralinguistic realm. As discussed below, he defends his idea of "problematization" against the charge of idealism, claiming that to problematize is not to invent something out of thin air but to give conceptual and social form to something that already exists. According to John Fraser, "Althusser sees reality as a theoretical object and appearance as merely empirical." See John Fraser, "Althusser: Science, Marxism, Politics," *Science and Society* 40, no. 4 (Winter 1976/1977): 438–64, at 455. For Foucault, this distinction is evidence of the metaphysical entanglements of Althusserian science. Fraser also discusses the problems associated with Althusser's ascription of an epistemological break to Marx. "First, according to Althusser, Marx's break is not final: only in the very latest texts does he avoid backsliding into Hegelianism." "Second, by following Bachelard and describing the break as epistemological, and established in theory, the problem of the political character of the break is left obscure." "Althusser both assures us that epistemology is not politics; yet he argues variously that class struggle, politics, may be present within epistemology, and that epistemology may be transposed onto the terrain of class struggle" (Fraser, "Althusser," 447, 448).

41. Althusser, *On the Reproduction of Capitalism*, 191–92; Althusser, *Lenin and Philosophy*, 175.

42. For the critique of empiricism's "real object," see Althusser and Balibar, *Reading "Capital,"* 37–39. By contrast with empiricism, "Marx provides us with the wherewithal to pose the problem we are concerned with: the problem of the cognitive appropriation of the real object by the object of knowledge [theoretical object], which is a special case of the appropriation of the real world by different practices, theoretical, aesthetic, religious, ethical, technical, etc." (66).

43. Sciences produce knowledge from their object by constituting it, and they produce knowledges of their objects in the specific mode that defines it, argues Althusser. The process of knowledge, as he reiterates his main "thesis" in *Essays in Self-Criticism*, takes place in abstraction: "If the process of knowledge does not transform the real object, but only transforms its perceptions into concepts and then into a thought-concrete, and if all this process takes place, as Marx repeatedly points out, 'in thought', and not in the real object, this means that, with regard to the real object, in order to know it, 'thought' operates on the transitional forms which designate the real object in the process of transformation in order finally to produce a concept of it, the thought-concrete." Louis Althusser, *Essays in Self-Criticism*, trans. Graham Locke (London: New Left Books, 1976), 192.

44. The realities through which the real object is at once grasped and transformed, we have seen, take place entirely within thought. But because the earlier work relied on the (positivist) idea of extrascientific criteria, provided by philosophy, with which to validate the relation of the theoretical to the real object, Althusser, against his antiempiricist intentions, ended up conflating the real and the theoretical object. See

André Glucksmann, "A Ventriloquist Structuralism," *New Left Review* 72 (March–April 1972): 68–92; Alex Callinicos, *Althusser's Marxism* (London: Pluto, 1976); G. Elliot, *Althusser: The Detour of Theory* (London: Verso, 1987).

45. Hristos Verikukis, "Knowledge versus 'Knowledge': Louis Althusser on the Autonomy of Science and Philosophy from Ideology: A Reply to William S. Lewis," *Rethinking Marxism* 21, no. 1 (January 2009): 67–84, 79.

46. Verikukis, 79, 80. The problem is not that Althusser was a "rationalist and idealist," argues Verikukis, but that the early work tried "to distinguish between [ideological and scientific] discourses in terms of objects: constructed versus 'given' objects. This distinction is unattainable even according to [the early] Althusser's own terms since no object is ever 'given.'" This leaves us unable to distinguish between the ideological and nonideological aspects of the different theoretical objects produced in science (Verikukis, 80).

47. Conant, "Subjective Thought," 256.

48. Drawing on Lenin, Althusser describes scientists as having "1) belief in the real, external and material existence of the object of the scientific knowledge; 2) belief in the existence and objectivity of the scientific knowledges that permit knowledge of this object; 3) belief in the correctness and efficacy of the procedures of scientific experimentation, or scientific method, capable of producing scientific knowledge." Louis Althusser, *Philosophy and the Spontaneous Philosophy of the Scientists, and Other Essays*, trans. Ben Brewster et al. (London: Verso, 1990), 133.

49. William S. Lewis, "Knowledge versus 'Knowledge': Louis Althusser on the Autonomy of Science and Philosophy from Ideology," *Rethinking Marxism* 17, no. 3 (July 2005): 455–70, at 464. See also Althusser, *Philosophy and the Spontaneous Philosophy of the Scientists, and Other Essays*, 106. For a critique of Lewis's reading of Althusser's later work, see Verikukis, "Knowledge versus 'Knowledge' . . . : A Reply"; Verikukis argues that Lewis reduces the later Althusser to a positivist (again) by claiming that he relies on the notion of the testability of scientific hypotheses by reference to reality as an "external check" on science's findings (80). See Lewis, "Knowledge versus 'Knowledge,'" 460, 463. Lewis himself claims that "when [concept] production takes place entirely in thought and the object that it works with consists exclusively of concepts, it is hard to see how such a practice can be externally verified" (460). Lewis seems to fall here into what Winifred Sellars famously criticized as the myth of "the given" that characterized (empiricist) sense-datum theories. "The point of the epistemological category of the given is, presumably, to explicate the idea that empirical knowledge rests on a 'foundation' of non-inferential knowledge of matter of fact." The given, Sellars argued, is ultimately incapable of establishing the normative distinctions required by any claim to knowledge. Wilfrid Sellars, "Empiricism and the Philosophy of Mind," in *Minnesota Studies in the Philosophy of Science*, vol. 1, *The Foundations of Science and the Concepts of Psychology and Psychoanalysis*, ed. Herbert Feigl and Michael Scriven (Minneapolis: University of Minnesota Press, 1956), 253–329, at 253, 255.

50. Althusser, *Self-Criticism*, 114.

51. The struggle, however, argues Verikukis, is not the earlier struggle to demarcate ideology from science but, rather, a new problem of choosing between problems science will solve. "Science can be subversive of the established order," or it can support that order. The problems it chooses to solve determines whether science facilitates or undermines class struggle. The form of philosophy that clears the way to solving problems of the first kind is called "materialist" versus "idealist" (Verikukis "Knowledge versus 'Knowledge' . . . : A Reply," 75, 77).

52. Filling in this account, Resch argues that Althusser's concepts of science and ideology as social practices "might be called a 'limited rationalism' . . . as opposed to the 'grand rationalism'" of his earlier thought. Philosophy is no longer described as "the science of sciences," as it is in positivism. Philosophy now abandons "epistemological rationalism" and defends scientific concepts "in terms of their adequacy rather than their truth." Resch continues:

> From such a limited rationalist position, the axiological superiority of science over ideology/error remains defensible in Althusser's materialist theses of ontological realism and epistemological relativism (without which the existence and intelligibility of science itself are incomprehensible). The assumption that the world postulated by both ideology and science is really there (that thought about the real logically presupposes the existence of reality independent from thought) justifies the claim that the thresholds of formalization that distinguish science from ideology/error provide not absolute truth (the abolition of the distinction between the real and thought about the real, the outcome of all rationalisms in the grand manner) but relative truth (affirmation of the distinction between the real and thought about the real, but also affirmation of the intelligibility and relative adequacy of thought—the modest but far from insignificant outcome of limited rationalism). Ontological realism and epistemological relativism cannot be proved by Althusser, of course, any more than they can be refuted by his opponents.

Robert Paul Resch, *Althusser and the Renewal of Marxist Social Theory* (Berkeley: University of California Press, 1992), 168–69. See also, Althusser, *Essays in Self-Criticism*, 168–69. For another attempt to fill out the possibilities for a nonrationalist historical materialism, see Verikukis, "Knowledge versus 'Knowledge' . . . : A Reply."

53. Althusser's rejection of his theoreticism, which sought to give a "*rationalist* explanation of 'the [epistemological] break' of Marx," writes Resch, contrasted "*truth* and *error* in the form of a speculative distinction between science and ideology in the singular and in general." Consequently, "from this rationalist-speculative drama the class struggle was practically absent" (Resch, *Althusser and the Renewal of Marxist Social Theory*, 163).

54. Conant, "Subjective Thought," 258.

55. Notwithstanding his self-criticism, writes Resch, "there is no point in denying a persistent tension between conventionalist and realist tendencies in Althusser's thought, a tension only summarily resolved by declaring the primacy of the latter over the former." To resolve this tension, "it was necessary for Althusser to act on the primacy of realism over conventionalism and relocate concepts of science and philosophy within historical materialism rather than outside it, to define science and philosophy [writes Althusser] 'not simply from the standpoint of the existence of Marxist science as science, but from the standpoint of Marxist science as the science of History.'" Redefined as a social practice, science is no longer described in terms of the "philosophical categories of truth or falsity." "The realist claim regarding the validity of knowledge effects cannot be proven (or disproven) apodictically by either philosophy or science" (Resch, *Althusser and the Renewal of Marxist Social Theory*, 161, 162).

56. Althusser and Balibar, *Reading "Capital,"* 87. "Thought about the real, the conception of the real, and all the operations of thought by which the real is thought and conceived, belong to the order of thought, the elements of thought, which must not be confused with the order of the real, the element of the real" (87).

57. Althusser, *Essays in Self-Criticism*, 193.
58. Althusser, 54.
59. Michel Foucault, *About the Beginning of the Hermeneutics of the Self: Lectures at Dartmouth College, 1980*, ed. H.-P. Fruchaud and D. Lorenzini, trans. Graham Burchelle (Chicago: University of Chicago Press, 2015), 26.
60. Michel Foucault, "Truth and Power" (1977), in *Power/Knowledge: Selected Interviews and Other Writings 1972–1977*, ed. Colin Gordon (1972; New York: Pantheon, 1980), 109–33.
61. Foucault, 118.
62. Michel Foucault, *Subjectivity and Truth: Lectures at the Collège de France 1980–1981*, ed. Frédéric Gros, trans. Graham Burchell (New York: Picador, 2017), 242.
63. Foucault, "Truth and Power," 118. As argued in the introduction and chap. 6, this discourse that is neither true nor false is what Wittgenstein calls "the picture" that lies at the bottom of any language game.
64. Cousins and Hussain, "Question of Ideology," 178.
65. Michel Foucault, "The Analytic Philosophy of Politics" (1978), trans. Giovanni Mascaretti, *Foucault Studies* 24 (2018): 188–200, at 192. See also Foucault, *Dits et écrits*, vol. 3 (Paris: Éditions Gallimard, 1994), 540–41.
66. Daniele Lorenzini, *The Force of Truth: Critique, Genealogy, and Truth-Telling in Michel Foucault* (Chicago: University of Chicago Press, 2023), 45.
67. Althusser, *On the Reproduction of Capitalism*, 197.
68. Foucault shows "that the scientific standpoint of truth, far from being 'pure,' is itself a regime of truth among others, that is, 'a system of ordered procedures for the production, regulation, distribution, circulation, and functioning of statements' that is linked 'by a circular relations to systems of power which produce and sustain it, and to the effects of power which it induces and redirect it'" (Lorenzini, *Force of Truth*, 23).
69. Lorenzini, 26. Contrast this with Althusser's focus on the state and its RSA and ISA.
70. Foucault, "Analytic Philosophy of Politics," 540–41.
71. Michel Foucault, *Psychiatric Power: Lectures at the Collège de France 1973–1974*, ed. Jacques Lagrange, trans. Graham Burchell (New York: Picador, 2006), 246.
72. Foucault, 246, 247. I discussed this "rarefaction of those who can know a truth that is now present everywhere and at every moment" (247) in the conclusion to chap. 2.
73. Foucault, 247.
74. Althusser, *Essays in Self-Criticism*, 193.
75. Althusser, 193.
76. Louis Althusser, "Marx in His Limits," in *Philosophy of the Encounter: Later Writings, 1978–1987*, trans. G. M. Goshgarian (New York: Verso, 2006), 7–162, at 135.
77. Althusser, 135.
78. Althusser, 137.
79. Althusser, 137.
80. Althusser, 138.
81. Laurence Gayot, "L'idéologie chez Marx: Concept politique ou theme polemique?," *Actuel Marx en ligne*, no. 32 (October 15, 2007): 1–68, 25. I agree with Gayot that the Marxian concept of ideology centers on the belief (in this unreflective sense) in the autonomy of ideas.
82. Because this is the fundamental ideological delusion and the core of all ideological illusions, Marx focuses his attacks on the imaginary conception of the autonomy

and priority of consciousness to the point that it can sometimes give the impression—as Althusser and other critics have complained—of simply reversing the determining relation between real life and ideas or representations of consciousness: "Life is not determined by consciousness, but consciousness by life." Karl Marx and Friedrich Engels, *The German Ideology* (New York: International, 1974), 47.

83. Marx and Engels, 47.

84. Isabelle Garo, *L'idéologie ou la pensée embarquée* (Paris: La Fabrique, 2009), 7.

85. Étienne Balibar notes, "Although he was constantly describing and criticizing particular 'ideologies', after 1846 and certainly after 1852, Marx never again used the term (it was to be exhumed by Engels twenty-five years later in *Anti-Düring* (1878) and in *Ludwig Feuerbach and the End of Classical German Philosophy* (1888), the works which mark his own appearance on the scene of the history of Marxism)." Étienne Balibar, *The Philosophy of Marx* (New York: Verso, 2007), 42. Whereas Balibar would have us understand commodity fetishism not as "a mere terminological variant, but a genuine theoretical alternative" to the classic but also the inconsistent concept of ideology in *The German Ideology* (Balibar, *Philosophy of Marx*, 42), Althusser argues that "the theory of fetishism . . . provides the springboard for all the 'humanist', or even 'religious', interpreters of Marx's thought" (Althusser, "Marx in His Limits," 127). Fetishism, argues Althusser, carries forward Marx's "basic conviction that *ideology consists of ideas*" (Althusser, 137).

86. Karl Marx, *Capital*, vol. 1, *A Critical Analysis of Capitalist Production*, ed. Frederick Engels, trans. Samuel Moore and Edward Averling (New York: International, 1967), 72.

87. Marx, 73. This point is brought out nicely in David Andrews, "Commodity Fetishism as a Form of Life," in *Marx and Wittgenstein: Knowledge, Morality, and Politics*, ed. Gavin Kitching and Nigel Pleasants (New York: Routledge, 2002), 78–94, 89.

88. Andrews, "Commodity Fetishism as a Form of Life," 89.

89. I. I. Rubin, *Essays on Marx's Theory of Value* (Sun Valley, CA: IndoEuropean, 2019), 59.

90. Althusser rightly criticizes those who read all of Marx through alienation and reification, but his own reading of the fetishism of commodities accuses Marx of "anthropological idealism" (*Essays in Self Criticism*, 70). In his "reader's guide" to volume 1 of Marx's *Capital* Althusser declares fetishism to be "a last trace of Hegelian influence" in Marx (*Lenin and Philosophy*, 95). And in "Marx in His Limits," Althusser argues that fetishism posits an opposition between persons and things that remains "trapped in the categories of the law or in the notions of juridical ideology" (129). In his 1973 critique of fetishism, Balibar likewise calls the "theory of 'fetishism'" in Marx "totally idealist." Étienne Balibar, "Self-Criticism: Answers to Questions from 'Theoretical Practice,'" *Theoretical Practice* 7–8 (1973): 56–72, at 57. His critique distinguished between a theory of fetishism and (Althusser's) theory of ideology, with the latter being "specific social relations really distinct from the relations of production although they are determined by the latter 'in the last instance'" (Balibar, 57). In later work, as Panagotis Sortitis notes, Balibar did not reject the theory of fetishism as had Althusser but argued that its focus on processes of reification was incompatible with the theory of ideology as a theory of power relations centered on the State. Panagotis Sortiris, "Althusserian and Value-Form Theory: Rancière, Althusser and the Question of Fetishism," *Crisis and Critique* 2, no. 2 (2015): 166–91, esp. 182–84.

91. Karl Marx, *Economic and Philosophic Manuscripts of 1844*, ed. Dirk J. Struik, trans. Martin Mulligan (New York: International, 1964), 108. For a discussion of these

points, see Geoffrey Pilling, *Marx's "Capital": Philosophy and Political Economy* (New York: Routledge and Kegan Paul, 1980), chap. 5.

92. Isabelle Garo, *Marx* (Paris: Éditions Seuil, 2000), 188.
93. "Preface," in Garo, 37.
94. Althusser, "Marx in His Limits," 17.
95. Althusser, 17.
96. Althusser, 18.
97. "Marx basically never abandoned the conviction that ideology consists of ideas as distinguished from the real and that the task of critique is to show that the real has primacy over ideas" (Althusser, 137).
98. Arendt explains:

> What makes a truly totalitarian device out of the Bolshevik claim that the present Russian system is superior to all others is the fact that the totalitarian ruler draws from this claim the logically impeccable conclusion that without this system people never could have built such a wonderful thing as, let us say, a subway; from this, he again draws the logical conclusion that anyone who knows of the existence of the Paris subway is a suspect because he may cause people to doubt that one can do things only in the Bolshevik way. This leads to the final conclusion that in order to remain a loyal Bolshevik, you have to destroy the Paris subway. Nothing matters but consistency. (*OT*, 458)

99. Hannah Arendt, *The Human Condition* (Chicago: University of Chicago Press, 1958), 171.
100. According to Peter Steinbrenner, Arendt's conception of logical reasoning "is rooted in human physiology." She presents "the brain as nothing more than a computational machine." Peter Steinbrenner, *The Concept of Political Judgment* (Chicago: University of Chicago Press, 1993), 63. I discuss Steinbrenner's reading and the problem of logic in Arendt's thought in Linda M. G. Zerilli, "'The Machine as Symbol': Wittgenstein's Contribution to the Politics of Judgment and Freedom in Contemporary Democratic Theory," in *Wittgenstein and Normative Inquiry*, ed. Mark Bevir and Andreas Galisanka (Leiden: Brill, 2016), 127–51.
101. Lorenzini, *Force of Truth*, 40.
102. Foucault, too, is interested in the worldly conditions of games of truth. For example, the game of truth called confession makes no sense apart from the rise of Christianity and its institutions.

Chapter Five

1. This project characterizes Jürgen Habermas's redefinition of the project of the Frankfurt School. See Seyla Benhabib, *Critique, Norm, and Utopia: A Study of the Foundations of Critical Theory* (New York: Columbia University Press, 1986), chap. 8. For a more critical discussion of Habermas's project, see Nikolas Kompridis, *Critique and Disclosure: Critical Theory between Past and Future* (Cambridge, MA: MIT Press, 2006); Linda M. G. Zerilli, *A Democratic Theory of Judgment* (Chicago: University of Chicago Press, 2016). The epigraph for this chapter is from Jürgen Habermas, *Justification and Application: Remarks on Discourse Ethics*, trans. Cioran Cronin (Cambridge, MA: MIT Press, 1994), 176.
2. Benhabib, *Critique, Norm, and Utopia*, 142. Although I find this characterization helpful, my argument disputes the idea that the "explanatory-diagnostic" function is

performed from the position of the "observer," which tends in Habermas's work to morph into the external standpoint criticized by Wittgenstein. See Zerilli, *Democratic Theory of Judgment*, chaps. 4 and 8.

3. Benhabib, *Critique, Norm, and Utopia*, 142.

4. Benhabib, 142.

5. This was the difference between traditional and critical theory. According to Benhabib, following Habermas, "after the *Dialectic of Enlightenment*, the critical theory of the Frankfurt School lost its explanatory-diagnostic dimension.... [It] continued as anticipatory-utopian critique alone" (Benhabib, *Critique, Norm, and Utopia*, 227). It fell to Habermas, in her view, to revive this first aspect of critical theory. I would agree with Nikolas Kompridis (in *Critique and Disclosure*), however, that Habermas has both lost track of tasks and redefined critical theory strictly as a procedural theory of justification. See also Max Horkheimer, "Traditional and Critical Theory," in *Critical Theory: Selected Essays*, ed. Matthew J. O'Connell et al. (New York: Continuum, 2002), 188–243.

6. See S. J. Methven, *Frank Ramsey and the Realistic Spirit* (London: Palgrave Macmillan, 2015), 1. In the view of Methven, Frank Ramsey—a brilliant mathematician, contemporary of Wittgenstein, and commentator on the latter's *Tractatus Logico-Philosophicus*—developed an outlook and practice of critique that he called realistic in spirit. *Realistic* is to be distinguished from *realism*. Methven explains:

> The right way to think about what it is to be *realistic* is along the lines of the way in which that term is used to describe fiction, films or painting. In that use, it characterizes both a certain absence—namely the absence of fantasy—and a certain presence—namely the presence of features which make the work, in some way or another, *true to the facts of our lives*. These facts may concern our cognitive and physical finitude, the limits of our conceptual capacities, our existence as creatures of nature and our lived experience of the world. The criticism of various forms of realism that Ramsey presses is that they are false to the facts of our lives as a result of their containing elements of fantasy, elements that deny or ignore one or more of the features of our existence. (5)

I agree with most of this description of what it means to be realistic in critical thinking. However, I would also argue that fantasy can indeed be put in the service of the realistic spirit, but it would be a form of fantasy that puts into question metaphysical realism. The use of counterfactuals to open the anticipatory-utopian dimension of critique, for example, can be realistic. See Geoffrey Hawthorn, *Plausible Worlds: Possibility and Understanding in History and Social Sciences* (New York: Cambridge University Press, 1991); Niall Ferguson, *Virtual History: Alternative and Counterfactuals* (New York: Basic, 1999). For a more critical reading of Ramsey, see Cora Diamond, "Realism and the Realistic Spirit," in *The Realistic Spirit: Wittgenstein, Philosophy, and Mind* (Cambridge, MA: MIT Press, 1995), 39–72.

7. Alice Crary, *Beyond Moral Judgment* (Cambridge, MA: Harvard University Press, 2007), 20, 21. I discussed Crary's argument in the introduction.

8. James Conant, "Subjective Thought," in *Cahiers Parisiens / Parisian Notebooks*, vol. 3 (Paris: University of Chicago Center, 2007), 234–58, at 240. I discussed Conant's argument about the subject dependence of objectivity in the introduction.

9. Stanley Cavell, "Knowing and Acknowledging," in *Must We Mean What We Say? A Book of Essays* (Cambridge: Cambridge University Press, 1976), 238–66.

10. Louis Althusser, *On the Reproduction of Capitalism: Ideology and Ideological State Apparatuses* (1969), trans. G. M. Goshgarian (New York: Verso, 2014), 176. I discussed this point is the previous chapter.

11. Wittgenstein continues: "Philosophers constantly see the method of science before their eyes, and are irresistibly tempted to ask and answer questions in the way science does. This tendency is the real source of metaphysics, and leads the philosopher into complete darkness. I want to say here that it can never be our job to reduce anything, or to explain anything. Philosophy really *is* 'purely descriptive.'" Ludwig Wittgenstein, "The Blue Book," in *The Blue and Brown Books*, 2nd ed. (New York: Harper and Row, 1960), 18.

12. Diamond, *Realistic Spirit*. I discuss Wittgenstein's critique of the metaphysical and skeptical tradition in *A Democratic Theory of Judgment*, chap. 1.

13. Nancy Streuver, *Rhetoric, Modality, Modernity* (Chicago: University of Chicago Press, 2009), 12. "Philosophy, with its duty of appealing to a universal audience by proclaiming the systemic coherence of its account, the universal as eternal, is predisposed to necessity as mode, and thus has deterministic proclivities," observes Streuver (71). The rhetorical tradition and rhetoric as a mode of critical inquiry are deeply relevant to modern debates on critique and can serve as a kind of antidote to philosophy's unfortunate affinities for necessity, thus determinism, which undermines political thinking.

14. One could argue that these terms are no longer relevant to understanding what is at stake in the current debate over the future of critical theory and, more broadly, critique. As I argue subsequently, the very crisis in which critique today seems to find itself is testament to the extent to which these philosophical categories continue to shape the horizon of critical thought. The very fact that social constructivists most always qualify claims such as gender is socially constructed but also socially real, while defenders of realism are quick to redefine it as commonsense realism or internal realism and take distance from all metaphysical varieties, speaks volumes to how embedded these terms are in our understanding of critique.

15. According to Toril Moi and Rita Felski, these otherwise diverse inherited approaches to critical thinking share the idea that critique entails suspending our ordinary beliefs and commitments to call into question the so-called natural and self-evident. Whether one thinks that there is a deep truth that needs to be uncovered (what Paul Ricoeur called the "hermeneutics of suspicion") or quotidian relations of power that reveal themselves as such ("surface reading"), there is a general sense that we need to be on guard against whatever appears as simply given to us in everyday life. Rita Felski, *The Limits of Critique* (Chicago: University of Chicago Press, 2015), esp. 25, 82–83; "surface reading": Toril Moi, *Revolution of the Ordinary: Literary Studies after Wittgenstein, Austin, and Cavell* (Chicago: University of Chicago Press, 2017), 179. The phrase, critically described by Moi, refers to an essay by Stephen Best and Sharon Marcus, "Surface Reading: An Introduction," *Representations*, no. 108 (2009): 1–21. Felski succinctly surveys the idea of critique within literary criticism. Moi brilliantly develops the work of Wittgenstein and Cavell to argue for an ordinary language approach to reading literary texts. Paul Ricoeur, *Freud and Philosophy: An Essay on Interpretation* (New Haven, CT: Yale University Press, 1970), 356.

16. In chap. 2, I discuss the two opposed approaches to critique represented by the names Habermas/Benhabib and Foucault/Butler. I also discuss different approaches to critique in Linda M. G. Zerilli, "Feministische Kritik als eine politische Praxis der Freiheit," in *Feminismus und Freiheit: Geschlechterkritische Neauaneignungen*

eines umkämpften Begriffs, ed. Barbara Grubner, Carmen Birke, and Annette Henniger (Sultzbach/Taunus: Ulrike Helmer Verlag, 2016), 128–38.

17. Linda M. G. Zerilli, *Feminism and the Abyss of Freedom* (Chicago: University of Chicago Press, 2005), esp. the introduction and chap. 1.

18. For a concise statement of these different positions, see Seyla Benhabib, Judith Butler, Drucilla Cornell, and Nancy Fraser, *Feminist Contentions: A Philosophical Exchange* (New York: Routledge, 1994). I discuss this debate in Linda M. G. Zerilli, *Feminism and the Abyss of Freedom*, esp. chap. 1.

19. Bruno Latour, "Why Has Critique Run Out of Steam? From Matters of Fact to Matters of Concern," *Critical Inquiry* 30 (2004): 225–48, at 232, 231.

20. Hubert Dreyfus and Charles Taylor, *Retrieving Realism* (Cambridge, MA: Harvard University Press, 2015).

21. I discuss this work in Linda M. G. Zerilli, "The Turn to Affect and the Problem of Judgment," *New Literary History* 46 (2015): 261–86; and in chap. 9 of *A Democratic Theory of Judgment*.

22. Felski, *Limits of Critique*.

23. Methven, *Frank Ramsey and the Realistic Spirit*, 2.

24. Zerilli, "Turn to Affect."

25. Cornelius Castoriadis, "Logic, Imagination, Reflection," in *World in Fragments: Writings on Politics, Society, Psychoanalysis, and the Imagination*, ed. and trans. David Ames Curtis (Stanford, CA: Stanford University Press, 1997), 246–72, at 271.

26. Didier Fassin, "The Endurance of Critique," *Anthropological Theory* 17, no. 1 (2017): 2–29, at 7.

27. Latour, "Why Has Critique Run Out of Steam?," 232.

28. Albeit in different ways, both James and Whitehead take for granted that our epistemic link with the world must be based on a causal foundation. In contrast, the realistic spirit, as I want to develop it through ordinary language philosophy, understands that conceptual link with the world as based on people's agreements about judgment concerning the world, and these are wholly ordinary in character. For an excellent comparative reading of Wittgenstein and Whitehead on this point, see Randy Ramal, "Realism without Empiricism: Wittgenstein and Whitehead," *Linguistic and Philosophical Investigations* 7 (2008): 260–83. I have explored the issue of realism and antirealism in *Feminism and the Abyss of Freedom*, chap. 1.

29. Latour, "Why Has Critique Run Out of Steam?," 231.

30. See Hannah Arendt, *The Human Condition* (Chicago: University of Chicago Press, 1989), 57–58.

31. Hilary Putnam, *Renewing Philosophy* (Cambridge, MA: Harvard University Press, 1992), 178. See also Nikolas Kompridis, "Disclosing Possibility: The Past and Future of Critical Theory," *International Journal of Philosophical Studies* 13, no. 3 (2006): 325–51.

32. Susan Hekman, "Truth and Method: Feminist Standpoint Theory Revisited," *Signs: Journal of Women in Culture and Society* 22, no. 2 (Winter 1977): 341–65, 342.

33. Hekman, 342.

34. Zerilli, *Feminism and the Abyss of Freedom*, chap. 4.

35. Seyla Benhabib, "Feminism and Postmodernism," in Benhabib, Butler, Cornell, and Fraser, *Feminist Contentions*, 25. Benhabib writes: "'How can we conceive a version of criticism without philosophy which is robust enough to handle the tough job of analyzing sexism in all its endless variety and monotonous similarity?' My answer [writes Benhabib] is that we cannot" (25).

36. John Gunnell, *The Orders of Discourse: Philosophy, Social Science, and Politics* (Lanham, MD: Rowman and Littlefield, 1998,) 20–21. Following Gunnell, I am using the terms *discourses* and *practices* interchangeably here, but strictly speaking, they are different.

> As concepts, practice and discourse do not have the same logical extension. When we use the phrase "orders of discourse," *discourse* is a more generic term than practice. Still, certain practices are often identified with or subsume particular discourses, or what might be called *discursive regimes*. A specific practice, such as one of the social sciences, often contains more than one level of discourse, while a certain mode of discourse may not be especially associated with any distinct practice. There were, for example, discourses on nature before there were differentiated practices of natural science, and there were discourses about politics [or feminist politics] that antedated the practice represented in the discipline and profession of political science [or the institutionalization of feminist theory and women and politics programs, etc.]. Practices are distinguished from discourses primarily by acquisition of institutional form. There are two fundamental types of discourses and practices—*first-order* and *meta*. (Gunnell, 18–19)

37. I draw here on Gunnell's point about the status of second-order practices such as political theory or social science generally (Gunnell, 21).

38. Gunnell, 21.

39. Gunnell, 31.

40. Gunnell, 32.

41. D. N. Rodowick, *Philosophy's Artful Conversation* (Cambridge, MA: Harvard University Press, 2015), 294–95. "Indeed our idea that Theory could represent a genre of critical discourse for the humanities, falling somewhere between criticism and philosophy, is fairly new, arising only in the 1960s" (295). Gunnell also offers a critical historical account of political theory and its fortunes within political science. Emphasizing the transformative influence of émigré scholars such as Leo Strauss, Gunnell tracks political theory's construction within American departments of political science as a distinct academic endeavor that claimed to be in conversation with, and to derive its authority from, the "great tradition" of political philosophy. See Gunnell, *The Descent of Political Theory: The Genealogy of an American Vocation* (Chicago: University of Chicago Press, 1993). A genealogical account of feminist theory too would show that the creation of a distinct object arises only after the institutionalization of women's studies programs in the 1970s and 1980s and the eventual "mainstreaming" of feminist scholarship in the traditional disciplines. The point here is not to denounce theory but to inquire, rather, why a certain conception of theory has taken hold in the humanities, social science, and feminism, and whether this conception is felicitous for gaining an understanding of the ostensible concerns and topics of these human endeavors.

42. Rodowick, *Philosophy's Artful Conversation*, 297.

43. "More generally, we may say that an important new theory—that of Newton, Einstein, Darwin, or Freud himself, not to mention those of philosophers—is never a simple 'induction,' any more than it is the mere product, 'by subtraction,' of the 'falsification' of previous theories. It is, *under constraint of the data* (this is what in fact empirical knowledge as well as 'falsification' amount to), the positing of a new imaginary figure/model of intelligibility" (Castoriadis, "Logic, Imagination, Reflection," 270–71). For a more extended discussion of this point, see Zerilli, *Feminism and the Abyss of Freedom*, chap. 1.

44. Gunnell, *Orders of Discourse*, 31; see also Nelson Goodman, *Ways of Worldmaking* (Indianapolis: Hackett, 1978).

45. Gunnell, *Orders of Discourse*, 40–41.

46. Gunnell, 41.

47. That which now answers to positivist verificationism is the concept of epistemic privilege, a kind of unique insight that standpoint theorists such as Nancy Hartsock first derived from Marx's account of the proletariat as the revolutionary class and later refined by other feminist standpoint theorists to reflect the crucial role of consciousness-raising (i.e., "the feminist standpoint" instead of "women's standpoint"). All knowledge is perspectival, but not all perspectives are equal; some can discern what is real and what is illusory. Nancy Hartsock, "The Feminist Standpoint: Developing the Ground for a Specifically Feminist Historical Materialism," in *The Feminist Standpoint Revisited, and Other Essays* (Boulder, CO: Westview, 1998), 105–32.

48. For a good account of why MacKinnon's epistemology is superfluous to her legal and political arguments, see Elizabeth Hackett, "Catharine MacKinnon's 'Feminist Epistemology'" (PhD diss., University of Pennsylvania, 1996).

49. See the comments on Hekman's essay by Nancy Hartsock, Sandra Harding, Patricia Hill Collins, and Dorothy Smith on Hekman's "Truth and Method" in *Signs: Journal of Women in Culture and Society* 22, no. 2 (Winter 1977): 367–98.

50. Patricia Hill Collins, "Comment on 'Truth and Method': Feminist Standpoint Theory Revisited'; Where's the Power?," *Signs: Journal of Women in Culture and Society* 22, no. 2 (Winter 1977): 375–81, at 375.

51. In previous work I argued that standpoint theorists, believing that feminist political claims are (some form of) truth claims, were focused on providing the proper criteria for their redemption. *Feminism and the Abyss of Freedom*, chap. 4. Here I direct attention to how a certain conception of theory assumes that such claims must be authorized by something outside the quotidian practice of claim making itself.

52. Nancy Bauer, *How to Do Things with Pornography* (Cambridge, MA: Harvard University Press, 2015), esp. 28–29. Bauer discusses how feminist concepts such as "sexual objectification" become part of a way of seeing the same things differently; for example, advertisements featuring scantily clad women to sell various products take on a whole new meaning as part of a system of representations in which women are depicted in (sexual) service to men.

53. For a good account, see Reva B. Siegel, "A Short History of Sexual Harassment," in *Directions in Sexual Harassment Law*, ed. Catharine MacKinnon and Reva B. Siegel (New Haven, CT: Yale University Press, 2003), 1–39. As Siegel explains, Cornell professor Lin Farley ran a course on women and work out of which a consciousness-raising group came up with the term *sexual harassment* and started to organize around it (8). Castoriadis, "Logic, Imagination, Reflection," 271; see also Susan Brownmiller's description of her involvement in the group: *In Our Time: Memoir of a Revolution* (New York: Dell, 1999), 279–94.

54. Siegel, "Short History of Sexual Harassment," 9.

55. Moi, *Revolution of the Ordinary*.

56. I address this tendency to construe all reflection on concepts in intellectualist terms in Zerilli, "Turn to Affect."

57. This imperative developed out of the so-called sex-plus doctrine, according to which discrimination "was on the basis of 'sex' 'plus' some other putatively *neutral* criterion (hair length, type of dress, mannerisms, orientation, or 'willingness to

furnish sexual consideration'). Courts elaborating sex-plus doctrine reasoned that the statutory prohibition on policies that discriminate 'on the basis of sex' applied to policies that affected (1) *only* class members and (2) *all* class members. A challenged practice would have to sort all employees into two perfectly sex-differentiated groups before the sorting operation amounted to discrimination on the basis of sex" (Siegel, "Short History of Sexual Harassment," 14).

58. See Siegel, 14, 16. "Sex discrimination law, like race discrimination law, pretends that it analyzes distinctions on the basis of physiologically, rather than sociologically, defined aspects of identity. In this way, antidiscrimination law represses the social history, social structure, and social meaning of the practice of sexual harassment in the very act of declaring the practice a legal wrong" (16).

59. Judith Butler, *Gender Trouble: Feminism and the Subversion of Identity* (New York: Routledge), 25.

60. Butler, 25.

61. Linda Martín Alcoff, "The Metaphysics of Gender and Sexual Difference," in *Visible Identities: Race, Gender, and the Self* (New York: Oxford University Press, 2006), 151–76, esp. 157–58. Alcoff tries to find some middle ground between the work of Sally Haslanger, who argues for specific modified objective criteria of gender, and Butler, who denies that such standards exist. See Sally Haslanger, "Feminism and Metaphysics: Negotiating the Natural," in *The Cambridge Companion to Feminist Philosophy*, ed. Miranda Fricker and Jennifer Hornsby (Cambridge: Cambridge University Press, 2000), 102–26.

62. I discussed this text in chap. 2.

63. Michel Foucault, "Questions of Method," in *The Foucault Effect: Studies in Governmentality*, ed. Graham Burchell, Colin Gordon, and Peter Miller (Chicago: University of Chicago Press, 1991), 73–86, at 76. "It is some time since historians lost their love of events, and made 'de-eventalization' their principle of historical intelligibility. The way they work is by ascribing the object they analyze to the most unitary, necessary, inevitable, and (ultimately) extrahistorical mechanism or structure available. An economic mechanism, an anthropological structure or a demographic process which figures the climatic stage of the investigation—these are the goals of de-eventalized history" (77–78).

64. Foucault, 76.

65. Simone de Beauvoir, *The Second Sex* (1949), trans. H. M. Parshley (New York: Vintage, 1989), 267.

66. Foucault, "Questions of Method," 76.

67. Foucault, 76.

68. Foucault, 77.

69. Michel Foucault, *Subjectivity and Truth: Lectures at the Collège de France 1980–1981*, ed. Frédéric Gros, trans. Graham Burchell (New York: Picador, 2017), 222. "How did the appearance of these games of truth came about? How was it that right within that experience one has of oneself as subject in a sexual relationship, the obligation of truth, the possibility and necessity of telling the truth appeared. You see that it is the same problem I wanted to pose with regard to madness, crime, and so on; how are games of truth connected up to real practices? And this is why analysis that consists in referring the game of truth to reality by saying: 'The game of truth is explained because the real is such,' however realistic it may seem to some, seems to me absolutely untenable and inadequate" (222).

70. For a discussion of what counts as feminist theory, see the essays by Sara Ahmed, Elizabeth Ermarth, and Bronwyn Winter in *Feminist Theory* 1, no. 1 (2000): 97–118.

71. Gunnell, *Orders of Discourse*, 42.

72. Gunnell, 161.

73. Kompridis, "Disclosing Possibility," 332.

74. Kompridis, 336.

75. Kompridis, 336.

76. Drawing on Wittgenstein, I discuss the role of this background in critical thought in *Feminism and the Abyss of Freedom*, chap. 1, and in *A Democratic Theory of Judgment*, chaps. 1 and 8. See also Kompridis, *Critique and Disclosure*.

77. Diamond, "Realism and the Realistic Spirit," 69.

Chapter Six

1. Common to the growing literature on "democratic erosion" is the thesis that democracies die without shared facts and a culture of argument that takes them for granted. Liberal democratic theory's focus on the relationship between citizens and the state has narrowed our understanding of the problem and what fosters a robust democratic culture of persuasive political speech. Within the American context, this narrowing arises as part of a debate between civil libertarians or "neutralists," for whom the democratic state cannot publicly voice its founding values of freedom and equality without violating its core commitments to freedom of speech, conscience, and religion for all citizens, on the one hand, and "militant democrats" or "prohibitionists," who reject viewpoint neutrality and endorse strict legal limits and punishments for those who engage in hateful speech and action, on the other hand.

2. Corey Brettschneider, *When the State Speaks, What Should It Say: How Democracies Can Protect Expression and Promote Equality* (Princeton, NJ: Princeton University Press, 2016), 10.

3. Brettschneider, 6. Brettschneider explicitly focuses on the idea of persuasive speech, specifically, the state speaking to its citizens in value-laden terms, and thus opens the question of the state-citizen relation within the register of language and evaluative judgment. He rightly sees that contemporary liberal political theory in general—though it holds that citizens as free and equal beings are entitled to justifications for the law by which they are governed—has been reluctant to directly engage citizens in reasoning or challenge them when they reject the democratic grounds of justification.

> Value democracy . . . introduce[es] the idea of democratic persuasion as a fundamental commitment of liberal society. Democratic persuasion extends the familiar principle that law, to be legitimate, must be widely publicized. It adds a further obligation that the state should publicize the justification for those rights protected by law—namely, their basis in the values of free and equal citizenship. When these values are attacked, the state should attempt to defend free and equal citizenship against the criticism of hate groups. The state's defense of democratic values should be persuasive in that it should aim to be convincing. This means that democratic persuasion should not merely recite the values that underlie rights; it should argue for them. The aim of democratic persuasion is to change the minds of the opponents of liberal democracy, and, more broadly, to persuade the public of the merits of democratic values. (6)

4. Brettschneider critically engages and modifies the stance of thinkers such as Habermas and Rawls, both of whom famously argue for the importance of reason giving in liberal democracies but reject as fatal any straying from state neutralism into the "normative attitude." Brettschneider writes: "The state should be neutral in protecting the right to express all viewpoints. But it should not be neutral in the values that it supports and expresses. Value democracy thus embraces viewpoint neutrality in protecting the right to free expression of all beliefs, but rejects neutralism as a theory of what the state should say. The state must favor some substantive values, namely the ideal that all citizens should be treated as free and equal." Corey Brettschneider, "Democratic Persuasion and Freedom of Speech: A Response to Four Critics and Two Allies," *Brooklyn Law Review* 79, no. 3 (2014): 1059–89, at 1060. "In sum, I propose democratic persuasion as a 'golden mean' between the prohibitionists who would ban hateful viewpoints and the neutralists who would have the state say nothing to criticize discrimination. It defends the standing of all citizens as free and equal while respecting their expressive rights" (1089).

5. Robin West, "Liberal Responsibilities," *Tulsa Law Review* 49 (2013): 393–20, at 404.

6. West, 405.

7. Robin West, "Introduction," in *In Search of Common Ground on Abortion: From Culture War to Reproductive Justice*, ed. Robin West, Justin Murray, and Meredith Esser (New York: Routledge, 2016), 1–18, at 11.

8. For Brettschneider as for Rawls, what matters in political life is not whether one's views are true but whether they can be defended as reasonable—that is, as being in accordance with the core political value of justice as fairness and the view of citizens as free and equal. The standard of correctness for engaging in democratic persuasion is reasonableness, not truth. Critics question whether the self-declared political liberal Brettschneider trespasses onto the territory of so-called comprehensive liberals such as Kant or John Stuart Mill, who put forward truth claims regarding politics and the good life. See Abner S. Green, "State Speech and Political Liberalism," *Constitutional Commentary* 421 (2013): 28, http://ir.lawnet.fordham.edu/faculty_scholarship/513.

I have discussed the problems with bracketing truth claims in the use of public reason in Linda M. G. Zerilli, *A Democratic Theory of Judgment* (Chicago: University of Chicago Press, 2016), chap. 5. My concern here is not whether truth creeps back into the political liberal worldview—if it was ever expunged in the first place—but whether the ungrounded beliefs that make up a worldview or comprehensive doctrine and shape its distinctive form of reasoning can be altered through democratic persuasion as Brettschneider characterizes it.

9. Within constitutional liberalism, these disagreements arise from what Rawls called competing "comprehensive doctrines." Such doctrines (religious, philosophical, and moral), Rawls argues, are at once incompatible and reasonable. They give rise to conflicting claims about the truth of certain human values and ways of living that belong to what Rawls calls "the free use" of human reason and the "burdens of judgment" specific to the pluralism of liberal democracy, claims that cannot be settled by shared criteria of proof. Recognizing the incompatibility of different "comprehensive doctrines" and their modes of reasoning, political liberalism would manage this problem by making reasonableness, not truth, the criterion of democratic persuasion. John Rawls, *Political Liberalism*, expanded paperback ed. (New York: Columbia University Press, 2005), esp. 54–59. Brettschneider explains that democratic persuasion

does not aim to impose a comprehensive doctrine but only to transform "those beliefs that are openly hostile to or implausibly consistent with the ideal of public equality" (Brettschneider, *When the State Speaks*, 14). It strains credulity, however, to believe that the deeply inegalitarian relations of, say, the patriarchal family rooted in a dogmatic Christian worldview could be transformed through the state's open contestation of false beliefs. Would one, for example, be open to prochoice arguments for abortion rights if one views the world as subject to God's will? Would not the very idea of choice be an arrogant usurpation of authority over spiritual questions regarding the good life (West, "Introduction," 11–12)? See also Robert J. Fogelin, "The Logic of Deep Disagreements," *Informal Logic* 7, no. 1 (Winter 1985): 1–8, at 5.

10. Fogelin, "Logic of Deep Disagreements," 5. For a useful discussion of Fogelin's reading of Wittgenstein, see D. M. Gooden and W. H. Brenner, "Wittgenstein and the Logic of Deep Disagreements," *Cogency* 2, no. 2 (Spring 2010): 42–80.

11. Fogelin, "Logic of Deep Disagreements," 6.

12. Fogelin, 6.

13. Similarly, Luigi Perisinotto writes: "All Catholics will admit that the colour of the wine, its taste, its chemical composition, etc., are the same before and after its consecration in the Mass; but, at the same time, they will claim that what now, after the consecration, fills the chalice is not wine but blood, the blood of Christ. Nothing has changed but, at the same time, everything has changed. Consequently, it will be of no use pointing out to a Catholic that a chemist will not detect the slightest difference in the consecrated wine because every Catholic will grant this without any problem." Perisinotto, "How Long Has the Earth Existed? Persuasion and World-Picture in Wittgenstein's *On Certainty*," *Philosophical Investigations* 39, no. 2 (April 2016): 154–77, at 170.

14. Likewise, West observes that "pro-life activists . . . view the exalted role of 'choice' in not just pro-choice but all liberal worldviews as an arrogant usurpation of authority over profoundly religious questions regarding the nature of the good life, while liberals and choice activists view the failure to plan one's parenthood as tantamount to grotesque irresponsibility" (West, "Introduction," 12).

15. Wittgenstein writes:

> The child learns to believe a host of things. I.e. it learns to act according to these beliefs. Bit by bit there forms a system of what is believed, and in that system some things stand unshakeably fast and some are more or less liable to shift. What stands fast does so, not because it is intrinsically obvious or convincing; it is rather held fast by what lies around it. . . .
>
> I do not explicitly learn the propositions that stand fast for me. I can *discover* them subsequently like the axis around which a body rotates. This axis is not fixed in the sense that anything holds it fast, but the movement around it determines its immobility. (*OC*, §§144, 152)

16. See Zerilli, *Democratic Theory of Judgment*, chap. 8, esp. pp. 212–13. See also Richard Rorty, "Introduction: Antirepresentationalism, Ethnocentrism, and Liberalism," in *Objectivity, Relativism, and Truth: Philosophical Papers*, vol. 1 (Cambridge: Cambridge University Press, 1991), 1–20, 15. Rorty draws on Wittgenstein's discussion of the limits of justification in *Philosophical Investigations*, §217. Wittgenstein writes: "If I have exhausted the justifications [for how to follow a rule] I have reached bedrock, and my spade is turned. Then I am inclined to say, 'This is simply what I do.'"

17. Fogelin, "Logic of Deep Disagreements," 6.

18. Fogelin, 7, 1.

19. Deep disagreements call for extraordinary measures to contain or transform them when seen as extraordinary because of their rootedness in incommensurable and groundless worldviews. These include the restrictions on speech and action that make up the prohibitionist case addressed by Brettschneider and the interdiction on public claims to truth that characterizes political liberalism and its highly restrictive conception of public reason. See my "Value Pluralism and the 'Burdens of Judgment': John Rawls's Political Liberalism," chap. 5 of Zerilli, *Democratic Theory of Judgment*, 143–62.

20. Peter Winch, "Persuasion," *Midwest Studies in Philosophy* 17 (1992): 123–37, at 129.

21. Ludwig Wittgenstein, *Culture and Value*, ed. Georg Henrik von Wright in collaboration with Heikki Nyman, rev. ed. of the text by Alois Pinchler, trans. Peter Winch (London: Blackwell, 1998), 95. Quoted with a different translation in Winch, "Persuasion," 130.

22. Winch, "Persuasion," 131.

23. Winch, 131.

24. Daniele Lorenzini, *The Force of Truth: Critique, Genealogy, and Truth-Telling in Michel Foucault* (Chicago: University of Chicago Press, 2023), 78.

25. Michel Foucault, *The Courage of Truth: Lectures at the Collège de France, 1983–1984*, ed. F. Gros, trans. Graham Burchell (New York: Picador, 2008), 14.

26. Lorenzini, *Force of Truth*, 78, 79.

27. Ernesto Grassi, *Rhetoric as Philosophy: The Humanist Tradition* (Carbondale: Southern Illinois University Press, 2021), 18–19.

28. Michel Foucault, *Lectures on the Will to Know: Lectures at the Collège de France, 1970–71*, ed. Daniel Defert, trans. Graham Burchell (Basingstoke: Palgrave Macmillan, 2013), 38.

29. Michel Foucault, *The Hermeneutics of the Subject: Lectures at the Collège de France, 1981–82*, ed. Frédéric Gros, trans. Graham Burchell (New York: Picador, 2005), at 381. Foucault is redescribing Quintilian's view of rhetoric here.

30. Foucault, *Courage of Truth*, 14.

31. Guido Niccolò Barbi, "No Truth without Opinion: The Root of Post-Truth in a Binary Conception of Truth," unpublished paper, 2022, 13.

32. Nancy Streuver, *Rhetoric, Modality, Modernity* (Chicago: University of Chicago Press, 2009), 4–5, 2.

33. Streuver, 1.

34. Streuver, 1.

35. Grassi, *Rhetoric as Philosophy*, 19.

36. Grassi, 19.

37. Grassi, 19–20.

38. Grassi, 20.

39. Grassi, 20.

40. Grassi, 20.

41. Grassi, 20.

42. Ernesto Grassi, "Roots of the Italian Humanist Tradition," in Grassi, *Rhetoric as Philosophy*, 1–17, at 8.

43. Grassi, *Rhetoric as Philosophy*, 33. Whereas "some authors limit the function of the metaphor to the transposition of words, i.e., of a word from its 'own' field to another," Grassi argues that "this transposition cannot be effected without an immediate insight into the *similarity* which appears in different fields. Aristotle says: 'A

good transposition is the sight of similar things.' Thus this kind of 'literary' metaphor already is based on the 'discovery' of a *similar nature*; its function is to make visible a 'common' quality between fields. It presupposes a 'vision' of something hitherto concealed; it 'shows' to the reader or to the spectator a common quality which is not rationally deducible" (33).

44. "We must remember . . . that the nonrational character of the principles is by no means identical with irrationality; the necessity and universal validity in the nonrational character of the *archai* impose themselves equally or to a higher degree than the universal validity and necessity effective in the deductive process and resting on the foundation of strict logic" (Grassi, 26).

45. Grassi, 26. Grassi goes on to show how Aristotle, among other Greek philosophers, comes to ascribe to rhetoric the job of providing "the emotive framework" in which primary belief is anchored. Rhetoric is to "'alleviate' the 'severity' and 'dryness' of rational language. To resort to images and metaphors, to the full set of implements proper to rhetoric and artistic language, in this sense, merely serves to make it 'easier' to absorb rational truth." This view of rhetoric is based on the distinction "between *content* and *form*," with rhetoric being "assigned a *formal* function, whereas philosophy, as *episteme*, as rational knowledge, was to supply the true, factual content" (26, 26–27).

46. For a discussion of these passages, see Lorenzini, *Force of Truth*, 78. Although Foucault clearly rejects the Platonic idea of true discourse, in which truth has a force all its own, he seems to accept the distinction between philosophical and rhetorical language that is said to originate with Plato. Accordingly, as Grassi puts it, "philosophy, represents the only true and valid rhetorical art." On this received account, "the fundamental argument of Plato's critique of rhetoric usually is exemplified by the thesis, maintained, among other things, in the *Gorgias*, that only he who 'knows' {epistatai} can speak correctly; for what would be the use of the 'beautiful,' of the rhetorical speech, if it merely sprang from opinions {doxa}, hence from not knowing?" This reading of Plato, however, fails to consider the *Phaedrus*, argues Grassi, in which we find that "the true philosophy is rhetoric, and the true rhetoric is philosophy, a philosophy which does not need an 'external' rhetoric to convince, and a rhetoric that does not need an 'external' content of verity" (Grassi, *Rhetoric as Philosophy*, 29, 28, 32).

47. In Foucault's reading of the *Apology*, Socrates "presents himself as the man of truth-telling without any *tekhne*." His speech refuses to "conform to any of the usual forms of oratory" and is instead "the language . . . [of] the public square, the market, and elsewhere. So the first difference from the language of rhetoric is that there is no discontinuity of vocabulary, form, or construction between Socrates' language and the everyday use of language" (*GS*, 312, 313). This reading of Socrates's language is clearly based on the disputed idea of rhetoric at issue in Grassi's critique.

48. Streuver, *Rhetoric, Modality, Modernity*, 2.

49. Streuver, 2.

50. Wittgenstein, *Culture and Value*, 97.

51. Wittgenstein, 73 (translation altered).

52. "If the true is what is grounded, then the ground is not *true*, nor yet false."

53. Immanuel Kant, *Critique of Judgment*, trans. Werner S. Pluhar (Indianapolis: Hackett, 1987), §8, p. 59.

54. Kant, §7, p. 55. For a more extensive discussion of these points, see Zerilli, *Feminism and the Abyss of Freedom*, 132–35.

55. As for Wittgenstein, the very idea of an absolute limit to what we might someday come to doubt belonged to the view of shared belief he would have us question.

56. Joseph J. Tinguely, *Kant and the Reorientation of Aesthetics: Finding the World* (New York: Routledge, 2018), 117n14.

57. Quoted in Tinguely, 121.

58. Tinguely, 103.

59. Tinguely, 18.

60. Arendt's refusal to provide normative criteria of judgment leaves "a yawning abyss between knowledge and opinion that cannot be closed with arguments." Jürgen Habermas, "Hannah Arendt's Communications Concept of Power," in *Hannah Arendt: Critical Essays*, ed. Lewis P. Hinchman and Sandra K. Hinchman (Albany: State University of New York Press, 1994), 21–229, 225. I have discussed Habermas's critique in Zerilli, *Feminism and the Abyss of Freedom*, chap. 4; and in Linda M. G. Zerilli, "'We Feel Our Freedom': Imagination and Judgment in the Thought of Hannah Arendt," *Political Theory* 33, no. 2 (April 2005): 158–88. As argued in the present book, Habermas and likeminded critics are focused on the problem of ideology and false belief, whereas I read Arendt as sharing Foucault's and Wittgenstein's concern with being held captive by a picture or perspective. This picture does not decide what is true or false but, rather, forms the system of reference in which statements or beliefs come to *count* as true or false.

61. Barbi, "No Truth without Opinion," 13. See also Guido Niccolò Barbi, "Technocracy and Political Truth: An Inquiry into the Singularity of Political Judgment" (PhD diss., Katholische Universität Leuven, 2022).

62. Hannah Arendt, *Denktagebuch*, vol. 1, *1950–1973*, and vol. 2, *1973–1975*, ed. Ursula Ludz and Ingrid Nordmann (München: Piper Verlag, 2003), vol. 1, workbook 16 (June 1953), 391.

63. Arendt, 391.

64. Barbi, "No Truth without Opinion," 14.

65. Arendt's original German text reads as follows:

> Zu den zwei λόγοι der Sophistin: Dies ist die eigentliche philosophisch-politische Entdeckung der Polis: In ihrem Zusammen zeigt sich, dass Pluralität wensentlich die Pluralität der Aspekte impliziert, dass πολιτευειν heist: es aushalten, dass jede Sache viele Seiten (nicht nur zwei, das ist schon eine logische Entstellung) hat. Seinen eigenen Aspekt durchzusetzen, was man innerhalb bestimmter Grenzen immer muss, heisst, fähig zu sein zu überreden. Darum wurde of Πειθώ eine athenische Göttin mit einem Tempel. Die entsprechende τέχνη, d.h. die Kunst, seinen eigenen Aspekte überzeugend darzustellen, war die Rednerkunst. Das ist der ürsprüngliche Zusammenhang zwischen Rhetorik und Politik. Die eigentliche τέχνη πολιτική ist nicht die Kunst zu herrschen, sondern zu "überreden" πείθεσθαι. Hier zeigt sich δόξα in ihrer eigentlichen Gestalt: Sie ist keine unverbindliche, unfundierte Meinung—dazu hat sie erst Plato gemacht, sondern der Ausdruck des δοκεῖ μοι: Im Unterschied zum φαίνεσθαι zeigt sich hier nur ein Aspekt, nicht das Ganze; aber diese Aspekt ist ganz und gar nicht *Schein*. (Arendt, *Denktagebuch*, 1:391)

Although I have left πολιτευειν untranslated because of the difficulty of translation, it means approximately to possess the status of a citizen and to engage in politics as an activity. Thanks to Patchen Markell for his help with the translation of this passage.

66. I owe the formulation of this insight to Patchen Markell.

67. Arendt, *Denktagebuch*, 1:391.

68. Winch, "Persuasion," 130–31. In his manifesto "On the Infinite," David Hilbert set out to defend infinitary mathematics, including Cantorian set theory. David Hilbert, "On the Infinite," in *Philosophy of Mathematics: Selected Readings*, ed. Paul Benacerraf and Hilary Putnam (Cambridge: Cambridge University Press, 194), 183–201. He proposed to regard all infinitary mathematics as a formal system in which the question of truth and falsity does not arise.

69. Criticizing Hilbert's defense of infinitary mathematics as a formal system and as Cantorian set theory, Wittgenstein argued against the view that mathematical systems had to be proven consistent before they were put to practical use. Alan Turning, who attended Wittgenstein's lectures, had objected that a faulty system could cause bridges to "fall down." Wittgenstein refuted the idea that a falling bridge speaks to a broader theoretical issue of inconsistencies in mathematics. Instead, it might reflect a faulty calculation in the bridge at hand. "Contradictions have no special status . . . in the practical applications of mathematics." See Ásgeir Berg, "Contradictions and Falling Bridges: What Was Wittgenstein's Reply to Turing?," *British Journal for the History of Philosophy*, October 1, 2020, 537–59, at 552, 538.

70. Stanley Cavell, "Austin at Criticism," in *Must We Mean What We Say? A Book of Essays* (Cambridge: Cambridge University Press, 1976), 95.

71. G. E. Moore, "Wittgenstein's Lectures in 1930–33," *Mind* 64, no. 253 (January 1955): 1–27, 19. "If, by giving 'reasons' of this sort, you make another person 'see what you see' but it still 'doesn't appeal to him,' that is 'the end' of the discussion" (19). But that does not mean that the discussion cannot start anew, only that I will have to find new "reasons" (e.g., new examples) if I hope still to persuade. I discuss these passages in Zerilli, *Democratic Theory of Judgment*, 77.

72. In addition to Wittgenstein's remarks in §11 of part 2 of *Philosophical Investigations*, other comments appear in Ludwig Wittgenstein, *Zettel*, ed. G. E. M. Anscombe and G. H. Wright (Berkeley: University of California Press, 2007), §§155–225; Ludwig Wittgenstein, *Remarks on the Philosophy of Psychology*, vols. 1 and 2, ed. G. E. M. Anscombe and G. H. Wright, trans. G. E. M. Anscombe (Chicago: University of Chicago Press, 1988); see especially vol. 1, §§411–36, 505–46, 860–90, 952–1137; and vol. 2, §§355–91, 435–97, 506–57. Remarks on aspects can also be found in the two volumes published as Ludwig Wittgenstein, *Last Writings on the Philosophy of Psychology*, vols. 1 and 2, ed. G. H. von Wright and Heikki Nyman (London: Wiley-Blackwell, 1994), esp. vol. 1, §§146–80, 429–613, 622–812; and vol. 2, 12c–19e.

73. Stephen Mulhall, *Inheritance and Originality, Wittgenstein, Heidegger, Kierkegaard* (Oxford: Clarendon, 2001), 154.

74. There are three relevant essays by Avner Baz. The first, "What's the Point of Seeing Aspects?" (*Philosophical Investigations* 23, no. 2 [April 2000]: 97–121), developed the critique of Mulhall under discussion here. The second, "Aspects of Perception," takes a significantly more radical position against what Baz sees as the conceptualist reading of Wittgensteinian aspects. For Baz, perception entails conceptualization whereas aspect seeing does not; the latter reveals the preconceptual, prejudged, and indeterminate "phenomenal world." Avner Baz, "Aspects of Perception," in *Wollheim, Wittgenstein, and Pictorial Representation: Seeing-As and Seeing-In*, ed. Gary Kemp and Gabriel M. Mras (New York: Routledge, 2016), 49–75. This preconceptual understanding of aspect seeing belongs to the broader idea of "nonconceptual embodied coping skills" advanced by thinkers such as Hubert Dreyfus, which I critically address in "The Turn to Affect

and the Problem of Judgment: Making Political Sense of the Nonconceptual," in *Democratic Theory of Judgment*, chap. 5, esp. p. 241. In a third essay, Baz further develops his nonconceptualist critique of Mulhall. Avner Baz, "On Learning from Wittgenstein, or What Does It Take to *See* the Grammar of Seeing Aspects?," in *Seeing Wittgenstein Anew*, ed. William Day and Victor J. Krebs (Cambridge: Cambridge University Press, 2010), 227–48. Mulhall responds in "The Work of Wittgenstein's Words: A Reply to Baz," in *Seeing Wittgenstein Anew*, ed. William Day and Victor J. Krebs (Cambridge: Cambridge University Press, 2010), 249–67.

75. Baz, "What's the Point of Seeing Aspects?," 99.

76. David Owen, "Criticism and Captivity: On Genealogy and Critical Theory," *European Journal of Philosophy* 10, no. 2 (August 2002): 216–30, at 217. I discuss the idea of "aspectival captivity" in the introduction, chaps. 3 and 4, and the conclusion.

77. Owen, 218.

78. Owen, 218.

79. Owen, 222, 218.

80. Owen, 227.

81. Jurgen Habermas, *The Inclusion of the Other: Studies in Political Theory*, ed. Ciaran Cronin and Pablo de Greiff (Cambridge, MA: MIT Press, 1998), 44.

82. Owen, "Criticism and Captivity," 227.

83. Owen, 227.

84. Owen, 227.

85. Owen, 227.

86. Brettschneider, *When the State Speaks*, 6.

87. Brettschneider, 10.

88. Owen, "Criticism and Captivity," 227.

89. Arendt, *Denktagebuch*, 1:391.

90. Hannah Arendt, *Lectures on Kant's Political Philosophy*, ed. Ronald Beiner (Chicago: University of Chicago Press, 1989), 40.

91. Arendt, 40.

92. Arendt, 41.

93. Thanks to Patchen Markell for this point.

94. Foucault, *Hermeneutics of the Subject*, 382.

95. Foucault, *Courage of Truth*, 13.

96. Lorenzini, *Force of Truth*, 77, 74.

97. Foucault, *Courage of Truth*, 14.

98. Foucault, 14.

99. Nicholas Dunn makes a compelling case for how to think about the problem of agreement in Arendt's thought through a fascinating reading of Kant's *Anthropology*. Dunn argues that Arendt focused not on agreement but on creating a shared world to sort better from worse judgments. She refused the idea that the goal of politics is reaching consensus, but she did not exclude the importance of understanding and judging diverse points of view. Drawing on *Anthropology*, Dunn rightly observes that Kant "chose to articulate his conception of pluralism in that text rather than in the *Doctrine of Right*. His pluralism is not the purely formal idea of another human being but the actual other with whom I share a world—this world." Keeping the particular "other" in view, Kant's approach to the problem of disagreement avoids treating a diversity of human beings as if they were "Man in the singular," as Arendt famously puts the subject of Western philosophy. Dunn convincingly shows that Arendt's idea

of plurality can be linked to Kant's worldly conception of pluralism to articulate an understanding of disagreement that rejects both simple agreement, on the one hand, and interminable disagreement, on the other. Nicholas Dunn, "Plurality and the Potential for Agreement: Arendt, Kant, and the 'Way of Thinking' of the World Citizen," *Constellations* 27, no. 2 (June 2020): 244–57, https://doi.org/10.1111/1467-8675.12449.

Conclusion

1. The chapter epigraph is quoted in James Conant, "Some Socratic Aspects of Wittgenstein's Conception of Philosophy," in *Wittgenstein on Philosophy, Objectivity, and Meaning* (Cambridge: Cambridge University Press, 2019), 231–64, at 232. See also Wittgenstein's letter to his sister Helene Salzer (née Wittgenstein) dated "Saturday [1934]": Ludwig Wittgenstein, *Gesamtbriefwechsel / Complete Correspondence*, Innsbrucker electronic ed., 2nd release, edited by Anna Coda, Gabriel Citron, Barbara Halder, Allan Janik, Ulrich Lobis, Kerstin Mayr, Brian McGuinness, Michael Schorner, Monika Seekircher, Anton Unterkircher, and Joseph Wang (Intelex, 2004 and 2011), www.nlx.com/collections/166.

2. Peter Winch, "Persuasion," *Midwest Studies in Philosophy* 17 (1992): 123–37, at 130. I discussed Winch and the Wittgensteinian idea of a picture in chap. 6.

3. Ludwig Wittgenstein, *Culture and Value*, ed. Georg Henrik von Wright in collaboration with Heikki Nyman, rev. ed. of the text by Alois Pinchler, trans. Peter Winch (London: Blackwell, 1998), 95.

4. Andreas Krebs, "Certainties and Rule-Following," https://doi.org/10.1515/witt-2022-0003,23, 29. Krebs explains: "If we would, for example, always or mostly disagree in the *results* of measurements, the distinction between correct and incorrect applications of the *rules* of measurement would also collapse. Analogously, this holds for colours as well. In *Zettel*, Wittgenstein [first] remarks: 'If humans did not in general agree about the colours of things, if undetermined cases were not exceptional, then our concept of color could not exist.'" Wittgenstein then adds, says Krebs: "No:—our concept of colour would not exist" (Krebs, 28–29). See also Ludwig Wittgenstein, *Zettel*, ed. G. E. M. Anscombe and G. H. Wright (Berkeley: University of California Press, 2007), §351.

5. Andreas Krebs explains: "Wittgenstein even considers it is conceivable that 'something *really unheard-of* happened.' For example, 'houses gradually turning into steam without any obvious cause,' or cattle ... 'speaking comprehensible words' [*OC*, §513]. In such a situation we *could* continue to hold on to our certainties and conclude, for instance, that we must be hallucinating. In this case, certainties would function like grammatical rules" (Krebs, "Certainties and Rule-Following," 25). They tell us what *must* be the case (e.g., cattle don't talk, therefore I am mistaken). "But they [certainties] also differ from the latter [rules]: while the sentence 'You do *not* play solitaire alone' is *nonsensical* since we do not use the word 'solitaire' that way, it is possible that I wake up after a surgery and find that this is *not* my hand, but a prosthesis. I could find out that this is *not* a tree if, for example, there is heavy fog.... The negation of certainties is *not nonsensical*" (Krebs, "Certainties and Rule-Following," 24, 25). According to Krebs, "certainties seem to be something *in between* rules and empirical propositions. They may oscillate between grammar and experience, and they can *change* their status" (25). "Certainties relativise the dualism of grammar and experience, belonging to the liminal space in between" (26). This means that certainties are at once the source of stability and change.

6. Michel Foucault, "The Analytic Philosophy of Politics" (1978), trans. Giovanni Mascaretti, *Foucault Studies* 24 (2018): 188–200, at 192. See also Michel Foucault, *Dits et écrits*, vol. 3 (Paris: Éditions Gallimard, 1994), 540–41. I referred to this passage in the introduction.

7. Wittgenstein's point here of course is not that things really are hidden but that they appear to us to be hidden precisely because they are in plain view.

8. Daniele Lorenzini, *The Force of Truth: Critique, Genealogy, and Truth-Telling in Michel Foucault* (Chicago: University of Chicago Press, 2023), 48.

9. John McDowell, "Wittgensteinian 'Quietism,'" *Common Knowledge* 15, no. 3:365–72, at 365. Wittgenstein writes: "If one tried to advance *theses* in philosophy, it would never be possible to debate them, because everyone would agree to them" (*PI*, §128).

10. McDowell, "Wittgensteinian 'Quietism,'" 366–67.

11. McDowell, 371.

12. McDowell, 369.

13. McDowell, 371.

14. Foucault, "Analytic Philosophy," 192.

15. Foucault, 192.

16. Foucault, 192.

17. David Owen, "Criticism and Captivity: On Genealogy and Critical Theory," *European Journal of Philosophy* 10, no. 2 (August 2002): 216–30, 221. I discussed Owen's argument in chap. 6.

18. I discussed this passage in the introduction.

19. I discussed Foucault's account of the Greek problematization of truth in the introduction and chap. 3.

20. See James Bohman, "Formal Pragmatics and Social Criticism: The Philosophy of Language and the Critique of Ideology in Habermas's Theory of Communicative Action," in *Jurgen Habermas*, ed. D. Rasmussen and J. Swindal (London: Sage, 2002), 297–313. Bohman argues that though Habermas's concept of "systematically distorted communication" seems to ignore ideology, it by definition includes ideology in the context of language use (297). Habermas writes: "Language is also a medium of domination and social power. It serves to legitimate relations of organized force. In so far as the legitimations do not articulate the relations of force that they make possible, in so far as these relations are merely expressed in the legitimations, language is also ideological. Here it is not a question of deceptions within language, but of deception with language as such." Jürgen Habermas, *Communication and the Evolution of Society* (London: Heinemann, 1979), 130.

21. Lorenzini, *Force of Truth*, 45.

22. Foucault, "Analytic Philosophy of Politics," 192.

23. Lorenzini, *Force of Truth*, 45.

24. Lorenzini, 37–38, and private correspondence.

25. Hannah Arendt, *The Human Condition* (Chicago: University of Chicago Press, 1989), 222. For a nuanced account of the politics of rule in Arendt's work, see Patchen Markell, "Politics against Rule: Hannah Arendt and *The Human Condition*," 2024, unpublished ms.

26. Arendt, *Human Condition*, 222, 223. For an excellent reading of these passages, see Patchen Markell, "The Rule of the People: Arendt, Archê, and Democracy," *American Political Science Review* 100, no. 1 (February 2006): 1–14.

27. Arendt, *Human Condition*, 223, 224.

28. Arendt, 226.

29. Arendt, 222.

30. Arendt, 225. Taking up "the equivocal significance of the word *archein*, which means both beginning and ruling," writes Arendt, "it is decisive for Plato, as he says expressly at the end of the *Laws*, that only the beginning (*archê*) is entitled to rule (*archein*). In the tradition of Platonic thought, this original, linguistically predetermined identity of ruling and beginning had the consequence that all beginning was understood as the legitimation for rulership, until, finally, the element of beginning disappeared altogether from the concept of rulership. With it the most elementary and authentic understanding of human freedom disappeared from political philosophy" (224–25). See Markell, "Rule of the People," for a compelling parsing of *archein*.

31. Arendt, 225.

32. Arendt, 225.

33. Arendt, 225.

Index

abortion, 150–51
absolute conception of reality, 67, 104, 128, 217n17
abstraction requirement, 128–29, 146–47
Academy (Platonic), 9–10, 40, 59–60, 86–87
acknowledgment, 64–68, 129
action, xiii–xiv, 24–27, 43, 68–76, 84–86, 90–93, 122, 211n38, 223n80
adjudication imperative, 149–53, 218n35
aesthetic judgment, 161–62, 167
affect theory, 132–33
Affordable Care Act, 131
Alcoff, Linda Martín, 142, 239n61
alethurgy, 77, 80, 108–10, 137–41, 219n43
alternative facts, xiii–xiv, 63–65, 74–75, 177, 218n35
Althusser, Louis, 97–105, 107–9, 111, 113–17, 123, 125, 129–30, 184, 227n40, 229n48
"anarcheology," 110–11
Andrews, David, 115
Anthropology (Kant), 247n99
anticipatory-utopian mode of critique, 127–28, 130–34, 142–46, 214nn52–53, 233n5
antirealism, and realism, 15–17
Apology (Plato), 222n72
appearances, realm of, 25, 28–44, 67–68, 118–25, 159–60, 162–66, 173, 210n29
Ardila, Camilo, 196n2
Arendt, Hannah: antipolitics and, 11–12; contingency and, 18–19, 56; critique and, 47, 57–61; *dokei moi* and, 4–15, 29–36, 70; factualism and, 18–20, 64–76; Foucault and, 4–5, 10–15, 83–84; ideology and, 118–25; on metaphysics, 29–36, 44–46, 187–88, 208n14; the ordinary and, 21, 26–27, 84–90, 168; originary freedom and, 54; persuasion and, 153–54, 160–66, 172–73, 223n80; politics as rule and, 4, 42, 46; skepticism and, 6–8, 199n30; thinking and contemplation and, 23–31, 38–44, 48–49; totalitarianism and, xiii–xiv, 5–6, 118–25, 198n21, 199n38, 233n98. See also *dokei moi; and specific works*
Aristotle, 14, 25, 158–59, 243n43
aspect-blindness, 169–71
aspect-seeing, 20–22, 66–67, 156–60, 163–72, 246n74
attention, 33
Augustine, 125
authoritarianism, xiii–xiv, 13. See also totalitarianism
Ayer, A. J., 161

Bachelard, Gaston, 101–2
Balibar, Étienne, 232n85, 232n90
Barbi, Guido Niccolò, 9, 157, 162–64, 202n58
Barnes v. Costel (1977), 141
Bauer, Nancy, 20, 139, 238n52
Baz, Avner, 168–69, 246n74
Beauvoir, Simone de, 140, 142–43
beginning, 71–76, 124–25, 187–88. See also action
Beiner, Ronald, 23, 209n17

Benhabib, Seyla, 127–28, 135–37, 145, 233n5, 236n35
Berkowitz, Roger, 46
Bernstein, Richard, 211nn33–34
Birmingham, Peg, 6
Biser, Ashley, 211n34
bivalence principle of truth, 9–15, 28–31, 34–36, 69, 100–101, 129–30, 162–63, 174–75, 177–83, 196n3, 201n57, 204n67
Blair, Tony, 66–67, 201n56
Bohman, James, 249n20
Borren, Marieke, 66–67
Bostrom, Nick, 198n26
"brains in a vat" thought experiment, 7, 198n24
Brettschneider, Corey, 149–50, 172–73, 240n3, 241n4, 241n7, 243n19
Bruch, Jean-Louis, 53
Bush, George W., 66–67, 81, 201n56, 217n14
Butler, Judith, 48, 51–55, 130, 141–44
"But Mom, Crop-Tops *Are* Cute!" (Haslanger), 96–97

Cambodia, 217n13
camera obscura, 114
Cantor, Georg, 167
Capital (Marx), 114–15, 227n40
Caplan, Bryan, 201n57
captivity to pictures, 16, 22, 150, 154–55, 160–66, 172–73, 175, 177–82, 206n88, 245n60
care for the self, 82–84, 91, 200n54
Carlson, Michael, 223n79
Carr, E. H., 202n60
Caruth, Cathy, 65, 72–73, 218n31
Castoriadis, Cornelius, 133–34, 137, 139–40, 237n43
causality, 142–44
Cavell, Stanley, 18, 129, 167, 198n25
certainty, 16, 20–21, 29–30, 44–45, 177–78. *See also* skepticism; truth
Chrysippus, 14
Cicero, 25, 158
Civil Rights Act of 1964, 141
cognitive determinism, 119–23
coherence theory of truth, xiv
Collins, Patricia Hill, 138–39

commodity fetishism, 114–17, 232n85, 232n90
commonplaces, 19
common sense, 6–8, 34–38, 41–42, 45–46, 111, 118–25. *See also* appearances, realm of; Arendt, Hannah; Kant, Immanuel; opinion; pluralism
comprehensive doctrines, 241n9
Conant, James, 9, 16–17, 31, 34, 102–3, 174, 200n40, 205n77, 227n39
consensus, 89
conspiracy theories, xiii–xiv, 95–97
contemplation, 23–25, 28–31, 33–36, 38, 40, 44, 56, 187
contingency: democratic politics and, 10–11; epistemic practices and, 1–2, 174; of facts, 66–67, 69–70, 74–75, 113, 212n45; Foucault on, 76–81; ideology and, 109–10, 118–25; judgment and, 55–56; perspectivism and, 57–58; rational problem-solvers and, 73–74; reality and, 17–19, 186–89; totalitarianism and, 14; truth-denial and, 4–5, 179
conventionalism, 103–4, 135–38, 230n55
Conway, Kellyanne, 63–65, 75
correct reasoning, 13–14, 129–30, 224. *See also* positivism; rule, politics as; scientism; verificationism
correspondence theory of truth, xiv, 9–10, 66–67, 88–89, 100–101
corrigibility, 21. *See also* persuasion
Cousins, Mark, 106, 227n33
Crary, Alice, 17, 20, 146–47
Crises of the Republic (Arendt), 65
criteria, 3, 123, 197n8
critical theory, 127–30
critique: democratic practices and, 1–4, 12–13, 47; feminism and, 130–38, 141–44; Foucault and, 47–61, 83–84, 89–90, 184–85, 187; genealogies of, 55–56; ideology and, 96–97; judgment and, 54–56; justification of, 127–30, 134–35; Kant and, 35–36; the ordinary and, 21–22, 116–17, 134–35, 144–47; *parrhesia* and, 13; public use of reason and, 56–58; realistic spirit and, 15–17, 185–89; as reflective disclosure, 146–47, 180–81; universities and, 59–61

Critique of Judgment (Kant), 162
Critique of Pure Reason (Kant), 37, 55, 161–62
cynicism, 6

Davis, Angela, 140
deep disagreements, 150–53, 161–66, 175, 243n19
democracy: aspect-seeing and, 20–21, 177–82, 246n74; common sense and, 6–8; as condition of true discourse, 10–11, 14–15; critique and, 1–4, 21–22, 48–50; epistocracy and, 10–11, 13–14, 185–86; factualism and, 8–9; Habermas and, 150; modern lies and, 4–9, 11; opinion and, 8–9; *parrhesia* and, 11–12, 76–84, 174, 220n59; persuasion and, 149–72, 174–75; plurality and, xiv, 1–9, 91–93; post-truth threats to, xiii–xiv, 1–4, 17, 182–89; rational truth and, 69; realistic spirit and, 15–22, 186–89; state's responsibility for supporting, 149–50; thinking and, 23–25, 38–44; truth and, 1–4, 6–7, 91, 182–86
denialism of post-truth, 90
Denktagebuch (Arendt), 163–64
Derrida, Jacques, 220n50
Descartes, René, 6–8, 44–45, 132–34, 198n23
description, 129–30, 137–47, 158–60, 167–68, 180, 237n41
desire, 41–42, 44, 54–55, 107–8
desubjugation, 51–58
determinative judgment, 55, 161–62
Dewey, John, 14, 201n57, 202n58
Diamond, Cora, 15–22, 28–29, 44, 106, 129–30, 179, 203n62, 204n68, 205n71, 205n75
Dietz, Mary, 63–65
difficulty of reality, 20–22, 43–44, 106
disinformation, xiii–xiv, 95–97
Doctrine of Right (Kant), 247n99
dogmatism, 128–29
dokei moi: common world and, 162–63; as inherently distorting, 111–12; persuasion and, 166–72, 175, 182; *phainetai* and, 9, 28–31, 157, 162–66, 174; public world and, 70, 87–90. See also appearances, realm of; democracy; pluralism; public world
Downing Street memos, 66–68, 81, 201n56, 217n14
doxastic solipsism, 173
Dreyfus, Hubert, 132, 246n74
"duck-rabbit" image, 168–69
Dummett, Michael, 199n29, 203n63, 205n71
Dunn, Nicholas, 247n99
Dworkin, Andrea, 140

echo chambers, 173
Economic and Philosophical Manuscripts of 1844 (Marx), 115
Eichmann, Adolf, 23–27, 38, 43–44, 46, 182, 207n7
Ellsberg, Daniel, 65–67, 73, 85, 216n8, 222n68
empiricism, 203n62, 228n42
epistemic democracy, 185–86, 201n57
epistemic privilege, 138–40, 238n47
Epistemic Theory of Democracy, An (Goodin and Spiekermann), 196n2
epistocracy, 10–11, 13–14, 187–88, 201n57, 250n30
Espionage Act of 1917, 85, 222n68
Essays in Self-Criticism (Althusser), 104, 228n43
Estlund, David, 201n57
etumos, 159–60
evaluative judgments, 161–62
eventalization, 142–44, 239n63
evidence, xiii–xiv, 2–4, 177–78; self-evidence and, 2; skepticism and, 6–8. See also factualism; games of truth; regimes of truth
expertise, 10–11, 13–14, 92–93
explanatory-diagnostic mode of critique, 127–32, 142–46, 233n2
expressivism, 161–62

FactCheck.org, 63, 196n2
factualism, 1–6, 13, 19–22, 26–27, 41, 63–96, 170–71, 182–83, 240n1
fake news, 4, 7, 177
false beliefs, 96–105, 109, 171–72, 241n9. See also ideology; post-truth

Fanon, Franz, 197n8
fantasies, 16, 29–31, 175, 234n6
Farley, Lin, 139–40, 238n53
fascism, 4–5
Fassin, Didier, 133
Felski, Rita, 133, 235n15
Feminine Mystique, The (Friedan), 140
feminism: critique and, 127–38; realistic spirit and, 20–22, 144–47; theory-politics division in, 134–47. *See also* standpoint theory; theory-practice divide
fetishism, 114–17, 232n85, 232n90
Fiorina, Cara Carleton ("Carly"), 95–96, 225n7
first-order discourses, 136–47, 237n36
Fogelin, Robert, 150–52, 165–66
For Marx (Althusser), 102
Foucault, Michel: analytics of truth and, 12–13; Arendt and, 4–5, 10–15, 83–84, 86; critique and, 47–61, 89–90, 184–85, 187, 218n37; eventalization and, 142–44; ideology and, 105–13, 120–21; the ordinary and, 21–22; *parrhesia* and, 11–12, 14–15, 76–86, 92–93, 156–60, 174–75, 200n54, 220n59, 221n61, 222n75; rhetoric and, 85–86, 156–60; truth's force and, xiii–xiv, 2–4, 9, 16, 77–81, 87–88, 91, 105–13, 116–17, 120, 178–79, 181–82, 184–85, 197n14, 200n49; Wittgenstein and, 179–82. *See also specific works*
Fox News Sunday, 95–96
Frankfurt School, 52–53, 98, 127–28, 184
Fraser, John, 227n40
free speech, 4–9, 11–12, 57–58, 67–68, 70, 81–84, 173. *See also isegoria*; liberalism (political); opinion; *parrhesia*
French Revolution, 55–56, 89
French Society of Philosophy, 48–49
Freud, Sigmund, 98, 137, 197n14, 227n26
Friedan, Betty, 140

Gaffney, Jennifer, 211n33, 212n45
games of truth, 2–11, 21–22, 52, 76–81, 108, 120, 123, 178–79, 184–89, 196n4, 200n49, 218n34, 219n44, 231n68, 233n102, 239n63

Garo, Isabelle, 100, 114
Gayot, Laurence, 114
gender, 53, 96–97, 130–34, 141–47, 185–86, 197n8
Gender Trouble (Butler), 142
German Ideology, The (Marx), 99–100, 113–14, 227n40
Gillot, Pascale, 98
Goodin, Robert E., 196n2
Goodman, Nelson, 137
Good Morning America (show), 95–96
governmentality, 47–50, 53–58, 89–90, 105, 107–9, 186–89
Government of Self and Others, The (Foucault), 81–84
Grassi, Ernesto, 156–60, 167, 174–75, 243n43, 244nn44–46
ground of critique, 127–28, 134–35, 154, 177–78
Gunnell, John, 16–17, 135–38, 140–41, 144–45, 205n75, 237n36

Habermas, Jürgen, 49, 51, 127–30, 146–47, 150, 162, 184, 204n65, 233n2, 245n60
habitus, 98
Harding, Sandra, 138–39
Hartsock, Nancy, 138–39, 238n47
Haslanger, Sally, 96–97, 115
"Hateful Society, The" (Brettschneider), 149–50, 172–73
Hegel, G. W. F., 38, 209n19
Heidegger, Martin, 23, 30, 38, 67, 88–89, 207n7, 209n19, 210n29
Hekman, Susan, 134–41
Hilbert, David, 167, 246nn68–69
History of Sexuality (Foucault), 105
Hitler, Adolf, 43–44, 119
Horkheimer, Max, 128
Human Condition, The (Arendt), 24–25, 119
Hume, David, 133–34, 161, 199n29, 225n9
Hussain, Athar, 106, 227n33
Hussein, Saddam, 66–67, 217n14
Husserl, Edmund, 209n19, 210n23

ideal theory, 127–30, 146–47
identity, 43–54, 95–96, 225n9

ideological state apparatuses (ISAs), 97–105, 111, 225n20
Ideologiekritik, 98, 116–17, 184
ideology, 171; Althusser and, 97–105; definitions of, 95–97; identity and, 225n17; logic of, 118–25; Marx on, 113–17; materiality of, 97–105, 113–17; as mere appearance, 105–13; mystification and, 64–65; the ordinary and, 106–13; science and, 101–5; subject-constitution and, 108–9, 121–24, 226n22; totalitarianism and, 118–25. *See also* captivity to pictures
If They Come in the Morning (Davis), 140
imaginary order, 227n35
intellect (and reason), 27, 37–38, 43, 56–57, 208n8
intentionality, 207n7
interpellation, 97–98, 226n22
intersectionality, 139
"Introduction *into* Politics" (Arendt), xiii–xiv
Iraq War, 65–68, 201n56, 217n14
isegoria, 12, 81–84, 220n59
isolation, 8–9, 122

James, William, 133–34, 236n28
Jaspers, Karl, 23
Jenkinson, Clay, 216n8
judging and judgment, 22–23, 37, 52–53, 55–56, 67–68, 128–30, 134–35

Kant, Immanuel, 24, 27, 32–44, 48–49, 55–58, 89, 118–19, 132–33, 161–62, 167, 173, 208n8, 213n40, 247n99
Klüger, Ruth, 18
knowledge-*connaissance*, 107, 156–60, 219n47
Kompridis, Nikolas, 145–47, 233n5, 234n5
Koselleck, Reinhardt, 59–60, 214n52
Krebs, Andreas, 248nn4–5

Lacan, Jacques, 98, 101–5, 226n24, 227n33
Landemore, Hélène, 201n57
Laos, 217n13
Latour, Bruno, 132–35, 147

Laws (Plato), 83, 221n61, 250n30
Lectures on Kant's Political Philosophy (Arendt), 26
legitimacy, 48–53
Levine, Steven, 204n65
Lewis, William, 102, 229n49
liberalism (political), 149–50, 241n4, 241n7
lies and lying. *See* modern lies
Life of the Mind, The (Arendt), 23–25
Lippmann, Walter, 14, 201n57, 202n58
Locke, John, 133–34
logic, 46, 69, 77–79, 96, 118–25, 129–30
loneliness, 8–9, 13, 122–24, 182
Lorenzini, Daniele, 3, 9–10, 77–79, 84–86, 108–9, 156, 180, 185, 219n44, 219n47
Luxon, Nancy, 197n14
"Lying and Politics" (Arendt), 65, 70–71
"lying the truth," 74–75

MacKinnon, Catharine, 139–41
Madness and Civilization (Foucault), 105
manifestations of truth, 108–10
Markell, Patchen, 245nn65–66
Marx, Karl, 99–100, 113–17, 119, 231n82, 232n85, 233n97
materiality, of ideology, 97–105, 113–17
Maxwell, Lida, 83, 93
McDowell, John, 180–81
McNamara, Robert S., 216n8
meaning, and truth, 25–27, 36–46, 66–67, 158, 182–86, 203n63, 210n29, 212n44
Mearsheimer, John, 202n60
Meet the Press (show), 63–65
Méndez, María Pía, 201n57
metadiscourses, 135–38, 144–45
metaphor, 158, 243n43
metaphysics, 15–17, 28–36, 44–46, 130–34, 142–47, 163–64
metapractices, 135–38
Methven, S. J., 133, 234n6
Mill, John Stuart, 241n7
misrecognition, 98–99, 103–6, 111, 184
modern lies, 4–9, 11, 14, 45–46, 64–65, 68–76
Moi, Toril, 21, 140, 235n15

Moore, G. E., 29–30, 167, 208n12
Morgenthau, Hans, 202n60
Mulhall, Stephen, 168–69
Musk, Elon, 198n26
mystification, 64–65, 119, 123, 129, 184

natality, 71–72, 124–25
naturalization, 96–97, 141
Nelson, Deborah, 19, 27
new materialism, 132–33
New York Times, The, 63–66, 196n2, 216n8
Nietzsche, Friedrich, 30–31, 34–35, 52
nihilism, 30, 41, 49
1984 (Orwell), 63
Nixon, Richard, 64–65, 91

Obama, Barack, 75, 95, 215n2, 215n6
objectivity: ideology and, 96; metaphysical realism and, 15–17; as Objectivity, 1–4, 8–9, 20, 22, 69, 100–103, 116–17, 128–29, 146–47, 153–54, 227n39; plurality and, 70–76, 138. See also bivalence principle of truth; perspective; pluralism
Okasha, Samir, 7, 198n25, 199n29
On Certainty (Wittgenstein), 151–52, 170, 178–79
On the Government of the Living (Foucault), 77, 106, 109, 120, 219n42
ontology of ourselves, 47, 52–53, 55, 57–61
opinion: common sense and, 14, 40–44, 87–90; epistocracy and, 13–14; fact-checking and, 67–68, 74–75, 90–93; objectivity and, 1–4; the ordinary and, 129–30; persuasion and, 149–53; Platonic view of, 9, 56–57, 59–60; pluralism and, xiv, 70–76; Socratic thinking and, 40–44; subjectivism and, 1–4, 9–15; thinking and, 28–31; truth and, xiii–xiv, 4–9, 14, 69–71, 78–79, 86–90, 100–101, 112. See also *dokei moi*
ordinary, the, 17–22, 26–27, 37–44, 46, 86–90, 96–97, 104–13, 129–30, 134–35, 137–38, 144–47, 153, 156–60, 186–89
ordinary language philosophy, 109, 180–82

orientation, 37, 44, 67–68, 88–89, 162–66. See also persuasion; pictures, Wittgensteinian
originary freedom, 51–54
Origins of Totalitarianism, The (Arendt), 6–7, 19, 124–25
Orwell, George, 63, 68–69
Owen, David, 22, 170–73, 181–82

Parmenides, 32, 35, 209n19
parrhesia, 11–12, 14–15, 76–86, 88–89, 156–60, 174, 177–82, 221n60, 222n75
Pashkov, Mikhail, 41
Pashkova, Valeria, 41
Pentagon Papers, 6–7, 64–68, 72, 91, 216n8, 217n13
performativity, 52–53, 84, 141–44
Perisinotto, Luigi, 242n13
perspective, 9, 40–41, 44–45, 67–68, 70, 86–90, 100–101, 110, 114, 116–17, 128–30, 163–66, 231n68
persuasion, 82–83, 85–86, 149–72, 177–82
Pfeifer, Geoff, 99
phainetai, 9, 28–31, 157, 162–66, 168, 174
phenomenology, 32
Philosophical Investigations (Wittgenstein), 16, 129, 167–68, 180–81, 188
pictures, Wittgensteinian, 16, 22, 129–30, 150, 154–55, 160–72, 175, 177–82, 206n88, 245n60
Pitkin, Hanna, 20–21
Planned Parenthood, 95–96
Plato: antipolitical dispositions of, 9–11, 13–14, 24–25, 29–30, 40, 56–57, 59–60, 83–84, 86–87, 187–89, 223n80, 250n30; bivalence principle and, 9, 157, 159–60, 162–66, 174, 196n3
pluralism: *dokei moi* and, 29–36, 59–60; Kant and, 247n99; loneliness and, 210n32; objectivity and, 1–4; seeing politically and, 153–54; spectatorship and, 56–57; truth and, 4–9, 69. See also democracy; public world
PolitiFact, 63
positivism, 66–68, 70–71, 102–3, 111–14, 138, 209n15, 228n44
postfoundationalism, 129–32, 135, 144–47

postpositivism, 138
poststructuralism, 49
post-truth: analytics of truth and, 12–14, 21–22, 80–81; aspect-seeing and, 170–72, 177–86; democracy and, 1–4, 17; fact-checking and, 1–4, 70–71, 90–93, 182–84; Foucault and, 3; ideology critique and, 125; modern lies and, 4–7; *parrhesia* and, 11–12; public world's destruction and, xiii–xiv; skepticism and, 8–9. *See also* factualism; relativism; skepticism
power, 3–4, 50–53, 96–97, 105–13, 120–21, 130, 146–47, 174, 184, 186–89, 231n68
pragmatic theory of truth, xiv
pragmatism, 32
problematization(s), 9–15, 57–61, 80, 87–88, 107, 111–12, 142–44, 180–81, 222n75, 227n40
propaganda, 95–97
Prozorov, Sergei, 78
publicity, 40–44, 56, 173
public world: action and, xiii–xiv; appearances and, 29–36, 86–90, 163–66; common sense and, 6–8, 34–38, 45–46; critique and, 47, 57–58, 116–17, 132–34; games and regimes of truth in, 3–4, 120–25; ideology and, 104–5; modern lies and, 84–86; pluralism and, xiv, 9–15, 67–68, 153–54, 173; Socrates and, 86–90; spectatorship and, 54–57; thinking and, 23–27, 36–44; truth and, 4–9, 44–45, 70. *See also* Arendt, Hannah; worldlessness

quietism, 180–82

Rajchman, John, 47–49
Ramsey, Frank, 128, 203n62, 234n6
Rancière, Jacques, 200n52
rationality, 154–55, 157–60, 230n52
rational problem-solvers, 73–74, 79, 218n31
Rawls, John, 201n57, 241n9
Reading Capital (Althusser), 102–4
realism, and antirealism, 15–22, 28–31, 33–34, 68–69, 103–4, 128–34, 141–44, 196n3, 202n60, 203n63, 227n40

realistic spirit, 15–22, 26–27, 33–34, 113, 128–30, 144–47, 179, 185–89, 202n60, 203nn62–63, 234n6
Realistic Spirit, The (Diamond), 15–17
reality, shock of, 19–20, 43–44, 65, 71–72, 82, 207n7
real objects, 101–5, 111–12, 143–44, 228n42
reason, and intellect, 27, 37–38, 43, 48–49, 56–57, 173, 208n8, 213n40
reason-giving, 149–55
regimes of truth, 2–5, 9–11, 21–22, 52–53, 76–81, 108, 120, 123, 178–79, 184–86, 188–89, 196n4, 219n44, 231n68
relativism, 1–4, 70–71, 75, 218n35
representative thinking, 40–41, 57–58, 160–66, 211n34
Resch, Robert Paul, 103–4, 230n52, 230n55
responsibility, for appearances and opinions, 160–72
rhetoric, 85–86, 88–89, 156–60, 174–75, 244nn45–46
Ricoeur, Paul, 235n15
Robinson, Spottswood, 141
Rodowick, D. N., 136–37, 237n41
Rorty, Richard, 152
Rubin, I. I., 115
rule, politics as, 4, 26–27, 42, 46–47, 100–113, 186–89
Ryder, Andrew, 227n40

scientism, 44–46, 73, 97–114, 123–35, 184, 196n4, 228n43, 229n48, 229n51, 231n68
second-order discourses, 138–41, 237n36
Second Sex, The (Beauvoir), 140
second-wave feminism, 141–44
seeing politically, 153–54, 158–66
Selberg, Anna-Karin, 198n21
self-evidence, 2
self-transformation, 47, 51–53
semantic theory of truth, xiv
sex-plus doctrine, 238n57
Sextus Empiricus, 14
sexual harassment, 138–41, 144–47
Siegel, Reva B., 140–41, 238n53, 239n58
Signs, 138–39

simulation theory, 198n26
skepticism, xiii–xiv, 6–8, 20, 29–30, 45, 74–75, 92–93, 128–34, 177–78, 198n24, 199n29, 206n87, 225n9
Sleat, Matt, 202n60
Smith, Dorothy, 138–39
social constructivism, 128–32, 134–35, 235n13
Socrates, as model of thinking, 17, 38–44, 59, 70, 86–90, 92–93, 211n33, 222n72
solitude, 122
Solon, 39–40
"Some Questions of Moral Philosophy" (Arendt), 37–38
sophists, 156–57, 163–64
Sortitis, Panagotis, 232n90
spectacle, 54–57, 114
Spicer, Sean, 63, 75, 215n6
Spiekermann, Kai, 196n2
Spinoza, Baruch de, 98
Stalin, Joseph, 119
standpoints, 40–41, 56–57, 67–68, 70, 86–90, 110, 128–29, 153–54
standpoint theory, 138–44, 238n47, 238n51
Stanley, Jason, 95–96, 225n9, 225n17
Steinbrenner, Peter, 233n100
Stephanopoulos, George, 95–96
stoicism, 54, 219n38
Streuver, Nancy, 129–30, 157, 235n13
subjectivation, 83, 90, 98–99, 185, 219n47, 226n22
subjectivism, 16, 199n30; feminism and, 134–35; normativity and, 40–41; vs. objectivity, 1–4, 101–4; opinion and, 9–15, 70, 163–66
submission, to truth, 2–4, 77–81, 105–13, 120, 123–24, 182, 184–85
Sunday Times, 66–67
supplement, truth as, 9–10, 16, 78, 88–89, 109, 112
surface reading, 235n15

taste, 161–62
Taylor, Charles, 132
Taylor, Craig, 203n62
testimony, 70, 74–81, 90–93

theoretical objects, 101–5, 111–12, 135–38
Theoria, 137–44
theory-practice divide, 130–32, 135–47
therapy, philosophical, 29
thinking (Arendtian), 16–17, 23–46, 59, 88–89, 182, 207n7, 210n30, 211n38
"Thinking and Moral Considerations" (Arendt), 38–39, 42–43, 209n15
third-wave feminist theory, 131, 135
thoughtlessness, 26–27, 45–46, 182
Tinguely, Joseph, 161–62
Todd, Chuck, 63–64, 75
totalitarianism, xiii–xiv, 4–5, 42–46, 70, 74–75, 118–25, 198n21, 199n38, 233n98
Tractatus Logico-Philosophicus (Wittgenstein), 204n68, 205n71, 234n6
traditional lies, 13
transparency, 106
Trotsky, Leon, 70
true discourse, 10–11, 76–84, 179
Trump, Donald, 63–65, 67–68, 72, 224n1
truth: action and, 68–76, 84–86, 124–25; analytics of, 12–13, 55, 76–81, 223n82; aspect-seeing and, 66–67; care of the self and, 82–84; certainty and, 16, 178–79; conspiracy theories and, 95–97; contingency of, 4–5, 9–15, 18–19; critique and, 21–22, 50, 130–34; democratic politics and, 8–9, 12–13, 91; demonstrations of, 59–60; difficulty and, 17–22; epistocracy and, 11–14; factualism and, 63–65, 81–86, 95–96; force of, xiii–xiv, 2, 9, 12–13, 19–20, 44–45, 52–53, 74–75, 77–81, 84–86, 91, 97–105, 108–9, 119–20, 122–25, 158–59, 181–82, 185; ideology and, 96–125; Kant and, 35–36; meaning and, 25–27, 36–46, 66–67, 158, 182–86; metaphysics and, 15–22, 28–36, 44–46, 69, 130–34, 163–64, 201n57, 204n67; opinion as, xiii–xiv, 4–11, 14, 28–31, 70–71, 78–79, 86–90; the ordinary and, 20–22; picture-captivity and, 151–53; Platonic view of, 9–15; pluralism and, xiv, 8–9; politics and, 69–76; power and, 3, 11–12; problematization and, 9–15, 76–81, 83–84, 87–88, 107, 182–86; rational vs. factual, 69; realistic spirit

and, 15–17, 76–81; reality and, 4–15; relativism and, 1–4; rhetoric and, 156–60; as supplement, 9–10, 16, 78, 88–89, 109, 112, 220n50; theories of, xiii–xiv; under totalitarianism, 4–6; as Truth, xiii–xiv, 1–4, 8–9, 100–101, 125, 153–54, 177–82. *See also* bivalence principle of truth; modern lies
Truth and Justification (Habermas), 204n65
"Truth and Politics" (Arendt), 69
truth-tellers, 61, 66–86, 91–93, 156–60, 174, 184, 197n14, 200n54, 218n34
Turing, Alan, 166–67, 171, 246n69

unconscious, the, 98
universities, 215n56, 223n81
unmasking, 96–105, 109, 119, 123, 128

verificationism, 198n25, 199n29, 205n71, 238n47
Verikukis, Hristos, 101, 229n46, 229n51
Vietnam War, 63–66, 74–75, 85, 91, 216n8
Visker, Rudi, 51
vita activa and *vita contemplativa*, 23–25, 30–31, 207n4
Vivian, Bradford, 11

Wallace, Chris, 95–96
Waltz, Kenneth, 202n60
warranted assertability, 203n63, 204n65

Washington Post, The, 63–65, 196n2
Watergate, 64–65
"Way of Truth, The" (Parmenides), 209n19
Weltbild, 151, 169. *See also* pictures, Wittgensteinian
West, Robin, 149–50
"What Does It Mean to Orient Oneself in Thinking?" (Kant), 40
"What Is Critique?" (Foucault), 48–50, 142
"What Is Enlightenment?" (Foucault), 57
"What Is Existenz Philosophy?" (Arendt), 32–33, 35
When the State Speaks, What Should It Say? (Brettschneider), 149–50
Whitehead, Alfred North, 133–34, 236n28
"Why Has Critique Run Out of Steam?" (Latour), 133–34
Williams, Bernard, 217n17
willing, 54
Winch, Peter, 154–55, 166–67
Wittgenstein, Ludwig, 15–22, 129–30, 146–55, 160, 165–82, 203n62, 204n68, 235n11, 242n15, 248nn4–5
worldlessness, xiii, 4–8, 13–14, 122–23, 133–34, 182
Wrathall, Mark, 67

Young Hegelians, 114

Printed and bound by CPI Group (UK) Ltd, Croydon, CR0 4YY
02/04/2025

14651940-0001